1974

Books by Nathaniel Burt

Novels

SCOTLAND'S BURNING

MAKE MY BED

LEOPARDS IN THE GARDEN

Nonfiction

THE PERENNIAL PHILADELPHIANS

WAR CRY OF THE WEST

FIRST FAMILIES

Poetry

ROOMS IN A HOUSE

QUESTION ON A KITE

First Families

First Families

The Making of an American Aristocracy

Nathaniel Burt

with illustrations

Little, Brown and Company—Boston–Toronto

Published simultaneously in Canada
by Little, Brown & Company (Canada) Limited

PRINTED IN THE UNITED STATES OF AMERICA

To Moe and Helen
with apologies and thanks

Contents

Illustrations

Illustrations appear between pages 120 and 121

Statue by St. Gaudens, marking the grave of Marian and Henry Adams. (*Photo courtesy National Park Service, United States Department of the Interior*)

Unfinished picture of the 1783 Peace Commissioners, by Benjamin West. (*Courtesy, The Henry Francis du Pont Winterthur Museum*)

Unfinished head of Abigail Adams, by Stuart. (*Massachusetts Historical Society*)

Thomas Biddle, by Sully. (*Courtesy of the Pennsylvania Academy of the Fine Arts*)

Portrait of Mary Hallock Greenewalt, by Eakins. (*Witchita Art Museum*)

Mrs. Theodore Roosevelt Jr., by Koch. (*Mrs. Quentin Roosevelt and Portraits, Inc.*)

Mrs. Nicholas Longworth, by Hurd. (*Mrs. Nicholas Longworth and Portraits, Inc.*)

Richard Lee, attributed to Lely. (*Frick Art Reference Library*)

Thomas Lee, artist unknown. (*Frick Art Reference Library*)

Richard Henry Lee, by C. W. Peale. (*Independence National Historical Park Collection*)

[xi]

Harry Lee, by C. W. Peale. (*Independence National Historical Park Collection*)

Admiral Samuel Phillips Lee, by Sully. (*P. Blair Lee*)

Pierre Samuel du Pont, engraving by Courbe. (*Eleutherian Mills Historical Library*)

Victor Marie du Pont, copy of an oil by Otis. (*Eleutherian Mills Historical Library*)

Charles Irénée du Pont, by Sully. (*Mrs. Victor du Pont and the Frick Art Reference Library*)

Eleuthère Irénée du Pont. (*Eleutherian Mills Historical Library*)

Edmond du Pont. (*Francis I. du Pont and Co.*)

John Quincy Adams, by Copley. (*Courtesy, Museum of Fine Arts, Boston*)

Henry Adams. (*Harvard University Archives*)

John Quincy Adams in 1844, by Brady. (*Harvard University Archives*)

Henry Adams, by Potter. (*Harvard University Archives*)

Nicholas Biddle young, by Trott. (*General Nicholas Biddle and The Historical Society of Pennsylvania*)

Nicholas Biddle later on, by Sully. (*C. J. Biddle and The Historical Society of Pennsylvania*)

Robert E. Lee, by Brady. (*Washington and Lee University*)

Robert E. Lee, by William West. (*Washington and Lee University*)

Theodore Roosevelt, about 1880. (*Franklin D. Roosevelt Memorial Library*)

Theodore Roosevelt, about 1884. (*Theodore Roosevelt Association*)

The Mount Rushmore Memorial, by Borglum. (*Theodore Roosevelt Association*)

Franklin and Eleanor engaged. (*Franklin D. Roosevelt Memorial Library*)

Eleanor Roosevelt in 1957 (*Mo-Bee Photo Service, Kansas City, Mo.*)

Churchill and Roosevelt. (*Franklin D. Roosevelt Memorial Library*)

Abigail Adams Homans. (*World Wide Photos, Inc.*)

Birthplaces of John Adams and John Quincy Adams. (*Quincy Historical Society, photo by Olberg*)

The Old House in Quincy, where John Adams died. (*Courtesy of C. L. Fasch Studios*)

Stratford, where Robert E. Lee was born. (*The Robert E. Lee Memorial Foundation*)

Arlington, where Robert E. Lee was married. (*Photo courtesy National Park Service, United States Department of the Interior*)

Eleutherian Mills, the first du Pont mansion on the Brandywine. (*Hagley Museum*)

Andalusia, where descendants of Nicholas Biddle live. (*Photograph by Cortlandt V. D. Hubbard for* Antiques)

Theodore Roosevelt's Sagamore Hill. (*Photo courtesy National Park Service, United States Department of the Interior*)

Franklin Roosevelt's Hyde Park. (*Franklin D. Roosevelt Memorial Library*)

I

In the Beginning

1

Family

FAMILY in America has always occupied a somewhat special position. Not of course "family" in the sense of the nowadays universally admired, not to say adulated, family group — Pop, Mom, Sis and Junior — but Family with a capital "F"; the clan, the name, the crest, the use of family in the sense of "first families." Such use of the word, involving hereditary distinction, privilege, position, prestige, has been, since the Revolution, officially and publicly outlawed and privately suspected. Americans are not permitted hereditary titles. There is no way to tell from looking at the name which of two Smiths is a man of Family and which is not.

There is in fact a whole large body of opinion and prejudice (enshrined in the cherished folk saying, "three generations from shirt-sleeves to shirt-sleeves"), of philosophy and feeling, which would tend to discredit the very idea of Family as being either foolish, nonexistent, obsolete or nefarious. There can be no question that this kind of capital F Family Feeling does run counter to the basically egalitarian and environmental current that moves behind much of our best democratic and progressive thought. For Family, in this sense, is uncompromisingly hereditary. It is quasi-aristocratic. It involves "blood," that quaint euphemism for genes and sex, transmitted superiorities, class connections. This whole concept of Family, then, will always be suspect in any democratic society; nowhere more so than in America.

Yet despite this there are no countries, modern countries at least, where family and men of family have played more important, more celebrated, more historic roles; few countries where, at all levels, such traditions of inherited worth are still more admired. The purpose of this particular book is to look at and compare five of the most excessively prominent of such families. Few others have been exhibited longer and larger on the American national scene; but these five are merely among the better known of thousands of others. Every village, town, city, state, region has its First Families; and the nation itself has, and always has had, family successions of prominence, political, intellectual, financial — Harrison, Lowell, Morgan. One has only to think of such recently conspicuous public figures and men of family as the late Senator Robert Taft, son of a President of the United States; Governor Adlai Stevenson, grandson of a Vice President; Senator Henry Cabot Lodge, grandson of another famous senator of that name; or such men of more recent, but no less family-conscious, clans as Nelson Rockefeller and John F. Kennedy.

True, the public scene is not and never has been in any way dominated by such men of hereditary distinction. America is not ruled by an aristocracy or an Establishment. The self-made man, the Truman, the Eisenhower, the Johnson, remains representatively American; but *equally* representative, no *more* so than the man of family. It is this equal division of honors between these two groups, the self-made men and the men of family, that must be emphasized. There is always a tendency to overstress the self-made man, the egalitarian, the man of the people, as being the *sole* representative of America, of "real Amurica," a tendency that dates from the Revolution, or at least the days of Jackson and de Tocqueville. The falseness of this picture of American leadership has created, by reaction, a tendency to think of America as secretly governed by an elite, an Establishment,* even a hereditary oligarchy; or a belief in the special efficacy of ruling classes. Certainly, if the American experiment has proved anything, it has proved that lead-

* See E. Digby Baltzell, *The Protestant Establishment*. New York, 1964.

[4]

ership can be summoned up from the people, from the bottom of the social pile, without even being properly processed on the way up (Lincoln).* A governing class is not a necessity. Society does not succumb to chaos and mobocracy without it, as was universally predicted by European and American reactionaries.

As we are basically a mixed economy of private and public enterprise, so we are a mixed society of personal mobility and traditional tenure. Nearly all societies in all ages previous to that established by the American Declaration had been run on the assumption of hereditary government. To base a government on the proposition that all men were created equal was wild radicalism. Yet from the beginning, American leadership was never totally egalitarian, and has always been half parvenu, half patrician. The Pantheon of our Founding Fathers perfectly exemplifies the split and the balance; and the paradoxes. Adams, Hamilton and Franklin were all self-made men. Jefferson, Washington and Madison, all kin, were all born into the Virginia aristocracy of planters. Adams, the self-made man, founded the one really long-lasting and distinguished family of the group. Hamilton, the self-made man, still remains America's prime defender of the rights of property and privilege. Jefferson, the greatest born aristocrat of them all, was the greatest radical and leveler. And Washington, father of his country, left no children. (Franklin's son was illegitimate, as was that son's son; and of course Hamilton himself was a bastard.)

Family, then, family in the special hereditary sense, is not now and never has been alien to America. Nor has it ever ruled the country as a whole, as opposed to certain localities and regions. Since the Revolution or at least since Jackson, there has never been a national Establishment, much less a real hereditary national aristocracy. Nor has there been, as, say, in England, much passive per-

---

* Lloyd George was the first "unprocessed" prime minister of England. Disraeli did not have the public-school education common to most prime ministers, but he was hardly a "man of the people."

sistence, merely by procreation, of sheer name and property without respect to persons. (As Lord Melbourne said approvingly of the Order of the Garter, it had none of this "damn merit" about it.) Due to the exigencies of the frontier and of a mercantile society, the supine transfer of greatness has not been characteristic. Family position in America has to be continually maintained and reearned, or it tends to disintegrate. Those families that have persisted in power and influence and reputation are usually those in which this process of reacquisition has been most successful. It is not just heredity, it is hereditary *merit* that tends to create Family in an American democracy. In all the five families looked at here, it is merit of one sort or another, exhibited steadily in succession, or popping up irregularly on the family tree, that has kept the names green.

The characteristic American man of family belongs essentially then to an hereditary meritocracy, not an hereditary aristocracy; the spectacle of a succession of persons who by their own efforts and through their own gifts, often in rebellion against their own family traditions, keep the family name burnished. Of course, family name as such certainly helps along the talent. Opportunities knock, doors are opened. Since one of the rewards and one of the bases of prominence in America, as elsewhere, is property, the moneyed advantages of education and social experience usually help the man of family along too. But unless talent and activeness are somehow "in the blood," the mere possession of money and position and advantages will surely decline. As the career of Henry Adams demonstrates, the man of family who stands about waiting to inherit his power may wait forever. Henry fortunately had other talents besides political ones. The traditional method of recouping family fortunes, a marriage to a rich girl, does help. (The Quaker prescription for a Family is: in the first generation, do well; in the second, marry well; in the third, breed well; then the fourth will take care of itself.) But a succession of merit counts most.

All these five families exhibit not just a tenacious ability to keep going and to hang onto money; they all owe their position, fame —

and money — to an ability to transmit ability. The pattern is quite different in each family, but in each family the phrase "hereditary meritocracy" best describes the process. How or why this happens is of course mysterious. Only a great expert or a rash fool would dare come up with a pat answer. Genes? Training? Conscious tradition? The rise in fortunes of a whole particular class or region? A fortune kept intact? Fate? These all surely have an enormous influence on such family tenure. But otherwise . . . a mystery. After all, so many families with all these things working for them do not become or remain First Families.

No two families follow exactly the same pattern, and all these five particular families are enormously different. Yet similarities do make them comparable. Adams, Roosevelt, Biddle, du Pont and Lee, naming them geographically from north to south, offer a study in contrasts; yet their histories are strangely parallel, and often interlocking.

What exactly, then, is a Family, and how does it begin? The American family, always composed of just private citizens, cannot be confused with the official titled aristocracy of Europe, which is either government itself, or an arm of government. Nor can the Firstness of these First Families be equated with plain tenure of land or wealth. The definition is more complex. Everybody belongs to a family, and all families go back to Adam. What distinguishes one as "first"? That such distinctions do exist, no one can deny. Any older locality has families — Cabots in Boston, Cadwaladers in Philadelphia — not famous so much nationally as locally. The really national family is distinctive. Often, in its own backyard, a national family like the Roosevelts will not be considered the peer of a more purely local family like the Van Rensselaers (Biddles and Cadwaladers, Lees and Randolphs). And it certainly might be questioned whether the Biddles or the du Ponts deserve to be really designated as "national," or even "first," at all.

No one could deny, however, that they are Families and have the stigmata that distinguish the special Family from the ordinary family. These are, as a rule: (1) conspicuous family founders, (2) excellent marriages with other Families, (3) conspicuous descendants, in more than one later generation, (4) conspicuous identification of long standing with one special locality, and above all, (5) the ability to keep going, keep up. For an example, more or less at random, of such a Family: Benjamin Rush rose from obscurity (his father was a gunsmith) to become America's most famous medical man of the Revolutionary and Federal period, Signer of the Declaration, etc. Rush was the man who, as good friend of both Adams and Jefferson, brought them together in their old age. His son Richard, first amiable and really accepted American minister to England, attorney general, secretary of the treasury, fixed the family fortunes. Dr. Benjamin himself married a Stockton (social) of Princeton and New Jersey. His son James, brother of Richard, married a Ridgway (rich), Philadelphia's most notable heiress. A twentieth-century Rush, deserting the family professionalism, became president of the huge Insurance Company of North America, and made money in his own right. All these Rushes were firmly based in Philadelphia, where there are Rushes today, one of them a prominent physician. The Rushes may not now be a truly national family, but they are certainly a family in Philadelphia.

What can be done in Philadelphia can be and has been done in Podunk. Every village has its special Smiths, acquires them as the decades roll by. Then there are families of statewide or regional or metropolitan fame. However, most of these lack the special, added dimension of national fame, which is what distinguishes these five families from most others. Sometimes the merit and the fame are not equivalent; still, not many families, in such a huge country, have managed to become and remain national. These five families are among the few.

Adams, Roosevelt, Biddle, du Pont, Lee: each of these families has not only, in an exaggerated degree, the kind of local-historical prestige exhibited in the Rushes, but to a varying degree, the more rarefied national prestige. Adams, Roosevelt, Lee, are names that it would be difficult for the average schoolchild to forget, though no doubt it can be done. Biddle and du Pont would be familiar to anyone truly acquainted with national affairs either historically or currently. Take, as representative, Samuel Eliot Morison's *Oxford History of the United States*. All these names are in the index, though being a New Englander, Morison has naturally reserved the lion's share for the Adamses. Beginning with the first timid emergence of a Roosevelt on page 76, we proceed with no appreciable large gaps to the final mention of Theodore Roosevelt and J. Q. Adams on page 1120. More than a hundred pages have been starred by the name Adams alone; and even the du Ponts, who do least well here, embellish at least four pages.* Of course Morison is a conservative historian who is partial to men of family; still, the echo of these family names from Adams to Roosevelt inevitably and unceasingly rebounds through the briskly bemarbled halls of his history. And the names still appear almost daily somewhere in some newspaper (FDR Jr., runs for governor of New York; Angier Biddle Duke transfers from chief of protocol to ambassador to Spain, following the footsteps of his uncle Tony; Lammot du Pont Copeland Jr. takes on another directorship; and another volume of another Adams diary appears in print, another study of R. E. Lee emerges).

Perhaps the best definition of "Family" can be made by example — these five examples. Their likenesses and their differences serve to define the terms. They have in common, first of all, tenure. They have been conspicuous, on a national or a large local scene, from the mid-eighteenth century to the mid-twentieth century. Those three indices of status, the *Dictionary of American Biography, Who's*

---

* An interesting comparison can be made with the Nevins-Commager *A Short History of the United States* (New York, 1966). Here the Adamses are scanted in favor of the Roosevelts, the Biddles are mentioned only once, and the du Ponts not at all.

Who and the *Social Register* are full of them,* an indication of their past and present prominence. All five families have nurtured not just one, but two or more men or women of outstanding talent. Through three centuries, eighteenth, nineteenth and twentieth, there has usually been someone about, from each family, with rank — a President or a senator, an ambassador or a cabinet member, a general or an admiral. In the twentieth century, for instance, a Charles Francis Adams was secretary of the navy; one Biddle was attorney general, another ambassador to Poland and Spain; one Lee was a senator, another an admiral; two du Ponts, T. Coleman and Colonel Henry, were senators too. And as for the Roosevelts. . . . Some of these have been not just respectable, but men to whom the word "great" could be applied, men who have had a role to play close to the center of affairs, and who have played it with distinction, if not necessarily with success. John Adams, Franklin Roosevelt, Nicholas Biddle, Pierre Samuel du Pont de Nemours, Robert E. Lee, may not all be equal in fame and attainments, but all of them had their turn at making history.

It is not the great men so much as their families as a whole that can be compared. All these families emerged at about the same time, the last third of the eighteenth century, but their trajectories since have been quite different, and make a different graph. Using liquid analogies, the course of each family could be compared to a course of water. The Adamses, for instance, represent the fall of a narrow but forceful jet from granite basin to basin, always downward from John the Founder. In each generation the principal holder of the name (each "basin," so to speak) has been thoroughly meritorious; quite apart from any family standards, he would be a personage in his own right. But compared to the Adams generation before him, he is less of a personage. The Adamses are now distinguished and successful Bostonians, but safely below the watermark of national fame.

* See Appendix II.

The Roosevelts exhibit exactly an opposite pattern, the upsurge of an artesian well from subterranean darkness to the light. Here it seems better to shift from water to fire and compare them to rockets, the slow ascent and the final outbreak in two successive bursts of color, Theodore and Franklin.

The Biddles exhibit a more relaxed Philadelphian pattern, a sort of constant simmer just above or just below the line of national significance. Rising through a group of members of some Revolutionary stature, the family fame fluctuates between the financial éclat and disaster of Nicholas Biddle, the decent legalism of George Washington Biddle, and the New Deal prominence of Francis, George and Anthony. Never very far up, never very far down, a random pattern of lights going on and off all over the family tree.

The du Ponts most obviously resemble a river, increasing vastly in bulk and content and force, yet perhaps always going downward from the high, absurd, Castilian source of Pierre the Founder.

And the Lees rise to two crests, a Revolutionary wave and then a Civil War one, waves that break and collapse afterwards.

2

Lee

How DID these families begin? Four of them "began" in America, one in France. Any American family usually has two beginnings, the date of emigration and the date of "emergence." This is true certainly for the four American names, Adams, Roosevelt, Biddle and Lee. In no case did the position, or lack of position, of

Engish Adamses, Biddles or Lees (or the Dutch position of the obscure Roosevelts) seem to have very much to do with the fortunes of the emigrating cousins.

This is a curious fact that separates the Anglo-American emigration from, say, the Spanish-American one. With the exception of a few proprietary and governing families (Calverts in Maryland, Fairfaxes in Virginia), almost no important American families depend for their luster upon European backgrounds. Even when the emigrant does happen to come from an English great house (usually of course as younger son disinherited by primogeniture), this fact doesn't continue to sustain him or his descendants across the water. Emigrants were pretty much on their own; as on any frontier, it was sink or swim. Good fortune was personal, not inherited.

Thus, whereas it seems Cuban families can still, even in exile, pride themselves on descent from the Dukes of Alba and on continuing connections with the court of Spain, North American families begin from scratch; *American* families, not offshoots of English ones. (All this despite late nineteenth-century efforts on the part of so many Americans to trace themselves back to Tudor gentility.)

This was certainly the case with the Lees. It was their position, from the beginning, as large Virginia landowners, that made them important, not any kinship with Lees in England. No doubt a coat of arms and money helped get them started; but after that it was land and tobacco, not a coat of arms, that counted. For generations, in fact, the actual details of kinship were obscured. Despite that coat of arms and various other Lee souvenirs of England, nobody remembered just where the first Lee came from, who his father was, what his wife's last name was. It was enough that he grew lots of tobacco.

Virginia itself did not begin as the one-crop, slave-holding aristocracy that it later became. At first, as in more northern colonies, it had a yeoman economy of mixed large and small farms growing a whole variety of crops. People were interested in finding out what would grow and what wouldn't. Governor Berkeley, for instance, planted mulberries, tried to encourage silk, and sent back three hundred pounds of it to the king. The smaller farmer depended on tobacco only to produce cash for a few imports and luxuries. There were large tobacco growers, there was slavery of a sort; but tobacco was not yet totally dominant, and the slaves were not yet Negro. Nor were the landowners noblemen, Cavalier favorites of the Stuarts granted immense tracts of land by royal whim. All these — one-crop economy, Negro slavery, grants to favorites — were to come later; but not in the 1640's when the first Lee arrived.

The original lands in Virginia were given not by royal grant but allotted by the headright system. This meant that any immigrant who managed to get himself over the water was granted fifty acres of land for himself, fifty for his wife and fifty for each servant he brought with him. He was required to settle on this land, clear it, and cultivate it. It was, in other words, much like the Homestead Act that settled the American Far West. The way to acquire large acreages was either by bringing servants, or by buying other people's headrights. These "servants" were really, in most cases, not servants but white slaves. That is, they were "indentured," poor people who sold themselves for a period of years, usually seven, in payment for their passage west. During these seven years they were the absolute property of their master, could be bought and sold and given as presents, just like any slaves. But after their period was up, they were free men. They could take up property themselves, and start off on their own, usually helped by their former masters. When they sold themselves, however, they sold their headrights too. That's the way it was possible for the evidently already fairly prosperous Richard Lee to arrive in America as the owner of a thousand acres of land in headrights: his own, his wife's and those of eighteen others, presumably such "servants."

So Virginia began, growing a variety of crops, and inhabited by a variety of persons: large landholders like the Lees, small landowners, freed indentured servants. Tobacco ruined this democratically developing society. From the time, as early as 1612, when Rolfe, the husband of Pocahontas and ancestor of the Randolphs, planted his first tobacco garden and discovered that tobacco could be profitably grown in Virginia and sold in England, the fate of the South was sealed. The appetite for the "filthy weed" (as King James I was among the first to call it) grew and grew in Europe. The supply in Virginia grew and grew to match the demand. Tobacco required certain things: lots of land, access to water, and a large, stable, unskilled labor force. Land was needed because the plant exhausted the soil, and new land had to be constantly opened up. The only decent transportation was by water. There were few or no roads; the tobacco was loaded directly at the tobacco-plantation wharf into ships that carried it to Europe. Riverside holdings were almost a necessity. Large acreages meant many hands. The Indians made poor slaves; they refused to work and died. The white indentured servants made poor slaves; they were too independent and soon became free, requiring constant replacement. The Negro could not leave, yet did not die. He worked, stayed, and bred, thus replacing himself. The supply, in any case, was cruelly abundant; replacements were always at hand. The answer then was the Negro.

So it was that the nature of tobacco growing formed the nature of the basic economy of Virginia — large riverside planters with many slaves prospered, while small inland farmers without slaves gave up and moved west. By 1700 the pattern was established that was to last till 1860. The tobacco plantation devoted to its single export crop, but otherwise almost self-sustaining, was the agricultural "economic unit," as the small farm was in the North. The Lees were among the big planter families that owned and ruled Virginia.

Who was Richard Lee, where did he come from? Until a few decades ago, nobody knew. There was that coat of arms, the main feature of which was three lines of checkerboard across the middle of the escutcheon, with little bricks called billets above and below it. On top sat a smug, small squirrel on its haunches, reaching for a nut on a twig. (This presumably represented frugality, a trait for which later Lees were not conspicuous.) Other families called Lee in Shropshire had similar arms. There were a few other clues, notably a silver cup. In Oxford at Queens College there still exists an elegant silver mug. It was the gift in 1658 of John Lee, eldest son of Richard the Founder, and has an inscription on it. The inscription says that John was born in CAPOHOWASICK WICKACOMOCO in Virginia (how those savage syllables must have thrilled the Oxonians of 1658), the firstborn of Richard Lee of Morton Regis in Shropshire. This, one would suppose, would have made everything simple; but unfortunately there is no Morton Regis in Shropshire. Nonetheless, this same Morton Regis is inscribed on the gravestone of Richard Lee II, John's brother (Merton, not Morton this time). Confusion and bafflement.

Finally in 1929 a family Bible turned up which had an authentic record of the parentage of Richard the Emigrant. It was *Nordley* Regis, not Morton, where the Lees came from. Someone had made a mistake in engraving the cup, and the mistake was copied in engraving the tombstone. Nobody cared. This pedigree discovered in 1929 was accepted by the English College of Heralds in 1930.*
Richard senior turned out to be a younger son of a Richard Lee, in turn younger son of a John Lee of the Lees of Coton, bona fide country gentlemen with large land holdings, an Elizabethan mansion called Coton Hall (mucked up by Victorians later), and a parish church (equally mucked up by Victorians) full of canopied Lee tombs. What more could an American family in search of genealogical roots desire? These English Lees, who'd been in Shropshire for some six hundred years when Richard left, continued to stay there for several hundred years more. They never did much of anything else.

What is really interesting about all this is that John, sent back to Oxford as early as the 1650's, a pattern followed in succeeding generations, did not seem to notice that his cup was incorrectly in-

* But strangely enough, not by most later Lee biographers, including Hendrick and Freeman.

scribed; and that the descendants of Richard II did not seem to care either. Later Lees, despite several inquiries of the eighteenth and nineteenth centuries, could not find out the facts. Though the Lees had continuing English connections of one kind or another, even with the Shropshire Lees, right down through the eighteenth century, their origins remained hidden. Obviously Elizabethan mansions and canopied tombs were a lot less interesting to early Lees than . . . land.

From Richard the Emigrant on, the Lees acquired and held great quantities of land. When Richard died in 1664 he owned something between thirteen and sixteen thousand acres. No one at that time owned more of Virginia. Not only was he busy acquiring land and making money from the tobacco he planted on it, but he became, under the patronage of Governor Berkeley, who liked gentlemen with coats of arms, a public figure. To this extent, at least, Richard's English family *was* important. His rise was steady. Emigrating in 1639 or early 1640, he was already in 1641 clerk of the quarter court; in 1643 attorney general of the colony, the first such on record; sheriff of York County in 1646, burgess of same in '47; in 1649 secretary of state; and finally, crowning glory for a Virginian, in 1651 a member of the Council.

The Council, of which Lees were to be members in each succeeding generation, was the senior of the legislative houses. As in other colonies, there were two branches, modeled upon the English Houses of Lords and Commons. The House of Burgesses corresponded to the House of Commons and was elective. The Council, corresponding roughly to the House of Lords, had members who were appointed, supposedly by the king, but actually at the will of the governor. The appointment was usually for life, and there were never more than twelve members. The scions of plantation families succeeded each other through the generations, and to be on the Council remained the highest honor in the colony until the body was finally dissolved in 1776 by the Revolution. The ancestry of our House and Senate is plain here.

Richard Lee's prosperous political career was interrupted by the dethronement and death of Charles I. Berkeley and his protégé Lee were both fanatical Royalists. When Cromwell took over England, Berkeley ceased to be governor. He retired to his plantation Green Spring (later a Lee property) and stayed there, cursing Cromwell and entertaining Cavaliers in exile. Lee, more cautious, was less conspicuously agin the government. He retired from politics, grew tobacco, and finally bought an estate in England and went to live there. The estate was at a place called Stratford-Langton near London, and he almost settled permanently. But just after the restoration of Charles II and just before his own death he returned to Virginia. He set up housekeeping at Cobb's Hall, on his lands at Dividing Creek on Chesapeake Bay, between the Potomac and the Rappahannock, and there he died in 1664. The English estate was sold, the Lees stayed in Virginia (most of them anyway); but it was a near thing. A year or two one way or another might have found them all in England for good.

By 1664 when Richard died, he and his family were firmly and flourishingly planted in America. There were eight children; but there was plenty of land to go around. To his widow (who later married again) went Cobb's Hall. To John went lands up the Potomac, where so many later Lee plantation houses were to rise. To Richard, the second son, was left Paradise, the first of his father's landholdings, on a creek inland from the York River. Francis, the next brother, settled permanently in London, but he too inherited lands, two parcels called War Captains Neck and Papermakers Neck (nobody knows why). Among the other children, William, Hancock, Charles, and the daughters Betsy and Ann, were divided the remaining properties on the Potomac, which included the site of the future Mount Vernon, land in Maryland, and leftover land on Dividing Creek. There was plenty for everybody.

Richard I, for all his contemporary prominence, is a vague character. Even his portrait tells nothing — a round-chinned, blank face, a full-bottomed wig. Whether it is the fault of the painter or the sitter, Richard remains a worthy cipher. Not so his two inheritor sons, John the gay bachelor, and Richard II, the morose, religious Royalist.

John, who gave his college the cup, died young. The most striking incident of a short life was his part in the building, in 1670, of a Banqueting Hall. Together with three neighbors, Isaac Allerton, Henry Corbin and Thomas Gerrard, he signed a contract to erect a place where, "for the better preservation" of their friendship, the four neighbors could meet to entertain their "men, masters and friends yearly." High doings, especially for seventeenth-century America; and more remarkable for having as a participant Allerton, whose father had come over on the Mayflower; and whose mother's name was Fear Brewster.* Imagine anything of that sort in Boston. Aside from his cup, his Banqueting Hall and his will — which lists amenities such as gray suits with silver buttons, gloves with silver tops, guns, fishing gear and pistols — nothing else remains of gay John; but this seems enough to sketch his character.

His lands were inherited by Richard II, who was as serious as John seems to have been frivolous. Richard moved into Mount Pleasant,† John's new seat on the Potomac, with a wife and a library. The wife, a Corbin, daughter of Henry, one of John's banqueting mates, was very much a catch, and established Richard as following the proper Quaker second-generation obligation: marry well. His offices as burgess, councillor and receiver of duties on the Potomac establish him as a man of some weight in colonial affairs. A catalogue of his library seems to indicate that he was a rather mel-

* Fear had a brother called Wrestling: Wrestling Brewster.

† The original house on the site may have been named Matholic, not Mount Pleasant, which was the name a George Lee, son of a Richard III, gave to a later house he built on this site. But the plantation nonetheless always seems to be referred to as Mount Pleasant whenever it is mentioned in Hendrick or Cazenove Lee.

ancholy student of religion — a Cavalier in politics, but a Puritan in faith. A dour portrait does nothing to contradict this impression of gloom.

Richard too, like brother John, had studied at Oxford; but his interest was the Church, and he was almost persuaded to make a career of it. He knew Greek, Latin and Hebrew. He read the works of Florus Franciscus, Paulus Orosius and Corderius, as well as such edifying books as *Learn to Die, The Mischief of Sin* and *Divine Breathings*. A man like that might well have been happy in Boston, except for his excessive loyalty to the Stuarts, as evidenced by *Power Communicated by God to the Prince*. He certainly had no use for Bacon and his rebellion of 1676, and supported his father's patron Berkeley during his disgracefully repressive second post-Restoration governorship.

Bacon's Rebellion began as Indian trouble. Just as in Massachusetts, the Indians of Virginia began to get restless at the encroachment of the whites. In 1675 settlers were massacred. Governor Berkeley, unpopular anyway since his restoration, failed to prosecute the war in a sufficiently bloodthirsty manner. Nathaniel Bacon, a young man of good family, cousin in fact of essayist Lord Bacon, took things into his own hands, and started killing Indians without the governor's permission. This led to a break with Berkeley, and then to a full-scale rebellion against the governor and all his supporters on the part of Bacon's following, which included not only poor whites but frontier landowners such as the contemporary William Byrd.

Richard Lee II was a member of the governing cabal against which Bacon and his supporters rebelled. Lee's name is on the specific list of nineteen whom Bacon charged with being "sponges" sucking up the public treasury and as "wicked and pernitious consillers." As such, Lee was imprisoned by the rebels for seven weeks. The insurrection collapsed after Bacon's death, and Berkeley took such a savage revenge on Bacon's followers that he was called back to explain himself to the more lenient Charles II. Shortly after, he died in disgrace.

Richard Lee stayed snugly in Virginia. When his beloved Stuart, James II, was exiled, he refused to accept the Dutch usurper William. William came to the throne in 1688, but at first Richard Lee would not take the oath of allegiance to him. Finally common sense prevailed. In 1690 he took the oath and was restored to the Council. Nothing much happened to him after that. Always eager in the service of despotism, Richard was the first Potomac landholder to acknowledge feudal obligations to the Fairfaxes, who had been granted proprietary rights to the Northern Neck by Charles II over the bitter opposition of the people who already owned land there. In fact, later on the Fairfaxes had their agency office right in Lee's own Mount Pleasant.

What most ingratiates Richard II to modern tastes is his kindness to his brothers and their heirs. He might have taken over their inherited lands on a legal technicality. Instead, in 1707 he confirmed their full ownership, signing over Cobb's Hall to Charles Jr., heir of his brother Charles, and neighboring Ditchley to his brother Hancock. Descendants or connections of these two branches of the Lee family own Ditchley and Cobb's Hall to the present day.*

Perhaps what made Richard II morose was the depression in tobacco caused by the Navigation Laws of 1661. Whereas before Virginia had traded with all Europe from Russia to Italy, now tobacco could only be sent to England on English ships. The result was disaster. Planters had overexpanded in the boom. Prices fell from fourpence a pound in 1650 to half a penny in 1667. The frontier bonanza gave way to a slump which lasted through the next two decades. It was America's first depression. Prosperity came again, as it usually does; and as usual, favored those who could survive it best,

---

* Cobb's Hall descended through five generations of Charles Lees to a Richard Lee, whose daughter married a Harvey; the Harveys, up through 1957 at least, still owned it. Ditchley passed from Lees to in-laws, the Balls, and has recently been restored by Mrs. Alfred I. du Pont, the former Jessie Ball. The Balls are all tied up with the Lees; George Washington's mother was a Ball.

the big businessmen. In this case it was the large landholders who managed to stay afloat, those who had slaves as cheap labor. But when Richard II died in 1714 he left an estate little greater than he himself had inherited. He was, unlike his father, no go-getter; and unlike his son Thomas too, who was the real establisher of the Lees as Lords of the Potomac.

Thomas (1690–1750) *was* a go-getter. Perhaps the fact that he was only the fourth son gave him an incentive his more well-endowed older brothers Richard III, Philip and Francis didn't have. In any case, he was the important Lee of the third generation; and he was the one who built Stratford, greatest and most famous of the Lee plantation houses.

As only fourth son, there was no Oxford education for Thomas. He had to acquire Latin and Greek (without which no Virginia gentleman could pretend to be considered acceptable) all on his own.* Whereas his brothers inherited rich land, he had to be satisfied with a mere thousand or so acres, most of it poor stuff in Maryland. While his uncles and brothers and cousins were comfortably settled at Ditchley and Cobb's Hall, secure as owners of Paradise or Mount Pleasant, Thomas had to fend for himself.

He was, like his grandfather, a born fender. In him the pioneer virtues of energy and acquisitiveness revived. Like his grandfather, he presents a certain lack of definite biographical character. Unlike his grandfather, however, he cannot be called "faceless." His portrait, in contrast to the bland nonentity of Richard I, shows a handsome virile swarthiness, largeness of nose and chin, full lips and big eyes, a face well able to carry off the heavy wig and satin gown of president of the Council; the outgoing, no-nonsense, sensual yet humorous face of a man riding zestfully on the crest of a particular wave, the high tide of eighteenth-century planter prosperity.

---

* "Fithian tells the story of young Bob Carter, sadly lacking in 'languages,' but much in love with Betty Tayloe of Mount Airy. 'The young lady's mother told him last Sunday that until he understands Latin he will never be able to win a young lady of family and fortune for his wife' " (Hendrick, *The Lees of Virginia*).

His father had been a child of depression. By the time Thomas had married a Ludwell in 1722 (an even better marriage than that of his father to a Corbin) and had leased Mount Pleasant from his brother Richard III who, like uncle Francis, lived in England, tobacco had made a recovery. Thomas Lee's own career began as resident agent of the Fairfaxes. Their proprietorship included some five million acres between the Potomac and the Rappahannock, the so-called Northern Neck. Thomas as their agent traveled all over the Fairfax land on horseback. It was not long before he began acquiring choice bits of it for himself, mostly to westward (sixteen thousand acres between the Great and Little Falls of the Potomac, forty-two hundred acres in Fauquier County where Warrenton is now, etc.).

He was particularly interested in the West, among the earliest of that race of entrepreneurs and visionaries who saw the possibilities of a continent. Virginia of course thought of its farthest boundary as "the Great South Sea, including California," supposed then to be an island. The fact that Spain and France had prior claims to most of this meant little to Thomas. Manifest Destiny called, and he wrote, "The French are intruders into this America," in a report he made to the Lords of Trade as president of the Council and acting governor of Virginia.

He bargained with Indians, in a conference at Lancaster, Pennsylvania, in 1744, and for a chest of knives, kettles and Jew's harps* got a treaty from the Six Nations granting to Virginia the Northwest Territory. In 1748 he organized an Ohio Company, a family affair with himself as president and various kinfolk, two sons, a nephew, a son-in-law, and Potomac neighbors Lawrence and Augustine Washington, Robert Carter Jr. and George Fairfax as partners. The Ohio Company was the first determined effort to organize that part of the western wilderness for colonization, and to create on the banks of the Ohio River an English, rather than a

* How did Indians manage with Jew's harps?

French Empire. The actual project ran into trouble; but the gesture was important.

This western real estate speculation was Thomas' one truly national effort. Otherwise he was busy at home, getting land, making money, and serving on the Council. By this time, the first half of the eighteenth century, that pattern of an oligarchy of slaveholders living on their riverside plantations and running the colony on an hereditary basis, was firmly established. The families had had time to marry each other through three or four generations, and nearly all of them were "kin" — cousins, in-laws, connections. They lived in handsome houses, the best of them built between 1725 and 1760, along the four great waterways, the James, the York, the Rappahannock and the Potomac, as well as such estuaries as the Piankatank and the Poropotank (the Red Man's Revenge). Many lived on or near Chesapeake Bay itself, on Mobjack Bay, Dividing Creek, the Wicomico River. They were served and supported by a great new army of recently imported slaves. From 1700 to 1730 the Negro population increased from six thousand to thirty thousand. White immigration had ceased. In fact, emigration, the emigration from Tidewater Virginia of the dispossessed poor whites, down to North Carolina or westward, was now the rule.

Those who stayed and prospered, like Thomas Lee, lived a very pleasant life indeed. This period, between 1700 and 1760, was the climax of Romantic Old Virginia, of mansions and boxwood and balls and carriages, trips to London, education at Oxford, the importation of fine furniture and china and horses, of lavish and continual hospitality.

All up and down the rivers lived the grandees — cousins, in-laws, connections. On the James were Carter's Grove, named by the builder in honor of his mother, daughter of "King" Carter of Corotoman; Green Spring, where Governor Berkeley retired to curse Cromwell, later inherited by the Lees through the Ludwells; Teddington of the Lightfoots (connections of the Lees as evidenced by names like Francis Lightfoot Lee); Claremont, where lived the Allens, and where a century later Edgar Allan Poe visited and got some of his tastes for decaying grandeur; Brandon (once owned by the brother-in-law of Shakespeare's daughter Judith) and Upper Brandon, both later on homes of Harrisons (kin by marriage to Carters, Fitzhughs, Randolphs and Byrds, and so of the Lees), the other family which, like the Adamses and Roosevelts, has supplied two Presidents to the Union; Flower de Hundred, whose odd name is the corruption of a lovely one, that of Lady Temperence Flowerdew, wife of the first owner, Sir George Yeardley; then, beyond Ducking Stool Point, most famous of all houses on the river, lordly Westover, built by the second William Byrd in 1730; next to Westover, Berkeley, earlier and most famous house of the Harrisons (how odd that both a President, Benjamin Harrison, and his succeeding Vice President, John Tyler, should have been born on neighboring plantations, Berkeley and Greenway; and been elected in the most shamelessly demagogic campaign in American history, based solely upon the fact that Harrison was supposed to be a hardy frontiersman who lived in a log cabin! "Tippecanoe and Tyler too!"); then the Forest, where Thomas Jefferson wooed and won Martha Wayles with his music; Appomattox, a name only too closely associated with later Lee history, home of the Eppes from 1635 on through three hundred years; Eppington, another Eppes place beyond, where John Wayles Eppes, Jefferson's son-in-law (Jeffersons related to Randolphs, Randolphs related to Lees) came from; Cawson's, birthplace of sinister John Randolph of Roanoke when his maternal grandfather Theodorick Bland (Blands were kin of the Lees) lived there; and then Shirley, equally famous along with Westover and Berkeley, acquired by John, eldest son of "King" Carter, from his wife, and home of his granddaughter Ann, the mother of Robert E. Lee; Turkey Island, beyond Shirley, where William Randolph settled in 1660. From his seven sons and two daughters descended not only Randolphs but Marshalls, Jeffersons, Blands and Lees, Lees, Lees (including Robert E.).

A similar trip up the shorter York River would have revealed Rosewell of the Pages (kin to the Lees through Carters, Tayloes, Grymes) with a stairway so wide eight people could sweep down it abreast. The York splits, upstream, into two tributaries, the Pamunkey and the Mattapony. Near the Pamunkey was the house of the Chamberlaynes, where George Washington first met Martha Custis of nearby White House, widow of Daniel Custis (Mrs. Robert E. Lee was a Custis). On up the Pamunkey and the Mattapony lived Dandridges (Martha was a Dandridge) and Braxtons, Robinsons and Corbins, all Lee entwined. On the Severn was seated Augustine Warner, ancestor of both George Washington and Robert E. Lee. Here, on creeks off the Chesapeake, were nestled sooner or later Landsdowne, Severnby, Eagle Point and White Mast, Level Green, the Shelter, Lowland Cottage, Hockley; White Hall, Glenroy, Goshen, Midlothian; Waverly, Newstead, Exchange and Toddsbury, sheltering their clutch of Taliaferros (Tullivers), Tabbs and Todds (Tabbs later on kin of the du Ponts).

Up the Rappahannock, the same thing: Corotoman, home of Robert Carter the "King," who sent out his children and their descendants to Shirley and Carter's Grove and Berkeley on the James, and to Rosewell on the York; sent out a Charles who married Anne Byrd of Westover, a Mary who married a Braxton and a Lucy who married a Fitzhugh of Eagle's Nest up on the Potomac. Thomas Lee's sister Ann also married a Fitzhugh.

The Potomac of course was the Lee river. Not only were there various Lee plantations along the banks, but many of the other houses contained Lee relations, like the Fitzhughs. At one time or another, beginning with Mount Pleasant, there were Lee Hall, Leesylvania, Chantilly and, grandest of them all, Stratford. Mount Vernon and Arlington both had strong Lee connections. Ditchley and Cobb's Hall were not too far away. Hominy Hall housed the first Mrs. Richard Henry Lee (an Aylett). Pecatone, where lived Corbins and Turbervilles (who kept their slaves chained in dungeons beneath the house), also had many Lee connections. Henry

Corbin of Pecatone was one of the Banqueting Hall neighbors. Nomini Hall, down the river from Stratford, was the home of Councillor Robert Carter, grandson of the "King," who survives so vividly in the diary of his tutor, Philip Vickers Fithian, the one truly living account of what this ample plantation life was like. Lees make frequent appearances there. George Washington's brother, John Augustine, lived in nearby Bushfield. Chantilly, Richard Henry Lee's house, was right across Nomini Creek. Beyond great Stratford was Wakefield, Washington's birthplace, now reconstructed. Close by, James Monroe was born, and the father of Chief Justice Marshall lived. Then came the Fitzhughs, who not only built Eagle's Nest, but Bedford, Marmion, Boscobel, Belle Air, Chatham and Ravensworth. Some of these still survive, and one of the estates, Bedford, has been in Fitzhugh hands in modern times. (An interior from Marmion is now in the American Wing of the Metropolitan Museum in New York, of which James Biddle of Andalusia has been the curator.) Hilton and Waterloo were two other Washington houses. Gunston Hall, on Mason's Neck, was the house of George Mason; Belvoir was the house of the Fairfaxes.

The greatest of all these Potomac houses, and of all these Lee houses, was Stratford. It is as the builder of Stratford, and father of sons brought up there, that Thomas Lee really touches fame. Since Thomas began to build it about 1725, Stratford has been the spiritual core of the Lee family's pride and affection. It is certainly one of the more grandiose of surviving Virginia plantation houses; less sheerly beautiful than say Westover, less gracious than many a smaller house; but then Stratford does not aim to be gracious. It aims to be, and is, impressive. There is indeed something formidable, frowning, castlelike, about its towering chimneys over the broad roof that comes down so heavily above the comparatively low story-and-a-half structure with its disproportionately high front stoop. It speaks of the seventeenth rather than the eighteenth century, of possible attacks by Indians, and of the morose royalism of

Thomas' father Richard rather than the enlightened radicalism of his son Richard.

There in Stratford, after 1730, Thomas lived. There his famous sons grew up. There his kinsman, but not descendant, Robert E. Lee was born. Before Thomas was able to move in, the older Mount Pleasant, where he had been living, burned down. His wife and child had to be thrown out of a window, a white servant girl died, and he himself was much scorched. Caroline, Queen of England, gave him several hundred pounds from the Privy Purse, which helped him to finish Stratford. The fire was probably set by "transported felons." Everything was lost, and the site has ever since been known as Burnt House Field.

A hundred years, less a decade, had passed since the first Lee came to Virginia. In another hundred years the Lees were to lose Stratford. The year 1730 marks the midpoint of their history as planters. The name Stratford was derived from the first Richard's estate in England at Stratford-Langton. Thomas himself had been there in 1716, and had probably studied the big house of the neighborhood, royal Ham House, built in the shape of an H like the Lee's own American Stratford. With the building and occupancy of Stratford, the summit of Lee prosperity was reached. Though later Lees were far more famous, no other Lee quite matched Thomas as sheer man of power: politically as president of the Council and acting governor of the colony, economically as agent of the Fairfaxes, western speculator and great landowner. The Lees and their cousins and their in-laws and their connections were all doing very well indeed.

3

Adams

IT IS indeed a comedown to pass from Stratford to Braintree and from the Lees to the Adamses. The contrast is great but salutary. It could not be greater if we studied two different continents, not merely two different colonies. Though the colonies were a thousand miles apart, they were even further apart spiritually. Massachusetts had been settled as a Holy Land, a place where those (and no others) who knew the Truth could dwell apart as upon a Sacred Mount. Virginia had been settled by people who hoped to become Gentlemen, rich and great gentlemen — quick. Such religion as they tolerated was an Establishment dependent on them, in a church headed by their King.

Massachusetts was settled in an orderly fashion largely by cohesive congregations who formed themselves into "towns" (what we would call townships). Virginia evolved its slave-owning, one-crop economy. Massachusetts had developed as a spreading patchwork of farm towns and seaports. Each town was a largely self-supporting organism, self-governed. These towns were not market villages for outlying farmers; they were instead quite tightly knit cooperatives *of* farmers built about church, school and the ownership of common lands. They were derived from various sorts of English village organizations; but the New England village was a new type and invention all its own. Villages varied, but most of them followed the same pattern: church members met at town meeting to elect a board of officers and lesser posts. The chief officers were the selectmen. They allotted lands, beginning with the very first settlement, decided boundary disputes, and managed the considerable affairs of common pasturage and woodlot, as well as those of church and school. The clergyman's salary and that of the schoolteacher were paid by the town. As compared to Virginia it was far more democratic, but perhaps less individualistic. Class distinctions in such a tight world were important but minute. The lowest villager, if a property holder and church member, was not far from the lordliest, sat on the same town boards and in the same congregation. The gulf in Virginia between the owner of thousands of acres and the poor white squatter was in the New England village reduced to that between the small farmer and the large one, between say a Deacon Adams and a Colonel Quincy of Braintree. Virginians had large horizons geographically, but narrow ones socially. They rode hundreds of miles to the seat of government at Williamsburg, but once there saw only their cousins. Guests were always welcome, hospitality endless; but otherwise they dealt mostly with slaves. Everybody in a New England town knew everybody else, rich or poor, prominent or obscure. Virginia stretched theoretically to the Pacific, and culturally across the Atlantic. Braintree was a boxed-up town surrounded by other, jealous, boxed-up towns. Boston was an enemy, and wicked; strangers were suspect. Yet from these two opposed backgrounds Richard Henry Lee and John Adams managed to get together and help found a country. What held them together was the British Empire and loyalty to its king, the English language, and traditions of freedom.

The little spot where the Adamses rooted and grew had an odd beginning. It was, ironically, Merrymount, America's pioneer pleasure resort. The first settlement had been as early as 1625, when Captain Wollaston brought thirty or forty colonists to the slopes of the Blue Hills south of Boston, cleared land, and built rude log shelters. The settlement was called Mount Wollaston, and though it soon failed, and Captain Wollaston removed to Virginia with most of his followers, the name stuck. The Quincy estate, where Abigail Adams spent so much of her childhood, was named Mount Wollaston.

This experiment lasted only about a year. What was left of the colony was then taken over by that almost legendary figure, the Royalist adventurer Thomas Morton. He changed the name to Merrymount, and there held forth with maypoles and other doings so scandalous that his Puritan neighbors sent Captain Miles Standish to arrest him. He was shipped off to England. In 1629 he returned, brought back by none other than Isaac Allerton, progenitor of Isaac of the Banqueting Hall. Morton was thereupon placed in the stocks and shipped right back to England again. His house was burned to the ground in the sight of the Indians "for their satisfaction," and that was the end of Merrymount.

This interlude rather put settlers off the locality; but in 1635–36 various grants were made to various worthies, such as Edmund Quincy and William Hutchinson (whose wife Anne was later excommunicated and went to Rhode Island). Reverend John Wheelwright, the as-yet unexcommunicated brother-in-law of Anne, secured a grant of 250 acres in 1637 to found a church. He erected what was called the "Chapel of Ease." This vital step having been taken, the settlement was now ready to set itself up as a town. This could only be done with a church as a nucleus and church members as citizens. In 1640 they were permitted to call themselves Braintree. Nobody is quite sure exactly why; Braintree is a town in Essex in England from which presumably some settlers came. Not the Adamses.

The town records begin with the setting aside of school lands. The second notice, in 1641, is "concerning a mill." "It is ordered that their [sic] shall noe other mill be built in the plantation without the consent of Richard Right." So on the basis of a church, a school and a mill was founded, as on granite, a "typical New England town." On these three, religion, education and, later on, industry, New England grew and prospered.

A Nathanill Adams is mentioned in 1640 (present at a meeting apropos a highway "layed through Brantry"): but that's not our family. Even then Adams was an uncommonly common name. But Henry Adams, the ancestor, was first keeper of town records, beginning in 1643. The first marriages recorded in Braintree were those of Henry junior in 1643 to Elizabeth Paine, and of his brother Joseph to Abigail Baxter in 1650. Henry junior and another brother Samuel both appear in 1646: "A grant of taking timber off of the common for a mans own use, but not to sell out of towne."

Henry, the father, had emigrated to Boston in 1636 with numerous children, and to Braintree shortly afterward. As in the case of the Lees, nobody knew where he had come from, or who his father was. In the beginning of course nobody cared; then in 1823, John Adams was moved to erect a monument to the aboriginal Henry, stating imperishably in stone that he "took his flight from the Dragon persecution in Devonshire." The Dragon of course was the Established Church. Then in 1853 a pedigree was published claiming not that Henry was descended from Adam, but that he was descended from an ap Adam ("son of Adam" in Welsh) and of the fine baronial ap Adam family from Stoke-Gabriel, Devon. Unfortunately both John's Dragon and the ap Adam descent were false; the ap Adam descent was a deliberate forgery. Charles Francis Adams II conjectured that Henry must have come from the original Braintree in Essex. Wrong again. Finally in 1923 a group of eager Americans bought an old farmhouse in Northamptonshire, believing *that* was Henry's ancestral home. This unfortunately was in all the newspapers, so when it turned out to be a mistake in 1925, it had to be denied in all the newspapers.

Finally, finally, about 1927, just about the time that the Lee genealogy got unraveled, the truth about the Adamses was revealed to a breathless world. Henry was a native of Barton David in Somersetshire, near Glastonbury. It had all been even more upsetting than the chase after the Lee origins; especially since in the end we get no manor houses or canopied tombs, but just a lot of farmers. A John of about 1500 is on the local muster rolls as among the "able bylemen fyndying harnys," which means he could afford to supply his own arms for military service, in this case a bow. These Adams farmers stayed farmers. There is a dim, fond hope that the plain Adamses of Barton David may, why not, be descendants of the Fitz Adams of the nearby manor of Charlton Adam. But alas, this is no more than a happy thought. However, one can always console oneself by calling one's ancestors "yeomen." Yeomen are always "sturdy"; farmers are only too frequently "dirt." There is no record whatsoever of persecution by a Dragon or by anything else.

The Squire family, that of Henry's wife, was a tiny bit more distinguished. Two sisters of Edith Squire Adams also emigrated, Anne and Margaret, Mrs. Aquila Purchase and Mrs. John Shepard respectively. This, not a Dragon, is probably what moved Henry across the water.

From 1646 on, the year in which Henry senior died, the name Adams appears with increasing frequency in the town records of Braintree. But not, in the early years, so very prominently. The Adamses were by no means first citizens. For every mention of an Adams in the early days, there are half a dozen of a Bass, Brackett or Veasey; and on almost every page a Quincy (then more properly spelled, as it is pronounced, *Quinsey*). From that first deeding of lands for a school in 1640 to the appointment of a committee in 1791 to "enquire of what became of the money Borrowed of Col. Josiah Quincy in the year 1775," an Edmund or a John or a Josiah or a Norton is recorded, usually as being elected or appointed to something. "Then Coll⁰ [Colonel] Josiah Quincy was nominated and Chosen Moderator" in 1762, a monotonous repetition through the decades. By 1734, it was Captain Peter Adams who was being chosen for this exalted honor, that is, the man who presided over the town meeting during elections, or the appointment of town offices, such as Assessors, Fire Wardens, Cullers of Staves, Sealors of Wood and of Leather, Surveyors of Lumber, Fence Viewers, Tythingmen and Hog Reaves. Almost everyone got into the act.

One can observe the rise of family by the kind of position the members of it held, the frequency of election, and the titles by which they are dignified. Joseph Adams, son of Henry, ancestor of John, made selectman, along with an Edmund Quincy in 1673; but there's no mention of him again till 1690, when he and Dependence French are referred to as the "late counstables." But an Edmund Quincy of one or another of the four generations of them turns up almost every year as Captain or Colonel or Honorable. It was easy enough to tell who was who, in Braintree, by looking at the record.

"Then voted that no Inhabitant of this town shall hereafter, Presume to Dig or carry off from the common Lands, any stone or stones whatsoever." With this sort of thing the august body, the Honorable Edmund Quincy presiding, concerned itself. An admirable, if usually petty, school of self-government. The weight of the town and its judgments and its prohibitions and permissions must have been ever-present and oppressive.

Strangers were *not* welcome. One of the earliest edicts, as of 1641, proclaims that "noe man that is not received as an inhabitant into the town shall have liberty to build any house" without the selectmen's approval. In 1653, "Upon Consideration of great ill conveniencyes that may come to the Towne of Brantree by persons coming into inhabite amongst us, it is therefore ordered that no person . . . shall come . . . without the Selectmen's consent upon the penalty of ninetene [sic] shillings fine for every three dayes they shall stay amongst us." By 1681 this penalty was reduced to ten shillings. And in 1792: "You are in the name of the Commonwealth of Massachusetts directed to warn . . . Francis Thayer of Boston in said County Merchant, and James Dill of Hull, Cordwinder . . . and unto Titus a Trancient negroman who have lately come into this Town . . . that they depart the limits thereof within fifteen days." New England hospitality mellowed through the years.

The Adams family grew. Henry's sons scattered abroad to Medfield and Chelmsford. Henry junior, the oldest of them, was killed by Indians in Medfield. This was in 1676 during the Indian War and the very same year during which Richard Lee II was thrown into jail by Bacon. Of all the Adams brothers, only Joseph seems to have remained in Braintree. Joseph in turn had twelve children; most of these, too, stayed in Braintree. The girls married neighbors (Bass, Webb, Savil). John, who married a Webb, went to Boston and became a sea captain and made money and was the grandfather of Samuel Adams. Son Joseph II stayed home and married three times (Chapin, Bass, Hobart). His brother Captain Peter stayed there too, and his name appears far more frequently in the town records. Only with Joseph's son, Deacon John of the fourth generation, does the Adams name begin to carry real weight there. Appearing brilliantly upon the town scene in 1722–23 as Sealor of Leather (John being a cordwainer, or worker in leather; and John Quincy, Esquire being at the time Moderator) he moves from honor to honor. While Captain Peter is already a Selectman, John moves up to Tithingman in 1724–25, Constable in 1728, and finally in 1734, Selectman (Captain Peter being Moderator), a position he was still occupying in 1758 shortly before his death in 1760. He is by then always referred to by his title of Deacon Adams. Deacon Adams and his family were progressing. He and his brother Ebenezer had both married Boylstons. The Boylstons in Boston were rich, as the various portraits of them by Copley indicate; and though this didn't seem to rub off on their in-laws in Braintree, it was a step upward socially. The Boston Adamses too were prospering. At least Captain John's son, Samuel the elder, was a merchant and a deacon and a selectman in the big city. Already the descendants of Henry had begun to swarm like locusts westward. The Reverend Joseph, elder brother of Deacon John, had actually gone to Harvard, class of 1710, first of his family there. Altogether some half-dozen Adamses went there before the century was done. Joseph was pastor of Newington, New Hampshire, progenitor of five children and innumerable grandchildren, so well known there and so long lived that he was facetiously referred to as the Bishop of Newington.

Adamses spread from Braintree out to Boston, Medfield, Chelmsford, Sherborn, Holliston, Framingham, Watertown, Medway, Hopkinton and Westborough. There were Adamses in Canterbury, Connecticut; Adamses up in the wilds of New Hampshire. One gets the impression, as of the third and fourth generations, and up through the eighteenth century, of a healthy and fruitful clan springing up and out from their center between the Blue Hills and the sea, bound to amount to something someday; though nowhere yet near to the possessions and position of the Lees. Farmers, selectmen, those half-dozen Harvard graduates (mostly country clergymen), money in Boston, connections with other money (Boylstons), but nothing very important yet.

One should expect, then, a sort of multifarious popping up in Revolutionary times like that of the Biddles, if not the Lees — two or three people of some real prominence, many others of worthy station. Actually this does not quite happen. Beginning with the generation of Deacon John, fourth in America, a curious fatality descends, rather awesomely, like some dim Hawthornian cloud, over the whole clan. True, Samuel, son of merchant Samuel, son of Captain John, does arise in Boston as firebrand of the Revolution. John junior, son of Deacon John, becomes our second President. From this John descends the Royal Line; but about this lonely eminence stretches a sort of barren waste, a blasted heath, a dearth of Adamses of merit. Samuel left no continuing family in the male line. *None* of Deacon John's other sons founded Adams families. The children of the deacon's brothers and uncles and great-uncles, though they did spread through Connecticut, New Hampshire, Vermont, New York State, Ohio, Iowa and points west in legions, never seem to have really amounted to much. One is appalled by the scarcity among them of even Harvard graduates.

Out of this sea of obscurity and often failure, emerges only the Royal Line itself: John, John Quincy, Charles Francis, his four sons, and their not very numerous or nationally prominent descendants. Of Deacon John there appear to be no other male descendants except for a mysterious stray sheep, John Quincy Adams, in the seventh generation (John 7, Elisha 6, Elihu 5, Deacon John 4, Joseph 3, Joseph 2, Henry 1). He was a printer, married to unknown females, and took off for New Orleans, where he may have had sons. Otherwise all the non-Royal Adams lines descended from Deacon John drifted off into females, married and unmarried, and into obscurity.

Of non-Deacon John Adamses we have Ladowick H. of Sempronius, New York (1840) and his brother Aristedes, sons of Loammi; or the Adams of Eden (Vermont), like Epiphanes Vespasian, and his brother Veranes, who ended up in Yankee Jim, California. There are the Adamses of Blue Mound, Kansas; or Jesse who married "a German lady," and his brother Festus Melancthon. None of these became very famous. The *Dictionary of American Biography* is indeed full of a random selection of Adamses, mildly distinguished in one way or another, and quite a few true-enough descendants of Henry of Braintree: Hannah the historian, one of the Medfield group, whose father, a bankrupt farmer, was so bookish he was called the "locomotive library." Hannah wrote a history of New England and a *Dictionary of Religions*. Or Alvin Adams of Andover, Vermont, pioneer in the express business (New York to Boston), which reaped great profits in the Civil War, shipping arms. "On his death he left few friends . . . and no monument save the great express business." William T. Adams, better known as Oliver Optic, wrote 126 books for boys that sold many more than a million copies. Unlike Alvin, his motto was "First God, then Country, then Friends." Another William Adams, president of Union Theological Seminary, was often regarded as the leading

Presbyterian of his time. He sprang from a nest of Adamses in Connecticut. They were all *Yale* graduates. Herbert B. Adams, historian, was one of the founders and long secretary of the American Historical Society, of which cousin Henry was onetime president. There are in fact quite a number of these stray Adams worthies; but evidently they don't count as being Adamses. That is, there are The Adamses; and then Adamses. Descent from Braintree is not enough. Somehow it's as though heredity had decided to concentrate all the exceptional Adams genes in one basket, rather than spreading them around. It's a purely father-to-son business for three generations, at that. Aside from this one lone shaft of eminence, the Adamses as a whole seem to be a peculiarly undistinguished family, considering their enormous number.

4

Biddle

IT IS logical to suppose that the Biddles would, in some fashion, fall halfway between the Adamses and the Lees. They do geographically; and in fact they do, by chance, socially and sociologically. That is, the family springs partly from the same large landowner roots as the Virginians, and partly from the same tradesman-religious refugee roots as the New Englanders. Like the first Lee, the first Biddle was a large landowner. Like a later Adams, he was also a cordwainer.

It's odd of course that this just-in-the-middle character should be so; a real coincidence. There were plenty of large landowners northward and religious refugees southward; but it does so happen that the Biddles were both planters and religious refugees, and in an area situated right between Braintree and the Potomac.

Alone among the four American Families, the Biddles did not begin where they have ended. They made their mark as a Pennsylvania family; but they began across the Delaware River in another colony, New Jersey. Like the Lees, they had great properties on a river, in this case the Delaware. Like the Adamses, they were part of a religious complex created around a village, Burlington, New Jersey, and a church, Quaker Meeting. Unlike either the Lees or the Adamses, they were real "proprietors." This sounds rather majestic and high-toned — Fairfaxes, Calverts, Penns. In New Jersey it wasn't. New Jersey, alone among the colonial states, managed to combine proprietorships and pettiness (trust New Jersey). Biddles were part of this.

The colonial proprietors were of course landlords, not settlers. Many of them never came to America, many that did come stayed a short time and then left. They were essentially real estate operators of a sort of feudal kind. Most of them were favorites of some king or other, given large tracts of land for their nice smiles, lands they in turn were permitted to sell or lease. They usually retained, however, various feudal rights over their grants. Those who bought from them had to acknowledge these feudal rights in one way or another, usually by paying an annual "quitrent." Proprietors also retained much political and administrative power. In Pennsylvania, where one family, the Penns, were proprietors of the whole colony, the situation was simple, if not satisfactory. The situation in New Jersey became both unbearably complicated and thoroughly unsatisfactory. Instead of one or two, there came to be literally hundreds of small proprietors. By a process of real estate subdivision (which has continued right down to the present day) original great tracts were divided and divided until the whole state was a crazy quilt of various kinds of ownerships. To be a "proprietor" then in New Jersey often meant no more than being a small farmer.

[38]

For half a century the white settlement of southern New Jersey had been confined to a scattering of Swedes, Finns and Dutchmen. Ownership passed back and forth between those two negligent colonial powers, Sweden and Holland, while the British continued to claim the whole area. They got it when they took Manhattan from the Dutch in 1664. The first real effort at English colonization in the area did not take place till 1675. A group of Quakers came to the east banks of the lower Delaware and were shortly followed by others. William Biddle, founder of his family, was one of these slightly later comers, arriving there around 1681. He was a leather-worker. As a Quaker, he had been jailed for his beliefs in London. He must nonetheless have been financially successful, since he arrived as a substantial property owner by virtue of various purchases made before he left London.

He was not only a property owner, but also one of these subdivided proprietors. The real estate operation of which he was the beneficiary had a long, complicated history. In 1664 King Charles, who wanted to make everybody happy without giving them any hard-to-come-by cash, bestowed on his brother James, Duke of York, a grant of lands that included almost all the territory now covered by the Middle Atlantic States, plus a few dividends such as Maine and Martha's Vineyard. In 1665 James in his turn granted the lands between the Hudson and the Delaware to two of his friends, John, Lord Berkeley, and Sir George Carteret. They had been faithful to the Stuarts in exile. Sir George had been governor of the Isle of Jersey during the civil wars and had sheltered Charles there at one point, so the new grant was called Nova Caesaria or New Jersey in his honor. The proprietors held the proprietorship jointly. Then Berkeley in 1674 sold his interest to one John Fenwick, a Quaker. With Fenwick was associated one Edward Byllynge, a London brewer and also a Quaker. Both these gentlemen were in a parlous financial position and took over the lands in New Jersey with the idea of salvaging their fortunes. Byllynge at the time was in fact bankrupt. Fenwick was little better off and had been in jail for debt.

However, they managed to raise enough money to pay off Berkeley. Then Fenwick and Byllynge quarreled.

New Jersey had been divided into East Jersey (northward section) and West Jersey (southward section). West Jersey in turn was divided again between Fenwick and Byllynge. Their unsavory fights over real estate, which involved William Penn as well as others acting as trustees for bankrupt Byllynge, ended with Fenwick getting a tenth of the whole, and Byllynge's trustees getting the rest of it. Biddle bought a sizable chunk of the Byllynge portion, a purchase which not only gave him land but a share in proprietorship. Of the hundred shares into which the whole province of West Jersey was divided, Biddle owned over one full share. This was probably more than forty thousand acres, so that William actually owned much more land than Richard Lee did. He was a large Lee-like, not a small Adams-like, property holder.

There was no tobacco boom in West Jersey, and land did not lead on to fortune, manor houses and finery. The fortunes of the Biddles, though they tend to parallel in some degree those of the Lees, did not proceed in such a flowery fashion. However, like the first Lee, the first Biddle was a worthy. He had his plantation, called Mount Hope, by his river, the Delaware, on the east bank just where Jersey bends back at the waist near present-day Bordentown. William too had his share of dull offices. He was on the Governor's Council, General Assembly, Council of the Proprietors of West Jersey (which still exists in a moribund fashion), sometimes as president of these bodies. He was a justice of Burlington for many years. He was active in Quaker circles and the Burlington Falls Quarterly Meeting was held at his house almost until he died in 1712. Unlike the case of Richard Lee I, Biddle's wife's last name, Kempe, survived.

And also unlike the first Lee, he left only one son. He seems to have had Biddle cousins in New Jersey, but all the Philadelphia Biddles are descended from William junior. William II did absolutely nothing except marry and live for the rest of his life at Mount

Hope, for thirty years from his inheritance of it in 1712 till his death in 1743. His wife was a Wardell, Huguenots twice refugee, first from France for being Huguenots, then from New England for being Quakers. One of them was said to have been burned as a wizard up there. Not many of us have ancestors who were convicted wizards. William Biddle II had even less public spirit than Richard Lee II and does not seem to have been on any significant committee. But then South Jersey during his lifetime was not an especially stimulating place. The settlement of Philadelphia was far more exciting. South Jersey became what it still is, a social and economic suburb of that growing metropolis. Ships went to Philadelphia, not to the little Jersey river towns of Salem, Gloucester and Burlington. Philadelphia, not the older meetings in Jersey, became the center of Quakerism. Emigrants went to Pennsylvania; West Jersey increased but slowly. Ambition and enterprise had moved, as they so very often moved, westward. The Biddles, in the third generation, moved too.

One of William junior's sons, Joseph, did stay in Jersey, and his descendants were lost to fame. They don't count as real Biddles, any more than the Adamses of Sempronius, New York, count as real Adamses. The Biddles that do count, Philadelphia Biddles, descend from William, the oldest, and John, the youngest of William II's seven children. Both went to Philadelphia, and both established families there; so that the Biddle family, like the Roosevelts, comes in two branches, the Williams and the Johns. The fact that they came to Philadelphia so late, somewhere between 1720 and 1730, has always made them a bit parvenu there, and consequently looked down upon by Morrises and Cadwaladers, who had arrived twenty to forty years earlier and were people of substance while the Biddle brothers were still struggling to get ahead in the big city. And they themselves never managed to get ahead very far. Only in their role as breeders of a fourth and more distinguished generation did they really succeed. William bred nine children; John five.

William, the oldest of his family, inherited Mount Hope, but had to sell it to his cousin Thomas Biddle. (Biddles owned Mount Hope until the Camden and Amboy Railroad bought it in 1834 to put their tracks through. Odd how the history of even one family does seem to head straight for the more prosaic, if permanent, aspects of New Jersey history — real estate, railroads, subdivisions, suburbia.) The truth is that by the third generation the Biddles had come down in the world. Whereas the modest rise of the Adams and Roosevelt families was continuous and that of the Lees a swelling progress, the Biddle proprietorship seemed to dwindle away. No longer presidents of councils, William and John were making their way as best they could.

William failed. His only successful venture was his marriage to Mary Scull. Mary was a woman of character, and the daughter of a modestly important man, Nicholas Scull, map-maker, Surveyor-General of Pennsylvania, well-known Indian interpreter. Scull was not wellborn or rich, but he was one of those "ingenious mechanics" who were friends of Franklin and spark plugs of Philadelphia's pre-Revolutionary Enlightenment. He was an original member of Franklin's Junto, that club devoted to talk and science. Franklin sketched him as a man "who loved books and sometimes made a few verses." The Scull connection was fortunate for William, who was fortunate in nothing else.

"I had nine children, one at my breast, when Mr. Biddle informed me one morning that he had involved himself and ruined me and his children. I was much shocked." So wrote Mary Scull Biddle at a later date. William had gone bail for a large sum of money for a certain Captain Turner. Hearing that Turner was about to skip without paying his debt, Biddle went round to Turner's lodging. There Turner had barricaded himself, threatening to kill anyone who came in. Biddle forced the door, Turner slashed him in the right arm with a cutlass and escaped. Biddle was not only permanently crippled, but had to pay Turner's debts and was also permanently ruined. He went into a decline, both financial and physical, and died.

Mary supported her progeny, until they were old enough to support her, by taking in boarders, tending the Fountain Tavern, and selling her late father's maps. Her example, and perhaps the maps too, started them off as ambitious and adventurous.

John, William's brother, had better luck. His wife was the daughter of Owen Owen, one of the many Welsh Quakers who came to Philadelphia, and like Mary, John also ran a tavern, his father-in-law's establishment, the Indian King. This was a rather famous place. John Fanning Watson in his *Annals* called it "the oldest inn in the city, and was in numerous years among the most respectable; when kept by Mr. Biddle it was indeed a famous house. There the Junto held their club, and it assembled such men as Doctor Franklin. . . ." Nicholas Scull, no doubt, too.

Later John went into dry goods at a shop two doors below the Indian King, assisted by his son Clement, and before he died could be thought of by himself and his descendants as a successful "merchant and importer," which takes some of the curse off that tavern. It was in the next generation that the Biddles, like the Lees and the Adamses, walked onto the national stage. In two branches, and in their fourth generation, the children of safe-and-sane John and bankrupt William established the Biddles in Philadelphia. As in the case of the Roosevelts, the two branches maintained their separate characters, while at the same time maintaining their close association. Like the du Ponts, the two branches intermarried at fairly constant intervals; yet the Johns remained, until the twentieth century, quiet, solid, prosperous people, important in law and banking, marrying into the highest echelons of Old Philadelphia and generally conducting themselves with rather stuffy decorum. The Williams, on the other hand, have been, again till the twentieth century, rather more inclined to violence and the picturesque. Beginning with William's attack on Captain Turner, these Biddles have found themselves blown up at sea, taken prisoner by pirates, killed in duels, spectacularly bankrupt and equally spectacularly married to and divorced from great heirs and heiresses. One of them kept alligators as parlor pets. Whatever they were, they weren't dull. The distinction between the John or Solid Biddles and the William or Romantic Biddles persisted down through the generations.

5

Roosevelt

THE Biddles and Lees arrived in comparative opulence and made their decent mark early in the annals of Nova Caesaria and Virginia. The Adamses, if hardly distinguished, began as integrated and recorded members of that most integrated and recorded of worlds, the Puritan township. But the Roosevelts were *obscure*. They leave a trace so faint as to be almost invisible. All we really know about their beginnings is that one Claes Martenzen van Rosenvelt (Nicholas son of Martin from the place Rose Field) and his wife Jannetje Thomas had six children: Christaen, who died an infant, Nicholas who survived, and four girls. These children were baptized in the Dutch Reformed church of New Amsterdam. Their parents, who owned a farm called Rose Hill in mid-Manhattan at the present level of Murray Hill, both died when the children were young, Claes in 1658. Guardians were appointed for the estate, and the children were reared by a hired woman, Metje Grevenraet. Claes was usually referred to by his nickname "Shorty" or "Little Claus," "Cleyn Claesjen." The daughters married various obscure

Hollanders. Only the son, Nicholas II, carried on the name — whatever it was: Martenzen, van Rosenvelt, or as Nicholas himself spelled it, Roosevelt.* Other spellings in that age of free spelling were Roosinffelt, Rosewelt, Rosewell, Raaswelt and Rosvelt. Like the Biddles, all Roosevelts that count are descended from this one surviving Nicholas.

That's all that really can be said about the first Roosevelt. Where he came from, when or where he married — all conjecture. There are Rosenvelts in Holland, but no record of their emigration. There is a village called Het Rosen Velt on the Island of Tholen, near Zeeland at the mouth of the Rhine. The "Thomas" in the name of Claes' wife would seem to indicate that she was English. There is a shadowy figure referred to as "Kleytjen" (Shorty) who had an adventurous career up the Hudson earlier in the seventeenth century as an explorer and a prisoner of the Indians. In 1638 a charge of slander was brought by Philip Teyler against Nicholas Martens. The complaint was dismissed. Kleytjen and Nicholas Martens and Claes Martenzen van Rosenvelt could all be the same. But whether Claes was really short or tall, light or dark, good or bad, Dutch or German, young or old when he emigrated and married and died, nobody knows. Of all our four American families, the Roosevelts begin most inconspicuously.

A bit more can be said about son Nicholas. He was born in 1658, he died in 1742. He really exists with some substance. As an orphan, his prospects in New Amsterdam were probably not promising. He moved upriver to Esopus (now Kingston) as a trapper and fur trader. He and his wife Heyltje Kunst (German stock) had children up there. Then in 1690, already in early middle age, he moved back down to the city.

It is at this point that the story of the Roosevelts can really be said

---

* Incredible as it seems, many Americans still cannot pronounce the name. It is, of course, "*Rose*-a-velt" not "*Rooz*-a-velt" (or anything else). Roseavelt, Quinzy.

to begin. Unlike the other three families, the farmer Adamses, the proprietor Biddles and the planter Lees, the Roosevelts made no headway as country folk. Only when they move to the city do they begin to rise. The New Amsterdam in which the Roosevelts settled was again as unlike New England as New England was unlike Virginia. The differences went deeper even than language and custom. Whereas New England and Virginia at least had king and tongue in common, New Amsterdam shared only Protestantism, and not too much of that.

The place was never really intended to be a settlement. The Dutch West India Company thought of it merely as a depot for their fur trade. It took on the qualities of trading post and seaport that it has maintained to the present. Dutch efforts at colonization were feeble and not very effective. While New England and Virginia were booming, New Amsterdam just barely struggled along. Badly governed (another continuing tradition) and poorly defended, New Amsterdam remained a muddy, polyglot, irreligious village, neglected by Holland and despised by its British neighbors. Up above it lay the reaches of the Hudson River, navigable to the earlier settled Fort Orange (renamed Albany by the British), which led to Indians and furs. There was none of the luxurious tobacco prosperity of the South, none of the tight organization and spiritual impulse of Quaker Pennsylvania and Puritan New England. New Amsterdam had a church and a court and a fort and a governor; but on the whole it was *fur* that counted (tobacco in Virginia; cod in New England).

There were two ways to get ahead in New Amsterdam. The most obvious of course was to make money in town as a businessman, trading with Indians for fur and with settlers for commodities. The other way was by acquiring lands, preferably along the Hudson. Two conceptions of New York aristocracy, the merchant prince and the patroon, were thus established early. The merchant of New York was like the merchant everywhere, but the patroon was something special. The myth of "patroonship" has in fact become central to the pride of New Yorkers, especially those of Dutch descent. Like the title of proprietor further south, patroon suggests feudal grandeur, and the term even in the colonial period was so popular that it was freely used to refer to any great Hudson River landowner. This was and is a misnomer. The patroonship was a special affair; there was, in fact, one true patroonship. The Van Rensselaer family was the only family under Dutch rule that was granted a patroonship and stuck with it. Others began but failed; later comers had manorial grants under English rule that somewhat resembled patroonships; but they were not actual patroons. The Van Rensselaers were *the* patroons, and hence have always claimed the right of being First Family in New York.

Like the Virginia Fairfaxes and their proprietorship, the Van Rensselaers had all sorts of rather confused feudal rights and privileges; and like the Fairfaxes they had enormous quantities of land — over a million acres on either side of the river at Albany. They held on to a good deal of it for two centuries, and they and their relations, the Van Cortlandts, Schuylers and Livingstons, etc., established themselves as a landowning aristocracy no less formidable and autocratic, if less expansive, than that of the South. They were joined by other Dutch families like the Philipses and Verplancks or English families like the Morrises of Morrisania, who also began to be considered and called "patroons."

The merchants down in New Amsterdam prospered as the advantages of their harbor became obvious, though in fact New York didn't really surge ahead till the nineteenth century and the building of the Erie Canal. During the Revolution it was smaller and less important commercially than Philadelphia or perhaps even Boston. The landowners benefited as more and more settlers moved in and their lands became more and more valuable. Merchant families and "patroon" families intermarried. Merchants like the Van Cortlandts bought properties up on the Hudson and became "patroons" by purchase. More and more this intermingling of money and land, Dutch and English, turned into a tight colonial oligarchy with a resemblance to that of Virginia or Boston. Most people in Virginia seemed to feel, at least after Bacon's rebellion, that rule by planter was the natural order. In New York people then, as now, were less amiable. Things were not made easier by the English conquest. The Dutch governors had been awful, but at least they were Dutch. The English sent over freaks like Lord Cornbury, who spent his time flaunting himself on the city wall dressed in women's clothes; his wife liked to steal things from the houses of people who entertained her. The fact that of all the original colonies New York was the only one that was conquered, rather than just merely settled, colored the atmosphere. It was a long time before the English became natives rather than merely overlords.

New Amsterdam by 1690, when Nicholas Roosevelt II moved back there, had become New York; but it was still a Dutch place, and continued to be so, especially for the Roosevelts. They spoke Dutch, worshiped Dutch, and married Dutch; almost up to the time of the Revolution English was foreign to them. Their children generally had Dutch names; those of Nicholas had names like Jennetje, Margaretta, Nicholas, Johannes, Elsje, Jacobus. The important ones, as far as family history is concerned, were Nicholas, Johannes and Jacobus.

Politics, however, in which Nicholas son of Claes (son of Martin) indulged, were already getting pretty American. Nicholas was involved in one of those upheavals which like Bacon's rebellion in Virginia foreshadowed the Revolution. Whereas Richard Lee II was firmly anti-Bacon and on the side of authority and the upper classes, as befitted a member of it, Nicholas Roosevelt II was equally firmly on the popular side.

In 1688 when William of Orange landed in England and James II fled to France, the colonial governors were obviously in a difficult position. News of the event did not reach America until the spring of 1689. Boston heard it first. The citizens there threw James' Governor Andros into jail, a "Declaration of Gentlemen, Merchants and

Inhabitants" was drawn up (foreshadowing a later Declaration), and William and Mary were proclaimed with enthusiasm. None of this Lee pro-Stuart sulking in Boston. Andros was governor in New York as well as in New England. His deputy in New York, Lieutenant Nicholson, in perplexity called the city fathers together. Most New Yorkers wanted to proclaim William and Mary, as the Bostonians had done. The city fathers, notably councillors Nicholas Bayard, Stephen Van Cortlandt and Frederick Philipse, representing the interests of the patroons, stood for James. After all, he had been the Duke of York after whom New York had been named. The people rose and a German militia captain, Jacob Leisler, was appointed by them as acting governor in place of Nicholson until the new government in England could be heard from.

Nicholson sailed off to England determined to vindicate himself and get Leisler put out. Meanwhile, a message from the king arrived (1) confirming Nicholson but (2) indicating that in his absence "such for the time being as were in power" were to take over the government. Nicholson was absent, Leisler was in power. Not till the fall of 1690 did the English see fit to send over a new governor for New York. Not till January 1691 did the first of his soldiers arrive, the governor himself having gotten lost en route. The commander of the redcoats, Major Ingoldsby, ordered Leisler to turn over the government to him. Leisler refused and shut himself up in the fort on the Battery. Ingoldsby besieged him there. Leisler's garrison fired on the soldiers, there was a battle; Leisler lost. At this moment, it now being March 1691, Governor Sloughter finally arrived. Leisler was tried for treason, and found guilty. All his worthy services as *pro tem* governor and supporter of William were outbalanced by the shots his men had fired from the Battery. He was hanged, his body cut down while still alive, disemboweled, beheaded and quartered. This was the usual punishment for traitors, familiar enough in London, but somewhat exceptional in the former New Amsterdam.

Eventually, a bit too late in 1702, Leisler was posthumously exonerated of treason by Parliament; but meanwhile New York politics had been split into a popular, pro-Leisler and an aristocratic anti-Leisler party, a cleavage which endured pretty much until the Revolution. Nicholas Roosevelt II, fresh from Esopus, became an alderman in 1700 and 1701, representing the Leisler party. He beat out a Schuyler (another connection of the Van Rensselaers) who represented the anti-Leislerians. He was aldermen again in 1719.

Nicholas turned from fur trading to flour milling. His children did well and bred well. Some even married well; one to a daughter of the very Schuyler he had defeated as alderman. No hard feelings. Nicholas lived to see over forty grandchildren, very much a patriarch.

Most prominent and interesting of his children was Nicholas III (born 1687). He was the oldest of three surviving sons, and a reputable gold-and-silversmith during that first half of the eighteenth century when New York silver, blending the Dutch, Scotch, French Huguenot and English traditions, was the most cosmopolitan made in the colonies. Unlike Paul Revere, his colleague in Boston, Nicholas Roosevelt was not colorful as a man. But his works are precious now as only American colonial silver can be. The fact that his name was Roosevelt does nothing to diminish a value based on fine craftsmanship. If you wanted to own a nice Roosevelt tankard or teapot, you would probably have to pay between five and ten thousand dollars for it, if you were lucky enough to get the chance. Meanwhile museums, notably the Museum of the City of New York, own Roosevelt pieces. The Metropolitan has a priceless bit of coral set in gold, once used by an infant for teething. Yale has a teapot. A handsome beaker exists, made as a communion cup for a church in Flatbush and inscribed "Spreek Dat Waar Is, Eet Dat Gaar Is, Em Drink Dat Klaar Is" (Speak what true is, Eat what well-cooked is, and Drink what clear is). This doesn't sound very churchly, even among Dutchmen, but such beakers were regularly used in Dutch Reformed communion services in place of the Popish chalice. Nicholas was the first Roosevelt to make his mark; literally. His mark was NR̄. One of his most important commissions came from the city, to make for them two gold boxes.

In 1769 an advertisement appeared in the *New York Gazette:*

"to be let . . . the house in which Nicholas Roosevelt now lives at the lower end of Thames Street, on the wharf fronting the North River. The conveniency and commodiousness of the situation excells any on the river. The house will suit a merchant . . . roomy and convenient . . . with seven fireplaces; a large yard, in which is a pump and cistern, and a garden and grass-plot . . . also to be sold by said Roosevelt, a parcel of ready made silver, large and small, Viz: silver tea pots and tea spoons, silver hilted swords, sauce boats, salts and shovels, soup-spoons both scollep'd and plain" and "sundry other small articles [any one of which would now be worth many times its weight in gold, much less silver] . . . which he will sell very reasonable, as he intends declining business, and to move in the country in the spring."

Evidently a "man of substance" in an age of competition. Silver-smiths (they often preferred to call themselves goldsmiths — it sounded richer) were in a way the bankers, or at least the savings accounts of that bankless time. It was safer and prettier to have one's spare cash turned into plate, with one's own crest or initials on it, than just to have coins lying around loose. Besides, it looked so impressive. Silversmiths flourished.

By 1771 Nicholas Roosevelt III was dead.

His other two brothers, Johannes and Jacobus, contributed less to their time than Nicholas; but it is through them and not Nicholas that the modern Roosevelts come down. Nicholas's Roosevelts seemed to evaporate, at least as far as New York history is concerned. Johannes, the elder of these two lesser brothers (born 1689), is the progenitor of the Oyster Bay branch and Theodore; Jacobus (born 1692), of the Hyde Park branch and Franklin. Exactly as in the case of the Biddle family, with its Williams (Romantic) and Johns (Solid), the two branches of the Roosevelts established and maintained a different character. In this case it was the elder branch that was, comparatively, perhaps more on the "solid" side, the younger the more "romantic." Actually the difference was that the Jacobites, or Hyde Parkers, emerged sooner into the upper classes — as much as two generations ahead of the Johannites. During their lifetimes, however, John and James were equals and often partners, and their descendants maintained close touch; but unlike the Biddles and du Ponts, did not seem to intermarry until the grand climactic union of Franklin and Eleanor.

Both Johannes and Jacobus, not specialized craftsmen like brother Nicholas, prospered in a modest way as entrepreneurs in real estate and linseed oil. Linseed oil was used in making paint. The Beekman swamp was a good place for tanneries. Johannes was instrumental in setting aside a bowling green for skittles down in lower Manhattan. There his bowling green is to this day, no longer suitable for bowling perhaps, but still a green oval park, still called Bowling Green, dominated by the rich facade of the Custom House with its wonderful statues, and with a vista out towards Fort Clinton and the bay. It is surrounded largely now by the offices of shipping lines. In the park itself is a statue not of a Roosevelt, but of a De Peyster, who was once mayor.

Jacobus, brother of Johannes, as senior elder of his church (Dutch Reformed of course) was one of the instigators of a move to hire a minister who could preach in English. By 1762 an exclusive Dutchness was becoming harder and harder to maintain. One might still talk Dutch at home, but in church many younger people could no longer follow the discourse. Along with Philip Livingston, and backed by a consistory (vestry) that included men with names like De Peyster, Brevoort and Beekman, Jacobus, often now called James, asked Amsterdam to authorize an English-preaching parson for their church. Over the bitterest opposition, Jacobus and his friends prevailed. The Reverend Archibald Laidlie, a Scotchman then holding forth in Flushing, was appointed. He was, fortunately, a good preacher. Galleries had to be built to accommodate the crowds that came to hear him. The English-speaking advocates welcomed him effusively. "Ah Dominie, we offered up many an earnest prayer in Dutch for your coming among us, and truly the Lord has heard us in English." Others, not so pleased, either deserted to the Anglican church, declaring, "If it must be English, let it be English," or continued, up to the Revolution, to listen to the Dutch sermons of Dominies de Ronde and Ritzema. De Ronde tried to compromise by preaching in a mixture of both languages. This was not a success. The Dutch Reformed Church still flourishes in New York today because of the good sense of Jacobus and his like.

So Johannes and Jacobus gradually merged into John and James, leaving some imprint on their city — a park in lowest Manhattan, a church that survived by adaptation. But they were most important as progenitors. Like contemporary Deacon John Adams, William and John Biddle, and Samuel Dupont, they would be of very little importance indeed if it were not for their descendants. Nicholas the silversmith has left his own small personal permanent reputation in the rarefied world of museums and collectors. John and James left only children, some money, and a middle-class respectability of position.

John married Heyltje Sjoerts. James married Catharine Hardenbroeck. As in the case of the Boylston-Adams and the Dupont-Montchanin marriages, the Roosevelt-Hardenbroeck union represented something of a social step up. Again, as in these other cases, this social superiority of the mother seems to be reflected in the son. The children of John were worthy but in no way distinguished. Isaac, son of James, was the first Roosevelt who could be called important. In the fourth generation, like the Revolutionary Biddles, he was the first to bring the name into any kind of prominence. The Hardenbroecks into whom the Roosevelts married were shopkeepers, but they were connected with the so-called "patroons." The original Hardenbroeck had been a German emigrant of the 1660's. His daughter married a Philipse. The Philipse family (associated incidentally with John in setting up the bowling green) were

Lords of Philipse Manor, had ties with the Van Rensselaers, and were very much quasi-patroons. This of course was not Catharine Roosevelt's particular family; but still her very own great-aunt was the formidable Lady of Philipse Manor, just as Nick Boylston was one of the richest men in Boston, or the Montchanins of Marzac were great nobles of the *ancien régime*. Remote, but glamorous, relations.

The Roosevelts then, at this time before the Revolution, had become worthy burghers. They were still thoroughly Dutch; they were civic-minded, and liberal as evidenced by father Nicholas' support of Leisler and by son James' support of English in the church. They were neither patroons nor merchant princes, but they were getting ahead. They were probably richer than either the Adamses of Braintree (if not those of Boston), or the Biddles of Philadelphia, but generally of the same prosperous lower middle class. Nicholas Roosevelt was a silversmith, Owen Biddle, son of John, was a watchmaker, as was Samuel Dupont in Paris. Mary Biddle kept a tavern, a Mrs. Roosevelt ran a boardinghouse or let rooms as of 1785. Unlike the Adamses or the Lees, they did not farm or plant. They were, at this time, purely town folk. Like all the other families except the Lees of Stratford, the Roosevelts were at this time totally inconspicuous. They had not yet even begun to emerge as a First Family.

6

Du Pont

WHILE the four families already rooted in America were establishing themselves in various degrees of prosperity — the Lees at the summit of colonial prestige and plantation riches; the Adamses cautiously moving up in Braintree towards Harvard and an alliance with the Quincys; the Roosevelts progressing from total obscurity to burgherish affluence; the Biddles, uprooted from their original background of modest proprietary position, trying their luck in America's boomtown — while these annals of peace were proceeding through the last half of the seventeenth and the first half of the eighteenth centuries, the Duponts were in France having a terrible time.

Nothing reveals the extent of the difference between American and continental European mentality and feelings than this contrast between what was happening to hardworking lower middle-class people in the two places. In America one might occasionally, on the frontier, have Indian or French trouble. Henry Adams Jr. was murdered in Medfield, Richard Lee felt safer moving south of the York in 1644, some of Hancock Lee's descendants were tomahawked in Kentucky. Depressions, such as the tobacco slump caused by the Navigation Act, wars like the Indian Wars of 1676 in New England, the French and Indian War of the mid-eighteenth century, even civil disturbances like Bacon's or Leisler's rebellions might scar the peaceful surface of life. There were endless and bitter political squabbles. Quakers and Catholics were maltreated. But when one compares the hundred and twenty years between 1640 and 1760 in Rouen and Braintree, for instance, one gets some idea of the humus of self-confidence, optimism and security that was built up in America during these comparatively happy years. Once the horrors of the very first waves of settlement were over, waves of ragged indispensable dispensables who died to make a foothold, American colonial history in the more settled areas seems from a modern perspective to come closer to Utopia (though still a long way off) than almost any comparative history anywhere before or since.

This could hardly be said of Rouen, where the Duponts came from. In these years, the Duponts were undoubtedly lucky. None seemed to have actually been persecuted. In earlier days none were burned at the stake, for instance, which had been the fate of many of their friends and connections before the Edict of Nantes in 1598. Exile and imprisonment were again the fate of many after the edict was so scandalously revoked in 1685. Politics, turmoil, war, persecution, religious bitterness and bigotry, all the mean and dreadful uses of tyranny (still unfortunately as familiar in the twentieth as in the tenth century) battered the Duponts. They lived through it all, and in a modest way did well, bred well, and married well. Some, but not our particular Duponts, emigrated. Most of them stayed in Rouen.

Three brothers Dupont began there: Charles, Jehan and Pierre. Though their descendant Pierre Samuel after he was ennobled liked to spell himself Du Pont, and his descendants prefer the even more distinguished-looking du Pont, the common form of this very common name is Dupont — "of the bridge" (any bridge). There is a tradition that the three brothers Dupont had come to Rouen from Brittany (even French families have such "beginnings"). In any case they turned Calvinist in the mid-sixteenth century, Charles for example about 1560. Their names are recorded on deeds, mortgages, loans. They obviously had some money and some property. They survived; and this was not so easy for a Calvinist in Rouen, since all during the brothers' lifetimes dangerous things were happening.

From the 1520's, when Calvinism first began to penetrate Normandy, persecution was constant and severe. For light offenses, such as expressing independent religious views or possessing any printed material attacking the Roman church, men and women were fined, imprisoned, publicly whipped. For serious crimes, preaching say, the punishment was burning alive in the very same square that had seen the execution of Joan of Arc a century before. Guillaume Huchon, apothecary, was so burned, suspended over a fire, his tongue first having been cut off. Giles Keefe, a Scotchman who got caught there, was merely hanged. Many others met similar deaths. This, needless to say, had no effect whatsoever. Calvinism boomed. Defying the authorities, seven thousand converts gathered in 1560 to hold an open-air service; and in 1562 civil war broke out.

The Huguenots, as these French Protestants were rather mysteriously called, were able to seize control of Rouen. Soon they were besieged. All through the summer and into October of '62 the citizens of the city held out. When finally the soldiers of Catherine de Medici took the city, they of course butchered everyone they could lay hands on, including kin of the Duponts.

The peace of 1563 forced concessions from the crown; Huguenots were permitted some religious freedom, but the terms of the peace were soon evaded by the government and there was a general Huguenot uprising in 1567. Another edict reaffirmed another promise of toleration. Then in 1572 came the Massacre of St. Bartholomew in Paris. Similar scenes were enacted in Rouen. A group of misguided Protestants, led to believe they would be safer in jail, surrendered to the prison authorities. A mob, encouraged by priests, called the prisoners out one by one and axed them down as they emerged. Altogether twenty thousand died in France as a whole. Civil war raged again. It is perhaps an example of retributive justice that two centuries later, during the Revolution, two hundred and fifty Catholic priests were killed in exactly the same fashion coming out of exactly the same Rouen jail.

Another siege of Rouen took place in 1591–92. This time the Catholics were inside, the Protestants outside. The siege was not successful. The Dupont brothers were refugees then as they had been before, but when at last the victorious Henry of Navarre proclaimed the Edict of Nantes, freedom for Protestant worship began, supposedly for all time. "Perpetual and irrevocable" toleration permitted the Duponts to return to their businesses and to prosper for a generation or two.

Though Cossart and Brière in-laws had died the death of martyrs, the Duponts got through safely. Jehan (generation Number 1), middle brother of this first three, married a Brière and had twelve children. His son (2) Abraham (the Huguenots, like the Puritans, went to the Bible for names but did not wander as far afield as Fear and Wrestling, like the Brewsters) married a Cossart and had five. By the time Abraham's son (3) Jean, of the third Rouen generation, born in 1631, had reached manhood, trouble began again. Despite the almost idolatrous loyalty of the Huguenots to the descendant of their liberator Henry, Louis XIV, that Grand Monarch, victorious in war and intoxicated with his own glory, turned against them. The Huguenots had supported him fanatically during that anti-Royalist rebellion known as the Fronde, and various edicts and declarations on the part of both Louis XIII and Louis XIV continued to declare the irrevocability of the Edict of Nantes. As late as 1652 Louis XIV was still praising his Protestant subjects for their affection and fidelity. By 1656 Louis, under the influence of palace priests, was already trying to destroy Protestantism in the first of a long series of memorials which gradually whittled away privileges. All persons who belonged to the "so-called Reformed Religion" were declared ineligible for public office; those already in were ousted. They could not be printers or booksellers, they could not be surgeons, physicians, apothecaries or even midwives. They could not employ a Catholic servant. All sorts of petty restrictions were placed on their worship. Gradually life for Protestants became more and more insufferable. Finally in 1685 the irrevocable and perpetual Edict of Nantes was revoked. All the 243 Huguenot churches not already harassed out of existence were to be destroyed, all Protestant meetings were prohibited, all ministers who refused to abjure were ordered to quit the country, all Protestant schools were to be closed and all Huguenot children brought up as Catholics.

The result, as in the case of the persecution of the Jews in Spain, was disastrous. A great emigration, estimated at between half a million to two million people, took place, despite desperate efforts on the part of the government to prevent it. (As early as 1669 all French subjects had been forbidden to emigrate permanently, under penalty of death and confiscation of their property.) The Huguenots who did nonetheless leave for good took with them a large part of French prosperity. Not only did they siphon off immense amounts of capital into the economy of France's Protestant neighbors, since then, as now, a great part of France's finance was in the hands of Protestants; but also more than two-thirds of the workshops and factories of the kingdom were closed. Many of Nicholas Roosevelt's rival New York silversmiths were of Huguenot extraction, as was Paul Revere of Boston. The middle class had been almost liquidated.

Various Duponts emigrated. Some went to London, some went to Holland. One branch, descendants of an Abraham (4), son of Jean (3) son of Abraham (2), went to South Carolina, where an eighteenth-century planter, Gideon Dupont, was famous for making rice a really practical cash crop there.

The Duponts who stayed in Rouen were forced to abjure their religion, and again like Jews or Moors in Spain, became always suspected fake Catholics. Rather than be burned at the stake like their ancestors, a punishment in any case rather out of date, they preferred to sign documents. A peculiar form of coercion called the *Dragonnade* was applied to them. Dragoons were quartered with Calvinist families and encouraged to break up the furniture, eat up the food, and molest the women until conversion to the True Faith had been accomplished. This is one reason why the "quartering of troops" was such an issue before the American Revolution; people hadn't forgotten the Dragonnade. Almost all the Huguenots abjured. They kept right on, of course, with their beliefs and their practices in secret. When finally in 1787 — a bit late — Louis XVI forced through the Edict of Toleration, over the opposition of Catholics, the Duponts were still Protestants. By then active persecutions were things of the past; but during the whole previous century Protestantism was officially considered not to exist in France, and no public or official Protestant marriages, christenings or burials were permitted.

It would be redundant to describe the sordid devices used by the government to destroy this underground Protestantism — kidnapping Protestant children and imprisoning them in convents, terrorizing the dying into deathbed conversions. Heresy nevertheless flourished, and the hardworking Duponts flourished, modestly, too. Three of Jean (3) Dupont's children, one of his brothers and a brother-in-law were driven from France by the Revocation. One son, Jean (4) junior, stayed. This Jean junior, great-grandson of the original Jehan, grandfather of Pierre Samuel, lived and died one of these secret and successful Protestants. He made money, he bought a country place called La Robinette, he sired eleven children, he died in 1731. His widow, née Marie de La Porte outlived him, and at the age of eighty-five fell off her horse and was killed.

One of Jean's sons, Samuel (5), went to Paris. As the first of his family to leave Rouen and the provinces for life in the capital, he made the first step towards fame for his family. He himself did nothing to bring his name to the world's notice. He was an industrious, skilled watchmaker; but he married a Montchanin, and he had a son.

Once again that familiar pattern appears: the marriage to a socially superior woman produces the illustrious son. As Deacon John

Adams married a Boylston and produced John, so Samuel Dupont married Anne Alexandrine de Montchanin and produced Pierre Samuel. The Duponts were petit bourgeois if ever there were petit bourgeois. The Montchanins were nobility; very minor nobility, for a long time impoverished, without lands or titles or prestige, but still nobility. It showed, if nowhere else, in Anne's name. One of the many ways in which Europe differs from America is in this matter of names. Most Americans have names that simply by themselves, without associations, fail to give away social rank. Robert Edward Lee and Charles Francis Adams, as sheer names, are no more than respectable; like say John Robert Smith. But in France, in the eighteenth century, there is an obvious physical difference between names like Marie Guis, Judith Auber, Jeanne Tranchepain (Marie de La Porte sounds fancier) and names like Anne Alexandrine de Montchanin. The first list suggests, accurately, the names of Protestant bourgeoises of Rouen who married into the Dupont family. Names like Anne's, or even more, some of the other names that married into the Montchanins, like that of Eléonore du Fay de La Tour-Maubourg, suggest, correctly enough, aristocracy. (These names turned out to be a fatal disadvantage, come the Revolution.) Eléonore was in fact the daughter of Jacques du Fay, Baron de La Tour-Maubourg, and third wife of Antoine de Montchanin, Comte de Marzac, Seigneur de la Garde, Collanges, Beauvernay Chassigny, etc. Antoine was the representative of the elder line of the Montchanins, and a long, long way off from Anne; but still, the same family.

Anne herself was the daughter of one Heliodore de Montchanin, who was the seigneur of nothing. He was the manager of an estate belonging to a distant cousin (or so Heliodore thought), the Marquis de Jaucourt-Epeuilles. The claim to kinship was awfully vague, but at least it got Heliodore his job. The Montchanins lived in an old castle surrounded by a moat, and Anne Alexandrine was born in these romantic but damp surroundings in 1720.

These particular Montchanins had come down in the world,

partly because they were younger sons of younger sons, and partly because they too, like the Duponts, were Protestants. Just like the Duponts, three Montchanin brothers had emerged from the mists and into recorded history; but somewhat earlier, about 1300. They had dwelt "from time immemorial" near Issy l'Evêque in Burgundy. The eldest of the three branches, descendants of Marc, moved to the Rhone and the Château de la Garde, where they became very grand indeed until the whole enterprise was liquidated during the Revolution, and the castle of La Garde sacked and destroyed. This was Antoine's branch. The youngest branch, descended from Girin, moved to St. Priest-La Roche near Roanne, and were lawyers for generations until the last one died there in 1836.

As our Duponts stemmed from the middle brother Jehan, so our Montchanins stem from a middle brother whose name is lost. Descendants of his, the Montchanins de la Nocle, stayed right around Issy l'Evêque, where they had been from that "time immemorial," and one of them, a Jehan, turned Huguenot. His son Elie was living in 1636 as a manager of the Le Nocle estate (this seemed to be more or less the family profession), which belonged to the fervently Huguenot La Fin de Salins family. Like the Puritans in England, not all the Huguenots were middle class; like the Duponts, the descendants of Elie also suffered for their religion after the Revocation. A château de Montchanin had to be sold. The sons of the family went off to fight in foreign Protestant armies — German, English. One of Anne's brothers in fact was killed, later on, by a cannonball in India, at the siege of Madras. Heliodore, Anne's father, fought for the Dutch; when he returned to France he appealed to his rich relatives the de Jaucourts, and so became manager of their estates.

Anne herself was subjected to an education which must have been fairly traumatic. Taken to Paris as an infant from her moated grange, she was brought up by the de Jaucourts-Epeuilles as one of the family. Trained for the haute monde, taught Italian and English, she found herself at adolescence thrown out into the wide world. The de Jaucourts felt they had done enough for her. If she wanted to continue with them as housekeeper . . . She chose rather to go to her brothers Pierre and Alexandre who (shame for the Montchanins) had become watchmakers. They put her to work painting watch faces.

The Rue de Richelieu, where both the Montchanins and Samuel Dupont lived, was a street of watchmakers. It was natural that Anne and Samuel should meet each other and marry. He was twelve years older than she, established in his profession. She was only seventeen, without prospects; she obviously had to marry somebody. They were both Protestants. He was handsome (five feet ten and a half inches tall with brown hair, blue eyes and an aquiline nose), fond of the flute and fencing. She was pretty (skin very white, eyes blue with dark lashes, the chin with a dimple) and accomplished.

Only as their child Pierre grew, and the variance in their ideas of what to do with him grew also, did the fundamental opposition of their natures and backgrounds begin to clash. He was a competent, obstinate, unimaginative watchmaker, proud of his craft, without further ambitions. He could conceive of no better life for his son than watchmaking. Anne on the contrary was "full of romance." She could never forget her descent from "time immemorial" and the Montchanin coat of arms (two golden chevrons and three silver stars on a red field). She brought up her son Pierre on tales of the three branches of the Montchanins and their great antiquity. On the basis of this clash and blend of the practical and the romantic — generations of Huguenot tradesmen and craftsmen versus folies de grandeur, coats of arms, useless accomplishments and "times immemorial" — were founded the fortunes of the du Ponts de Nemours, who eventually managed, in a most practical way, to achieve considerable grandeur.

Summary

Here then were five contemporary families, totally unrelated, living in totally different settings. There were the various Lees in their fine waterside plantation houses, Stratford, Ditchley, Cobb's Hall, Mount Pleasant, Lee Hall, Leesylvania; over in Maryland the Lees of magnificent Blenheim. Further north were the two families of Biddle, having lost their lands in New Jersey, now struggling in the Quaker boomtown of growing Philadelphia. John, tavernkeeper and merchant, was doing well. Mary, widow, was just keeping her chin and her children above water. Up in Braintree, and in numberless neighboring towns, various Adamses were Sealors of Leather, Selectmen or even Moderators of their towns, church officials like Deacon John, exalted village clergymen like the Reverend Joseph, Bishop of Newington. Samuel Adams senior in Boston had come up in the world almost as far as Deacon John's in-laws, the rich Boylstons.

The Roosevelts, unlike those other three families, still not absorbed into an English culture though New York had become an English colony, were making silver and linseed oil and money. They were separated by a considerable distance from the oligarchy of great merchants and so-called patroons; but the gap was closing.

And over in Paris Samuel Dupont and his wife were quarreling over how to bring up son Pierre — honest watchmaker, or would-be courtier and intellectual. Not one member of any of these families could have imagined what the future was to bring to them; nor that they would all someday be more or less relations by marriage.

This history of the Potomac, Delaware and Hudson, of Braintree and Rouen is in the nature of prehistory. None of these families, with the exception of the Lees, had so to speak stepped on stage. Even Thomas Lee, though acting governor of Virginia, builder of Stratford, president of the Ohio Company, the most important man of the most important colony of the most important empire in the world, would not now be remembered except for his descendants.

The curtain was about to go up. Adamses, Roosevelts, Biddles and Lees were all to be propelled on stage by the American Revolution, some as stars, some as supernumeraries, but all with at least speaking parts. Pierre du Pont, in another country and another revolution, was also to play a fairly outstanding role. In this one generation — fourth from their foundation in America for Biddles and Roosevelts, fourth and fifth for the two different branches of the Lees, fifth for both John and Samuel Adams, sixth for the Duponts from their establishment in Rouen — fame, riches, honor, position, power and prestige were to come, in some degree to some members of all these families. All lower middle class except for the already aristocratic Virginians, all were to find themselves firmly and permanently members of the gentry of their particular locales, Boston, New York, Philadelphia, Delaware and Virginia, from at least 1800 on. The effect is rather like that of the simultaneous blooming of flowers of the same species in the same season. A change in the world's weather, about 1760, brought them all out.

II

The Rebels

1760–1800

1

Adams

JOHN, Abigail and Samuel Adams; Isaac Roosevelt; Clement, Owen, Edward, Nicholas and Charles Biddle; Pierre Samuel du Pont de Nemours; Richard Henry Lee and his brothers Francis, Arthur, and William; his cousin Henry ("Light-Horse Harry") Lee and *his* brothers Charles and Richard Bland (and over in Maryland another cousin, Thomas Sim Lee) — these are the principals of the play during that first act in the lives of these five emergent families. They were all revolutionists. All the Americans were in possible danger of being hanged, if they had been caught; and one of them, Charles Biddle, was a prisoner, though he was not hanged. Pierre du Pont very narrowly escaped death by guillotine.

As in any play, some actors are stars. The star of stars here is John Adams of Braintree. This is not to denigrate the position of the others; but John alone of this group has a firm and final place in American history as a Founding Father.

In the mind's eye and imagination of almost all literate Americans there floats a curious structure: the Pantheon of the Founders. It is surprising that it doesn't physically exist somewhere in Washington, D.C. This pantheon can be visualized, very concretely, as a neoclassic structure in the Federalist style, awesome but jaunty, grave but elegant, noble but a bit naïve. At the center of it is a circular domed rotunda, obviously modeled on the prototype in Rome, but smaller and very white. Marble steps lead up to the columned portico (Doric) over which a gilded eagle spreads his wings.

Through the tall portal is the rotunda itself. The rotunda has four doors: the entrance from the west, another facing door on the east leading to a similar but less impressive chamber (minor founding fathers) and two doors north and south that proceed in long colonnades to outlying pavilions. In the center of the rotunda, under the light from the cupola, stands a monumental statue, half classic, half eighteenth-century. It is, of course, George Washington. In four niches set into the rounded sides of the building between the four doors are large but lesser full-length statues; and over the four doors are arches containing monumental portrait busts. The floor is of black and white marble radiating from the foot of Washington's pedestal. The ceiling is coffered in white and gilt, with golden stars (fifty of them, we presume, at the moment) on a sky-blue background. There are a few, too few, marble benches for the weary tourist.

In the four niches, more eighteenth century than classic, looking at each other with unconcealed asperity, are the other four inevitable chief occupants of the Founder's pantheon: Jefferson, Franklin, Hamilton . . . and Adams. The most prominent bust, that over the east door, shows forth the wizened yet boyish face of James Madison, elevated but disembodied. To north and south are the features of the Revolution's two chief firebrands, Samuel Adams and Patrick Henry. Back of them stretch northward and southward those colonnades, lined with the statues of statesmen, soldiers and even authors. One culminates in the Lincoln pavilion, where the President broods in his chair, surrounded by generals and senators; the other corridor ends in the Lee pavilion where the general rides Traveler, surrounded by his command and associates, Jefferson Davis the only civilian among them. Over the west portal, facing Madison, but almost indistinguishable in the shadows, is the seldom observed simulacrum of Richard Henry Lee.

Jefferson, Franklin, Hamilton, Adams — these four surround Washington in his center, great satellites, universal geniuses, but compared at least to Washington, flawed spirits. Their very flaws, their partialities make them rather more savory and human than Washington in his weighty near-perfection. Though they may be less, they are certainly livelier. We may deplore their quarrels and prejudices; but what style! It is only by comparison with a paragon that they seem less virtuous. They had virtue enough; they simply had failings of character.

They have not only come to symbolize human qualities such as Imagination, Wisdom, Enterprise, Integrity; but they also stand for regions, the South, the Middle States (Philadelphia and New York respectively), New England.

It is with one of these American demigods that our Revolutionary story must begin. John Adams, the caustic, overbearing, thin-skinned, narrow-and-high-and-tough-minded, funny (consciously and unconsciously), learned, exasperated Puritan lawyer. But it is primarily as a Family Founder that he is presented here. With John and his cousin Samuel, and John's wife Abigail and her cousin-in-law John Hancock and her cousin Josiah Quincy, the Adamses as a family certainly emerged as definitely as possible from obscurity into fame. They were of course the product of the times; but they made the times, and seldom has there been a more marvelous con-junction of men *and* times.

This most crucial period in American history from 1760 to 1800 is neatly spanned by John Adams's active legal-political career. After 1760, when he first began as a lawyer, to 1800, when he was tum-bled into private life again, no event of importance, except the purely military actions, is untouched by his presence or his influ-ence. Even military, especially naval, history is colored by his im-portance as a member of the Revolutionary Board of War (Defense Department). Even at the Constitutional Convention, held while he was abroad, his presence hovered and his advice, set forth in his turgid book, *A Defense of the Constitutions of Government of the United States of America,* was influential. The career of John

Adams from 1760 to 1800 can be used as a sort of ruler against which all the events of the period, all the activities of other men of the period, can be measured.

This obviously isn't the place to mount a full-scale biographical account; but very briefly, as a standard which can be referred to, here is the agenda:

1735: Born in Braintree (later Quincy), Massachusetts, son of Deacon John and Susanna Boylston Adams, daughter of Peter Boylston of Muddy River (later Brookline), Massachusetts, niece of the famous Doctor Zabdiel Boylston, pioneer in smallpox inoculation, granddaughter of Dr. Thomas Boylston, first of that name in America. Two other Adams sons, Peter and Elihu, were born to Deacon John. The Deacon's brother Ebenezer also married a Boylston, Anne, sister of Susanna.

1755: Graduated from Harvard College. The first Adams there was his uncle, the Reverend Joseph, Bishop of Newington, New Hampshire, class of 1710. Joseph's sons, Dr. Joseph (1745) and Ebenezer (1747) also preceded John, as well as cousins Jebediah (1733) and Samuel (1740).

1755–58: After graduation, John went to Worcester, Massachusetts, where he taught school and studied law. In 1758 he returned to Braintree and was admitted to the bar of Boston along with college friend and future cousin-in-law Samuel Quincy. He began practice in Braintree and participated in local affairs.

1764: Married Abigail Smith, daughter of the Reverend William Smith, pastor of neighboring Weymouth, and his wife Elizabeth Quincy Smith, daughter of Colonel John Quincy of "Mount Wollaston," leading figure of Braintree. This brought him into contact with the well-born and well-connected Quincys. John Hancock, next to Adams the most prominent, and also richest, of Bostonian patriots, married Abigail's cousin Dorothy Quincy. Jonathan Sewall, lawyer and best friend of John Adams, later a Tory refugee (like Samuel Quincy), married Dorothy's sister Esther. Hannah Quincy, another cousin, had been previously courted by John

Adams but married elsewhere. Of Abigail Smith's two sisters, Mary married Richard Cranch and Elizabeth married first John Shaw and then Stephen Peabody. Their brother William Smith, after an active Revolutionary career, ended a vagabond, drunkard and bankrupt, thus introducing his tarnished strain into the inheritance of the Royal Line.

1765: Born: Abigail, first child of John and Abigail Adams. She was followed by John Quincy (1767), named after his great-grandfather Colonel John Quincy who died that same year; Susanna (1768) who died an infant; Charles (1770) who, like his uncle William, died a drunkard and bankrupt; and Thomas Boylston (1772). All four surviving children married and had children. Of the whole lot only John Quincy's son Charles Francis was in any way distinguished.

1760–1774: Adams' public career followed the course of events in Boston from the victorious end of the war with France in 1763 to the calling of the First Continental Congress in Philadelphia in 1774. Victory over France meant the end of the French Empire in America and its threat to the English settlers. It also meant the beginnings of a new English colonial policy. A "century of salutary neglect," during which the colonies had learned to govern themselves, was to be superseded by a policy of tight and efficient imperial control under the rule of Parliament. This began, already before the end of the war, with an attempt to enforce England's various navigation laws. These laws had been on the books all during that century of neglect, but Americans had disobeyed them, greatly to their profit. Now it was time to amend and implement them properly. What could be more reasonable? Americans had never really objected to the laws; how could they object to their decent execution?

So began a program of revised taxation and renewed enforcement against violations — smuggling, nonpayment of duties, etc. The long series of conflicts which began in 1760 with the renewal of the so-called Writs of Assistance and became acute in 1764 with the revisions of the so-called Sugar Acts made Americans realize two things: that the English government intended to govern America, but that Americans had no voice in and no control over that English government. The actual causes of the fight were trivial — the Stamp Act of 1765, the Townshend Acts of 1767, the Tea Act of 1773 — but the principle was certainly fundamental. The English voter might unseat a Parliament he didn't like. Americans could do nothing but protest.

None saw this more clearly than the two Adamses. John Adams first began to see it in 1761 when as court recorder he heard the Boston lawyer James Otis arguing against the Writs of Assistance. These Writs were all-purpose search warrants that permitted customs officials to break in anywhere, anytime, looking for contraband. It was with this issue and Otis's attack that, according to Adams, the Revolution actually began. "Here this day . . . the child Independence was born."

The true leader in the battle towards such independence was not John but his cousin Samuel. It was Samuel, politician and pamphleteer, who organized the objectors into a party for liberty, pressed the cause, stimulated the grievances. John Adams was a commentator, not an organizer. It was Samuel, for instance, who stage-managed the Tea Party of 1773. John merely applauded.

Whereas Samuel directed the Revolution in Boston, John was, so to speak, its legal adviser. His articles in newspapers, his motions in town meeting, such as the influential Braintree Instructions of 1764 against the Stamp Act, were all concerned with establishing a sound legal basis for opposition to English tyranny. Obviously government and taxation by a body in which America had no representation whatsoever was, for Americans, "tyranny" by any proper *English* standards.

His most famous single act during this period, however, was of a rather counterrevolutionary sort. He defended the British soldiers involved in the Boston Massacre of 1770. The massacre was evidently something of a put-up job. The radical leaders, Samuel

Adams no doubt among them, did everything they could to stir up trouble between the people of Boston and the British troops quartered there to prevent just such troubles. When a mob attacked the soldiers, the nervous fellows fired on them and killed several (including a mulatto named Crispus Attucks). John Adams obeyed his legal conscience and risked his future and his popularity with the patriots by defending the Britishers. They were acquitted. Samuel Quincy was the prosecutor, Josiah Quincy was Adams's partner in the defense. Despite vicious attacks in the press, some by Samuel Adams himself, John was elected to the state House of Representatives (General Court) in 1770.

1774: Both John and Samuel Adams were among the delegates from Massachusetts to the first and second Continental Congresses in Philadelphia. The Adamses were thus exposed to the larger world of national affairs. John's name in particular can be associated with specific acts of importance. It was he who conspired, and first moved in 1775, to make George Washington Commander in Chief of the American Army. It was he who helped inspire, and seconded, the motion in 1776 of Richard Henry Lee that "these colonies . . . ought to be free and independent states." He was on the committee to draft the Declaration, though, of course, Jefferson did the actual writing. It was Adams who led the debate in Congress for its adoption.

As chief figure of the Board of War he is always considered the Father of the Navy (of which Nicholas Biddle was one of the first five captains). He served altogether on more than ninety different committees, and was chairman of more than twenty-five of them.

1778: A second career as diplomat kept Adams abroad for ten years. On resigning from Congress, he was appointed in 1777 one of the three commissioners to France, taking the place of recently recalled Silas Deane. He joined Benjamin Franklin and Arthur Lee, the other two commissioners, in Paris in 1778 and became involved in their quarrels, that of Arthur Lee with Franklin and that of Arthur Lee with Silas Deane. Adams suggested to Congress that they avoid this kind of thing by appointing only one commissioner. Congress followed his suggestion. They appointed Franklin, and this left Adams without a job.

1779: He returned briefly to America, where he had time to write the new constitution for the state of Massachusetts, but was immediately sent back to Europe as peace commissioner. Blocked in his earlier efforts to get things moving by the caution of Vergennes, the French minister, and by the refusal of King George III to consider independence as a basis for peace, Adams, on his own initiative, removed to Holland in 1780 where he negotiated a profitable loan and a favorable treaty with the Netherlands. Returning to Paris in 1782, he signed preliminary articles of a peace with England which was formally concluded in 1783.

1785: Upon the signing of the peace, John Adams was appointed the first minister to the Court of Saint James's (a post later held by his son and by his grandson). Abigail joined him abroad in 1784, living with him first at Auteuil, outside of Paris, then removing with him to London in 1785. Frustrated there in his attempt to achieve a favorable commercial treaty with the English, he wrote the confused but learned *Defense of the Constitutions* etc. This was his principal contribution to the debate over the new Constitution.

1788: Returning to America, he was immediately elected to Congress. However, beginning in 1789, he became for two terms the first Vice President of the United States, in New York and then in Philadelphia, under George Washington. When Washington retired, he succeeded him as President in 1797 and directed his principal efforts to preventing a formal declaration of war against France, now under the belligerent rule of the revolutionary Directory. Despite the machinations of the French, which included the attempt to bribe American envoys (the XYZ affair) and the intrigues of the English, supported by Hamilton and his coterie; despite the treachery of his own Cabinet, notably of Secretary of State Timothy Pickering, who was secretly dealing with Hamilton and entirely under his direction, Adams managed by his own efforts to keep the peace. Meanwhile Adams made himself almost universally unpopular through the oppressive Alien and Sedition Acts, war emergency measures against vituperative newspapers and seditious foreigners of French sympathies.

Hamilton, who wanted war with France and alliance with England, and also wanted to run the administration, destroyed Adams's political career by writing, on the eve of the election of 1800, a letter violently attacking Adams. The split in the Federalist party between Adams and Hamilton assured the election of their rivals, the Republicans (i.e., Democrats). A tie between Jefferson and Burr was broken by the House of Representatives in favor of Jefferson. Adams, first President to live in the White House in Washington, refused to stay to greet his former friend and victorious rival. He hurried back to Braintree (that part of it now renamed Quincy in honor of his wife's family), where he lived the rest of his life in conspicuous seclusion, publicly bitter, privately contented. Before his death on July 4, 1826, he mellowed sufficiently to carry on a long and illuminating correspondence with Jefferson. They both died on the same day — the fiftieth anniversary of Independence — surely one of the most symbolic and touching and extraordinary coincidences in all history.

This is a most cursory outline of a long, busy life. There was hardly a month between 1760 and 1800 when John Adams was not involved in something that had a bearing upon the history of the nation. Though not famous for any one outstanding thing as, say, Jefferson was famous for writing the Declaration of Independence, he was continuously prominent and busy, first on the local, then the state, then the national and, finally, the international scene. He was a learned and acute lawyer, perhaps the foremost in America of his time. He was an equally learned and forceful speaker, and a most influential one, particularly in his debates in Congress.

He was also a voluminous writer. He kept a diary, with entries beginning in 1753 and ending in 1804. He wrote a rather messy, self-justificatory autobiography, which is in turn boring, unpleasant and vivid. He wrote endless letters, some of the best of them to his wife Abigail, who wrote him back. He also wrote books and pamphlets. Whereas in diary and letter he could be pungent and striking, in formal writing he tended to be pompous, verbose and disorganized, though sometimes noble. But none of his book-length works — *Dissertation on the Canon and the Feudal Law* (1765), *Thoughts on Government* (1776), *A Defense of the Constitutions of Government of the United States of America* (1787–88), *Discourses on Davila* (1791) and other newspaper and legal contributions — makes for stimulating reading. Yet they are frequently sensible and often profound. He was, like his compeers Franklin, Jefferson and Hamilton, something of a writer *manqué*. If he hadn't been so busy doing things, he might, like the rest of them, have written more and better. At his best, in passages of diary and letter, he is tart, funny and forceful, a keen sketcher of human character.

It is in his informal asides that John Adams lives as a person. There he embodies that quintessential New Englandness — prissy, pursy, schoolmarmish, meddling, prejudiced, parochial and touchy, but also rock-bottom honest, clear-sighted, large-viewed and pertinacious. Few men could have been more exasperating personally. "Your Mr. Adams . . . is the most ungracious man I ever saw," said Sir John Temple, English diplomat, as quoted with relish by John himself in his own diary. Yet few public men have ever left a fresher spoor in history.

John Adams had an eye for human frailty. This may have made him a less than amiable acquaintance at times, but it makes him a lively diarist. As of 1774 in Philadelphia:

"In Congress, nibbling and quibbling — as usual. There is no greater Mortification than to sit with half a dozen Witts, deliberating upon a Petition, Address, or Memorial. These great Witts, these subtle Critics, these refined Genius's, these learned Lawyers, these wise Statesmen, are so fond of shewing their Parts and Powers, as to make their Consultations very tedius."

As true now as then. He gets down to personalities. "Young Ned Rutledge is a perfect Bob o'Lincoln — a Swallow — a Sparrow — a Peacock — excessively vain, excessively weak, and excessively variable and unsteady — jejune, inane, and puerile."

He could be kind and genial; especially when well fed. Another gathering in the same year, 1774, also in Philadelphia, pleased him better. "Dined at Mr. Willing's, who is a Judge of the Supreme Court here, with the Gentlemen from Virginia, Maryland and New York. A most splendid Feast again — Turtle and every Thing else. Mr. Willing told us a Story of a Lawyer here, who the other Day, gave him upon the Bench the following Answer, to a Question Why the Lawyers were so increased.

> *You ask me why Lawyers so much are increas'd*
> *Tho most of the Country already are fleec'd*
> *The Reason I'm sure is most strikingly plain*
> *The Sheep are oft sheared yet the Wool grows again*
> *And tho you may think e'er so odd of the Matter*
> *The oft'ner they're fleeced, the Wool grows the better*
> *Thus downy-chin'd Boys as oft I have heard*
> *By frequently shaving obtain a large Beard.*

"Mr. Willing is the most sociable, agreeable Man of all. He told us of a Law of this Place, that whereas oysters, between the Months of May and September were found to be unwholesome food, if any were brought to Market they should be forfeited and given to the Poor.

"We drank Coffee, and then Reed, Cushing and I strolled, to the Moravian Evening Lecture where we heard soft, sweet Music and a dutchified English Prayer and Preachment."

He had his sublime moments also, as for instance his raptures over the conduct of the Boston Tea Party. "Last Night three Cargoes of Bohea Tea were emptied into the Sea. This Morning a Man of War sails. This is the most magnificent Movement of all. There is a Dignity, a Majesty, a Sublimity, in this last Effort of the Patriots, that I greatly admire. The People should never rise, without doing something to be remembered — something notable and striking. This Destruction of the Tea is so bold, so daring, so firm, intrepid and inflexible, and it must have so important Consequences, and so lasting, that I cant but consider it as an Epocha in History."

It is indeed startling to find this sort of noble rhetoric suddenly intruding into the minutes of the town records of Braintree, when Adams's Instructions appear there: "In all the Calamities that have ever befallen this Country, we have never felt so great a Concern. . . . " This in the midst of trivia about roads and taxes.

Best of all are the various travel diaries, written either at home, or while passing through Connecticut, or going to Europe by sea, or while on the Continent itself. Even the most ordinary details have salt. His description in his autobiography, for instance, of his first leave-taking on February 13, 1778:

". . . Captain Samuel Tucker, Commander of the Frigate Boston, met me at the House of Norton Quincy Esquire, in Braintree, where We dined. After dinner I bid Adieu to my Friend and Uncle Quincy, sent my Baggage, and walked myself with Captain Tucker, Mr. Griffin a Midshipman, and my eldest Son, John Quincy Adams between ten and eleven years of Age, down to the Moon Head where lay the Bostons Barge. In our Way We made an halt of a few minutes at the House of Mr. Seth Spear of Hoffs Neck, where some Sailors belonging to our barge had been waiting for Us. The good Lady, who was an Adams, came out very civilly to invite Us in. We had not time to spare and excused ourselves. She was an aimiable Woman, with very delicate health, much afflicted with hysterical complaints, often a little disarranged in her imagination. At this time she was somewhat flighty and accosted me in an alarming manner. 'Mr. Adams you are going to embark under very threatening signs. The Heavens frown, the Clouds roll, the hollow Winds howl, The Waves of the Sea roar upon the Beech,' and on she went in such a Strain that I seemed to be reading Ossian. I thought this prophecy of the Sybill, was not very cheering to one whose Acquaintance with the Sea, had been confined to a few Trips to Half Moon a gunning and one to Cohasset rocks a fishing when he was a Boy. . . ." *

As for John Adams and his trip abroad, his Sibyl cousin was quite right. They had a most exciting trip. Terrible storms, during which the mainmast was struck by lightning and a seaman killed; pursuit by a British man of war; capture of a British prize — all vivaciously set forth by JA in both diary and autobiography. When he finally reached Paris, his tartness did not desert him, and his Puritanism got many a shock.

". . . We Were invited to dine at Monsieur Brillons, a Family in which Mr. Franklin was very intimate, and in which he spent much of his Time. Here We met a large Company of both Sexes and among them were a Monsieur Le Vailliant and his Lady. Madam Brillion [*sic*] was one of the most beautifull Women in France, a great Mistress of Musick, as were her two little Daughters. The Dinner was Luxury, as usual in that Country. A large Cake was brought in with three flaggs flying. On one of them 'Pride subdued': on another 'Haec dies, in qua fit Congressus, exultemus et potemus in eâ.' Mr. Brillon was a rough kind of Country Squire. His Lady all softness, sweetness and politeness. I saw a Woman in Company, as a Companion of Madam Brillon who dined with her at Table, and was considered as one of the Family. She was very plain and clumzy. When I afterwards learned both from Dr. Franklin and his Grandson, and from many other Persons, that this woman was the Amie of Mr. Brillion and that Madam Brillion consoled herself by the Amitié of Mr. Le Vailliant, I was astonished that these People could live together in such apperent Friendship and indeed without cutting each others throats. But I did not know the World. I soon saw and heard so much of these Things in other Families

---

* A footnote in the invaluable Adams papers adds family richness to this statement. " 'Cohasset Rocks,' a few miles east of Braintree . . . remained a favorite fishing and shooting area throughout the 19th century. As an example of the continuity of family habits it is worth remarking that in 1880 two of JA's greatgrandchildren, JQA2 and CFA2 [Adams-papers shorthand] who had as boys gone on fishing jaunts there with their father, bought shares in a private summer colony, the Glades Club, whose property helps form Cohasset harbor, and that in the 1960's *their* great-grandchildren still swim, fish and sail off 'Cohasset Rocks.' "

and among almost all the great People of the Kingdom that I found it was a thing of course. It was universally understood and Nobody lost any reputation by it. Yet I must say that I never knew an Instance of it, without perceiving that all their Complaisancy was external and ostensible only; a mere conformity to the fashion; and that internally there was so far from being any real friendship or conjugal Affection that their minds and hearts were full of Jealousy, Envy, revenge and rancour. . . . There were none of the delightful Enjoyments of conscious Innocence and mutual Confidence. It was mere brutal pleasure."

It was of course with Abigail that John enjoyed this Mutual Confidence, and along with his diaries, her letters make an equally bright spot of color on the annals of the Revolution. Since she has become so famous — a top best-seller of 1965-66, *Those Who Love* by Irving Stone being a fictionalized biography of her — and her vignettes, like that of Mme. Helvitus, one of Franklin's female friends, wiping up her little dog's nuisance in the drawing room with her rather soiled petticoat, etc., having been so often repeated, more quotation, though tempting, must be resisted.

Obviously, someday, the two Adamses should be rescued, first from the Victorian embalming and bowdlerizing of pious Charles Francis Adams (how one does learn to loathe the "delicacy" of the Victorians!) and then from the admirable welter of *everything* in the Adams papers, where the best is lost amid the worst. What the Adamses need is a good editor to prune and extract without distorting. Then it will finally be recognized that they are among the liveliest writers of the eighteenth century, and their record of men, events and homely details invaluable.*

One of the most important acts of John Adams's life, especially as a founder of a family, was his marriage into the Quincy connection. It illustrates, very specifically, the importance to these families of the Good Marriage.

---

* Adrienne Koch and William Piden's *Selected Writings of John and John Quincy Adams* (Knopf, 1946) is a good step in the right direction, but still based on the nineteenth-century editions.

The idea of the Good Marriage is rather repugnant to modern tastes. We have been so saturated with romantic ideals (one must marry only for love) and with philosophies of rebellious individualism or utopian socialism that the very idea of "marrying well" is shameful. Such is above all the effect of literature, particularly, as per example, the traditional English novel, in which again and again from Jane Austen through Trollope it is asserted that true feeling is a better basis for marriage than money and fortune. (Of course, it is nice to have all of them.)

Nonetheless in all these families, in almost all generations, a Good Marriage, in the thoroughly worldly sense, has helped establish and maintain family fortunes; and bad marriages have helped undermine them. Of all these good marriages, none was more obviously useful in this way than the marriage of John to Abigail. It was, at the same time, also equally obviously a love match, and continued to be one. There are not many records of continuing marital affection more winning than that of this quaint couple. Yet the fact remains that in marrying as he did, John Adams certainly enhanced his position, just as much as if he had done so with cold calculation. One aspect of a family's hereditary meritocracy seems to be the ability to attract outstanding spouses.

The Quincys were the first family of Braintree. They were not the first family of Massachusetts. They represented not the topmost ruling clique of the colony, such earlier families as Winthrop, Bradstreet, and Dudley, or such later oligarchs as the Hutchinson-Oliver faction, but "provincial squirarchy." That is, Massachusetts being organized in "towns," each such township had its organized class system. At the top were the preacher, the professionals (lawyers, doctors, schoolteachers) and above all the squire. The squire lived in the largest house on the biggest acreage, represented the township in the state governing bodies, acted as colonel of the local militia, and was elected year after year as the moderator of town meeting. One member of the family would be a judge. The squire, beyond other members of the town, would have connections with a larger world, friends, relations and equals in other townships, even in other colonies.

The pattern was repeated all over Massachusetts. In Worcester, for instance, where Adams taught school, the Chandlers were such a family of squires, as is abundantly clear in reading his diary for the period. In Braintree it was the Quincy family. These squires had something of the status that prominent planters had down south in their own parishes; but up north they had to compete for power not only with the already established official classes (Winthrops, Hutchinsons) but with the merchants and professionals of Boston (Boylstons) and of the other rising seaports like Salem. These were strictly mercantile and urban, as contrasted to the basically rural and agricultural squirarchy.

Of such members of the provincial aristocracy, the Quincys seem to have been rather special, as Braintree itself was a rather special town. They were an old family, having emigrated in 1633, and from the beginning the important one locally. They had connections with the scholar-theocrats who so dominated Massachusetts in its earliest years. Abigail's great-grandfather Daniel, already in the third generation of the family's American foundation, had married the daughter of Thomas Shepard, leader before the Lord. Daniel's son Colonel John (after whom John Q. was named) had married a Norton, of the same breed and eminence. Another Quincy had married the sister of President Hoar of Harvard. This meant that the family was tied to the leadership of church and state by kinship.

By education the Quincys began in 1699 to cement relations with Harvard; rather late as Massachusetts families go. Edmund the third graduated in that year and so prepared the way for generations of Quincys and for a Josiah who became president of the institution in the nineteenth century.

Through Abigail, John became a member of this first family of his native Braintree; and in fact it was a thoroughly Braintree coalition that led the patriot party in Revolutionary Massachusetts. Samuel Adams, their chief, had a Braintree grandfather. John Hancock, his coadjutor, financer and rival, had been born the son of a poor Braintree clergyman and married a Braintree girl; it was only when his uncle Thomas, "richest man in Boston," died, leaving him sole heir, that Hancock began to strut upon the stage of Boston and the nation. Josiah Quincy would certainly have been one of the important men of his period if he had not been cut off so early by consumption. He had gone to England in 1774 on a secret mission, and died on the way home. The secret of his mission died with him. Only the Otis-Warren family combination and the mercantile complex of the Essex Junto (Cabot, Lowell) approached the Braintree group in influence.

The Revolution liquidated many of the older colonial families of Massachusetts. Winthrops petered out and Mathers came to a Tory end after four generations of declining significance. Hutchinsons and Olivers were exiled. Into the vacuum there then stepped these patriot families, the Braintree group of Adamses, Hancocks, Quincys; and the Essex Junto. Unlike Virginia, where the planters continued to run things after the war as they had before it, a new order began for New England.

In the end John Adams fought with everyone, even his cousin Samuel, and so brought his party to national defeat and to local domination by the Essex Junto. But the alliance with the Quincy strand remained firm; it attached the Adamses to pre-Revolutionary aristocracy and provided a political and social nucleus for the whole Braintree faction.

This pattern, that of the Good Marriage, with its linkage of new blood and old, a past era and a present one, has been followed in various degrees and generations by all these families; most notable and parallel being the marriage of Isaac Roosevelt to Cornelia Hoffman. Moderns may not quite like or approve of it, but the pattern persists today as one of the most important ingredients that go into the making of any First Family. The Adamses, meritorious, independent and conscientious as they were, still followed the formula faithfully.

2

Roosevelts

IN OUR CAST of Revolutionary characters, our patriot portrait gallery, the Adamses are the most conspicuous. The Roosevelts are the least. Only one Roosevelt, Isaac, really did anything, and he didn't do much. He definitely belongs in a third tier, not as a Great Founder, nor even a Lesser Founder, but merely a Local Worthy. However, he has earned his sobriquet of "The Patriot," he was pretty important around New York, and he did elevate the family from middle to upper class by his success, and by his marriage.

Isaac was the son of that Jacobus who had married a Hardenbroeck and who had brought English into the Dutch Church (Hyde Park branch). Isaac, born in 1726, spent the major part of his life as a "successful merchant"; that is, he refined sugar, being one of the first to do so on a large scale. He sired ten children.

As far as Family is concerned, his marriage was probably more important than his personal success, and needs more comment. As Adams married into the squirarchy, so Roosevelt married into the so-called Patroonship.

As has been suggested, New York was dominated by its "patroonocracy" as Virginia by its "plantocracy." The New York group differed from the Virginians in that it was so much smaller and tighter; and that it was *Dutch,* not English. It was the only aristocracy in all of the original thirteen states that was predominantly *not* of English origin. This gave it a peculiar cast of exclusiveness and conservatism; but also perhaps a feeling of alienation and inferiority. This may account for the contradictory fact of Dutch Revolutionary patriotism. The oligarchs certainly weren't democrats, and they had nothing to say for Liberty, Equality and Fraternity. Property, Consanguinity and Seniority was more the idea. As in any country of immigrants, those who get there first have a certain automatic status, and these Dutch firstcomers were well aware of this. Nonetheless it was this group, this family complex, that largely led and commanded the Revolution in New York. This despite the fact that it meant the end of the various patroonships, lordships and manors to which they owed their position.

The four families already mentioned — Van Rensselaer, Schuyler, Livingston and Van Cortlandt — form the very core and center of this group. Added to this were other Dutch or Dutchified families, also most of them landowners, such as the Beekmans, De Peysters and Bayards. The Beekmans were German (Beckmann), the Bayards were originally French, the De Peysters Flemish and city folk, not upriver landowners. Nonetheless, all had become thoroughly Dutch in culture and tradition. Somewhat to one side, but linked by many strands, were the Morrises, who as lords of Morrisania were also "patroons," but English, not Dutch.

With these few names alone one could play genealogical cats-cradle, attempting to follow down through the generations just how knotted the various bloodstreams got to be. They married each other and married each other right up through the nineteenth century, when at last the money and the vigor gave out, and the lands were sold off.

These families are indeed incredibly cross-fertilized; but it would be tedious to trace the actual kinships. Suffice it to say that in the most conspicuous fashion down through the generations, leading members of the Van Rensselaer family married Van Cortlandts, Livingstons, Schuylers and De Peysters; Van Cortlandts in turn married Schuylers, Bayards, Beekmans and Livingstons; Schuylers married Van Cortlandts, Van Rensselaers, Livingstons and Bayards;

Livingstons (who were actually Scotch, but had emigrated to Holland before they came west, spoke Dutch, and were therefore quite acceptable) married Van Rensselaers, Schuylers, De Peysters and other Livingstons; and Bayards, connected already with the Stuyvesants, married Van Cortlandts, Livingstons and Schuylers. It would be impossible for these families to be more consanguineous than they were unless, like the Ptolomys, they had married their own brothers and sisters. They came close.

These families and their kin produced most of New York's Revolutionary leadership, political and even military. To start with the Schuylers: Philip John, in the fourth generation (his mother was a Van Cortlandt, he married a Van Rensselaer) was appointed in 1775 one of the four major generals in the first Continental Army under Washington. He wasn't very good. He was in the state senate. He supported the Constitution. He was one of the first two senators from New York in the new government. Alexander Hamilton was his son-in-law.

Stephen Van Rensselaer, another son-in-law, eighth patroon (his mother was a Livingston, he married a Schuyler), was a state assemblyman, then senator, then lieutenant governor. He ran for governor but was defeated by George Clinton. He was a general in the War of 1812 (he wasn't very good), and was in the U.S. Congress. He cast the deciding vote that elected John Quincy Adams as President. But he was really more famous as a sort of genial "last of the patroons," who treated his tenants nicely, founded Rensselaer Institute, and was the foremost citizen of his state.

Pierre Van Cortlandt (whose mother was a De Peyster and who married a Livingston) was the first lieutenant governor of New York and held down the job for eighteen years, mostly under George Clinton. His son Philip (whose mother was of course a Livingston) was brevetted a brigadier general for bravery at Yorktown and served sixteen years in Congress. But he never married.

As for the Livingstons, they were all over the place; as ubiquitous as the Lees. Philip signed the Declaration of Independence. William, one brother, was first and semipermanent governor of the new state of New Jersey. William's son Brockholst ended up on the U.S. Supreme Court. William's daughter Sarah married John Jay, first Chief Justice. Robert R. Livingston (married a Beekman whose mother was a Livingston) was a patriot judge and had a son, Robert R., who was a member of the Continental Congress, but who missed signing the Declaration, though he was one of the five-member committee that drew it up. He was secretary of foreign affairs for the Congress. He was chancellor of New York and as such administered the oath of office to Washington in 1789. Robert's brother Edward was a congressman, senator and finally secretary of state under Jackson and then minister to France. Four Livingstons all told were at the Continental Congress (there were six Lees there). Many of the other prominent New Yorkers were cousins or in-laws: John Jay (mother a Van Cortlandt, wife a Livingston), James Duane (wife a Livingston), and of course Alexander Hamilton. As for the Morrises, they were almost as busy as the Livingstons. One signed the Declaration, alongside a Livingston . . . but we really needn't go into them.*

Where were the Roosevelts? Well, a Hardenbroeck had married a Philipse, and the Philipses were also lords of a manor; one of Isaac's aunts married a Schuyler; one of his first cousins married a

---

* To give a more definite impression of the weight of the patroonship in Revolutionary affairs: Of the four New York signers of the Declaration of Independence, one was a Livingston, one was a Morris (The Livingston who signed, Philip, was of course not the one, Robert R., who helped draw it up.); of the four New York signers of the Articles of the Confederation, one was a Morris, one was a Duane; the only New Yorker made president of the Continental Congress (John Hancock of Massachusetts was one, R. H. Lee of Virginia was another) was John Jay; of the thirty-some New York members who served in the Continental Congress, at least one-third belonged to the Patroonship, either directly (Livingston, Morris, Schuyler) or by marriage (Hamilton, Duane, Jay); Hamilton was the only signer of the Constitution from New York, but a Livingston signed for New Jersey, and a New York Morris for Pennsylvania; Philip Schuyler and Philip Van Rensselaer were Revolutionary generals; of the two first U.S. senators from the state, one was a Schuyler; there was either a Van Cortlandt or a Van Rensselaer in each of the first twelve U.S. Congresses except the second; John Jay was first Chief Justice of the United States, the only other New Yorker of the earlier years to serve on the Court being Brockholst Livingston, his brother-in-law. And so on.

De Peyster. This however did not seem to count, any more than the Adams' marriages to Boylstons seemed to count. What *did* count was that Isaac himself married a Hoffman. Uncle Nicholas made a very nice silver wedding tankard for them in 1758. The Hoffmans were minor "patroons." They were Swedish, sort of. That is, the original Martinus Hoffman came from Revel on the Baltic, which at the moment was part of Sweden. (It is now Tallinn, the capital of Estonia, and an unwilling part of Russia.) Hoffman ended up in the seventeenth century along the Hudson with lots of land (but no manor); a stone mansion was built, children were born, slaves were bought. The Hoffmans had more slaves than anyone else around, which isn't saying much. They had ten. Martinus, third of the line, married first a Benson, the Bensons also being Swedish too and minor patroons.* Martinus then married for a second wife an Alida Livingston. She was of course merely Cornelia Roosevelt's step-mother, but that was close. Somewhat like the Quincys, the Hoffmans weren't the most important of New Yorkers, but they were related and connected with those who were. In any case, the marriage served to make this branch of the Roosevelts appendages to the patroonship, and to direct their interests up toward the Hudson River Valley.

Isaac, as well as marrying, also did things; the right things. He was in both the Provincial Congress and on the Committee of One Hundred, stopgap attempts at government after British authority ended in 1776. He was in the convention that created the state's constitution in 1776–77 and was one of the first state senators in the newly created government. He capped his career by becoming the second president of America's second bank. This is less of a coup than being the first president of the first bank, a privilege reserved for Thomas Willing of Philadelphia, whom John Adams found so very agreeable at dinner in 1774. But nowadays Roosevelt's bank is

* An Egbert Benson was prominent in the Revolution and represented the patroonship in that second U.S. Congress otherwise denuded of patroons.

the oldest surviving one in the country, the Bank of New York. The bank was the brainchild of Alexander Hamilton, and the first president of it was crusty General Alexander McDougall of the Revolution. He lasted only a short time; the bank was founded in 1784 and McDougall died in 1786. Roosevelt was president from 1786 to 1791.* In 1794 Isaac died.

Meanwhile, there was politics. The world of state politics in which Roosevelt acted was as thoroughly dominated by the patroonship as anything else. It was continuously a family affair. The divisions were along family lines; before the Revolution between Tory De Lancey-Philipses and Whig Livingston-Schuylers, and after the Revolution between Federalist Schuyler-Hamiltons and Republican Livingston-Clintons. The De Lanceys were ruined and exiled. The Federalists won their first great battle over the adoption of the Constitution, but lost most of the local battles afterward.

Isaac was a Whig before and a Federalist after. He played an active, if never very conspicuous, role throughout the period. When the British occupied New York in 1776, he became a refugee, leaving his handsome house on Queen Street and his sugar mill behind him. There was a certain amount of real sacrifice involved. He moved up to Hoffman territory on the Hudson, and though he had no active military career (he was, after all, in his fifties), he did join a militia regiment. He was busy during the war in currency control jobs; not glamorous, but useful. He returned to the city when the British evacuated in 1783, and immediately became one of Hamilton's partisans, a political and financial supporter.

The politics of the post-Revolutionary period were as much a family affair as they had ever been before the Revolution; more or less the same families too. On one side were now ranged, as conservatives, Hamilton and his Schuyler in-laws. On the other side were the Clintons, joined by the Livingstons. Hamilton, naturally, repre-

---

* There is another candidate for second president, who presided in the interregnum between McDougall's death and Roosevelt's election, but he has not usually been recognized as legitimate in company history.

sented Property. He also supported the Constitution. The Clintons represented the People. They were violently opposed to the Constitution, which they regarded as an instrument of reaction, oligarchy and Government Control. Isaac Roosevelt, as a staunch Hamiltonian, was one of the delegates to New York's Constitutional Convention in 1788. He was keeping the best company there; other delegates included John Jay, Richard Morris, Alexander Hamilton, R. R. Livingston and James Duane, Family men all.

The Hamiltonian forces won this battle; but the Clintonians won most of the others. From 1777, when George Clinton defeated Philip Schuyler to become first governor of New York, till 1828, when his nephew De Witt died in office as governor, the Clintons and their allies, including Aaron Burr, ran the state. The Clintons, though they came from up the Hudson too, did not belong to the patroonship. When George was first elected, his political enemy John Jay made it pretty clear what the Hamilton wing of the patroonship thought of the Clintons. Jay said, "Clinton's family and connections do not entitle him to so distinguished a pre-eminence," which gives some idea of what these people thought the qualifications for a state governor in a democracy were (Property, Consanguinity, Seniority). That didn't stop the Clintons. George remained governor through the Revolution, being elected for six successive terms, till 1795, and then for another extra term in 1800. After that, like a later governor of New York, Theodore Roosevelt, he went on to become Vice President of the United States; but unlike TR, failed to become President, though he tried. Like his nephew De Witt, he also died in office.

Isaac, being a Federalist, was therefore generally on the losing and conservative side of the fight, so unlike his descendant Franklin. But he was able to set up said descendant both ancestorally and financially as a member in good standing of the post-Revolutionary patroonship.

His wife Cornelia died in 1788, and her death was the occasion of setting a precedent. Washington was asked to the funeral — "Received an invitation to attend the funeral of Mrs. Roosevelt (the wife of a Senator of this State)" — but declined "because the propriety of accepting an invitation of this sort appeared to be very questionable and secondly . . . because it might be difficult to discriminate in cases which might thereafter happen." Cautious fellow, George. A pew at the Roosevelt funeral was one place where Washington did not sleep.

Isaac Roosevelt is no meteor across the skies of the national firmament, but in him the family for the first time emerged from petit-bourgeois security into the high finance and high society of the period. By the time Isaac died, respected, rich, well connected, everybody in the city knew who the Roosevelts were.

Other Roosevelts fought and served. James, Isaac's first cousin (Oyster Bay branch), had a son James who served in the Commissary Department without pay. This was noble of him, but not very exciting. Until Theodore came along, the Roosevelts in either branch were not famous as fighters.

3

Biddles

THE Adams family was founded by one man, John Adams, and from him descend all the Adamses that, as Family, really count. Isaac Roosevelt elevated his particular branch of his particular family into the New York upper classes. There they stayed, largely on the basis of tenure and connection, rather than achievement, until the days of Franklin Delano. The other branch soon caught up, but not during the Revolution. The du Ponts, too, are a "one-man family" in this sense. The Biddles and the Lees are not. The Lees emerged from local into national esteem on a broad front, in a band, a squad, a complex. So, in a somewhat similar though considerably less startling fashion, did the Biddles.

William and John, progenitors of the two Philadelphia branches, are certainly obscure enough; yet no less than six of the Biddle sons achieved some reputation or position; at least three of the daughters made "good marriages." Some, though not all, of this success could be said to be on a national, not merely a Philadelphia level. Some, but not all, of the families descended from this success have kept their places down to the present.

On the whole, the children of William, the older brother, are more interesting than the children of John. However the grandchildren of John, at least, were perhaps a bit more securely embedded into the matrix of Old Philadelphia by marriage and kinship. There is not the time lag that exists between the two branches of the Roosevelts, nor the economic differences that existed between the two American branches of the du Pont family. The two Biddle branches emerge simultaneously and equally. The difference is rather one of character than quality. The John Biddles (Solid) were sober folk. The Williams (Romantic) were a bit more violent and spectacular.

They all started pretty much from scratch, though the family of John, successful tavern-and-storekeeper, was certainly better off than the bankrupt family of widow Mary Scull Biddle. Neither family could have had any pretension to social position or distinction; this again in a colony, like Massachusetts or New York or Virginia, where social distinctions were already thoroughly stabilized.

Like Roosevelts or Adamses, the Biddles had to rise up into an already established aristocracy. It differed from that of Massachusetts, New York, and Virginia, in that the aristocracy of Philadelphia was almost exclusively urban and mercantile. The source of wealth was shipping — importing and exporting. Philadelphia was

America's greatest port, surrounded by its richest farmlands. From the beginning of the settlement, life had been easy and prosperous. No trouble with the Indians, as long as Penn's benevolent Indian policy lasted; no struggles with extremes of either heat or cold. No dependence on one cash crop like tobacco, but a rich variety of trade and even craft manufacture. Those who profited most from this were the merchants. Like his counterpart in Boston, the Philadelphia merchant lived in a fine house and controlled the city's political and social life. Unlike the merchant of Boston, he did not have over him a distinct, rather separated group of political families, Winthrops or Hutchinsons, who dominated the whole colony on the basis of tenure in office; nor a powerful group of churchly intellectuals who dominated thought and morals, like the Mathers. Unlike the merchant in New York, there was no group of all-powerful upstate landowners who must be fought or placated. And of course there was no oligarchy of planters. Only the large ironmasters, rich farmers and small traders of the countryside and provincial towns provided any competition to the dominance of the Philadelphia merchant, Quaker or worldly, in the state's councils. Later on, the Scotch-Irish of western Pennsylvania grew restive, demanding a voice in said councils.

All that really stood between the oligarchy of merchants and almost complete local rule and local independence was the Penn family. As proprietors of all Pennsylvania, they theoretically had almost absolute rights over their private property. Only theoretically. The politics of Pennsylvania and of Philadelphia consisted of a long, drawn-out conflict between Proprietor and People. For the proprietors it was a consistently losing battle; and one odd result of this battle was that the direct rule by the British government tended to look pretty good to many Pennsylvanians by comparison.

Since the Penns did not live in Pennsylvania, except occasionally, their influence was not present, direct and personal. The social and political vacuum thus created was filled by Americans, a somewhat heterogeneous collection. Some were representatives of the proprietors, some were antagonists. Some were Quaker, some were Anglican. No one single group, like that of the patroons or the planters, dominated; not even the Quakers, after the first few decades. Though the influence of the outlying towns, like Reading and Carlisle, and of the counties was felt, there was no powerful rural aristocracy to balance the city aristocracy.

There was however a special quirk to Philadelphia mercantile oligarchism. Though the economic base of the city's wealth and growth was obviously mercantile, and its merchants obviously pre-eminent, "being in trade" was always just a trifle déclassé. The very highest place in the city's esteem was always reserved not for the merchant himself, but for the professional, at least the doctor and the lawyer. And though the money came from the city, Philadelphia's rich people set their hearts on country estates. Thus, almost from the very beginnings of settlement, the chief representatives of the chief families were usually not actually businessmen themselves, but medical practitioners or legal lights, judges in particular. The money might come from trade or real estate; the status came from the distinctions of the learned professions.

The world, then, into which the Biddles rose was an almost strictly urban, mercantile world dominated by professionals who spent much of their time living in the country. The obvious object of any Philadelphian who wanted to get ahead was to make enough money from shipping and trading so that he could acquire a country estate and send his sons to Edinburgh to study medicine, or to the Temple in London to study law. This in fact is what families like the Shippens, the Cadwaladers and other such pre-Revolutionary first families had done.

So the typical Philadelphia grandee of the mid-eighteenth century presented a picture that might be painted thus: Of a Quaker family emigrating in the 1680's, and that had prospered greatly in the following decades in, say, the West India trade, the present representative of the family had by now been converted to the Establishment. Sent abroad by his father to study law or medicine and take the Grand Tour through France and Italy (bringing back a picture or statue), he returned home elegant and Anglican. He then proceeded to marry the heiress of a southern plantation. An elegant new house in town, an elegant new country house on the Schuylkill completed the picture. Devotion to social life, politics, profession and business affairs in about that order, occupied time and energies; as well as the patronization of science, art and good works of all kinds. This affluent state of affairs coincided with the flowering of the Virginia river life, though perhaps it was at its height later, after 1750 rather than before. Those that stayed Quaker, though they may have disapproved, led about the same sort of life; only more circumspectly. They did not attend dances like the Assemblies that became traditional after 1748. They were warier of art and the Grand Tour. They did drink Madeira and fox-hunt though, like their Anglican cousins. The politics of both Quakers and non-Quakers were violently split along pro- and anti-proprietory lines.

Two families might be used as specimens here to stand for Philadelphia's colonial aristocracy in comparison to Quincys, Hoffmans and Lees. The Shippens became kin of the Lees. The Cadwaladers, later on, of the Biddles. Both families were important, first in medicine, then in law (judges).

The Shippens came to Philadelphia from England via Boston, and to Anglicanism from Quakerism via Presbyterianism. Edward Shippen, first of his line, made a fortune in New England; but in 1694 he left, because of Quaker persecution. He came to Philadelphia, and there quickly established himself as a great man; in fact as "the biggest man with the biggest house and the biggest coach" in the city. He was Philadelphia's first true mayor in 1701. Though a pillar of the community, he "anticipated the marriage relation" with his third wife, which caused him trouble in Meeting; but the Shippens had a faculty for rising above such clouds. Not his son Joseph, who doesn't seem to cut much of a figure except as a literary dilettante, but his grandson made the proper leap into medicine. Doctor

William Shippen senior was a dominant personage in local practice and a member of the Continental Congress. His son William junior went to the nascent College of New Jersey, of which his Presbyterian family was a patron, then on to London and Edinburgh (M.D., 1761), then the Grand Tour through France, with medical overtones, and home. He was chief of the medical department of the Continental Army during the Revolution, and one of America's very first professors in its first medical school at the University of Pennsylvania. He married Alice Lee, sister of Richard Henry, and delighted John Adams by giving him a "comprehensive Lecture upon all Parts of the human Frame. This Entertainment charmed me." William's cousin Edward Shippen, converting to Anglicanism, became chief justice of Pennsylvania after the Revolution, although he'd been a Loyalist during it. Again, Shippens were able to rise above such trifles. They were, after all, connected not only to the Lees, and so to everybody in Virginia, but also to everybody in Philadelphia. Edward Shippen's daughter Peggy married Benedict Arnold, which was *not* a good marriage.

A similar pattern was followed by the Cadwaladers. A Quaker John ap (son of) Cadwalader came to Philadelphia from Wales in 1697, bearing with him a genealogy traceable right back to God (via Adda ap Duw, Adam son of God). His son, Thomas Cadwalader, followed in the wake of the Shippens. On his mother's side, Thomas was related to a nest of Welsh doctors, earliest of their profession in Philadelphia. He started his apprenticeship with an uncle, Dr. Evan Jones, and then went abroad, to England and Rheims rather than to Edinburgh. When he got back, he demonstrated the new European methods of dissection for Dr. William Shippen senior, inoculated skeptical patients for smallpox, a daring thing to do in the 1730's (as Dr. Zabdiel Boylston found out when he tried it in Boston and was mobbed), and married an heiress, Miss Lambert from Trenton. He passed his time between his inlaws' estates on the Delaware and his own near the Schuylkill. He was an active patriot, and wrote an *Essay on the West-India Dry*

Gripes, a form of poisoning that came from drinking rum distilled through lead pipes.

Two of his children, Lambert and John, were dashing militia officers in the Revolution. Lambert was captain of the Greens, John of the Silk-Stockings, two companies of high-toned volunteers, to whom Madeira was served during drills at the expense of the Cadwaladers. Lambert was captured by the British, but John was active at the battles of Princeton, Brandywine and Germantown. He declined the offer by Congress to make him brigadier general of the Continentals in command of the cavalry. During the so-called Conway Cabal against Washington, Cadwalader shot and nearly killed Conway in a duel. Washington admired him. John's son Thomas, also a militia general, married a Biddle, and their son John was a famous judge. So it went.

Everybody of course had lots of land and money, and like John and Lambert, indulged occasionally in "mercantile pursuits." Above all they had beautiful houses. Edward Shippen may have had the biggest house in his time; John Cadwalader had the handsomest. He remodeled one on Second Street in downtown Philadelphia for his bride, a Lloyd of Maryland, and when he moved in during the winter of 1770–71 it was the last word in native elegance. All the furniture was American-made, in the culmination of Philadelphia Chippendale, in itself the culmination of American taste and opulence; in fact a sort of culmination of eighteenth-century taste, a golden mean, much more sober and simple and "old-fashioned" than contemporary English or European decor, less flamboyant and ostentatious, but more lavish than anything else native to the colonies.

Not so very sober or simple though. Cadwalader's bed was, for instance, an awesome affair, crowned with plumes, swathed in betasseled curtains. His light green coach with crests and a border of "proper colour'd flowers" on the gilded panels was equally awesome. Asleep or about, the Cadwaladers made a brave show. New Englanders, when they attended the Continental Congress, were impressed in spite of themselves. Said Silas Deane, "I dined yesterday with Mr. Cadwallader [*sic;* actually it's only one *l*, and this is terribly important] whose furniture and house exceeds anything I have seen in this city or elsewhere." John Adams was more restrained. "We visited a Mr. Cadwallader [those two *ll*'s again!] a Gentleman of large Fortune, a grand and elegant House and Furniture."

From the day of Edward Shippen's biggest house and coach, or of John Cadwalader's plumed bed, tasteful opulence has been the *sine qua non* of a Philadelphian's status. The Cadwaladers set the standard to which the Biddles must aspire. Achievements, however, came first. Plumed beds and beflowered coaches cost money. Professional rank was the result of educational advantages. Even captaincies of militia often meant that the captains had paid for all the uniforms. The Biddles had very little money. Nonetheless, in the Revolutionary generation they managed to produce a lawyer, a doctor and a variety of captains.

Clement and Owen Biddle were the two sons of John who distinguished themselves, and a very worthy pair of worthies they were. They were both Quakers until the fighting began. Clement never returned to the fold; Owen did. He apologized in Meeting, after the war, for his part in it, and was taken back in. Actually he hadn't really done any fighting; he had just been an ardent patriot on belligerent committees. He signed the nonimportation agreement alongside brother Clement, and served on the local Committee of Safety and Board of War. This was enough, however, to make him a warmonger among Friends. His real fame was as a scientist, a "great mathematician" as John Adams, who met him, put it. He was, like Nicholas Scull, one of those gathered about Franklin and was active in his Philosophical Society, oldest and still one of the most famous of American learned societies. Owen began as a clock-and-watchmaker, and branched out as an astronomer and importer. He observed the transit of Venus in 1769 from Cape Henlopen on

the Delaware, and in 1778 an eclipse of the sun. David Rittenhouse, America's foremost astronomer, was his friend.

George Washington was Clement Biddle's friend, and Clement
had a much more active and distinguished and dangerous war career
than Owen. He helped organize the Quaker Blues, another of those
militia regiments, and actively fought at Trenton, Brandywine,
Germantown, Monmouth and other places. He was delegated to
receive the swords of the surrendering Hessians after the battle of
Trenton. He was aide-de-camp of General Greene, quartermaster
general at Valley Forge. He was mainly useful as a forager. Lack of
supplies was always the one thing that most plagued Washington as
Commander in Chief. Biddle, at Valley Forge and elsewhere, was
invaluable in this capacity. When he tried to resign in 1780 Washington personally intervened to prevent him. They corresponded till
Washington died, and the great man gave him a set of a dozen
chairs as a present, which the family still owned into modern times.

Before and after the war both Clement and Owen were busy
businessmen, with varying success. Clement did very well indeed.
Owen did well, then nearly went bankrupt, then did well again.
But it was Clement who became the rich man of the family. He
married a Rebekah Cornell, daughter of the lieutenant governor of
Rhode Island, and his descendants were always the moneyed,
marrying Biddles. Clement had the most respectable descendants,
Owen had the most numerous. But as Francis Biddle, descendant
himself of Clement, rather spitefully puts it, their careers are the
"stuff from which the arid bricks of history are baked." Francis was
much distressed that he didn't come down from the far more dashing and desperate Romantic Biddles, the Williams. The thing he
liked best about ancestor Clement was his one human weakness, a
fondness for using cologne in his bath.

The Williams were worthy enough; but they were not dull. No
observing the transits of Venus or foraging for them. They were out
getting blown up. Of Widow Biddle's nine children, one, James the

eldest, became a judge and local personage; another, Thomas the youngest, short-lived and unmarried, became a doctor. A third son, John, became a loyalist and left the country.* But none of these brought real fame or fortune to the family. Three other brothers, Edward, Nicholas and Charles, made the name prominent. All three were rather violent characters, particularly in view of their father's Quaker background.

Edward, fourth child, third son of William, should have been the great Biddle, rival to the Adamses and the Lees, and in any case, a more distinguished figure than Isaac Roosevelt. He was the political Biddle and seemed destined for great things. He joined the provincial militia at the age of sixteen, and in 1763 when the French wars ended, he emerged a captain, with five thousand acres of land as a bounty. Then he took up law, in Reading, Pennsylvania, and in no time was in the Assembly. By 1774 he was the speaker of that body, a more elevated position, say, than any that John Adams had occupied before the Revolution. Like John Adams, he too was a member of the first and second Continental Congresses, and evidently all for independence. But one fatal incident robbed him of health, wealth and glory.

As his brother Charles Biddle, an eyewitness, tells it,

"Coming to Philadelphia in January 1775 from Reading by boat, he fell overboard. I was in the boat with him. We got him in immediately and went ashore to a tavern that happened to be near where we landed. In order to prevent his taking cold he drank a great deal of wine and stood before a large fire in his shirt to dry it. The landlord being a Tory, and saying something about what Congress had done being improper, he beat him severely. With his passion and wine he became ungovernable. He ordered a blanket to be brought in . . . and laid down in it damp before the fire. The next morning he was very ill, and in a few days broke out all over his body and face [in] large blotches. He had one in his eye that deprived him of the sight of it. Although he lived nearly five years afterward, he had scarce a day's health."

* He had a descendant called Biddle Boggs.

With his military experience, his friends and family expected him to receive a commission "next in command" to Washington. He had married a Ross, niece of George Ross, an important lawyer of the Reading region and signer of the Declaration of Independence; but he himself missed that immortality, not because he wasn't for it but because of ill health. He was a delegate to the Congress again in '78 and '79, but the accident by the river effectively ended his career. Bad luck pursued his children too. His daughters married men of misfortune and had no descendants; Edward had no sons. He failed to be a proper Biddle family founder.

So did his brother Nicholas. He too came to a sad end, after a short life, and left no little Biddles. However, his career was so active and his end so spectacular that he definitely adds glamour to the name. His life, short though it may have been, was crammed with adventure and except for the finale would certainly make a ripe historical novel.

Following the footsteps of his brother Charles and his brother-in-law, salty Captain McFunn of the British navy, Nicholas went to sea at thirteen. On his second trip out, to Honduras to fetch mahogany, his ship was wrecked on a reef, and Nicholas was marooned for two weeks on a desert isle, while brother Charles went for help. Later on, in his twenties, he was a midshipman in the English navy and went on a naval expedition towards the North Pole, where his ship was nearly crushed by the ice, and where Horatio Nelson was one of Nicholas's co-explorers and acquaintances. When he returned to America in 1774, war and independence were brewing, and when John Adams and the Naval Board set out to create the infant American navy, Nicholas Biddle was the third captain to be commissioned. It was a struggle, since Adams and the other members of the committee wanted to give all the commissions to New Englanders. In fact most of them went to the members of one family, that of the then chairman of the Naval Committee, Stephen Hopkins of Rhode Island. Stephen's brother Esek Hopkins was made commodore; other commissions were given to Esek's son John

Burroughs Hopkins and to a Hopkins brother-in-law, Abraham Whipple. Esek was old and incompetent, his kin not much better, and it was only because of a few youngsters like Biddle, John Paul Jones and John Barry, none of them, incidentally, New Englanders, that the American navy had any pluck or luck at all. Even so, the record was fairly inglorious.

The first American navy consisted of five brigs converted from merchantmen — the *Alfred, Columbus, Cabot, Providence* and *Andrea Doria* — of which Dudley Saltonstall (brother-in-law of Silas Deane, another New England member of the Naval Committee), Abraham Whipple, John Burroughs Hopkins, a mysterious John Hazard and Nicholas Biddle were the respective captains. The *Alfred* was Esek Hopkins' flagship. "The first American fleet that ever swelled their [*sic*] sails on the Western Ocean," as a rhapsodic editor put it, was finally able to leave ice-bound Philadelphia on January 4, 1776. The fleet proceeded to Nassau and captured a large store of ammunition. It is interesting that America's very first "naval victory" was in fact an amphibious operation in which marines did the fighting, such as it was.

The second, and last, engagement of this little fleet was not so fortunate. It attacked, in a body, H.M.S. *Glasgow*, near Block Island. The *Glasgow* got away, more or less unscathed, and all the captains, except Biddle, displayed degrees of ineptitude or cowardice. John Burroughs Hopkins was wounded and put out of circulation. Hazard was court-martialed and dismissed from the service. Whipple insisted on a court-martial to clear his name of vicious rumors. He was acquitted, but he, Esek Hopkins and Saltonstall had to report to Congress in Philadelphia to "answer for their conduct." This left Biddle, the only captain whose reputation was unchallenged, as senior officer of the fleet. The marine committee of Congress cleared Saltonstall and Whipple. Poor old Esek Hopkins was censured and later relieved of his command.

So that was the end of the "first American fleet that ever swelled their sails on the Western Ocean." Individual ships went about capturing prizes, notably the *Providence,* now under the command of J. P. Jones; but there were no more concerted actions.

Congress then ordered a real navy to be built: thirteen new frigates. Some two-dozen captains were appointed to command the frigates and other vessels of this second, more genuine, American navy, and proper seniority among them was determined. Biddle ranked number five, next after Saltonstall. His ship, the *Randolph,* was the first of these frigates to get to sea. It soon developed that a rotten spar had been used for the mainmast. It broke, and the *Randolph* had to put into Charleston, South Carolina, for a new one. There, after endless delays, and after two masts in succession had been struck by lightning, a third mainmast was fitted, with lightning rod attached. (Why not think of this the first time?) The *Randolph* finally put to sea again. After one very successful prize-taking expedition, the *Randolph,* accompanied by some smaller vessels, met up with the formidable sixty-four-gun ship of the line *Yarmouth.* Though the *Randolph* sported only thirty-six guns, Biddle and his little fleet took on the battleship. The fight, despite the odds, was going all in favor of the *Randolph;* though Biddle was wounded in the thigh, he continued to direct the operations from a chair on deck. Then suddenly and inexplicably, the *Randolph* blew up. All but four of the crew were annihilated along with their ship and its captain.* The *Yarmouth,* undamaged by the blast, but in sorry shape from the fight, limped off. And so, in 1778 when the war had just begun, Biddle's promising career in the navy was dramatically cut short. Though it could hardly be considered an American victory, it was at least an action of gallantry. The fact that Biddle was young and handsome and engaged to the daughter of a rich South Carolinian, old plantation and all, added to the pathos. It caused a tremendous stir, added excitement to the hitherto thoroughly drab history of the navy and made the name of Biddle famous. Nicholas was, after all, *the* very first American naval captain who could pos-

* Including John McDougall, nephew of General McDougall, first president of Isaac Roosevelt's Bank of New York.

sibly be considered a "hero." All the newspapers were full of the matter, and Philip Freneau, America's foremost Revolutionary poet, wrote a rather spectacularly bad ballad about it:

> *What distant thunders rend the skies*
> *What clouds of smoke in columns rise*
> *What means the dreadful roar?*

or, in another verse, apropos the battle,

> *T'is Biddle wings those angry fires,*
> *Biddle, whose bosom Jove inspires,*
> *With more than mortal rage.*

As for the other captains of the "first American fleet that ever swelled" etc., they came to more inglorious naval ends. Esek Hopkins and Hazard had of course already been disgraced. John Burroughs Hopkins, best of his family, was dismissed in '79 for disobeying the orders of Congress. Whipple was captured in the same year and sat out the rest of the war on parole. Saltonstall, also in '79, ruined himself in the failure of an expedition to Maine and was court-martialed and dismissed too. Only the triumph of Jones in his *Bonhomme Richard* later in that same fatal year redeemed the record of this original group of naval officers. Of the first five captains, Biddle was incomparably the best.

The true foundation of the Romantic branch of the Biddle family was left to brother Charles. Fortunately, unlike Edward, Nicholas, or Thomas the doctor, he survived and had sons; he was a patriot, unlike John, and distinguished himself in various ways, though never actually a judge like James. Charles had the good sense to write an autobiography in his old age, so that we know something about him. It compares favorably with those of Adams and of du Pont, in that it is completed and more or less consistent. It describes a life of wonderful seafaring adventure, followed by a remarkably sudden legal and political success ashore. Charles was anything but literary. Perhaps just because of this, his straightforward and vigorous account of his early days gives a hair-raising picture of what life at sea meant to professionals of the period. A wonder any of them ever followed such a dangerous career. It was an arduous approach to plumed beds, flowered carriages and country seats.

Born in 1745, and something of a juvenile delinquent as a boy (they called it "mischief" then), he too took off after brother-in-law Captain McFunn at the age of seventeen. For twenty years and through more than a score of voyages he experienced just about every calamity possible to the human being except death. Almost every trip was attended by its individual disaster. As a mere sample, almost at random, on his second voyage in winter to the Azores:

"A few days after we were out we had had a most violent gale . . . About 3 p.m. the mate desired me to go below and bring him a drink; I was on the ladder, just going to hand it to him, when a tremendous sea broke on board and cleared the decks of everything upon them but the masts and pumps. There were two men with the mate upon the deck. The seamen had, fortunately, taken hold of a rope the moment the sea struck us, and by that means were saved. The mate was lost. As he was fond of liquor and surly, the crew did not much regret his loss. A coop broke when washed overboard, that had some geese in it; they appeared atop the waves to enjoy very much their liberty. A large dog was in the midst of them; he swam to the vessel and we took him on board."

The ship was then wrecked off Fayal in the Azores.

"We were drawing fast upon rocks that the sea broke over in such a manner that death appeared inevitable. As I swam remarkably well, I was determined as soon as the vessel struck to commit myself to the waves . . . Grant [the Captain] from the quarterdeck, seeing me naked, called to me. He represented to me the impossibility of my being saved by swimming while there was such a dreadful surf. When he found this had no effect, he begged me not to leave him. . . . When I looked at him, I perceived tears in his eyes. . . . This was one great inducement for me to stay. . . . We were now driving fast on shore, which had a horrid appearance. . . . When we first struck, I expected the vessel would have gone to pieces; however the second heavy sea . . . hove her so far on the beach that when the sea left her she was almost dry. In this situation we dropped from the end of the bowsprit and . . . reached the shore in safety."

This might have discouraged some from following this particular trade, but not Charles. On the next trip to the West Indies he was involved in a violent battle with the crew of another ship over a cargo of wood, and saw a vision by night of his dying sister, a splendid instance of a psychic phenomenon. The fourth voyage was the one where Nicholas was marooned on the island after the ship went on the reef. Charles also witnessed the burning at the stake of a Negro slave he was fond of who had murdered his master. The fifth voyage took him through a hurricane, and on the sixth voyage, Biddle by now being captain himself, he fought a duel with a friend over fighting cocks.

"We fired at the distance of ten paces and missed, and had agreed to fire the next shot at five yards, but before we were loaded an old gentleman, at whose house we had been, came down and prevented us firing a second time, and soon persuaded us to be reconciled. This difference . . . was of service to me afterward, and it was a caution not to lose my temper in a dispute with a friend."

Each voyage had its adventure — a pilot attempted to stab Biddle in Portugal, he struck a postearthquake plague in Haiti, there were more duels, wrecks and other varieties of mayhem. During the Revolution he continued at sea and was captured by the British. However, this seemed to cause him little real discomfort; in fact, it rather endeared the British naval officers to him. Though he had trouble with some of his captors, he still thought them "generally the best of seamen; and brave, generous and humane," which was seldom the feeling most American prisoners of war had about army officers.

Finally in 1783 after marrying a woman named Hannah Shepard from New Bern, North Carolina (no mention of old plantations here), he returned to Philadelphia, and in a twinkling of an eye found himself vice president of the state's supreme executive council. How this was done is something of a mystery. All Charles says is,

"I employed myself during the fall and winter [of 1783] in keeping a small store of goods [in Reading, Pennsylvania]. I thought Philadelphia would answer me better than Reading, and therefore intended . . . to move there, but some of my friends in Berks [County] wishing me to remain in Reading until the fall, when there was to be an election . . . I agreed."

Simple as that. For a short time he was acting governor of the state, like Thomas Lee of Virginia. This transformation from sea dog to statesman surprised no one more than Charles himself, since he seems to have had no experience or qualifications except force of character and the reputation of his brothers Edward and Judge James. "An uncommon circumstance," he says of himself, "that a man brought up to the sea, and who . . . was left without a fortune, should so early in life be raised to such a station." He was not quite forty. When Franklin came back from France in September 1785, he was of course elected president of the state, and Charles Biddle vice president "almost unanimously." "President" was equivalent to governor, vice president to lieutenant governor under the radical, unicameral, first state constitution of Pennsylvania of which John Adams so highly disapproved.

His career from then on was landlocked, legal and spiced only by an intense interest in the various murder trials in which, as a member of the Council, he seems to have been concerned, such as that of the unfortunate Elizabeth Wilson, executed at Chester in 1786 for the murder of her twin infants. (She didn't do it.) Charles died, full of years and honors, rich and respected and surrounded by a numerous progeny, in 1821, and founder of the other branch of Philadelphia Biddles that has best maintained its prestige and kept its money, along with the descendants of Clement.

One thing that helped spice Charles' later life was his connection with the Burr-Wilkinson complex. On the whole, this generation and branch of Biddles was not terribly fortunate in its marriages. Charles' own bride seems to have been a fine woman, but not an heiress of any kind. His brothers and sisters did no better. Captain McFunn, for instance, was a hearty fellow but not a man of fame or fortune. Two sisters, Abigail and Mary, died unmarried. Abigail was the one who appeared to Charles in the vision in the Caribbean.

The daughters of John did do better. Sarah married a Penrose, and thus into a family of weighty shipbuilders and merchants. Lydia married Dr. James Hutchinson, one of the most heroic of Philadelphia doctors, who gave his life tending the sick in the great plague of 1793; but they had no descendants. Ann, Clement's other sister, married General James Wilkinson, certainly one of the most prominent and peculiar personages of the Revolutionary period and after. His success is both sinister and incomprehensible. How did such a mucker ever get so far? He must have had vast reserves of charm and plausibility, though from his own recorded statements he was a ludicrous blowhard. A brief chronicle of the high spots of his career sounds most impressive: brevetted a brigadier general in the Revolution at the age of twenty for his services under Benedict Arnold and as aide-de-camp of Gates; brigadier general again under Wayne out West in '92, and after Wayne's death the ranking officer of the U.S. Army; occupier of Detroit when the English gave it up in 1796; sharer with Governor Claiborne of Louisiana of the honor of taking possession of the Louisiana Purchase in 1803, and himself a governor of the Territory of Upper Louisiana in 1805–06; and finally the man who revealed the Burr conspiracy and was chief witness against him. All this sounds great, but in between he shows the most suspicious record of treachery, intrigue and deceit. He left the Revolutionary army under a cloud for his part in the Conway Cabal against Washington. He became a leader in Kentucky politics by defaming and ruining George Rogers Clark, savior of the

West. He swore secret allegiance to the king of Spain and, while he was actually second in command of the U.S. Army fighting Indians in Ohio, received a Spanish "pension," or bribe, for his efforts to detach Kentucky from the Union. And, finally, as chief witness against Burr, his character was so bad and his testimony so unreliable that he helped Burr get acquitted. He ended in a glorious burst of disaster, when an expedition he led against Montreal in 1813, as major general, was routed. He was court-martialed, but acquitted and honorably discharged. Nobody at the time knew he had actually received doubloons from Spain, though everyone suspected it. He ended his days in Mexico. John Randolph, a man for the vivid phrase, called him a villain "from bark to the very core." His wife, the only connection this story has with him, stuck by her husband through thick and thin, East and West, until her death in 1807. It is an almost overmastering biographical temptation to skip off after this handsome, nefarious character and all the incredibly picturesque people he dealt with in the West — Benjamin Sebastian, honored judge of Kentucky, who was exposed as a Spanish agent; Joseph Street, the Honest Editor and violent partisan, who exposed him and was hounded from Kentucky as a result; Samuel Swartwout, associate of Burr who challenged Wilkinson to a duel, which so pleased Andrew Jackson that he made him collector of the Port of New York, whereupon Swartwout stole a million dollars from the city; and dozens of equally dashing and despicable persons. Then, of course, there was Burr himself, with whom Wilkinson had the most intimate and mysterious dealings.*

The other connection of the Biddles with all this was the friendship of Charles Biddle and Burr. When Burr shot Hamilton in their

---

* Wilkinson has his defenders. A great-grandson, James Wilkinson of the Louisiana bar, wrote an impassioned brief for the defense in 1935, redolent with the magnolia of Southern Patriotism. A far more telling blow in his favor was the objective book of Hay and Werner in 1941, *The Admirable Trumpeter,* which almost manages to make Wilkinson dull and respectable. Not quite. He was, after all, in the pay of the Spaniards while a senior officer of the U.S. Army on active duty. You can't get round that. He certainly would have been shot if he had been caught.

famous duel, it was to the house of Charles Biddle in Philadelphia that Burr fled for refuge. Biddle to his dying day would never believe Burr meant to be a traitor; and maybe he wasn't a traitor. Certainly anyone who made an enemy of Wilkinson must have had some good in him. Brothers-in-law grave Clement and pious Owen must have had second thoughts about the man their sister married, though they helped him in his first ventures in Kentucky, and Owen corresponded with Wilkinson about Indians. Wilkinson's marriage was considered a big step up for him, which shows how the Biddle family fortunes had advanced after the Revolution.

So the Biddles, though they had not yet reached the apogee of Cadwalader plumed beds, flowered coaches and regiments equipped with casks of Madeira, or total Shippen medical and legal security, were on their way there. In the next generation the sons and daughters of Clement and Charles achieved the early nineteenth-century equivalent of all this; in the Revolutionary generation, more famous than the Roosevelts, but far less so than the Adamses or Lees, the Biddles reached national prominence in Captain Nicholas, and respectability all along the line, with the exciting exception of the in-law Wilkinsons. Since someday, someone will have to edit a representative *selection* of the letters and diaries of John and Abigail Adams, so a new edition of the autobiography of Charles Biddle, properly annotated, is called for. Even as it stands in its somewhat disorganized, privately printed 1883 version, it exhibits an extraordinary panorama of eighteenth-century seafaring life and of pioneer success on land. Charles Biddle, that violent, hearty, healthy family founder is very much alive in it.

4

Du Ponts

THE DU PONTS, like the Adamses, and unlike the Biddles, defi-
nitely have a one-man family foundation. The sole and pre-
eminent originator of the American house is that fantastic figure,
that almost-great Frenchman who was born plain Pierre Samuel
Dupont and who ended up as Messire Pierre Samuel du Pont* de
Nemours, noble of France, onetime President of the Constituent
Assembly and of the Council of Ancients, Councillor of Baden,
Chevalier of the order of Vasa of Sweden, friend of Madame de
Pompadour and Madame de Staël, of Lavoisier and Louis XVI, correspondent of Voltaire and Franklin, acquaintance of every great
person in France before the Revolution.

He provides a marvelous biographical opportunity, with one
grave exception; his rise to fame and comparative fortune was spectacular, he knew everybody, he was in the thick of everything. But
what did he *do*? What did he really accomplish? His life is an historical doughnut, rich in surrounding incident, but with a sort of
vacuum in the middle. He was either in the government or in jail,
he published numberless books and pamphlets. None of his posts
were terribly important, none of the books have endured. What is
he famous for? In the end, he is important as a disciple, a publicizer
of the ideas of others; and as the founder of his family.

His life, character and achievements make a most curious parallel

---

* Actually Pierre himself spelled it "Du Pont." See page 124.

and contrast to those of John Adams. They were almost exact contemporaries. In many ways they were dealing with similar problems, and as conservative revolutionaries, approached the problems in a similar fashion, Adams through law, du Pont through economics. Though Adams in fact feared and detested du Pont as a Red and subversive, their policies and attitudes were really quite alike. And they were both defeated in the end as honest moderates crushed between the collision of two extremes. The extremes in the case of du Pont were far more extreme, the collision far more violent. Adams lost his political influence. Du Pont nearly lost his head.

If, as compared with the life of Adams, the earlier biography of du Pont has some of the quality of a romance, it is because he wrote it himself. The chief source for knowledge of both men's formative years is their respective autobiographies; but where that of Adams is full of tart common sense, that of du Pont is lurid with drama. They were born within a few years of each other, Adams in 1735, du Pont in 1739. One was the son of a farmer and cordwainer, the other of a watchmaker.

At this point their careers diverge. Adams of Braintree had the most conventional of New England educations. Du Pont of Paris had a very peculiar education indeed. His romantic mother, disappointed in marriage to dull, obstinate, bourgeois Samuel, took the usual revenge: she devoted herself to her son. He rewarded this devotion by proving himself an infant prodigy, much to his father's annoyance. Samuel just wanted Pierre to be a good watchmaker. Anne Alexandrine had other ideas, and so did Pierre himself. After early vicissitudes of health and nursing, which left Pierre stunted and rickety, with a broken nose and, later on, pockmarked, his mother found for him a brilliant tutor named Viard. The father allowed his son this unnecessary brush with learning only on condition that he stay away from poetry. Viard used the brilliant boy to attract more pupils for himself. He arranged a public exhibition. Pierre had to learn by heart the Institutes of Justinian and the laws of French grammar, and then display his talents before an audience of four hundred people by answering questions on French and Latin grammar, translating extracts from Latin authors, and carrying on a "dissertation on logic, rhetoric, the Apologue, the Eclogue, the epistolary style and Roman Law." Even his father wept for joy at this pyrotechnic display. His fellow students organized a torchlight parade for him, and Viard planned a second such happening.

Scheduled for August 12, 1752 (the year after Adams entered Harvard), this sequel was to take place before all the professors of the university. But the Rector, jealous of Viard, refused his permission. Samuel too decided this kind of education had gone far enough. Back to the watches. Young du Pont's taste for public appearances and applause was determined for life. His mother managed to mitigate the evils of apprenticeship by suggesting he study mathematics, useful even for watchmakers. This encouraged Pierre to become a military engineer; meanwhile his father kept him on the workbench. In the end, the inevitable break took place, but not before poor Anne, weakened by giving birth to two short-lived daughters in one year, herself succumbed at the age of thirty-six in 1756. Her last words were an appeal to her husband and son to make each other happy.

After a series of bitter fights which involved Pierre's associations with girls as well as his distaste for watches, Pierre left home. He pursued the illusion of a career as a military engineer. When he found he couldn't make a go of this, he decided, after an attempt at suicide, to pay his father back. He settled down to his apprenticeship again, and eventually, in 1763, produced a magnificent timepiece. On New Year's Day he presented it to his father, inscribed "Du Pont filius composit, fecit, dedicavit patri suo." He never made another watch.

Pierre meanwhile determined to find some other and nobler career. He studied medicine, but worked at it so hard his health broke down. Besides, he didn't really feel he was suited to the profession. He had a fling at amateur theatricals, and at one time, despite broken nose, pockmarks and rickets, posed for a drawing class of which his sister Anne Alexandrine was a member. Another girl in the class was a dazzling demimondaine named Jeanne Beçu. She turned out later to be Madame du Barry, and unlike du Pont, did have her head cut off. Du Pont remarked that he was, alas, "not among the numerous predecessors of King Louis XV." He wrote tragedies, went to dances, planned to go to Corsica with a friend to help the revolution there, and got himself engaged. Above all, he began to think about agriculture and economics.

Both his engagement and his interest in economics were the result of trips to the country. His friends the Dorés lived in Nemours, forty miles southeast of Paris. There he met a cousin of the Dorés, Nicole-Charlotte-Marie-Louise Le Dée de Raucourt. Who could ask for a more imposing name? She was, however, merely the daughter of a minor government official. She and Pierre were friends, but not yet in love. Suddenly Mme. Doré announced that she had arranged a marriage between Marie Le Dée and the local tax receiver, a widower of fifty-five. After a good deal of soul-searching, du Pont offered himself as a substitute. Marie was ecstatic. However, they would have to wait at least two years until he could establish himself; at the moment he had no prospects at all — a craft which he despised, no profession.

His trips to the country provided him not only with a wife, but with this necessary profession. He became interested in agriculture from a philosophic, economic, scientific point of view. He had always been interested in everything from a philosophic, economic, scientific point of view except, oddly enough, watchmaking, which might have led him into astronomy as it did Owen Biddle (optical instruments).

Everybody of course at that time in France, as in America, was writing and reading pamphlets. One of the more popular was called *La Richesse de l'Etat* by Roussel de La Tour. It was full of radical suggestions for tax reform. Du Pont believed they were erroneous and in 1763 he sold to a publisher for two louis (which he never collected) a pamphlet of his own which was a rebuttal to the

Richesse de l'Etat. His "research" on agricultural affairs had so far consisted of conversations with cart drivers as he went to and from Nemours and various chats with his father's cook. Another similar pamphlet followed. These works brought him to the attention of Madame de Pompadour's doctor, who as physician to the king's mistress of course had great national prestige; and so the fortunes of Pierre Samuel Dupont, late watchmaker, were made. That's how things were done in the *ancien régime*.

Quesnay, Pompadour's doctor, was no ordinary doctor. He was an economist, usually considered, because of his influence on Adam Smith, as the real founder of the dismal science of scientific economics. He was the prophet of a special school whose theories dominated French economic thinking in the eighteenth century. He was the originator of the so-called Physiocrats, and Du Pont was one of his chief disciples, and indeed is credited with giving the theory its name. Just at the time that John Adams was emerging as a young Bostonian who wrote on law (*Canon and Feudal Law*, 1765) and was getting married to Abigail, Pierre, then Dupont, was emerging as a writer on economics and was getting married to Marie Le Dée. In both cases they were fortunate in their wives, and in both cases their thought was tinged with ideas which led to revolutions.

The ideas of the Physiocrats seem today more reactionary than radical, but in eighteenth-century France they were evidently dynamite. They came closer to Henry George's single-tax theories than anything else. Basic to the theories was a rather romantic, Rousseau-like worship of Mother Earth. The only true basis of human life and culture was the soil and farming, the only true wealth, Natural Surplus. Everything else was a "sterile" manipulation of these fruits of the earth, either in the form of manufactures or trade. This fact of life therefore set up an essential "order of nature," which was that all wealth, and hence all rights and all duties of the commonwealth, centered in land and in the landed proprietor. Every difficulty of modern France was due to a distortion of this natural order of things, a distortion resulting from mercantilism, and producing sterile commercial, feudal, and clerical arrangements, elaborate and damaging restrictions, monopolies, privileges and taxes.

Abolish them all! Tax only the surplus of agricultural produce and nothing else. Turn all government over to a hierarchy of landed proprietors, and landed proprietors only, headed by a hereditary monarch considered as a sort of "landed proprietor" of the whole nation — and *voilà!* all your problems are solved. Solved as permanently as simply, too, since this state of affairs was the real essence of nature's own laws. Everlasting peace and plenty would be the result. Various extensions of this theory turned the Physiocrats in the direction of free trade and industrial laissez-faire, since they thought of all restraints of trade as in the interests of "sterile" commerce. Exactly how watchmakers fitted into this beautiful agricultural universe is not clear. Somewhere down at the bottom. Quesnay, the doctor, was the founder of the sect. His chief allies were Victor, Marquis de Mirabeau, father of the Revolutionary Mirabeau, and Anne Robert Jacques Turgot, a provincial administrator who tried to put these doctrines into practice. (Anne was of course a man, despite the name. Most male French aristocrats of the time had at least one female name. Lafayette's, for instance, was Marie.) Du Pont was intimate with all three — Quesnay, Mirabeau and especially Turgot — and his career followed the ups and downs of theirs.

It was an uncertain thing being a pamphleteer and politician in France. Mirabeau had been the first to suffer. In 1760 he wrote a book, again about taxes, called the *Théorie de l'Impôt.* For this he was imprisoned and then exiled to his country estates, where he kept right on writing and publishing, suing his wife and getting his son put in jail. Quesnay lasted a few years longer. His position in the world depended entirely on the power of Madame de Pompadour. When she died, he was out. As a disciple of the favorite of La Pompadour, du Pont had also been generously received at court. Madame called him "our young agriculturist." In gratitude, he dedicated to her the first of his books that really became famous. It bore

the thrilling title *De l'Exportation et de l'importation des grains*.
Pompadour died in 1764 before the book came out. Quesnay's enemies were now in power, and any friend of Madame was no friend
of theirs. Du Pont was urged to change his dedication, but he man-
fully refused. "Woe to the man who would fear to fling a few
flowers on the tomb of those to whom he offered his incense," he
added to his dedication. The book was a best-seller. Not only did it
make his reputation as an economist, but it also brought him to the
attention of Turgot, who took Quesnay's place in the life of Pierre
du Pont as hero and patron. Can one imagine what the Adamses,
newlyweds in 1764, would have thought of making one's reputation
with a book dedicated to the king's mistress? A best-selling, provoca-
tive book on the import and export of grain. What a fantastic world.

Pierre, too, was soon to be married, but only after an excruciating
engagement marked by the worldly fickleness of his beloved's
family. In the beginning they were dead set against du Pont. When
they found he was in favor with Pompadour, they suddenly became
more than kind. But when she died, her "young agriculturist" was
no longer welcome in Nemours. Marie's parents forbad Anne to see
him. The usual *opéra bouffe* of young lovers began. Kindly old gov-
ernesses and great-aunts carried secret messages, drunken gardeners
were bribed. It was like a scene of Fragonard. A light was placed in
a certain window and dried peas thrown against the windowpane.
Meanwhile du Pont did not neglect society, and in fact, gaiety — a
round of dinners and parties in the houses of economics-minded
notables — began to interfere with his search for a career. Finally,
late nights and hangovers became so distracting that he impulsively
seized a pair of scissors and cut off half his hair. This very effectively kept him out of the salons and in his room writing.

Even in his writing he failed to keep to the subject, that is, economics. He read a successful play of the season of 1764–65 called
the *Siege of Calais* and proceeded to send the happy author a vast
letter containing some 580 "corrections" of the author's barbarous
verse. He was really surprised when the playwright failed to reply.

This did not of course stop du Pont from writing bad verse-dramas himself. A few years later he wrote a terrible one about Joseph II, the current Emperor of Austria. His patron Turgot suggested he put it aside and stick to taxes.

At last he got a job; two in fact. One was to conduct an extensive survey of farm properties in Soissons. The other was the editorship of a *Journal of Agriculture*. He was now ready to be married. The father put up one last objection. He would not have a Protestant son-in-law. Pierre said, truthfully enough, that he was not a Protestant. Indeed by this time he was nothing much except a benevolent deist. The couple were married at Saint-Sulpice in Paris on January 28, 1766. He lost his editorial job almost immediately, but it had served its purpose. His marriage was the most fortunate event in du Pont's life. Not only was his wife amiable, charming and devoted to him, but she had a good business head. Like many an economist, this was something that du Pont conspicuously lacked.

From then on, until the great events of the Revolution threw him into the whirlpool of elective politics, du Pont made himself useful and even moderately famous and modestly rich by his writings, his editorships and above all his positions in the commercial-financial bureaus of the government. The high point of this bureaucratic career came in 1774. In the same year that John Adams left the smaller scene of Boston for the larger one of the Continental Congress, Louis XV, once so "well beloved," now so well detested, died. Rule by mistress was a thing of the past. A new young king, earnest, simple, sober, kindly, fat, took over, and the golden age was to dawn. One of the first acts of the new king and of his golden age was to elevate du Pont's master Turgot, preeminent economic theorist of the kingdom, first to minister of the navy and then to controller general of finance. What an opportunity for Physiocrats, what a chance to create heaven on earth!

Unfortunately just at this juncture du Pont was in Poland. His pamphlets were even more famous abroad than at home. It was the

*Augustus St. Gaudens' enigmatic statue marks the grave of Henry Adams
and his suicide wife Marian.*

This picture of the 1783 Peace Commissioners by Benjamin West (John Adams seated to the left) remained unfinished due to the chagrin of the British signers.

Gilbert Stuart's head of Abigail also remained unfinished. He did a later, completed and more famous version.

Thomas Biddle, brother of Nicholas, by Thomas Sully, is the very model of the Buck. Where else could he end but on the Field of Honor?

Mary Hallock Greenewalt is one of Thomas Eakins' most seriously beautiful subjects. Crawford Hallock Greenewalt, the ornithologist, was also president of the Company.

Mrs. Theodore Roosevelt Jr. (the "other Eleanor") by John Koch, at Old
Orchard surrounded by daughter-in-law and granddaughters.

Princess Alice in 1966, by Peter Hurd (kin of the Wyeths).

Richard I; portrait attributed to Sir Peter Lely.

A PRIDE OF LEES

Thomas; portrait from the British school, eighteenth century, artist unknown.

Richard Henry; miniature by
Charles Willson Peale.

Harry; miniature by Peale.

Admiral Samuel Phillips Lee,
by Thomas Sully.

*Pierre Samuel; engraved by
Courbe from a portrait
by Gras.*

A PERSISTENCE OF DU PONTS

*Victor Marie; copy of an
oil by Bass Otis.*

Eleuthère Irénée

Charles Irénée, who
married so well, twice; by
Thomas Sully. Note
eyebrows.

Edmond, present chairman
of the board of Francis I.
du Pont and Co. Note
eyebrows.

John Quincy Adams, by John Singleton Copley; or, from nice young diplomat to . . .

Henry Adams as Harvard undergraduate.

... "bruiser." John Quincy Adams photographed in 1844 by Matthew Brady.

The results of an Education: Henry Adams later on, by Potter.

Nicholas Biddle young, lover of Greece and Byron. Portrait by Benjamin Trott.

Nicholas Biddle later on, by Thomas Sully. Note the hair on America's foremost banker.

Robert E. Lee, by Matthew Brady. The Great God of War.

The Marble Model; young Robert, by William E. West.

Theodore as dude, about 1880. Hair parted in the middle?

Theodore as mountain man, 1884.

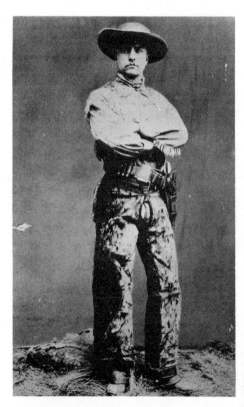

Theodore as mountain — the Mount Rushmore memorial by Gutzon Borglum. TR third from left.

Franklin and Eleanor engaged, snapped on the porch at Campobello.

Eleanor triumphant over time, 1957.

Franklin, with Winston, triumphant over the Axis, but not necessarily over Joe and time.

An Adams also triumphant over time: Abigail Adams Homans in 1969.

Where it all began: John Adams was born on the right, John Quincy on the left. Both houses preserved now in Quincy, Massachusetts.

Where most of it ended: the Old House in Quincy, where John Adams died and the family lived till 1927.

Stratford, where Robert E. Lee was born.

Arlington, where Robert E. Lee was married.

The first du Pont mansion on the Brandywine, the so-called Eleutherian Mills.

Andalusia, where the descendents of Nicholas Biddle still live.

Theodore Roosevelt's Sagamore Hill.

Franklin Roosevelt's Hyde Park.

period of enlightened despots. One of the smaller of these, the German Margrave of Baden, had met du Pont in Paris, been impressed by him, and appointed him an "Aulic Councillor" and arranged for him to visit his capital, Karlsruhe. More magnificent was an offer, early in 1774, to come to Poland and tutor the four-year-old son of Prince Adam Czartoryski. The terms were extravagantly generous, a salary of ten thousand francs a year with living quarters, carriage, traveling expenses, plus a bonus of one hundred thousand francs. He could hardly refuse. Thirty thousand francs of this bonus were paid him in advance and with it he bought a landed estate called Bois-des-Fossés at Chevannes near Nemours, in the *pays* of his wife (as Adams lived in Quincy and the Roosevelts went up the Hudson to Hoffman territory). After years of writing about the land, he finally owned some.

He was not very happy about going way out there to barbarous Poland however, and was even less happy when he finally arrived. His grandiose schemes for reorganizing Polish education got nowhere, he was bored with tutoring; and besides, lavish Prince Czartoryski had imported about ten other tutors for his two children.

When Turgot came to power he insisted on having his beloved du Pont at his side. Pierre was officially recalled from Poland, a settlement was made which permitted him to retain Bois-des-Fossés, and du Pont was appointed inspector general of commerce. Glorious days! A new monarch as earnest and virtuous as his grandfather had been frivolous and lecherous, and carte blanche to rejuvenate the finances of a country bled white by the luxuriousness of the court, the antiquated privileges and benefices of nobility and clergy, the maladministration and corruption of tax collectors. Turgot started to sweep clean. Du Pont threw himself into his job with violent enthusiasm, collecting statistics, writing out programs and proposals.

There is a chance that if perhaps Turgot had been allowed to stay in office, and if his New Deal had worked, France might have been saved from ruin, the Revolution might have been averted, Louis might not have been decapitated. Turgot, for all his theories, was a practical administrator with long experience. Everyone hated him but Louis. All those who thrived on the abuses which were ruining France combined against him. The king was weak; and just at this juncture the harvests were bad. There was a shortage of bread. People blamed it on Turgot's reforms. Groups of hoodlums were hired to go about from town to town stirring up riots against the government. Meanwhile at Versailles Marie-Antoinette, who didn't like having her spending money cut down, and Prime Minister Maurepas, a wily septuagenarian, saw to it that certain letters fell into the hands of the king. They purported to be from Turgot to a friend in Vienna full of uncomplimentary remarks about the king and queen. Maurepas, as prime minister, vouched for their authenticity. They were complete forgeries. Louis hesitated and hemmed and hawed, and then, inevitably, did the wrong thing. In 1776 he dismissed Turgot. Du Pont lost office along with his chief.

That was the end of Turgot's public career. He died in 1781, without ever regaining favor. Du Pont was grief-stricken, and in 1782 reproduced a *Mémoires sur la vie . . . de Turgot*. It was the end of French solvency too. Under the direction first of the Swiss financial magician Necker and then under the French speculator Calonne, desperate remedies were tried: money was borrowed, false accounts published and flamboyant claims made, but nothing helped. France sank deeper and deeper into financial disorder.

It was not the end of du Pont however. Though he was out of favor and could hardly hope for great things, he was just too useful and knowledgeable to fire. Under both Necker and Calonne he held posts in the department of commerce; but he was no longer a member of the inner circle, or a right-hand man. His estate at Bois-des-Fossés, under the sensible administration of his wife, helped support the family. He solaced himself for his political disappointment by translating Ariosto's *Orlando Furioso* into French verse (his father's insistence that he stay away from poetry had of course done no good), and he entered into correspondence with King Gustavus of Sweden. He felt in general, though, that his opportunities to save his country with honor and glory were frustrated.

His two sons, Victor Marie, born in 1767, and Eleuthère Irénée, born in 1771, grew and prospered. Mirabeau was the godfather of the oldest, and the boy was named for him (note the Marie). Turgot was the godfather of the youngest, and it was he who suggested the Greek-inspired names of Eleuthère and Irénée, "in honor of Liberty and Peace," appropriate to either a girl or a boy, names which have persisted down to the present not only as peculiarly family names, but embedded, a whiff of the Enlightenment, in the title of the Company itself.

In America the Revolution progressed, and was aided by France. The Comte de Vergennes, that foreign minister with whom Adams had so much trouble during his peace-making days, was a friend and supporter of du Pont. Franklin was another.* Adams was not. Adams held Physiocracy in abomination, and had a particular animus against the ideas of Turgot, though he rather admired him as a person. His weighty book on the *Defense of the Constitutions* was in fact an answer to certain criticisms made by Turgot on the American system of checks and balances as embodied in various state constitutions, such as that of Massachusetts. Adams and du Pont must have met during Adams' various stays in Paris. As a friend of Franklin and Vergennes, du Pont was hardly likely to be very sympathetic to Adams.

Life was not a complete disappointment for du Pont. In 1783, for instance, two signal honors came to him. His friend the margrave of Baden appointed him ambassador to France (that is, *chargé d'affaires*). This unusual arrangement by which a foreign nation was represented in France by an official of the French government

---

* Franklin wrote to du Pont in 1770: "Would to God I could take with me [to America] Messrs. du Pont, Dubourg and some other French friends, with their good ladies. I might then, by mixing them with my friends in Philadelphia, form a little happy society that would prevent my ever wishing again to visit Europe."

was looked upon askance even in France, where unusual arrangements were the rule. But it was permitted, and though it didn't do du Pont much good, it was an honor.

Much more exciting was the patent of nobility granted him in December of 1783, through the influence of Vergennes. He got no title, and he had to swear he was a Catholic (which he did, though he wasn't) but it gave him many useful privileges: he could call himself "Messire," somewhat equivalent to the English "Sir," and it permitted him to adopt a coat of arms. He chose one with a column on it, the motto "Rectitudine Sto" (stand upright) and an embellishment of ostrich plumes with a lion and eagle as supporters.* It's all somehow rather like John Cadwalader's bed. Another such honor had already come to him in 1775, when he was made a Knight of the Royal Order of Vasa of Sweden. It was after his ennoblement that he began to write his name Du Pont (now usually written with a little *d*, du Pont),† rather than plain Dupont. He never missed an opportunity to call himself "Chevalier of the Order of Vasa." It is engraved on his tombstone in Delaware.

The history of France during this period makes a curious, and saddening, contrast to that of America. Almost exactly the same set of events, over almost exactly the same length of time, led to diametrically different results. The French drama was played out just about ten years later than the American one. The American Revolution began with England, flushed with victory over France in 1763 and inspired by the virtues of a new young king, embarking on a program of colonial reform that resulted in the loss of the colonies. The French Revolution began in 1774 with a new young king attempting a program of internal reform that resulted in the loss of

---

* The crest the family now uses is a plain column, with a helmet above and the motto below. No lions or eagles.

† It is nowadays correct to use "du Pont" for both family and company. Even though Pierre himself used "Du Pont," I have stuck to "du Pont" after the "Dupont" was dropped. See page 113.

the king's head. France's parallel victory over England occurred of course in 1783. With the loss of America, the British Empire had presumably been destroyed, as the French Empire had been destroyed in 1763 by the loss of Canada. Both America and France, almost simultaneously just before 1790, began parallel constitutional struggles. In America a sound republican government was established which has lasted, with some vicissitudes, to the present. In France everything broke down in a welter of bloodshed and disorder. Fifteen years after the American Presidency was established, justifying the American Revolution, Napoleon made himself dictator, then emperor, thus making a mockery of the French Revolution.

The two parallel careers of these revolutions are like the passage of two very different crafts through white water. The American log raft, loose-jointed and primitive, but steered by woodsmen who knew what they were doing, somehow survived, was salvaged and reconverted into the Ship of State. The gorgeous barque of the French monarchy, all gilded figureheads and flapping pennants topside and rotten timbers below waterline, gradually, inexorably, plunged down the current. A succession of captains rushed about wildly, spouting contradictory orders, the passengers continued to make love and gamble under their awnings, and, as the crew mutinied, the whole thing smashed onto the rocks, killing most of the passengers and half the crew.*

Du Pont could not be called a captain, but he certainly stood on the quarterdeck giving advice. To continue the simile a bit too far, he moved from the staff to the line. That is, instead of being a government functionary and bureaucrat, he became an elected official.

In the process of changing from an almost-absolute monarchy†

---

* The simile of the ship and the raft occurred to Fisher Ames. His wry complaint was that on the raft one's feet were always wet.

† There were, to be sure, some annoying local bodies called Parlements, who

governed by ministers appointed directly by the king himself, into a would-be-absolute democracy, a series of Assemblies, each one more powerful and more radical than the last, decided the Destinies of France (the Revolutionary style is catching). First came the Assembly of Notables (1787–89), a sort of rump parliament appointed by the king, composed mostly of nobility, and purely advisory. It was supposed to help the desperate finance minister Calonne out of his hopeless embarrassments. Instead, it devoted itself to attacking the king in the name of the nobility. Du Pont had lots to do in drafting the program of reform the Notables were supposed to approve and in organizing the show. It was a fiasco. Calonne was disgraced and dismissed, and that Assembly was dissolved.

In its place was erected a far more formidable affair, the Constituent Assembly (1789–1791). This began as a real parliament, a House of Lords, House of Bishops and House of Commons combined in one body composed of three so-called "Estates." The Commons or "Third Estate" was elective, and du Pont was named to this as from Nemours, though he was of course by now a nobleman. Since there were other Duponts in the Assembly, notably a well-known Dupont of Bigorre, Pierre tacked on the "de Nemours," usually in parentheses. Of course it did make his name look fancier; du Pont de Nemours is certainly more inspiring than even plain du Pont. Still, he had a legitimate reason.

The Assembly turned out to be earthshaking. The Commons, or "Third Estate," took over. It created a constitution, it made the king in effect a constitutional monarch, and in general it combined the functions of the American Continental Congress that declared independence with the American Constitutional Convention. Du Pont was as busy here as Adams was in Congress. He was a member of committees too — Agriculture and Commerce, National Treasury, Examination of Accounts, Public Assistance, Public Taxes, Imposts, Finance, Tithes and what have you. It was as glorious as

could effectively obstruct the king's ministers when they chose; but they were very reactionary, even in the France of that period.

the days under Turgot in 1774. Du Pont incurred the fury of all by being a moderate. The Royalists and the Jacobins hated him equally.

Endless pains were taken, endless ingenuity was devoted to creating a framework which would probably never have functioned in the best of circumstances; and France was in the worst of circumstances. For example, the king was made the executive and given a veto. Naturally Louis used the veto to help his friends and thus completely discredited the idea of a royal veto, and indeed separate executive power in general.

Already mobs were at work, forcing the king and the Assembly to move to Paris and then harassing them there. Already the nobility and conservatives were emigrating. When the king himself tried to escape, and failed, the influence of the monarchy was totally destroyed. Still, a constitution had been created, and in 1791 a third body, the Legislative Assembly, met to take over the government. A brilliant provision was that no one who had served in the old Constituent Assembly could serve in the new Legislative Assembly. This meant of course that all those with experience and knowledge, all those who had created the Constitution, were prevented from putting it into action. The result was again — total disaster.

Du Pont, who had been president of the old Assembly for a short period in 1790, now found himself completely unemployed. His wife Marie had died back in 1784, and he had had to bring up his sons by himself, helped by a faithful tutor-disciple called Philip Harmand. Together with Harmand, and helped by young Irénée, who had inherited all his mother's good sense and then had married an equally sensible Sophie Dalmas, du Pont started a printing business. It was actually quite a success, though never very remunerative. Du Pont confessed himself "happy to finish as Franklin began," a printer. It was no hand-art press. It employed as many as forty-four printers and seventeen others and did enough government business to survive all the tumults of the Terror until the plant was finally wrecked in 1797. True, Irénée did most of the actual work, but his father edited and wrote for it, and it was his name that gave it tone and brought it business. But du Pont's personal misadventures were just beginning.

Du Pont, for all his radical ideas and fervent love of liberty, was a firm monarchist and loyal to Louis. This loyalty almost cost him his life. The Assembly of Notables mounted a revolution of the nobility against the king and his ministers. The Constituent Assembly mounted a revolution of the bourgeois of the Third Estate against the nobility. The Legislative Assembly fell victim to the mob and its leaders. Public safety and order disappeared. As a result, many of the citizens of Paris organized themselves into armed vigilante groups. Du Pont was one of these. He formed a band of some fifteen relatives and friends, to whom others attached themselves, and hoped to attack and destroy the Jacobin Club. The Jacobins were too well protected.

On August 10 the du Pont Irregulars had their day (they actually called themselves the "Grenadiers and Chasseurs of the Army of Paris"). Louis was increasingly unpopular, especially since he had an Austrian wife and France was at war with Austria. He was attacked in the Tuileries by another mob. Du Pont and his band went to his defense. The king walked out on his defenders and took refuge in the chamber where the Assembly was sitting. According to family legend he passed du Pont on the way. "Ah! Monsieur du Pont, one finds you always where one has need of you," he is supposed to have said. The king was saved, this time, but most of his defenders were massacred. As only eight of the du Pont band were left, including du Pont himself and Irénée, it seemed advisable to leave. They marched off pretending to be a routine Revolutionary patrol, and so escaped.

The Jacobins were masters of Paris and the nation, and du Pont was, especially after this rash display of loyalty, an Enemy of the People. He had to hide. Faithful tutor Harmand knew Lalande, chief of the Paris Observatory. Here du Pont secreted himself, Harmand bringing him whatever food he could. On September 2 he had a chance to escape from the city. The suspected Royalists in the prisons were being slaughtered, and in the joyful excitement the gates of the city were left open for a few hours. Du Pont managed to get out and walk ten miles to the village of Cormeilles, where Harmand owned a cottage. He stayed there till November, pretending to be an elderly physician, his face half-hidden by an eyeshade, writing prescriptions. His early training in medicine came in handy.

Finally he returned to Bois-des-Fossés and was able to live there for more than a year unmolested. His daughter-in-law Sophie took care of him, Irénée continued to run the press. Pierre, with characteristic aplomb and energy, devoted himself to a work called, quite simply, *Philosophy of the Universe*. Being proscribed by the government could not be expected to interfere with the play of the mind. The *Philosophy* is an elaborate presentation of deism, and contains the famous simile of God as the Great Watchmaker always used as representative of the Enlightenment's conception of the Deity. "If I am a watchmaker, I, with my little spirit," says du Pont, "the great clock of the Universe has also a clockmaker."

Once again he was to have difficulty with a dedication. His *Philosophy*, which actually got published, was dedicated to his dear friend Lavoisier, foremost chemist of Europe, and the man who had educated Irénée in powder making. In May 1794, Lavoisier, because he had once been a tax collector, was executed. "The Republic has no need of scientists," said the gentleman in charge. Du Pont's turn came in July.

Robespierre was in the final throes of his bloodbath. Every last one of the Enemies of the People must be eliminated. Du Pont's name came up. On July 22 he was hustled off to the prison of La Force in Paris, Sophie following him. There in jail he spent his time cheerfully giving lectures on economics and devising plans of self-defense in case the jails should be mobbed as they had been in '92. Then on July 27 Robespierre himself fell, and du Pont was saved.

Soon the French government was reorganized again, with still another constitution, this time along more reactionary lines; there were even property qualifications for voters as in the U.S.A. Under the Directory, as it was called, a vaguely American system of two houses and an executive branch was created. There was a Council of Five Hundred, corresponding roughly to the House of Representatives, a Council of Elders (or Ancients), 250 men over forty years old and either married or widowed, and five directors chosen by the upper house from a list prepared by the lower house. Du Pont was a member of the Council of Elders. Once again speeches, reports, statistics, committees. Once again, and again briefly, he was president of this council as he had been of the Constituent Assembly. Once again everything went wrong, du Pont antagonized everyone with his forceful moderation. Once again there was a coup d'état. President of the council in July 1797, by that very September du Pont was in jail again, in the same prison, La Force. This time the prisoners were not to be guillotined but sent to French Guiana, the future Devil's Island. Irénée was jailed with him. Due perhaps to the influence of his powerful friend Madame de Staël, he and Irénée were promptly released, but not before the du Pont printing establishment had been wrecked.

They were put out of business. This, decided du Pont, was enough. The golden age was obviously *not* going to dawn in France. He decided to emigrate to America. It took him two full years to prepare himself, his new wife, formerly the widow Poivre, and his two sons and their families for this momentous step. Finally on October 2, 1799, the *American Eagle*, an old American ship seized by the French and left to rot in the harbor of New Rochelle, set sail.

This was not hasty flight but an elaborate resettlement. There were, all told, eighteen people in the du Pont party: du Pont himself, his son Victor with wife Josephine and two children, his son Irénée with wife Sophie and three children, the daughter of Madame Poivre, a Madame Bureaux de Pusy with her newborn infant, and Charles Dalmas, brother of Irénée's wife Sophie. There were also three nurses, a manservant and a stableboy ("a jockey of thirteen or fourteen years old"). The enormous baggage included several pianos. Pierre's new wife and her son-in-law de Pusy had already gone ahead to prepare the way.

Thus ended the story of the du Pont family in France. Pierre Samuel returned there and held later positions in the government, but his effective career as statesman and publicist was over. The sons, Victor and Irénée, settled in America. They and their children and their grandchildren became Americans. Active as both Victor and Irénée were in the latter half of the eighteenth century, their story really belongs to the nineteenth, and is tied up with the founding of that great preserver of the du Pont fame and fortunes, the E. I. du Pont de Nemours Company.

5

Lees

Richard

THERE IS no phenomenon in American history quite like the Revolutionary Lees. The Livingstons, Morrises, Biddles and others were numerous. John and Samuel Adams, even John Hancock, are more famous than any single Lee; but for a combination of numbers and distinction, there is nothing quite like the Revolutionary Lees.

The Lees had already developed to a formidable extent that characteristic proper to any well-developed First Family tree — branches. All these families except, notably, the Adamses, quickly developed at least two: the Oyster Bay versus the Hyde Park Roosevelts, the Solid versus the Romantic Biddles, the Irénée versus the Victor du Ponts. By the time of the Revolution the Lees had sprouted half a dozen flourishingly separate branches, but only two, those of Stratford and Leesylvania, figure prominently in history.

No less than four sons of Thomas of Stratford and three sons of Henry of Leesylvania achieved some degree of national distinction. Besides this there was Thomas Sim Lee of Maryland, famous locally. Various other Lees of these and other branches had more modestly patriotic roles in state affairs. Actually, however, the real history of the Lees in the Revolution can be centered about three men, Richard Henry and Arthur of Stratford, and Harry of Leesylvania. Each one of these men had, as a sort of satellite, a lesser accompanying brother. Richard's shadow was amiable Francis Lightfoot of Menokin; Arthur's was his elder and outspoken brother William; and Harry's was sound, quiet, loyal, legal Charles. Harry's other well-known brother, Richard Bland, is, like Thomas Sim Lee, a sort of leftover.

The two oldest brothers of Stratford, Philip Ludwell and Thomas, played no role in the Revolution. Philip the heir, his mother's favorite, inherited Stratford and the Lee position on the Council. He leaves an ambiguous trace. Educated, delighting in music and the charm of his two daughters, the "divine Matilda" and the younger Flora, hospitable and impressive, he was a model of the Virginia grandee. There are also unfortunate evidences of his meanness and his arrogance. Unlike his grandfather Richard II, who was just and kind to his family in matters of inheritance, Philip refused to pay over to his youngest brothers their father's meager bequests. William was still dunning Philip for his money twelve years after it was due. He is also recorded as being rude to inferiors. He refused to participate in any of the various Lee pre-Revolutionary anti-British activities, and if he hadn't died, he would perhaps have found himself a Tory exile. No love was lost between Philip and his younger brothers.

Thomas was, on the contrary, the most popular of them all; said in fact to be the best-loved man in the state. He settled in Stafford County at Bellview and was content to stay there, active enough in state affairs, a firm patriot, but refusing to play the larger national role that might have been given him.

Other Lees, not of Stratford — Squire Richard of Lee Hall, a John Lee Jr., George Lee of Mount Pleasant — figure in letters and petitions, or as holders of offices; but of these obscure yet active Virginia Lees, Thomas is the least obscure. Of the Lees of Ditchley or Cobb's Hall one hears nothing.

Over in Maryland, Thomas Sim Lee of the Blenheim line had a career and descendants. He was the second governor of the new state of Maryland, succeeding the more famous Thomas Johnson (uncle of John Quincy Adams's wife Louisa Johnson), and a generally substantial character. But the true glory of the Lees must begin with Richard Henry, third son of great Thomas of Stratford.

Richard Henry, born in 1732 and so the first son definitely to see the light in Stratford itself, was as positive towards a career in public affairs as his older brothers were negative. His whole education seems to have been merely a preparation for what he himself, as a classicist, undoubtedly thought of as the "forum." He went to England for schooling, at a place called Wakefield (the vicar of which was supposed in fact to be a model for Goldsmith's). He was back in Virginia by 1752, following a European tour. Then after devoting several years to self-instruction in the classics, history and law in the library of Stratford, where he lived with his brother Philip, he entered upon his inevitable career. In 1757 he married neighbor Anne Aylett of Hominy Hall, and in 1758 he became a member of the House of Burgesses.

From this time until his retirement a couple of years before his death in 1794 he was a politician. Except for a small flurry as a militia officer (he was involved in routing a British force that came ashore at Stratford Landing), he devoted his whole life to the "forum." He was of course a planter, building a house of his own on the Potomac called Chantilly; but unlike John Adams, he had no learned profession, much less a trade like Pierre du Pont and his watchmaking. He was an orator, he was a statesman, he was a patriot. He was a Founding Father; and yet, somehow, rather like his men-of-action forbears Richard I and Thomas, he is, well . . . faceless. Not literally. There are portraits, and quite vivid contemporary descriptions of his face and mannerisms. We know how he looked: tall, thin, hawk-profiled, elegant in dress and so graceful in gesture that his enemies accused him of practicing before a mirror. His voice was forceful and melodious, the Cicero of Virginia.

But as a real man, a flesh and blood figure, he is, so unlike Adams or Franklin, unknowable. The lesser Lees, Arthur and Harry, are human enough. Richard, more truly important than either of these, keeps in a shadow. We know what he did. It is hard to sense what he was. A certain Lee austerity and inscrutability, inherited perhaps from his father, passed on perhaps in the next generation to Robert E. Lee, cloud him.

What he did was simple and important enough. Hand-in-hand with his great friend Patrick Henry in Virginia, and that other similar team in Massachusetts of Adamses, he is the author of American independence. He bears somewhat the same relationship to Patrick Henry that John Adams does to Samuel. Patrick Henry was the firebrand, the impetuous forerunner. Richard Lee was the calm but forceful consolidator, the establisher. Whereas Henry roused, Lee confirmed, just as Samuel Adams used newspapers and mobs to stir up opposition, while John found legal precedents.

Like the Adamses, the Lee-Henry team moved, one step at a time, through the series of pre-Revolutionary events that came closer and closer to rebellion. Each British act brought its increasing response. By the time the two teams from Virginia and Massachusetts converged in 1774 in Philadelphia, they were both really, though still secretly, revolutionists. Lee's supreme moment, the true climax of his life, came on June 7, 1776, when under instructions from his state, he moved: "That these united colonies are, and of right ought to be, free and independent states; that they are absolved from all allegiance to the British crown, and that all political connection between them and the state of Great Britain is, and ought to be, totally dissolved." John Adams seconded him. The Lee motion, passed on July 2 (not 4), created the United States of America. Lee was the man responsible for that motion. Glory enough for anyone. The actual Declaration, of which he was a Signer, was intended merely as an explanation of Lee's motion. It incorporated Lee's sentiments, but he had no hand in writing it. Why he was denied the privilege, and why Jefferson became author of it, goes back into the past history of Richard's Virginia career. The fact that he did move the resolution should make him immortal. The fact that he did not write the Declaration cheats him of real fame. Everybody knows who Jefferson was. Few know Richard Henry Lee.

All his career up to this moment, and after it, is a preparation and an implementation. There is something Roman in the directness and simplicity of his life; grand, but not really very intriguing or appealing or curious.

His first step towards immortality had been a significant one. In 1759 he proposed, on the floor of the Virginia House of Burgesses, that the state tax out of existence the importation of slaves. Though this motion was defeated, it is notable that he was received with applause; not lynched, as he might have been a century later. The fact was, though Virginia's wealth was based firmly on slavery, many planters of the Enlightenment felt badly about it. Most of the great Virginians of the Revolution — Washington, Jefferson, Madison, George Mason, Patrick Henry and the Lees — expressed their hatred of the system. The introduction of slavery and the firm British support of the slave trade were parts of the grievance that Americans had against England. Still, to make such a speech in a house composed almost exclusively of great slave owners was a bit on the brash side. Some must have frowned.

All frowned at Richard's next and most notorious motion. This occurred five years later in 1764 (the same year in which John

Adams married Abigail). Though trouble with Britain was brewing abroad, trouble was brewing at home in Virginia too.

Theoretically, Virginia should have been the ideal of the Aristocratic Commonwealth. Here was a dominion governed entirely by gentlemen, educated gentlemen, free of the corruptions of King and Court on one side and of commercialism and popular mobocracy on the other. They were almost independent, since the king's representative, the governor, could usually be managed or thwarted to their satisfaction. It was a government supported passively and willingly by the lower classes. There was nothing to disturb the pure intent to manage the affairs of the colony in a seemly manner. Theoretically, these gentlemen could be guaranteed to be above dishonesty and corruption.

The final answer to this theory, and to all such theories of aristocratical government, with this as an example, is that these gentlemen proved not to be above dishonesty. Without "checks and balances," human nature triumphs. Unchecked and uncontrolled, the Virginians lined their pockets like other more unfortunate statesmen. A racket worthy of, say, New York City at its Democratic dirtiest was flourishing; it involved the best blood of the state.

John Robinson had held the offices of Speaker of the House and of treasurer since 1738. Everybody loved him. "The highest model of elegance and fashion," "sound political knowledge," "benevolence . . . sincerity . . . decorum . . . comprehension and perspicacity . . . a column"; this sort of verbiage decorated his reputation. Under his administration, Virginia had issued government notes to help pay the state's expenses in the French and Indian Wars. A certain number of these were redeemable each year for cash, paid for by a special tax. The redeemed notes were supposed to be burned by Mr. Robinson himself, personally. Instead, Mr. Robinson quietly passed them on to cronies who owed him money, so that they could be redeemed, presumably, again and again. Suspicions dawned. A new group of burgesses, elected mostly from the western counties, had coalesced into a radical, anti-aristocratic, anti-tidewater, anti-great-planter party. Richard Henry Lee, for all his background, had joined Patrick Henry there. He proposed in the House that the sacred Mr. Robinson be investigated. Consternation and horror (and guilt) shook the House. "The speaker fixt his eyes with a dark and terrible frown upon Mr. Lee," but the resolution was adopted. After six months, a committee of picked friends of Speaker Robinson exonerated him — a thorough whitewash. All was serene until most unfortunately, a year later, Robinson died. In the course of settling his estate the financial irregularities came out; the colony had to sell his plantation to get its money back, and the scandal became public. His beneficiaries, however, escaped scot-free; their names were not even known. But from that time on, the great tidewater plantation owners, the aristocratic wing of Virginia politics, were deadly enemies of Richard Henry Lee.

The Revolution proceeded: Stamp Act, Townshend Acts, non-importation agreements, trouble and troops in Boston. Through it all Richard remonstrated, petitioned, orated, combined. He is given credit for first suggesting the Committees of Correspondence, an idea so welcome to Samuel Adams, and the origin of American union. As Adams in 1765 wrote his much-applauded Braintree Instructions for his town meeting, so in 1766 Lee wrote his Westmorland Resolves for his county. "We do determine at every hazard, and paying no regard to danger or death, we will exert every faculty to prevent the execution of the said Stamp Act." Seditious, fiery words, prelude to friend Patrick Henry's "liberty or death." The document of these resolves was signed by six Lees (Richard, brothers Thomas, Francis and William, cousins Richard and John junior), and has five Washington signatures.

It was inevitable that Richard Henry should be delegated to the first Continental Congress. Almost everyone who went with him was a kinsman, except Patrick Henry, his friend. Peyton Randolph led the group; others were George Washington, Richard Bland, Benjamin Harrison and Edmund Pendleton. Except for the base-born Henry, the blood lines of the others were totally entangled. Randolph and Harrison were in fact brothers-in-law. The Second Congress, which added Jefferson, Thomas Nelson, George Wythe and Francis Lee, was no less consanguineous. Of these first delegates from Virginia, Peyton Randolph became first President of the Congress, and so de facto first executive of the United States, George Washington became its first commander in chief, and Richard Lee the first to declare independence.

The reason he was not made a member of the committee to draft the Declaration, though he should by rights have been chairman of it, was because he had made enemies during the Robinson affair. Benjamin Harrison, leader of the conservatives in the delegation, was chosen by a coalition of his conservative colleagues to be Virginia's representative on the committee in place of Lee. In order to forestall this, and since Lee was unacceptable, the comparatively unknown Jefferson was chosen as a compromise candidate. Lee left Congress and returned to Virginia to help set up the state government. He returned to serve his country for many years, despite constant poor health. Like John Adams, he was on innumerable committees, often as chairman. He was even President of Congress, like Randolph. Later came his election as one of the two first senators of his state, and his championship of the Bill of Rights as added to the Constitution by amendments.

But still, his great moment had come and gone. As in the case of the other two important Revolutionary Lees, his triumph was embittered, his luster dimmed by the action of enemies. As mover of independence he should be famous; as framer of the Declaration he would be famous. Jefferson popularly (and properly) gets most of the credit, whereas Lee remains almost unknown. (It pays to be a good writer.)

The real trouble with Richard Henry Lee is exactly that: he was not a good writer, and what he did write was dispersed and neglected. His most famous speeches went unrecorded. His grandson, another Richard Henry Lee, was pious enough to write the first, and still (incredibly) last and only, biography of the man, but impious enough to hand out all his sources to friends as presents, including an original copy of the Declaration of Independence which, if kept in family hands, would have paid many times for the restoration of Stratford. Richard's one book, *Letters from the Federal Farmer,* a reasoned and cogent diatribe against the adoption of the Constitution from the already nascent position of states' rights, is nonetheless a pretty labored and clumsy affair, particularly when compared with its urbane model, Dickinson's *Letters from a Farmer in Pennsylvania.* Richard's own letters are well expressed, but so to the point — domestic or public business — that they contain few of the touches that make the Adams letters so delightful, none of the wit that flavors Franklin's. The result is that nobody has been interested enough in Richard Henry Lee to write a modern biography of him. Yet surely he deserves one.

Surely along with Patrick Henry and Samuel Adams, he has his niche above the doors of that central rotunda in the Pantheon of the Founding Fathers; but somehow the sunlight from the cupola never seems to strike him.

Arthur

Whatever you can say of Arthur Lee — and most of the things said of him have been uncomplimentary — no one can accuse him of being "faceless," or of lacking character. The youngest of the sons of Stratford, he was also generally considered to be the most intellectually gifted. Since he could not expect to benefit much by inheritance, the four older brothers getting most of the estate, Arthur and his next older brother William were expected to make their own way in life. William seemed to have been destined early to assume that quasi-hereditary position of tobacco agent in London, filled in the second generation by a Francis, and in the third by a Richard. He and Arthur spent most of their adult lives in England. Arthur went to Eton when he was ten, then went on to Edinburgh to study medicine, on the personal advice of Doctor Johnson himself who, though he despised the Scotch, still thought their teaching of medicine more practical, if less learned, than that of England. In fact most American doctors, like Arthur's friend and future in-law William Shippen, studied up there. Arthur returned to Virginia, after getting his M.D. in 1764, but he found provincial practice back in Virginia dull, so in 1768 he returned to London to study law. William went with him.

Unlike Arthur, William had had no English schooling. His particular college of hard knocks was his brother Philip, who used the boy as an estate manager when Philip went to Council meetings at Williamsburg. This bred him to business, as Arthur was bred to professional life. Both Arthur and William soon made themselves modestly successful careers in London.

These careers were not only professional, but also political, and were tied to that lurid comet in English public life, John Wilkes. William stuck to the tobacco business, married his first cousin Hannah Ludwell, and prospered. Arthur, however, seemed to spend less time with the law than he did with Wilkes, and the association determined the whole course of his not very successful or happy, but certainly very lively, life.

John Wilkes was essentially a revolutionist who was cheated of his revolution. Living in either America or France he would surely have been a leader. In England he seems to have been largely a brilliant agin-er who made the Establishment tremble with fury, but who seems to have actually accomplished little. He was a focus, however, for varieties of discontent; among these, of colonial discontent. He was one of the most prominent English champions of America (in his honor, and that of another such American supporter, Colonel Barré, the Pennsylvania town of Wilkes-Barre was named). Arthur Lee was a friend of Wilkes.

Various things came of this Lee-Wilkes association. The first was a curious Lee flurry in city government. Wilkes was a perennially elected member of Parliament; but Parliament refused to seat him, and in fact Wilkes spent much of his time in jail, imprisoned on charges of seditious libel. He lived very well there on the bounty of friends and entertained his circle freely. Meanwhile he also managed to become lord mayor of London. This pompous office was then a powerful one; the lord mayor could act as a sort of Tribune of the People, and as such challenge King and Parliament with petitions, remonstrances and mobs.

As a member of the Wilkes party, William Lee also found himself elected to city offices, first as one of the two sheriffs of London, the other sheriff being his business partner, the American Stephen Sayre, and then in 1775, while the fighting had actually begun in America, as alderman. Alderman was one step below mayor, the office was for life, and William Lee was the only American elected to the post in all history. His election as an American in time of rebellion indicates how strong the pro-American sentiment must have been among the citizens of London. He didn't resign the office until 1780, in mid-war, and after he had left London for diplomatic adventures in Europe.

More important for the future of Arthur and William was another aspect of their association with John Wilkes. Wilkes, as the center of a racy and convivial group, attracted to him certain French refugees. Of these certainly the most peculiar and mysterious was that odd bisexual, the Chevalier D'Eon. The most peculiar and mysterious thing about him was his sex. By order of the king of France he was not allowed to set foot in his native country except in woman's clothes. There he was usually referred to in the feminine as the "Chevalière" and strode about cursing, smoking and drinking in hoopskirts. In 1775 he was a refugee in London, a friend of Wilkes, and a worry to the French government. His letters were supposed to be dynamite, and if made public might start a war between France and England.

Sent to get these letters from D'Eon, and so prevent their publication, was another equally picturesque Frenchman, Pierre Augustin Caron de Beaumarchais, watchmaker like Du Pont, musician, courtier and above all playwright. He had gotten into a complicated legal-financial scandal involving the bribery of a court of justice and had been stripped of his French citizenship. To redeem himself in exile, he was busy on various secret missions. First he silenced a blackmailer called Morande, who had written a dirty book about Madame du Barry. This success sent him back to London to silence D'Eon.

D'Eon, Beaumarchais and Lee all met at the rowdy if stimulating soirées held by Wilkes, in or out of jail; and Beaumarchais added a new secret mission to his portfolio — aid to America. For Arthur Lee, admitted to the English bar in 1775, then appointed successor to Franklin as the agent for Massachusetts in England, had now been named secret representative of Congress abroad; as such, America's very first diplomat — and first secret agent.

He and Beaumarchais together arranged a large loan from France, later supplemented by another from Spain. War supplies were sent off at last in 1777, consigned to a fake importing house in the West Indies, a blind for Beaumarchais, called Rodrique Hortalez. The arms reached the American army in time to be crucial in the victory of Saratoga later in 1777. The victory at Saratoga in turn was crucial in persuading the French to come out openly as allies of America in 1778. And without this French aid and the French fleet, Cornwallis could not have been defeated at Yorktown; and so the War of Independence might not have been won.

Thus the cloak-and-dagger mysteries of the Lee-Beaumarchais deal were definitely of importance, and marked the first successful bit of American wartime diplomatic strategy. The happy result should have made Arthur Lee's reputation and assured his career. It was, in fact, the real high-point of it, as the motion for independence was for Richard. But here again, as in the story of all three of the great Revolutionary Lees, the Enemy stepped in and dashed the Cup of Triumph, etc.

In this case, the Enemy was Silas Deane, member of Congress from Connecticut, in-law of the Saltonstalls, former schoolteacher, thriving businessman. Arthur Lee had been appointed secret agent in the fall of '75. In February '76 Beaumarchais sent a memorial to the king which determined the course of French action in favor of America. In May the French officially approved a loan of one million livres. In June the Spaniards duplicated the French subsidy. Congress, however, did not hear of it (and then only verbally, for fear of interception) till October '76, the supplies themselves not arriving until '77.

Meanwhile, in March of '76, Congress had appointed Silas Deane as its official business agent in Paris. He arrived there in July '76, and Beaumarchais immediately switched his dealings from Lee to Deane. Lee, after all, was in London and had no official standing. Deane was now in Paris and did have official standing. He turned out to be far more sympathetic to Beaumarchais than Lee. Both of them saw no harm in making as much money as possible privately while aiding their country publicly; and in fact nobody much else did at that time, except Arthur Lee. They both proceeded to do so.

However, there was this one small matter. When Lee had secretly arranged for the "loan" from France he had thought that there had been no question of repayment. It was a free gift, and Beaumarchais and Lee were merely intermediaries. Now suddenly, as the supplies were on their way, Beaumarchais began to demand payment for them from Congress, saying that he and friends had raised the money privately. Deane supported him in the fraud — or misunderstanding. He probably knew little or nothing about the consultations with Lee. Arthur, never a man to dodge issues, indignantly informed Congress of what he considered the deceit. Congress, always willing to save money, chose to believe him. Beaumarchais was naturally not pleased. Still, Beaumarchais and Deane between them got most of the credit for the deal, and Lee's part in the affair was more or less ignored.

Friendship between Deane and Lee having thus been firmly established, Congress then had the wit to appoint, in the fall of '76, three commissioners to France to arrange an alliance. They were Franklin, Deane and Lee. So began the famous Deane-Lee feud that split Congress into two parties and ended by ruining the diplomatic careers of both men. If the quarrel had involved only Lee and Deane, it might not have been important. Unfortunately it involved a personage greater than both of them put together, the third commissioner, Benjamin Franklin.

Lee had already formed a jealousy of that paragon in England. Having drawn attention to himself on both sides of the water by a series of newspaper "letters" signed Junius Americanus, Lee became the protégé of Samuel Adams. The two knew each other only by correspondence, and in fact never met face to face until 1781, but were thoroughly of one mind. Arthur Lee became the Adams' source of confidential information from abroad. When in 1770 the then agent for Massachusetts died, Adams nominated Lee to take his place. Franklin, however, was in London and got the job. Lee was appointed his assistant and successor; but Franklin stayed on and on, and Adams and Lee were miffed. They both thought Franklin too pro-English.

Thus, when Lee got to Paris late in 1776 as third commissioner, he was already suspicious of both Franklin and Deane. All his suspicions were confirmed. It was made very clear that Mr. Lee was not wanted. He was sent off on a diplomatic mission to Spain, which was successful and another to Germany, which was not. The first mission persuaded Spain to add subsidies to those of France. On his mission to Germany, where the Prussian government made clear its lack of interest in America, he had all his papers stolen and copied. The copies still rest in the British official files.

When he returned from Berlin he found that there was really nothing for him to do in Paris except make a nuisance of himself. This he proceeded to do. Franklin was completely and successfully in charge of all diplomatic affairs, he had turned over all business affairs to Deane; so Lee appointed himself Inspector and Investigator of the conduct of affairs on the part of Franklin and Deane. He discovered, in fact, that the conduct was very lax. Things were working well enough, but they were in an awful mess. No proper books or accounts were being kept, nepotism was rife, juicy commercial plums were falling into the hands of Deane or of the friends and relations of Franklin. Deane was obviously out to make his fortune; and worst of all, the office was crawling with strange characters, undoubtedly spies. One man in particular, Edward Bancroft, roused Lee's suspicions.

Edward Bancroft, acting as private secretary to Deane, had been a Connecticut student of Deane's in his earlier school-mastering days. He was an M.D. and a scientific and literary amateur of just the kind Franklin liked and admired. He lived in the same house with Deane and Franklin and had access to all their correspondence and conversation. Franklin trusted him, and never knew during his whole lifetime that Bancroft was, in fact, a spy. Nobody knew for sure, even the suspicious Lee. Proof only became available in 1889 with the publication of British Secret Service archives. Letters, supposedly love letters written by Bancroft, were bottled and placed in a hole at the foot of a tree in the gardens of the Tuileries. They were picked up every Tuesday evening by a member of the British Embassy. In the spaces between the gallant sentiments information was written in invisible ink. By this means everything that went on in the American commission was known to the English.

Arthur Lee brought to his associate's attention the disgraceful disarray of office routine. He warned them that Bancroft and others were probably spies. He told them not to trust the French. He was perfectly right. He was honest, conscientious, efficient. He was inspired by the highest motives. He was also officious, tactless, irritable and irritating, a typical "fussy bachelor." Franklin and Deane paid no attention to him, though he was supposedly their equal in power and responsibility. They ignored his suggestions, warnings and protests. Proud Arthur was livid.

Franklin had sound reasons for his complaisance to all the irregularities Lee pointed out to him. He knew what he was doing: cementing friendship with the French and getting them to help the Revolution. Smaller details should not be allowed to interfere with the main object. He was grateful, perhaps too grateful, to Deane for taking over from him all the burdensome financial and commercial details of the mission. If thoughts of private profit kept Deane happy and busy, so much the better. Franklin hated business matters. Arthur Lee's efforts to draw his attention to Deane's irregularities were just a nuisance.

As for spies, Franklin may not have known that his good friend Bancroft was one; but he obviously did not care to know. "It is impossible to discover in every case the falsity of pretended friends," he wrote. "If I was sure therefore that my valet de place was a spy, as he probably is, I think I should not discharge him for that if in other respects I liked him." Franklin liked Bancroft. Franklin did not like Lee.

When it came to handling the French, Franklin knew exactly what he was doing. Lee did not. He was more than a nuisance, he was a liability. The French adored Franklin. They detested grim Monsieur Lee.

So built up one of the most famous of the feuds of the American Revolution, that time fertile in feuds. Arthur wrote home to his powerful friends, the Adamses, his brothers Richard and Francis. Congress soon split into two factions, Deane versus Lee, and this split was one of the beginnings of a division that colored all American political thinking for the next fifty years. The Deane faction was pro-Franklin and pro-French. The Lee faction was anti-French and somewhat pro-British. The pro-French faction, led by Franklin and Jefferson, inclined towards political radicalism, idealism and democracy. The anti-French party, which included John Adams (sometimes) and Hamilton, leaned towards political and financial conservatism, balance of powers within the government, pessimism about the nature of man and resumption of trade with the British as soon as the war was over. These leanings persisted for decades, in fact in some ways still persist embedded in American liberalism and conservatism. Men shifted from side to side,* and so did issues, but the American two-party system evolved in part and in embryo like a pearl about the tiny scruple of this personal feud.

In 1778 the French, almost entirely due to the persuasiveness of Franklin and the victory at Saratoga, signed a formal treaty of alliance with the revolting colonies. The three signers for America were Franklin, Deane and Lee. Almost immediately Deane left for home, where he was forced to explain his conduct, and John Adams took his place in Paris. At home, the investigation of Deane by Congress was frustrated by the fact that Deane had brought none of his papers and accounts with him; he claimed he had left in too much of a hurry. The friends of Lee pounced on this and demolished Deane's reputation. Deane in turn took to the newspapers and demolished Lee's reputation. Everyone finally came to the sensible conclusion stated by John Adams that one representative to the French court was enough. Arthur Lee had the impudence to suggest himself for the post in place of Franklin. Instead he was recalled, Adams lost his job too, and only Franklin survived the wreckage.

Deane went back to France to try and straighten out his accounts and justify himself. While there he wrote discouraged letters suggesting that America better give up the impracticable idea of independence. These remarks were published in a Tory newspaper in occupied New York. Deane was really ruined now, and he died abroad bankrupt and disgraced.

Arthur Lee did better. After his return to America he was elected in 1782 to the Continental Congress (where brothers Francis and Richard had already served, and where cousins Richard Bland, Harry and Thomas Sim also served — a record for any one family, approached only by the four Livingstons). Later he became one of three commissioners of the treasury and retired comfortably to his

* The Constitutionalists and Federalists, for instance, tended to belong to the Lee faction. Yet Richard Henry Lee was the foremost champion of the anti-Constitutional party, and there joined Jefferson, leader of the pro-French party. Things got mixed up.

plantation Landsdowne, there to plant orchards, correspond with his favorite niece, Nancy Shippen Livingston, and vainly court various unsusceptible ladies. He died a bachelor, bitter against the Ingratitude of the Republic, firmly convinced that monarchy was the solution for the proper conduct of American affairs, and hating Franklin, "that wicked old man" as Richard Henry called him, to his last breath.

A career that promised much, and accomplished something, came to a rather subdued end. Arthur Lee has certainly been wronged by history, as a brief examination of biased sources like Van Doren's life of Franklin would seem to reveal, or even the Dictionary of American Biography. It is possible that he was right — right about Beaumarchais, right about Bancroft, and right about Deane to a certain extent: Deane was indeed one of the most careless administrators in American history. John Adams believed in Arthur Lee and considered him greatly wronged, "A man of whom I cannot think without emotion." But then Adams and Lee belonged to the same political cabal and shared the same virtues and vices: uncompromising honesty, unbounded self-righteousness. There was in fact something neurotic about Lee's brand of self-righteousness. Not only was everyone else wrong, but they were all in a *plot* against him. Franklin spotted this paranoiac streak and, with his usual insight, in a letter which he may after all not have sent Lee, specifically warned him to beware of "your sick mind, which is forever tormenting itself with its jealousies, suspicions, and fancies that others mean you ill. . . . If you do not cure yourself of this temper it will end in insanity, of which it is a symptomatic forerunner, as I have seen in several instances. God preserve you . . . and for His sake suffer me to live in quiet."

"This man," as John Adams wrote in 1819, "never had justice done him by his country in his life time, and I fear he never will have by posterity." John Adams was right. As in the case of Richard Henry Lee, there is only one biography, again written by that careless later Richard Henry Lee in 1829. Yet surely a career of such picturesque incident should attract some modern writer, even if the subject is not noticeably endearing.

Lesser Lees

Among the lesser or underbrush Lees, William has at least one supremely peculiar incident to his credit. He too, like Arthur, left his cozy and prominent niche in London as tobacco agent and alderman, and followed brother Arthur into what John Adams called "militia diplomacy." In a sort of forlornly hopeful gesture, Congress sent representatives to various European courts on the chance that they might be recognized and money be lent. They weren't and it wasn't. William was so appointed to the courts of Berlin and Vienna, where nobody paid any attention to him.

In his spare time, of which he had much, he scouted Europe for possible friends of America, and found some sympathy among the Dutch. The ruler of Holland, the stadtholder Prince of Orange, was not among these, being a cousin and good friend of George III; but the burgomasters of Amsterdam wanted to help. A representative was appointed to get together with Lee and work out a "treaty of alliance" between America and Holland. Of course this "treaty" was about as binding as one between the Board of Aldermen of New York and a minor Dutch foreign attaché would be; but still, in a most devious way, it did in the end serve the intended purpose.

A copy of this private treaty was sent back to Congress. Two years later Henry Laurens of South Carolina, former President of Congress, was sent on a mission to Holland. He took along with him a copy of this Lee-Amsterdam treaty. En route, his ship was captured by the British. He dutifully threw all his papers overboard in weighted bags, but the bag containing the "treaty" failed to sink. The British picked it out of the water and used the rescued treaty as an excuse to break off relations with Holland. Though the Dutch government feverishly disowned this bit of amateur diplomacy, in the end it did the trick, and America gained Holland as another prosperous ally. Poor Mr. Laurens spent his time as a prisoner in the Tower of London, until he was exchanged for Lord Cornwallis, captured at Yorktown.

The other "underbrush Lees" had no such picturesque incidents to star their worthy courses. Richard Henry's brother Francis Lightfoot affixed his name to the Declaration of Independence, thus making Richard and Francis the only pair of brothers to do so; but he was a retiring gentleman whose attitude toward public affairs was summed up by his pithy statement, "What damned dirty work is this politics!" He backed up Richard Henry at each stage of his career and retired to Menokin as soon as he decently could. One gets the impression that his charm acted as oil on the waters in the rather stormy wake of stern brother Richard, and that he made friends and mended fences after Richard had broken them.

As for the lesser brothers of the Leesylvania line, Charles was third attorney general, succeeding cousin Randolph and collegemate Bradford. He lasted from Washington's second administration through Adams' stormy presidency and was one of the few cabinet members who was loyal to the President and not a secret agent for Hamilton. His public career ended when Jefferson took power.

His younger brother, Richard Bland, was one of Virginia's initial congressmen, as Richard Henry was one of its first two senators. He is not otherwise very distinguished. His vote, however, determined the fate of the city of Washington. A deadlock over Hamilton's financial program was broken by a political deal: the federal capital would be located southward on the Potomac, if a Virginian would vote pro-Hamilton. Richard Bland was that Virginian. Hamilton got his way, and Washington, D.C., ended up on Foggy Bottom.

It was during this Revolutionary generation that the Lees began to intermarry inordinately. Both of Philip Ludwell Lee's daughters, the divine Matilda and Flora, married Lees. Matilda married Light-Horse Harry, and Flora married her first cousin, Ludwell Lee of Belmont, a son of Richard Henry. Two daughters of Richard Henry also married Lees — two brothers of Light-Horse Harry, Charles the attorney general and Edmund Jennings Lee. Things were getting pretty damn close-knit.

Henry

Of the three famous Lees, the most famous, the least faceless, and the most thoroughly disappointed was Henry, grandson of a Henry who was the younger brother of great Thomas of Stratford. This Henry married a Bland (whose mother was a Randolph) and lived at Lee Hall. He in turn had a son Henry who married a Grymes (reputedly an old flame of George Washington) and lived at Leesylvania. His son was the Revolutionary Henry, Light-Horse Harry Lee, who married first a Lee and then a Carter, and who lived, until he went bankrupt, at Stratford.

Harry was handsome, Harry was brave, Harry was even learned. He was a native military genius, a lover of Latin, one of Washington's best personal friends, though so much younger; everything, in fact, except a man of ordinary common sense. He Thirsted for Glory, and also, alas, for riches. The combination brought him, and indeed the family fortunes of the Lees, crashing. He and brother Charles graduated from Princeton, where politician Madison, poet Freneau (he of the Biddle ballad) and writer Brackenridge were all friends, and all crossed his path decisively in various ways later. The first tragedy of Harry's life was that he lived before the United States existed, with its army and its military academy. Harry would then have been happily set for life. He was a man of war, pure and simple. In civilian matters he was usually a fool.

Fired with patriotism like most of his college-mates and kinfolk, he began his career in the Revolutionary War as a captain of the Light Dragoons organized by his cousin Theodorick Bland. Sent north, he served in New Jersey and Pennsylvania as a most skillful skirmisher, scout and seizer of supplies from the British, and here acquired the nickname of Light-Horse Harry by which he was ever afterward known. Between October and December of 1776 he conducted at least fifteen raids on the British, most of them spectacularly successful. His only casualties during this period were two troopers wounded and one horse shot. Then and later, such actions earned him a good reputation and the admiration of Washington; but this was not quite the Glory for which he Thirsted. It was all very well to gallop about in fancy uniform (helmet with horsehair plumes, short blue cape, etc.). What he needed was a specific, important, one-man victory.

His chance came, or rather, was manufactured. By now a major, he suggested he be allowed to direct a special assault on one of the forts guarding British-occupied New York. Anthony Wayne had become America's darling by his successful and incredibly daring capture of Stony Point, a fort north of New York. Lee had had a vital part in the preparation of this assault, but got no credit for it. Now he would capture, with equally incredible daring, a fort south of New York. This time he *would* get the credit for it, and become America's darling too. He was given permission and direction by Washington.

The fort at Paulus Hook was on an isthmus surrounded by water, the Hudson River on one side, the Hackensack on the other. The nearest bridge was twelve miles upstream. The Royal Navy patroled the rivers, and a creek had been widened into a fortified ditch, cutting the isthmus above the fort, and crossable only by a drawbridge. Paulus Hook seemed impregnable.

Lee's plan of attack was to march his cavalry and supporting infantry down the Hackensack to a point opposite the fort, set up a prefabricated bridge there, cross river and ditch and take the fort by surprise. Although he was delayed by getting lost on the march down, he made the crossings successfully by dark and caught the redcoats sleeping. In no time at all they had surrendered. More difficult was the retreat by daylight burdened with prisoners, but this too was accomplished, though much of his men's powder had been soaked and ruined fording the fortified ditch. Also, a fleet of boats that was supposed to take the raiders back across the water failed to keep its rendezvous. However, even an attack en route by British cavalry was repulsed, and Henry made it into the American camp late in the afternoon with nearly four hundred prisoners. Only one of his own men had been killed during the entire operation.

Washington immediately sent a letter of commendation to Congress and one to Harry himself. Lafayette joined in the chorus of praise that came from other leaders like Wayne, Greene and Knox. Even the enemy general, Sir Henry Clinton, said, rather ungrammatically, "I wish I had a few more officers of my own who display Major Lee's spirit."

Glory enough, one would have supposed. But here again the Fate of the Lees intervened. Instead of being commended by Congress, Lee found himself court-martialed! Enemies again; various disgruntled officers accused him of various irregularities and malfeasances. A Major Clarke who served under him claimed he was really senior officer present and should have been in command instead of Lee. He was accused of cowardice in having retreated too soon, and of negligence for not having been able to destroy the fort's arsenal. All these matters were cleared up at the trial by Washington himself, who had specified everything in his secret verbal orders to Lee before the battle. Lee was acquitted and completely exonerated. Congress, needled by cousin Richard Henry, struck a special medal for Harry, and presented it to him in the presence of Washington. It has been considered one of the first Congressional Medals of Honor and as such the ancestor of the present decoration, though there is no real connection. This was Glory, but the court-martial and the delay in recognition rankled. Bitterness in the cup.

Lee's next and really more important field of action was in the South. He was sent down to help General Greene dislodge the British from Georgia and the Carolinas. In the long and hard-fought battles that followed, the boyish apparatus of galloping raids and plumed helmets was absorbed in real warfare. Lee became Greene's right-hand man in the campaign that eventually led to Yorktown and the final defeat of the British. The credit for maneuvering Cornwallis into the trap belongs to Lee.

In essence the strategic decision was: how could the feeble and outnumbered American forces in the South handle the threat of Cornwallis's army, larger and better equipped, in control of the seacoast, where the British transports and supply ships could come and go as they pleased? Should Greene retreat north and leave Cornwallis in control? Should Greene confront Cornwallis in a decisive battle? A third and eventually successful course of action was suggested by Lee. Let Greene bypass Cornwallis and move south, permitting Cornwallis to move into Virginia unopposed, and so into the arms of Washington and his French allies. Cornwallis took the bait, moved north, and was checkmated at Yorktown. Greene's army meanwhile moved south and, largely under the leadership of Lee, captured the backcountry British forts, confined the British to the seacoast, and liberated Georgia and the Carolinas. Though it was a while before this seacoast foothold was dislodged, and before Adams, Franklin and Jay signed the final treaty of peace in 1783, the war was really won in October 1781 at the surrender of Yorktown.

Harry Lee was there for the ceremonies. He had been sent north by Greene to beg Washington for more men and supplies to finish off the British in the South. He was thus able to witness the fruition of his grand design. Yet here again, Glory escaped him. It may have been his plan that accomplished victory, but it was not his name or rank that counted at the surrender. He was a mere observer, and he was not yet even a general.

The return to the South, with its fag-end fighting, was an anticlimax. Everyone wanted to go home. Finally in January 1782 Lee sent Greene an unfortunately sour letter of resignation: ". . . the indifference with which my efforts to advance the cause of my country is [*sic*] considered by my friends, the persecution of my foes . . ." — all rather in the vein of cousin Arthur. Greene was terribly upset, and wrote a long letter of praise and consolation; but to no avail. Harry was through with military life.

Somewhat as Samuel Adams, his real task of independence over, retired to a career of outward honor as governor of Massachusetts, but really to a decline of forces and reputation, so Harry Lee, his real task of victory done, retired to a spurious effulgence as master of Stratford and governor of Virginia. On the surface, life after the Revolution seemed to offer him everything.

He became master of Stratford by his marriage in 1782 to cousin Matilda, who had inherited from her father Philip. They had two surviving Lee-Lee children, a Henry, fourth in direct line, and a Lucy. Stratford thus was never actually owned by Harry senior, but passed direct from Philip to Matilda to Harry junior; but the father lived there during the minority of his son.

Matilda died in 1790 and two years later Harry married again. His second marriage was as brilliant, socially and even financially, as his first. Ann, the daughter of Charles Carter of Shirley, was seventeen years younger than her husband. Like his first wife, she too was an heiress, in spite of the fact that her father had more than twenty other children. As in the case of Matilda, her family also took the precaution of seeing that Harry couldn't get his hands on her money.

The truth was that Harry was as reckless a spender and investor as he was a canny military tactician. Like many other Virginians, including Washington, he believed the state was on the verge of a great commercial and land boom, and that a canal built down the Potomac would channel trade from the West. He invested heavily in the site of a future town at the Great Falls of the river. The canal never got properly built, there was a flaw in the title of the lands, western trade did not get channeled, and the city never was started. But throughout the remaining years of the eighteenth century, Harry's civilian career seemed glitteringly prosperous. A friend of

Washington and Madison and ardent supporter of the new Constitution, he had patronage and power as a Federalist. He served prominently as delegate to the Virginia Constitutional Convention, and was governor of the state as well as congressman. He dispensed lavish hospitality at Stratford or from the so-called "mansion" of the governor at Richmond. Children were born to him, though his favorite, Philip, the oldest of Matilda's children, died suddenly, as did the firstborn child of Ann.

Despite his successes and friendships in high places, he spoiled it all by a genius for political tactlessness. His blunders were usually due to the noblest motives, usually in defense of a friend, but they were still blunders. For an example (one of many) of his maladroitness: He and Madison set up a newspaper to counteract the Northern-financial bias of the Hamiltonians championed by John Fenno in his *Gazette*. They naturally picked their mutual friend and college-mate, the poet and pamphleteer Philip Freneau. He too started a *Gazette* (Freneau versus Fenno) and in no time this became the mouthpiece of the Jeffersonians and mounted the most vicious attacks on two of Harry's best friends, personal and political, Hamilton and Washington. Both of them blamed Harry for Freneau's attacks.

Meanwhile, he had offended cousin Jefferson, whom he never liked anyway, in a far more direct way. He reported to Washington derogatory remarks that Jefferson was supposed to have made (evidently not in Harry's hearing) about the President at a small private dinner. His letter to Washington somehow fell into Jefferson's hands. Jefferson never forgave him. Thus, while he was governor of Virginia, he managed to alienate simultaneously both centers of American national political power, Hamilton and Jefferson, by meddling in matters which were of no immediate concern, just to help a friend — Madison, Freneau, Washington. It is remarkable that any man of such enormous political naïveté could have survived as long and prominently as he did. He makes John Adams seem like Machiavelli.

There were still moments of Glory, however — his victorious defense of the Constitution at the Virginia convention,* backed by Washington, but attacked by the two greatest orators of the state, Patrick Henry and Richard Henry Lee; his election to governor for three terms as a protégé of Madison; his final election to Congress in 1799 as a Federalist, his election being carried largely because George Washington appeared in person to vote for him. In Congress he achieved a curious immortality. He placed before that body a resolution honoring the death of Washington, containing those words "first in war, first in peace, and first in the hearts of his countrymen." Even here though, that curious quirk of circumstance, the Fate of the Lees, spoiled things a bit. When it came time to present the resolution, Harry was so overcome by emotion that his seconder, John Marshall, had to read it for him — and so, at the time, got the public credit for originating the famous words.

There were even military exploits, though not exactly glorious ones. When in 1794 the backwoods farmers of Pennsylvania, stirred up considerably by the propaganda of classmate Henry Brackenridge, rose in revolt against a tax on their precious staple, whiskey, and began to manhandle revenue agents and organize themselves into armed bands, Washington decided to put down the incipient rebellion with a strong hand. The strong hand consisted of an army of fifteen thousand men, more than Washington himself had ever been able to get together during the Revolution. Harry, promoted at last from lieutenant colonel to major general, was given command. It was not an exciting campaign. It rained. The backwoodsmen gave up without a struggle. Friend Brackenridge was exonerated; those who were found guilty of sedition were sentenced to be hanged, but were pardoned by Washington. When Harry got back to Virginia, he found himself attacked because he'd

---

* One of the most vivid portraits of him describes his debut on that occasion. "A young man, thirty-two years of age, rose, and standing within a few feet of the chair was recognized. Six feet tall, beautiful of face, with the resounding and fearless voice of a warrior, Henry Lee looked the part which reputation had assigned him."

gone off on the expedition while still governor. He was not re-elected. But at least he got his coveted rank of general out of it; and how ironic that the father Harry led the first Federal army against civil rebellion, whereas the son Robert led the last rebellious army against these same Federals.

When Harry's archenemy Jefferson became President, Harry was through with politics. He went out with the eighteenth century on his burst of perdurable rhetoric and into a new era of shame and misfortune. His financial collapse followed his political one. Again, he had helped a friend. He lent forty thousand dollars to Robert Morris, who as financial dictator of the Revolution and "richest man in America" should have been a safe bet; but Morris went bankrupt and to debtors' prison. Lee lost all his money. Living miserably, in poverty and loneliness at Stratford, the door chained against creditors, poor Ann bore child after child. Finally the inevitable could no longer be forestalled. In 1809, while his kinsman, college-mate and friend Madison assumed the dignities of President of the United States, Harry went to jail. Like Morris, Lee also was declared bankrupt and sentenced to debtors' prison. Here he improved his leisure by writing his memoirs of the Revolution in the South. He hoped the book would make money. It didn't, but it is a valuable record, and achieved later editions, one in 1827 edited by his eldest son, Harry junior, and one in 1870 edited by a younger son, Robert Edward.

During this lowest ebb of Lee fortunes, in 1807, while Harry dashed about the state trying to raise money and Ann was sequestered in decaying Stratford, this unwanted child Robert Edward was born. In him the Fate of the Lees and the Glory for which his father so thirsted both achieved their simultaneous apotheosis.

Meanwhile, in 1810, when Harry got out of jail, it was decided to move the family to Alexandria. Harry junior took over Stratford. Harry senior's family had to rely on Ann's modest capital for survival. Broken in health and spirits, Harry tried to emigrate to the

West Indies, but even Madison couldn't get him through the British blockade.

One final glory and one final blow of fate were to attend Harry Lee before his death. Again, both were due to loyalty and to friends. In 1812, just after war with England had been declared, Lee happened to be in Baltimore (nobody yet knows quite why). Then, as now and always, the war was unpopular with a vocal minority. One of the most vocal was a young editor called Alexander Hanson, son of a friend of Harry's. Hanson insisted on airing his views in the face of mob action, and Harry called on him at the moment when he was about to barricade his house against such a mob. Harry immediately took charge of the military defense. In one of the most shameful bits of administrative cowardice on record, Mayor Johnson of Baltimore broke up the fight by escorting the besieged editor and friends to jail, and after promising to safeguard them there, permitted the mob to sack the jail and torture the prisoners. Two were killed outright, the others all rendered unconscious. Harry's face had been gouged with a knife and he had been seriously injured internally. He lay near death all summer, and when he got out he was a permanent cripple. President Madison, Secretary of State Monroe, and Chief Justice Marshall all visited and tried to console him; but Lee was beyond consolation.

The final irony of his career occurred next year, in 1813, when Madison offered him the command of the U.S. Army. By now it was too late. Harry was an invalid. Though the war was still in progress, this time Madison was able to get permission from the British for Lee to go to Barbados for his health. There in the Caribbean he lingered, enjoying the occasional society of British officials, writing forlorn letters to his family, drifting from island to island in clothes grown threadbare, always hoping to return to Alexandria.

Finally in 1818 he managed to board a ship heading north; but he was by then too ill to finish the trip. He was put off on the coast of Georgia, where the widow of his old commander General Greene lived on a plantation called Dungeness. There the dying man was coddled and cared for, surrounded by orange trees and the admiration of his hostess's family and of young officers from the nearby garrison. There he died in 1818 and was buried with military honors.* No relatives were with him; not until 1862, when his son Robert was stationed nearby during the Civil War, did any members of his family visit his lonely grave.

Henry was certainly an extreme example of the kind of fame and failure which in general characterized the careers of the more distinguished individuals of all these families during this formative period — John Adams, plunged into political obscurity by his own party; Nicholas Biddle, blown up on his ship at the moment of victory; Richard, Arthur and William Lee all to some extent cheated of their rightful political deserts. Only the lesser figures, the comfortable Isaac Roosevelt, the vigorous Charles Biddle, the modest Francis Lightfoot, earnest Charles and accommodating Richard Bland Lee seemed to survive the turmoil with fortune and reputation securely intact. Pierre du Pont also had been roughly treated by French history.

From the family point of view, however, these greater figures were all vital. Though perhaps in the end personal failures, they added to their names that special essence and luster that cannot be achieved by mere money, tenure, worthiness and social position. Four of the families — all but the Roosevelts — had now some national or even international reputation. All had position. Roosevelts and Biddles had wealth.

Above all, they were launched, like ships of the line, as Families — vessels of different build and size, ready for the voyage through the nineteenth century. For the next twenty decades nobody could be born in America with the names Adams, Roosevelt, Biddle, du Pont or Lee (common as the names Adams and Lee are) without calling up references based on family rather than just personal reputation; family reputations still prestigious today without regard to the individual worth of contemporary bearers of the names.

* There was a marine guard from the frigate *John Adams*.

III

Full Flood

1800–1900

1

The Nineteenth Century

WITH the beginning of the nineteenth century, true family history really starts. For the first time, the men of these particular families are no longer, so to speak, on their own. Except perhaps, and only perhaps, for the Lees, the careers of the eighteenth-century personages — John Adams, Charles Biddle, Isaac Roosevelt, Pierre du Pont — were very much individual careers. These men were ancestors, not descendants. Even for the Lees, active revolution could hardly be considered an hereditary pattern. But beginning almost to the date in 1800 everything, or nearly everything, changes. The careers of nineteenth-century Adamses, Roosevelts (with notable exceptions), Biddles, du Ponts and Lees are to an excruciating extent the careers of sons, grandsons and great-grandsons; people caught inexorably in traditions and attitudes not of their own private making. Careers, that is to say, of Men of Family.

The nineteenth century also represents for these families, as continuing entities, a full span of one hundred years of active, prominent existence. In 1700 there were no true Adams, Roosevelt, Biddle or du Pont families, or rather Families, as such. By 1800 there definitely were; and by 1900 there still definitely were. (Will we be able to say the same thing as of 2000?) The nineteenth century then is the true exhibit, test tube, showcase, demonstration, of the interaction between Family and Democracy. Here the story really begins. From now on we can trace causes and observe effects, and history up to this point has really been only prehistory.

A new cast of characters of course: three generations of Adamses, from John and Abigail's son John Quincy to his son Charles Francis to his sons John, Charles, Henry and Brooks; a random collection of Roosevelts of various branches; Biddles of whom a Nicholas is pre-eminent; du Ponts, both Company and non-Company; and the culminate Lee, Robert Edward. Almost all of these were fated from birth to respond to certain conditions not of their own choosing. They had to act and react as they did because of "who they were." As at the beginning of the Revolution, a curtain comes down and a curtain goes up; the actors of that stirring scene clear the stage, the new ones enter, almost exactly as the century itself changes.

Two events in particular occurred to mark this change. Most conspicuous was the defeat of John Adams in his bid (if it can be called a "bid") for second term as President. As he left the White House in 1801, the first to do so, he was not only dragging his party into permanent eclipse but also, it would seem, the political fortunes of his family. It looked as though the Adamses were done for. John had recalled his son John Quincy from his diplomatic post in Berlin, and he too was out of a job.

The other event, far less publicly notorious, but still noticed, that marked the beginning of a new era was the arrival in Newport, on January 1, 1800, of the du Pont family, that emigration of over a dozen people, du Ponts, in-laws, relations of in-laws with their children, servants, luggage and pianos. They had had a terrible trip of ninety-odd days, been reduced to eating soup made of boiled rats, and they landed in Newport only because the captain had lost his way. They arrived in an ice-packed harbor almost starved to death. They went ashore looking for food and shelter. According to legend (and legend accrues thickly about these early days of du Pont history), they stopped at the first inhabited house to ask for assistance. Nobody was home, but there was a cheery fire and a holiday feast spread out. The owners were off, perhaps on a New Year's call. In any case the du Ponts could not resist the temptation; they went in and ate the whole spread, leaving before the owners returned. There is some disagreement as to whether or not they also left money to pay for this impromptu meal.

Other less distinctive events mark the break between centuries. The defeat of the Federalists finished not only the political career of John Adams, but those of Light-Horse Harry Lee and his brother Charles, former cabinet member. The Stratford Lees were already dead. A second generation of Biddles appeared, in miniature, on the public stage. Nicholas Biddle, precocious son of Charles, delivered the valedictory to the senior class of the College of New Jersey (Princeton), of which he was a graduate in 1801. He was fifteen and the youngest ever to graduate from the college before or since. As for the Roosevelts, Isaac was dead, and nothing in particular seems to mark off the Age of the Revolution from the Age of Steam for them until in 1811 a Nicholas Roosevelt was the first man to puff down the Ohio in a steamboat.

In general then, the nineteenth century was a new world, and this new world can be thought of as divided into three phases, three family generations. There was first of all, after the Golden Age of Independence and the Constitution, a Silver Age, from 1800 to 1830, an age of consolidation and of rule by gentlemen, of ignominy and glory on land and sea during Mr. Madison's inconclusive war of 1812, and finally the rout of the old order, as represented by John Quincy Adams and Nicholas Biddle, by Democracy under that madman from the West, Andrew Jackson.

The second phase or generation, the Iron Age, saw the beginnings of the most dreadful of national issues, the battle over slavery, and the beginnings of the most extraordinary of national changes, the transformation of America from a rural to an industrial nation. The period climaxes of course in the Civil War and its immediate aftermath. Its most significant family member is, equally of course, Robert Edward Lee, who led the wrong side for the right reasons so gloriously to defeat; and, opposing him, that coldly successful diplomat, Charles Francis Adams.

A new, third, less elevated phase must be dated from the accession of Grant to that of Theodore Roosevelt, roughly 1870 to 1900, the Gilded Age. This was the longest low ebb in American political and spiritual and esthetic morality, yet it witnessed the final triumph of industrial capitalism and the building up of the forces of reform.

Of these three phases, only the first could be said to be conceivably a period dominated by men of family.

Until the Jacksonian Revolution, the country was run under the shadow of the Founding Fathers, either by founders themselves, like Jefferson and Madison, or by their disciples and heirs. For a government supposedly the most progressive and radical and experimental on earth at the time, it was a peculiar situation. All the first five Presidents after Washington — John Adams, Jefferson, Madison, Monroe and John Quincy Adams — succeeded each other over a period of forty years as though by right of office rather than by election. First the Vice Presidents succeeded the Presidents (Adams, Jefferson), then the secretaries of state (Madison, Monroe, J. Q. Adams). They were all Virginians or Yankees, and in fact all from two family clans, the Virginia Oligarchy and the Braintree Faction. All were from the same small social circle of born or self-made gentlemen. There was certainly an atmosphere of collusion and exclusion, of hereditary laying on of hands; awfully conservative for a democracy based on a revolution. The regimes of Monroe and John Quincy Adams, of the hand-picked disciple and the favorite son, seemed to exaggerate and exacerbate the feeling, particularly strong in the West and the Middle States, that America was going to be run forever by the members not just of a club, but of two family groups.

It is therefore natural that during this curiously aristocratic half century the Gentleman should have come to one of his finest and most fulsome American flowerings. There existed in the period between 1800 and 1830 two rather antagonistic ideal prototypes of this American Gentleman. One was the Dilettante, friend of arts and letters, patron of politics and science, of agriculture and industry, who might dabble in commerce, scribble a drama, grow trees, serve a term or two in Congress, go on a diplomatic mission abroad, and meanwhile be sure to run a fine town house and country place with dashing carriages and an heiress for hostess and wife. This type, modeled on the eighteenth century as exhibited in the Cadwaladers and representative principally of the middle states, had its counterparts to the North and South. Josiah Quincy of Boston, aristocrat of all trades, choleric individualist; George Washington Parke Custis of "Arlington" in Virginia, playwright, painter and planter; various Roosevelts and Biddles and du Ponts all conform in a degree to this image. The other ideal was that of the Buck, the ridin', drinkin' and above all shootin' hero of army or navy, side-whiskered, high-booted, tight-trousered, the *beau sabreur* whose honor was so delicate that almost any incident could turn into a fatal duel. At his best in war, where he terrorized the British and Algerians, at his worst in politics, where he usually ended up taking pot shots at political opponents, this handsome, heady creature also finds embodiments in various Lees and Biddles.

2

Nicholas Biddle

CERTAINLY the most perfect example of one of these ideals of the time, that of the Gentleman Dilettante, can be found in Nicholas Biddle. Son of tough sailor Charles, Nicholas himself was very much the suave man of the world. Poet, editor, politician, connoisseur of art, one felt he could have turned his hand to anything. In the end, and almost as a matter of chance rather than choice, he took up banking, and became before he was done the benevolent despot of the American economy. So brilliant as a boy that he had to be sent to two colleges in succession to keep him busy, first the University of Pennsylvania, then Princeton, he emerged at that ripe age of fifteen with no very fixed ambitions except a bent towards "law and literature." He could and did write verses, elegant, rather frivolous things, but adept. He was considered one of the best American judges of art, his tastes running in the direction of the antique, the grandeurs that were Greece, and he personally helped to imprint on the youthful Republic a taste for columns and Doric pediments. He not only knew ancient Greek, but modern, picked up on an adventurous trip; he has been called the first American tourist in Greece. He was familiar with Europe, but as the first editor of the journals of the Lewis and Clark expedition, knew more than most Americans about the western wilderness of his own country. He was a diligent horticulturist, a successful progressive farmer, an amateur of sciences. He had his experiences as diplomat, journalist and legislator.

The only really incongruous thing about him is that he should ever have gone into finance. He was certainly as far as possible from being a money-minded go-getter interested only in acquisition, or a hard-headed businessman who scorned fripperies for the practical. Yet he became the unquestioned leader of his profession, and next to President Jackson, he was at one time perhaps the most powerful individual in the country. "I have been for years in the daily exercise of more personal authority than any President habitually enjoys," he answered a friend who suggested that he try for that same presidency. The steel hand in the silk glove, the will under the smile, were part of the act, and though he played the part of dilettante admirably, he became very professional indeed in the intricate swordplay of money and politics.

As one of the half-dozen most important American figures of the second quarter of the century, the Jacksonian era, Nicholas is certainly the most important of the Biddles. But as the Revolutionary generation produced a whole cluster of mildly notable Biddles, so the generation after it was also full of notables of one kind or another. The two main branches, the descendants of sober Clement and of salty Charles, dominated the family chronicle. There were those other branches, but when Victorian Philadelphians thought of Biddles, they thought of the Clements or the Charleses, the Solids or the Romantics.

No other Biddles, even those of the two main branches, had the position and prominence of Nicholas the banker. Yet some of these others were pretty prominent. The sons and daughters of Clement, as might be expected, stuck to Philadelphia and the safe and sound. Thomas, the first son, founded an estimable private banking house, which though of course never as exhilarating as the Bank of the United States has managed to survive into modern times as the investment-brokerage house of Yarnall, Biddle. Brother John joined him in the firm, and battened down the hatches by marrying his cousin Mary Biddle, daughter of Charles. Clement Cornell, still another brother, was a founder and president of still another bank, the Philadelphia Saving Fund Society (PSFS), to this day one of the pillars of Philadelphia respectability and capital. One of the brothers, the youngest, an Edward, disgraced himself by running off to New York and hence beyond the Philadelphia pale, and another went further: George died young and was buried in Macao beside the China Sea.

Clement's daughters, if possible, did even better. Mary eloped with a Cadwalader, son of fancy John, which definitely brought the Biddles into the plumed-bed category. Their children and grandchildren have formed the very core of Philadelphia's nineteenth-century legal old-family complex. Another daughter, Rebecca, married medically, Dr. Nathaniel Chapman, first president of the American Medical Association.

Worthy. Solid.

The contrast with the Romantic branch is illustrative. The children of Charles were restless and active, not safe and sane. Two of them became military heroes, James in the navy and Thomas in the army. Four of them moved westward, with attendant pioneering. James, for instance, carried on the seafaring traditions of his father and his uncle Nicholas. If the War of 1812 accomplished little, at least it did produce heroes, especially naval ones. James was among them. He began the new century by going to sea at the age of seventeen, along with his brilliant brother Edward. Edward died of a fever, but three years later James, still a midshipman, was one of those unfortunate Americans aboard Bainbridge's stranded *Philadelphia* who were imprisoned for nineteen months by the pirates of Tripoli.

James' real career began with the War of 1812. As first lieutenant of the sloop *Wasp,* he led the boarding party that captured the British *Frolic,* only to be recaptured by the British battleship *Poictiers* and again imprisoned, this time in Bermuda. Finally, after being exchanged, Biddle, now captain of the sloop *Hornet,* ran her out of the harbor of New London through the enemy blockade and sailed down to the South Atlantic. There he took on the brig *Penguin* and reduced her in twenty-two minutes to a sinking hulk. As he stood waiting to receive the surrender a British sailor shot him in the chin; but he survived, and captained the *Hornet* in an exciting escape from another pursuing battleship, the *Cornwallis.* The only trouble with this glorious victory of *Hornet* over *Penguin* was that, like the battle of New Orleans, it took place after the peace had been signed. In fact it was the last regular action of the war. Though useless, it added another sweet touch of glory at sea to that achieved by Jackson on land. The eagle screamed.

The rest of his active life was spent cruising all over the world on quasi-diplomatic missions. He sailed round the Horn and up to the Columbia River, where he officially took repossession of the Oregon Territory, occupied by England during the war. He went to Turkey as commodore of the Mediterranean squadron to negotiate a commercial treaty with the Ottoman Empire. He went to China to conclude the first commercial treaty with the Chinese Empire, and he was one of the first to try to break the wall of isolation surrounding Japan. In 1846 he attempted to negotiate with the Japanese government in Tokyo harbor, the first American to do so; but he was not allowed ashore. En route he stopped off to repair the tomb of his cousin George at Macao.

Finally he was given command of the Pacific squadron in the Mexican War (a war which James himself described as that "unjust war we have provoked with Mexico") in a campaign that soon brought California into the Union. The Pacific coast altogether owes quite a debt to James Biddle — Oregon, California. In 1847 at San Francisco he turned over his command to Commodore Shubrick (in-law of the du Ponts; a granddaughter of Pierre married a brother of Commodore Shubrick) and sailed home for good. He died the next year.

He makes the impression of a game, humorous, crusty little fellow (five feet four and a half inches) with much of his father's verve. He never married, but was a devoted uncle to the daughters of Nicholas, and made up for one of them a delightful little autobiography in the form of a sketch-album, depicting his career from his first voyage out in 1800 to his final laying up in drydock in 1848. Throughout the series the commodore is always shown with his back turned.*

Brother Thomas was less prominently heroic and less amiable. He went into the army, as James went into the navy, and ended up a major distinguished for wounds and bravery in two of the few reputable land battles of that same War of 1812, those of Lundy's Lane and Fort Erie along the Great Lakes. He was also one of the four brothers to go West. He ended up in St. Louis in the 1820's as army paymaster, married a local heiress, and got involved in local politics. So involved, in fact, that it killed him. He fought a duel with a congressman from the newly created state of Missouri, one Spencer Pettis. The issue was brother Nicholas's Bank of the United States, the direct cause a beating which violent Thomas gave Pettis in bed, marching into his lodging and pulling off his bedclothes. They repaired to Bloody Island in the middle of the Mississippi. Thomas, being nearsighted, chose pistols at five feet. The two gun barrels clanked against each other. Naturally both duelists were killed, a high price to pay for not wearing spectacles. Hundreds of people came out to watch, and Thomas's widow erected a handsome monument to his memory. It was a most spectacular exit. One of Sully's handsomest portraits shows Thomas as the very model of the Buck, one of the ideals of that period, dashing and dangerous. The duel was certainly his appropriate medium of expression.

As for the other brothers of Nicholas, they too scattered about. In fact Nicholas and his childless, recessive, older brother, the lawyer

---

* See "Commodore James Biddle and His Sketch Book," N. B. Wainwright, *Pennsylvania Magazine,* Vol. XC, No. 1, Jan. 1966.

William Shepard, were the only males of this family to stay in Philadelphia. John, for instance, who also became a major in the War of 1812, went to Michigan. He settled in Detroit and emerged as a founding father of the state. He was the fourth mayor of the city, a delegate to the U.S. Congress from the territory and president of the Michigan Constitutional Convention. He sired a stray but most distinguished branch of Michigan Biddles, who have been conspicuous down to modern times in the army and in medicine. There are still descendants in Michigan. The Biddles in Philadelphia do not seem to have cared much.

Richard, another brother, went to Pittsburgh and to Congress, and wrote a book. Charles failed in business in Philadelphia, moved to Nashville, and finally wound up on the Isthmus of Panama as President Jackson's personal representative in an early attempt to create a crossing there; rather remarkable that a brother of Nicholas should have been Jackson's representative anywhere. The two sisters, Mary and Ann, did almost as well as the daughters of Clement. Mary married her banker cousin John; Ann married a Hopkinson, son of Francis, Signer and poet, which in Philadelphia has always been a good thing to do.

All this would have been enough to keep the Biddles bubbling prosperously in their second, post-Revolutionary generations, and to assure them of continuing First Family status, at least in Philadelphia (and Detroit). But the Great Man of the family, the person who perhaps brings the family up towards the level of the other four, is Nicholas the banker.

Nicholas presents an odd autobiographical problem not met with in these other family chronicles. He was unquestionably a most important man; more questionably, a great one. But whereas no one has any doubts nowadays of the greatness of the great Adamses, Lees and Roosevelts, or of the importance of the du Ponts as a family, Nicholas Biddle's reputation is still in the making. He is a person that might well seem more famous in twenty years than he is now. He labors under the awesome disadvantage of a career in finance, so that no really scholarly or detailed description of his life is comprehensible to a layman.

He labors under still another grave disadvantage. He cannot easily be made the hero of a modern party. Whereas Jackson has been set up, rather dubiously, as a primitive New Dealer, Biddle won't really do as a modern "conservative" banker though he may be. He was a conservative in a true sense perhaps, but not in the perverted sense of being an advocate of "free enterprise" or speculative capitalism. In fact he didn't much approve of unlimited "free enterprise" and his business as bank president was to curb and control it in the general interest. He was a liberal Jeffersonian in politics and even voted for Jackson twice; yet he was, in the end, the most violent of anti-Jacksonians, and the leader of good society in that enmity. He was in fact that always difficult character, the aristocratic liberal. Like his friend John Quincy Adams, he did not and does not fit easily into either wing of the present political spectrum. He had as many enemies on one side as on the other, and his economic program was really more New Deal than was Jacksonian laissez-faire. His personality and associations, however, were definitely Bourbon.

Biddle has other, minor claims to fame — the editorship, for instance, of America's first truly intellectual magazine, the *Port Folio*, and his editing of the Lewis and Clark journals, an edition still something of a classic; but of course his chief claim to remembrance is as president of the second Bank of the United States. Banking was something of a novelty in the United States, even in 1819 when Biddle's banking career began. America's very first true bank had only been founded in Philadelphia in 1781, under the influence of Harry Lee's unfortunate friend Robert Morris. The second was Isaac Roosevelt's Bank of New York, brainchild of Alexander Hamilton. The first Bank of the United States was also Hamilton's idea. He and his followers backed it; Jefferson and his followers naturally fought it. From the very beginning politics was just as important to the idea of the Bank as was finance.

The Bank was organized, just like any other private bank, with headquarters in Philadelphia and branches elsewhere. It had private depositors, private shareholders who received dividends, private directors and a privately elected president. What made it different was that all the U.S. government funds were put into it, and that the government was represented by five directors of the twenty-five on the board. This, of course, gave the Bank tremendous capital and an advantage over any other private bank in the country, but also subjected it to government supervision as well as to all sorts of partisan attacks. Its originators intended it to be a stabilizing influence. It is hard to conceive of such a situation, but at that time there was no universally accepted national paper currency. Any bank could issue bank notes almost at pleasure, and did. The notes of the Bank of the United States became the one sound money in general circulation, and the Bank by its power and policies did serve to keep the economy steady.

The first Bank lasted until 1811, when its recharter failed to pass through Congress. The economic distress that followed led to the establishment of a second Bank in 1816. In 1815 Nicholas Biddle, as a state representative of Pennsylvania, had made a stirring speech in behalf of the institution. He was appointed a government director in 1819 by his old friend President Monroe, and in 1822 succeeded to the Bank's presidency.

There is certainly something odd in the finances of a country being run by a private corporation. When the corporation in turn is run by a private individual, as was the Bank by Biddle, the situation is even more undemocratic and potentially dangerous. If that individual should turn out to be either incompetent or power-mad, the threat to the country in such a situation would be obvious. In fact, Biddle was neither incompetent nor power-mad, though certainly fully power-conscious. He did a superlative job, guided the Bank and the economy through all sorts of ticklish situations, and set up a model of how the American economy might have been organized, and indeed still might be: that is, government charters to private companies run for profit but supervised and checked by the government. Natural law and laissez-faire had very little to do with either the conception or operation of the Bank. The economy was managed, under Biddle, and managed very well indeed, but it was by no means "free."

Unfortunately, the Bank had its hereditary enemies. The tradition of Jefferson and Democracy had always been strong against this threat of oligarchical and central financial control. Jackson and his supporters and the West in general shared this prejudice. The result was a constant campaign alleging that Biddle was in fact incompetent and power-mad, which he was not, and that the Bank, the "hydra-headed monster," was a menace to freedom, which it could easily have been. By "freedom" most of the Westerners meant freedom for speculation, and many Easterners, especially New Yorkers, meant freedom from domination by Philadelphia and freedom for domination by New York. Since Jackson was a Westerner and his chief aide, first secretary of state and then Vice President Van Buren was a New Yorker, both East and West combined against the Bank.

The story of Biddle, the Bank, and its battle is involved, turgid, and not easy to assess or even to describe. The issue dominated the politics of the country during the 1830's. In the end Jackson wrecked the Bank by vetoing a recharter and by withdrawing the government funds. Actually the final blows were delivered by such non-Jacksonians as the Bank of England and a group of the Bank's own directors. Finally, in 1841, Biddle's bank failed. Biddle himself was ruined, the American economy collapsed into cycles of bust and boom that lasted for years, through the 1830's and '40's and '50's, and the system, or lack of system, of economic jungle warfare that led eventually to the corruptions of the Gilded Age and the depression of 1930 was inaugurated. Only when the New Deal began once again to attempt to subject the American economy to some sort of government control was the Biddle-Hamilton theory in part and to some extent vindicated; but of course all under the leadership of Jackson's direct political descendant, that Tribune of the People, Franklin Roosevelt. It is a complicated, century-long bit of historical irony.

Biddle is a personage quite apart from his role as president of the Bank; and "role" here is the proper word. He seems to have been a natural and consummate role player. No one else on the public stage at the time quite so perfectly plays this particular part. He was of course handsome, in youth a perfect curly-headed Byron, though later he got fat. He not only was rich and married an heiress, but he became even richer as a banker. He lived in style — a town house and a beautiful country place on the Delaware called Andalusia, belonging to his wife's family but made over Grecian by him — a style of life quite equal to John Cadwalader's. He gave elaborate parties and indulged in good works and speeches. He was much in the public eye. As Jackson represented both the Buck and the Frontiersman, so Biddle represented Urbanity. James Silk Buckingham, one of the many supercilious Tory Englishmen who visited America to despise, exempted him, conspicuously, from general condemnation. Speaking of the people who had tendered him hospitality in Philadelphia, he wrote,

"Among these I cannot refrain from naming, especially, Mr. Nicholas Biddle . . . because he appeared to me to present the most perfect specimen of American gentleman I had yet seen in the United States. To a mind of great force and originality he added the advantage of an excellent education, highly polished manners, great urbanity, and a perfect freedom from all those peculiarities which, more or less, mark the citizen of every class in this country. His early residence in Europe, and employment in a diplomatic station, was no doubt in part the cause of this exemption from national characteristics; yet while his private hospitalities were conducted in the best possible European taste, and in a style that the most fastidious would admire, his patriotism, frankness, simplicity, and application to business, were thoroughly American, and made him altogether one of the most agreeable, as he is one of the most accomplished members of the community."

A stately if typically backhanded sort of English tribute.

Americans (if they were not Jacksonians) were no less charmed. Even John Quincy Adams was and remained a close friend, a most unusual circumstance. "He liked to be irresistible," as one of his more friendly biographers, Bray Hammond, so aptly put it. The Philadelphia diarist Sidney Fisher gives the picture: "Wherever he appeared there was a sensation and a crowd immediately formed around him. His manner was gracious, smiling, easy, gentleman-like, a little condescending and exhibited supreme self-satisfaction and elation." He was a sparkling conversationalist and expansive host. It was his wide range of interest and talents that so distinguished him from the average businessman and made him, in fact, suspect in ordinary financial circles. John Jacob Astor thought his presidency of the Bank would "not add much to the stock." One gets the impression of an allegorical progress, a darling of the gods moving through flowery financial meads, surrounded by fiddling cherubs, and dispensing largesse — all leading of course towards the dark debacle. As a young man he described his "usual habits of laborious indolence . . . mineralogy and the theater, chemistry and clubs, the laws of nations and the rules of tea parties." Currency problems were among these studies; but only among them. All this elegance and social flair certainly did not endear him to those who adulated rugged Old Hickory. In fact as personalities Jackson and Biddle very aptly symbolize the two permanent polarities of American thought and feeling, the silk stocking and the leather stocking, the East and the West, Henry James and Mark Twain. In fact, if one wanted to track down an original for the *New Yorker*'s Eustace Tilley, that symbolic figure in top hat, high collar and supercilious eyeglass who stares down a butterfly each year in February on the magazine's cover, Nicholas Biddle would do very well indeed.

All these princeling airs enhanced a very real and effective knowledge and interest. Even his hobbies were influential. His great greenhouses at Andalusia, where he raised silkworms and rare grapes, were famous, as were his thoroughbred horses, cattle and sheep. He put the stamp of his esthetic taste permanently on his city and country. Three important Philadelphia buildings, his own house Andalusia, the building of his second Bank and the complex of Girard College, remain as monuments to the Neo-Grecian style he admired. Thomas U. Walter, his pet architect, went on to design the Roman dome of the capitol, so furiously imitated all over the country, probably the nation's most famous architectural landmark. Washington, D.C. is itself a sort of stepchild of Biddle's patronage. Certainly it was Biddle's influence that fastened the Doric column on banks, exemplified by the building on Chestnut Street, as somewhat ironic symbol of stability.

In literature he also had a real, if never properly developed, flair for Anacreontic verse, the late-Regency light touch. The "Ode to Bogle" is the best specimen of his skill, a *jeu d'esprit* that is the very model of Tom Moore sophistication.*

By 1841 Biddle was a ruined man. The Bank had failed, dragging down with it the country's prosperity. Biddle was blamed for the disaster caused by his enemies. John Quincy Adams had dinner with him in November 1840, just before the crash. "I dined with Mr. Nicholas Biddle en famille. . . . We sat after dinner settling the nation . . . little satisfied with the result . . . Biddle broods with smiling face and stifled groans over the wreck of splendid blasted expectations and ruined hopes. A fair mind, a brilliant genius, a generous temper, an honest heart, waylaid and led astray by prosperity, suffering the penalty of scarcely voluntary error — 'tis piteous to behold."

Whether his fall was the proper chastisement of hubris, the result of his excess of pride, of that "self-satisfaction and elation," whether

---

* Dedicated to his four-year-old daughter Meta, it celebrates one of those ubiquitous Negro caterers, as familiar today in Philadelphia as in 1829, without whom no ceremonial occasion is complete. It typifies period and man, and shows a nice skill and a pleasant humor. See Appendix IV.

the Bank was the black citadel of oligarchy stormed, like the Bastille, by the people in the name of freedom; or whether, on the contrary, Biddle did more than any human being to stem the flood of chaotic speculation which caused the depressions of the 1830's, '40's and '50's remains a matter of controversy almost as intense now as then. If you read Schlesinger's popular but wholly biased *Age of Jackson* you get the picture of Jackson as an early FDR and of Biddle as a malefactor of great wealth. If you read economists like Bray Hammond and the equally biased Thomas Govan you get the impression of Biddle as an early New Dealer battling in vain against ruthless laissez-faire speculation. Granted that Schlesinger's interpretation is totally one-sided, still — the Bank *was* a threat, actual or potential, Biddle *did* go in for some pretty devious and ruthless politics, reactionaries *were* back of him, fighting Jackson and democracy too.

In any case, at least Biddle was a far more important and interesting figure than he has generally been given credit for being. He belongs in the great line of American financiers that stretches from Robert Morris and Hamilton to the Morgans through Stephen Girard, Astor, Drexel, Jay Cooke. They were very powerful, they were very colorful, most of them were ardent and practical patriots who saved the country in desperate need (incidentally, of course, making fortunes themselves). Quite a few of them — Morris, Biddle, Cooke — were ruined. It is a panorama that should be properly painted. In this panorama Biddle would be the most important figure of his particular era. So far the story has been told either by political historians like Schlesinger, usually with an axe to grind, or by economists who are difficult to understand. Someday we can hope for more light, and in that light Biddle's stature will probably increase. Meanwhile he remains a representative figure of his period, and the greatest of the Biddles.

There were other, later Biddles crowding the nineteenth century. The family was nothing if not prolific. The third generation followed the Quaker formula faithfully and bred well. None of them, however, recaptured the heights held by Nicholas as national figure. In Philadelphia, which as far as Philadelphia was concerned was all that mattered, Biddles of one branch or another filled every available niche: presidents of banks, clubs and societies, leaders of the right balls and the right causes ("the laws of nations and the rules of tea parties"). A curious example of their numbers and influence is the list of nineteenth-century Biddles who were members of the American Philosophical Society, then as now the oldest and one of the most august of our scientific bodies. Founded by Benjamin Franklin, it included as members not only bona-fide scientists like David Rittenhouse and Franklin himself, but also Founding Fathers like Washington, Adams, Hamilton, Jefferson. Of Revolutionary Biddles four were members (Owen as scientist, Clement, Judge James and Edward as, presumably, Founding Fathers). In the next century there were no less than a round dozen. Not one of them was a scientist, not one a Founding Father: such men as banker Nicholas, banker Thomas, banker Clement C; sixteen Biddles all told. It was obvious that the reasons for inclusion were purely Family reasons. Biddles had to be included, along with all their relations like the Cadwaladers (seven all told), Rawles (six), and many other not really very philosophical types. By 1900 it was no longer individual Biddles who counted so much as the total mass. In the Philadelphia Club, Philadelphia's best and the nation's oldest, there have been some forty Biddles, which must be an American club record for one family. Even to this day no charitable or institutional board in Philadelphia is complete without its Biddle, male or female. It is hard to think of any city of equivalent size quite so permeated for quite so long by one name — Lowells in Boston, Tafts in Cincinnati?

Out of this nineteenth-century mass, however, though there are plenty of characters and plenty of worthies, there were not many really famous individuals. The Solids are more numerous than the Romantics, since the latter were represented only by the sons of

Nicholas. A proper Romantic might be Charles John, his second son, who kept the flag flying by becoming a hero in the Mexican War. This was more rare than heroism in the War of 1812. At the siege of Chapultepec, when he was left behind by his regiment, ill with tropical fever, he found an old horse that had also been left behind, rushed to the scene of battle clutching only a ramrod for a weapon, and was the second American to set foot on the ramparts. During the Civil War he gave up a commission as colonel in the army to serve as a Democrat in Congress, and afterwards became the editor of a Democratic paper in Philadelphia, stronghold of Republicanism. He managed to survive even this, and had seven children. Everybody seemed to love him in spite of his politics.

It was a Solid Biddle who came closest to Civil War heroism in the family. A Henry was an adjutant general of reserves and died of wounds received before Richmond in 1862. On the whole the Biddles were not as conspicuous in this war as they had been in previous ones. The Solids could be best represented not by military men but by George Washington Biddle, grandson of Revolutionary Clement, son of PSFS Clement C. George Washington Biddle was Chancellor of the Bar Association and the leader of his profession in Philadelphia during his eminent maturity. In Philadelphia that's just about as eminent as one can get. He translated Greek for fun.

From a Family, rather than a purely individual point of view, the most spectacular event of the century was the marriage of a grandson of Nicholas, an Edward, to Emily Drexel. Edward was the son of another Edward who had married a Spaniard, and the Biddle-Drexel nuptials were considered to be of awe-inspiring dynastic importance, a by-now old name linked to one of the most impressive of new ones. There used to be jokes around Philadelphia about the city's being founded at the confluence of the Biddles and the Drexels. Francis Drexel had been an itinerant Austrian portrait painter, who made money rather mysteriously in South America and then settled in Philadelphia before the Civil War to found one of the world's great investment houses. It still exists today, still famous;

under its wing the great Morgan sheltered for years as junior partner and New York representative before he finally set up on his own.

Drexel-marrying Edward Biddle was of course by now in the fourth generation from the family's establishment (Charles, Nicholas, Edward, Edward). The marriage of Mary Biddle, daughter of Clement, in the second generation of affluence, to Thomas Cadwalader was exactly the opposite. Then it had been the older Cadwaladers marrying the new Biddles; now it was old Biddles marrying new Drexels. Exactly the same pattern was followed, one generation sooner, when the brand-new John Adams married into the old Quincys, and when the third-generation old Adamses married the second-generation new Brookses. Unlike Charles Francis Adams, Edward Biddle never particularly distinguished himself, but he was progenitor of one of the more spectacular twentieth-century Biddle lines, that of madcap Anthony, happiest of millionaires, and his children.

America, however, was and is full of other Biddles, as it is full of Adamses, who are actually true Biddles, descendants of the original Jersey settlers. Opposed to the du Ponts, where every du Pont (but not Dupont) is a genuine family member, or to the Roosevelts, where almost anyone named Roosevelt is assumed to be kin, opposed on the other hand to the Adamses where the only Adamses, no matter how distinguished, who are considered to be true Adamses are the scanty handful of descendants of the two Presidents, the Biddles, all through the nineteenth century came in three groups, like a sociological study: Upper Biddles, Middle Biddles and Lower Biddles. Principal Upper Biddles were and are the Solids and Romantics, but there were many others. There were the Reading (Pennsylvania) Biddles, descendants of Judge James, the eldest line, once prominent in Berks County but now extinct; or the Carlisle (Pennsylvania) Biddles, who were really McFunns. These were sprung from that old salt-in-law Captain McFunn of the British navy, whose example and advice started the whole Biddle naval tradition. His son, William Biddle McFunn switched his name around to McFunn Biddle, and henceforth all his children have been accounted true Biddles. By now they are thoroughly embedded in Philadelphia upper-class circles.

The Lower Biddles have had no such luck. They were Biddles who stayed in New Jersey instead of moving to Philadelphia. Most of them in later generations moved westward to Pittsburgh, to Indiana, Colorado, Oregon. There were, and no doubt are, hundreds of them, though never as many as Adamses, and like the vagrant Vespasian and Veranes of that family, no one ever heard of them in the East again. Some became dentists, some became grocers, most were farmers. One of these in a later time, an Arney Biddle born of a westward-moving branch, emerged in the twentieth century into *Who's Who* as a prominent Presbyterian clergyman in Jersey City. This did not make him an Upper Biddle.

The case of the Middle Biddles is more ambivalent. These were the descendants of Owen, the scientific Quaker watchmaker. They remained very much Quakers, and for several generations watchmakers or the equivalent — druggists, hardware merchants, silversmiths. They were a God-fearing lot, totally secluded from the worldliness of cousin Nicholas or the Cadwaladers. Their biographies are full of homely touches. Of a William Biddle it was said, "His father's sudden death during a summer thunderstorm in 1815 may have helped the nine year old boy to decide that he too would be a retail druggist." Of Clement, devout Friend of Chadds Ford, it was said that "As a very young man he gave up fancy vests and the much loved study of chess" to pursue the Inner Light. Poor Anne became "the typical benevolent maiden aunt. . . . Owing to the extreme care which her father took of his health . . . the family retired to bed so early that no opportunity was given to Anne when young to entertain suitors."

But gradually riches and worldliness overtook these simple folk, and from being thunder-inspired retail druggists they became presidents of small railroads. The famous firm of silversmiths, Bailey, Banks and Biddle,* was established and grew into one of Philadelphia's traditions. John Biddle, president of the Locust Mountain Coal and Iron Company, "in late life . . . became so devoted to the study of genealogy that those ignorant of it sometimes tired of his talk on it"; and Robert, a big man in hardware, "more than most members of the Society . . . combined a Grecian appreciation of beauty . . . with the . . . ideals of Quakerism." Robert moved back to New Jersey, and at Riverton, right opposite Andalusia on the Delaware, established his own pleasure dome. It is doubtful if the Biddles across the water recognized him as kissing kin. Marriages and fortunes, however, were made, and by 1900 these Middle Biddles were all over the place, connected with other rising Philadelphia families, many of them also Quaker like the Canbys from Wilmington, the ubiquitous Rhoads, the more dashing Griscoms and Clays or the German Fitlers, family of the present Mrs. Nelson Rockefeller.

A startling butterfly to flutter from this branch was a James Canby Biddle-Cope, who "owing to visits to England when a boy . . . conceived a great love for the mother country and her ancient social distinctions." In a somewhat desperate effort to achieve true Britishness, he hyphenated his name, dabbled with Oxford, the Church, the army. He bought beautiful old country places. Finally he wrote novels. One of these, laid in Philadelphia, dealt "with characters apparently drawn from old acquaintances," which "did not produce at all a favorable impression among these circles." Finally, despairing of an English peerage, he turned to Rome and was made a papal nobleman and an Italian baron, calling himself the Marquis Biddle-Cope.

But he broke with this church too. "Domestic difficulties, in which his friends could not at all sympathize . . . led to a somewhat wandering life": Australia, Fiji, the Alps, Asheville, North

* In *The Perennial Philadelphians* I intimated that these Bailey, Banks Biddles were not true Biddles. They are.

Carolina. One of his daughters married a Baron Calenda di Tavani. It was all a far cry from giving up fancy vests.

So by now these Middle Biddles have caught up socially to the others, and are all over Philadelphia, counted as genuinely Upper Biddles. A very recent headline in the social pages of the *Philadelphia Inquirer* announced "A. P. G. Biddle Chooses Best Man" (to hell with the bride, a non-Philadelphian). This Augustus Peabody Gardner lived in a place called Canby House and is the son of a Henry Canby Biddle II. Days of thunderstruck retail druggery are long past.

Nonetheless, from the collapse of the Bank and the ruin of Nicholas, no Biddle has ever again been as influential and prominent in American history; 1841 marks the crest in the history of this family, as does 1865 in the history of the Lees. The Biddles, and indeed most upper-class Philadelphians, had learned their lesson: stay out of politics. From this time forth, until Teddy Roosevelt, it began to be considered degrading to serve the nation as an elected official. The triumph of Jacksonianism put an end for many decades to the benevolent rule by aristocrats and by gentlemen dilettantes. When Biddle shut the classic doors of Andalusia behind him, living there in scholarly seclusion till his death in 1844, he closed an era. Not until Franklin Roosevelt did Biddles again appear prominently on the national stage.

3

John Quincy Adams

"I MUST STUDY politics and war that my sons may have liberty to study mathematics and philosophy. My sons ought to study mathematics and philosophy, geography, natural history and naval architecture . . . in order to give their children a right to study painting, poetry, music, architecture, statuary, tapestry and porcelain." This, one of the most famous quotations from John Adams, is one of the most revealing. It is, quite obviously, a proposal for the development of America as a whole; also as obviously the legacy of a self-made man to his children. The fact that Adams identified America and the Adams family is typical Adams. In fact America was already way ahead of John Adams, had already produced some of its best painters (Stuart, Copley, Peale), some considerable poets (Freneau, Barlow), and even a few musicians (the Moravians, Hopkinson, Billings). All these were contemporaries of Adams. He knew some of them but was not able to make just estimates. American architecture and craftsmanship, in such people as goldsmith Roosevelt, had reached an all-time high. Even more to the point, his own family outstripped his predictions. John Quincy Adams in his proper person summed up all the stages of his father's educational program.

John Quincy Adams was in fact another potential specimen of the Gentleman Dilettante of the Silver Age, quite on the order of Nicholas Biddle. He was not natively as gifted. His poetry, for instance, is far less elegant, though often surprisingly similar in tone. He had no noticeable taste in the fine arts. Scientifically, however, he accomplished a great deal more. Though his experiments in tree growing went no further than Biddle's silkworms and glass houses, his report on weights and measures, completed in 1821 while he was secretary of state, is a true accomplishment, and his persistence as congressman in the foundation of the Smithsonian Institution is a monument to his foresight and obstinacy. But like Nicholas Biddle, he too responded to the whole world of culture and affairs with some of the same many-sidedness. He had after all been educated in the courts and diplomatic circles of Europe, he was passionately fond of the theater, a most un-Puritan trait, and knew it in various languages, notably French. He was formidably self-educated in literature and read Latin, Greek, French, German, Italian and even Dutch and Spanish. He seriously loved poetry and as seriously wrote it. But . . . he was poor; he was a Puritan; he was an Adams. Whereas Biddle was rich, was an epicure, and felt no need to follow in his father's rugged footsteps, was in fact happy to preen in the sun of second-generation affluence, poor John Quincy was a hag-ridden, hypnotized, duty-whipped victim of compulsions and obligations — mostly family ones. Like any good Puritan he never felt truly happy unless he was doing something that made him utterly miserable. But at least he knew he was *right,* that God was on his side. Only this conviction could have kept this tortured soul afloat. Where his brother Charles sank under the weight, succumbing to speculation and drink; whereas his other brother Thomas, after a promising start as a diplomatic assistant, business adviser to the family, and lawyer (he was briefly [1809-11] Chief Justice of Mass.), also succumbed to middle-aged alcoholism, John Quincy Adams survived. He did his duty; that is, he followed in his father's footsteps.

It is impossible not to like prim, pursy, fussy, funny John and his apple-cheeked romance with Abigail. For all his pettiness, jealousy, touchiness, meanness, self-righteousness, he is hard to hate. The beautiful sunset reconciliation with Jefferson gives a benedictory glow to this enemy of optimism and liberalism, from the one quarter that might have remained unreconciled, and cancels out much of the possible animus against him. But John Quincy is something else again. He is admirable. One can be terribly sorry for him. One can smile with or at his terrible saber attacks on the Devil, as embodied in the persons of those who disagreed with him. But I defy anyone to really *like* him. Respect, pity, a glow of heart for the stubborn fight for freedom of speech with which he ended his days, for his honesty, for his integrity; but he is so grim, so pathological a hater, so devastatingly obtuse and cruel, especially as a father, and such a total, deliberate failure as a politician. However, as a person, he is undoubtedly interesting. In that wonderful gallery of heroes and hams strutting through American history in the first half of the nineteenth century — Clay, Calhoun, Webster, Biddle and Jackson — Adams is outstanding.

What did he do? Well, he did *exactly* what his father did. Exactly. This is the uncanny, the really incredible, indeed the supernaturally coincidental pattern of his career. Fate? Chance? The Hand of God or Providence? Family tradition and genes? There is an odd, Mephistophelian whiff of sulphur to it. Compare the careers of father and son, step by step, date by date:

1735; 1767: Born in Braintree (later Quincy), Massachusetts, son of a John Adams. Of three brothers, one died young, one lived on into obscure mediocrity, neither leaving any distinguished Adams descendants; and one became a national figure.

Early Schooling: The patterns diverge. John received his education at home in local schools; John Quincy abroad in Paris and the Low Countries. At fourteen, JQA went to Russia as secretary to the diplomat Francis Dana, and had almost no more formal pre-college schooling.

1755; 1787: Graduated from Harvard.

1758; 1790: Admitted to the bar of Massachusetts after studying law in a provincial town (Worcester; Newburyport).

1764; 1797: Marriage, after breaking off a previous affair (Hannah Quincy of Braintree; Mary Frazier of Newburyport), to a woman with a plain name (Smith; Johnson) but prominent connections, Abigail Smith being kin of the Quincys of Braintree; Louisa Johnson niece of Thomas Johnson, first post-Revolutionary governor of Maryland (Johnson was succeeded by Thomas Sim Lee).

1765 on; 1801 on: Children. A daughter that died an infant. Of three sons, one died young (and disgraced), one lived on into obscure mediocrity, neither leaving any distinguished Adams descendants; and one became a national figure.*

1760–74; 1791–1803: An early public career of law and the writing of anonymous letters in Boston newspapers. However, here too there is a divergence, parallel to that of early education. John spent all these early years in Boston, active in American politics; John Quincy's first steps up the ladder were in Europe. He was appointed minister to the Netherlands by Washington in 1794, then minister to Prussia.

1774; 1803: John, after a brief spell as a state representative (member of the General Court) in 1770–71, went to Philadelphia and the Continental Congress. John Quincy, after a brief spell as state senator in 1802, went to Washington as senator from Massachusetts.

1778; 1809: Sent abroad as a diplomat; JA to France, JQA to Russia.

1782; 1814: Appointed peace commissioner; signer of a treaty

---

* Another divergence here. John Adams had a daughter Abigail who lived. She married a Smith (no kin) so that whereas Abigail Smith became Abigail Adams, Abigail Adams became Abigail Smith. Daughter Abigail Adams Smith also had a niece, daughter of her ne'er-do-well brother Charles Adams (he having married Abigail's sister-in-law, a Smith). This niece, Abigail Adams, married a Johnson (no kin), important people of Utica, New York. The son of Abigail Adams Smith, a William Steuben Smith Jr., married Catherine Johnson, sister of Louisa Johnson Adams. Abigail Adams Johnson of Utica in turn had a son William Johnson who married a Louisa Adams, daughter of JQA's son John and his first-cousin wife Mary Hellen, daughter of another sister of Louisa Johnson Adams. Clear? See Appendix V.

with England (along with Frank*in*, J*ay*; Gall*atin*, Cl*ay* — men whose names end with "in" and "ay").

1785; 1815: First postwar minister to England (aged fifty; forty-eight).

1789; 1817: Assumes place of second in command and heir apparent in the U.S. government (Vice President for two terms under Washington; secretary of state for two terms under Monroe).

1797; 1825: President of the United States, for one term only. Destroyed largely by the disloyalty and machinations of men of his own party, and defeated by an adversary, once a friend, but by now a bitter enemy (Jack*son*; Jeffer*son*. Their names both begin with "J" and end in "son"; carrying this a bit too far?). Both father and son deliberately refused to attend the inauguration of their successors. Only Andrew Johnson among other Presidents seems to have done likewise.

1800; 1829: The gloom of political defeat was aggravated in each case by the almost simultaneous death of a favorite son in disgrace, Charles as ne'er-do-well, George as suicide. Plunged into political obscurity, both men retired to Quincy. Neither John nor John Quincy Adams (nor, in fact, any later Adams) ever again held an important elective office; but JQA was almost immediately elected (1831) to Congress as representative for his home district and had a glorious and cantankerous career, for seventeen successive years, as defender of freedom of speech and freedom of petition against the slave oligarchy. When the South, by means of the notorious Gag Rule, tried to prevent antislavery petitions from being presented in Congress, John Quincy Adams fought them to final victory in 1844 with the repeal of the Gag Rule. Though always an antiabolitionist, he became one of the earliest political leaders against the divisive and tyrannical power of slavery in the U.S. government.

1753–1804; 1779–1848: Kept a diary.

July 4, 1826; February 23, 1848: Died; buried in Quincy.

Of how many fathers and sons is it possible to sketch such a minute double history? In other words, except for three periods in the two respective lives — boyhood educations, early career, and final phase — the paths of father and son run exactly parallel. It is really too much, especially those crucial years — service in the state legislature, election to the national legislature, diplomatic appointment to Europe, signer of a peace treaty with and then minister to Great Britain, second in command at home, President, defeat after one term — and death of a favorite son in disgrace! This all just can't be "mere coincidence"! In an elective democracy, even such a limited one as America then was, the odds against a son being able to so duplicate a father's public career are astronomical. Yet JQA did it — and, one feels, hated every minute of it. Only at the last, when he Drank the Cup (which is certainly how he felt about it) of the presidency and was pitched into limbo, bitter yet relieved (just like father), was he at last a free man. It is from then on that he emerges as the champion of freedom that he had it in him to become. One of the most curious Family histories in history. Along with John's death on July 4, this incredible parallelism of Adams careers has something *fated* about it. One of the essential characteristics of great families, like great individuals, is that they have this "fatal" character, generation after generation.

His actual accomplishments, aside perhaps from his defeat of the Gag Rule, are really rather unimportant. He was an excellent diplomat, perhaps the best in America at the time, and did much to lay down the course of America's foreign policy for the century; but his residences in Holland, Prussia, Russia and England were not characterized by any specially notable single incidents or achievements. His role as peace commissioner was important, but no more so than that of Gallatin or Clay. Notably, again just like his father, he secured the right of the North Atlantic fisheries for New Englanders from British attempts to curtail them. As secretary of state, his part in molding the Monroe Doctrine was important, but not all-important. He secured Florida for the United States, helped secure the Northwest, and did much to establish the Canadian boundary. As President he was able to do nothing, and spent perhaps the most useless years of his useful career. Yet this presidency, which of course it was his duty to achieve if he hoped to catch up to Father, cost him the most precious possible piece of Adams jewelry, integrity. He came near to selling his soul to get the presidency, and he paid for it.

The story of John Quincy Adams' elevation to the presidency has all the flamboyant trappings which seemed to surround the events of that flamboyant period. It was at once the zenith and nadir, crux and collapse of the fortunes of the Adams family. That is, President Adams was the only son of a President ever to be President; and after him no Adams was President, or anything else elective except congressman. As a crisis in family fortunes it compares with Appomattox for the Lees, or the ruin of the Bank for the Biddles.

America, for the one time in its history, was a one-party country. As a result, the election of 1824 was scattered among various favorite sons. Of these, four emerged as preeminent, but no one preeminent enough. They were of course all "Republicans," i.e., Democrats. Andrew Jackson was the popular figure, not because of any political experience, but just because he was Old Hickory, victor of New Orleans. He got the biggest vote. Next came John Quincy Adams, not because he was popular, but because he was heir apparent to Monroe, having been secretary of state. Two others, Crawford and Clay, were prominent politicians. Crawford's ill health eliminated him.

The election was thrown into the House of Representatives, where the vote went by states, not by number of votes. Two things became obvious: Jackson deserved the presidency on the basis of his popular plurality; anyone who got Clay's votes in the House of Representatives would probably win. Clay hated both Adams and Jackson, but Adams needed Clay more than Jackson did. What happened was that Clay and Adams had a little conference. Both swore that no promises were made. Probably none were; but significantly, this interview is one of the curious gaps in the monumental Adams diary. Hundreds of routine official and diplomatic conversations are summarized or quoted there. This, the most important conversation in John Quincy's life, was not. Probably nothing was said; but Clay's votes went for Adams, Adams became President, Clay became secretary of state and hence heir apparent. No doubt Clay's fear of Jackson would have made him turn to Adams in any case. No doubt Clay was best qualified for secretary of state, and would have been appointed in any case. But . . . for an Adams it all came much too close to politically corrupt compromise to be comfortable.

Actually the final vote for Adams was determined by God, as was of course appropriate. Old Stephen Van Rensselaer, last of the patroons, and representative from New York, was undecided. Van Buren had almost persuaded him to vote against Adams. Since Van Rensselaer was a brother-in-law of Hamilton, this was not too difficult. He went to his seat in the chamber, bowed his head in prayer to ask for divine guidance, and when he opened his eyes, saw an Adams ballot lying on the floor. God having so spoken, he picked up the ballot and voted for Adams. The votes of New York thus went for Adams, and the presidency too.

The infuriated Jacksonians, feeling quite justly swindled out of the office, made the most of the Clay-Adams rapprochement. It was called everywhere a "corrupt bargain." The label stuck. It destroyed the political careers of both men, and made Jackson President in the next election. John Randolph, who hated everyone, made a memorable speech in which he compared the brilliant Clay to rotten mackerel by moonlight that "shines and stinks and stinks and shines," and spoke of the 'corrupt bargain' as a combination "unheard of till then" of Blifil and Black George, the "Puritan with the black-leg." All educated Americans of course knew their *Tom Jones* well enough in those days to get the allusion immediately. Clay challenged Randolph to a duel. Nobody was hurt, though Clay's bullet punctured Randolph's coat. Senator Thomas Hart Benton thought it the "highest toned" duel he had ever witnessed, though he witnessed many. Monroe's Era of Good Feeling was definitely over.

Adams' vision of being a President not of a party but of a whole nation — of embarking on a course of increased governmental revenues from the proper management of the sale of public lands, which revenues were to be devoted to internal improvement — all came to nothing. This was another project that had to await FDR. His proposal for government-sponsored observatories, "lighthouses of the skies," was laughed to scorn. When time came for reelection, he was done for. This presidency, for which he had come so close to cheating, was of all his disappointments the greatest. Still, he had followed his father's footsteps, right to the bitter end. He had done his duty, miserable though it made him. His debt to the ambitions of the Adams family was paid.

Now he could retire to letters and leisure. For all this time, through years of diplomacy and politics, John Quincy Adams fancied himself as a writer. He *was* a writer. He was the only man to sit in the presidency who could be called "a poet." He was not a very good poet, but he was a poet, not merely like Biddle an occasional writer of verse. It seems very odd that this fact has not been more emphasized and studied. There is, for instance, no full collection of his poetical works, no full study of his poetry. As in everything else, he approached poetry with dogged, disillusioned devotion. He wrote stern, religious sonnets, mostly secreted in his diary. He wrote gay, graceful album pieces, most un-Puritan. More expectedly, he made many a dreary metrical version of the Psalms. He translated the German poetical romance *Oberon* by the once-popular Wieland.* This is no fragment or pastime, but a solid, laborious achievement. When finally printed in 1940 it came to some 314 pages of rhymed poetry. It is the only full translation into Eng-

* As Pierre du Pont translated *Orlando*.

lish of this influential and unreadable work. He himself also wrote
and even had published a poetical romance, a queer little epic called
Dermot Mac Morrogh, all about early Ireland. His most popular
poem was a queer half-cynical, half-moralistic piece called "The
Wants of Man," partly in the flippant Biddle style, partly in a prosy
Puritan vein. It reveals, like so many of his works and deeds, this
conflict of irreconcilables — the worldly, European-educated, thea-
ter-loving dilettante; the tortured, God-fearing, father-loving-and-
hating New Englander. What is one to make, for instance, of the
Byronism of his otherwise seriously intended epic? Lines like (p.
22, Canto I, xvii):

> *Dermot Mac Morrogh cast lascivious eyes*
> *On Dovergilda, wife of Breffny's prince.*
> *This need not startle readers with surprise;*
> *Such things have happen'd both before and since.*

Or (p. 48, Canto II, xli):

> *In fresh pursuit of Dermot fifty men*
> *Had been dispatched, but he their search eluded;*
> *For refuge fled to forest, wild, or glen*
> *Or climbed an oak, as once, Charles Stuart, you did.*

One is constantly baffled by alternations of the solemn and the silly.
Nonetheless, his *Poems of Religion and Society* sold over four thousand copies, good for a poet anywhere, anytime.

Actually, as poet of a low ebb in American poetry, post-Freneau
and pre-Poe, he is not all that bad, comparatively. In his diary he
quotes a list of the chief contemporary American poets — Percival,
Halleck, Dana, Bryant, Peabody, Willis. With the exception of
Bryant, Adams is perhaps their equal or even superior. His rock-
bound sonnets have sincerity and weight, his album pieces grace.*

And then, as a writer, there's that diary. It is unquestionably a

---

* Perhaps his best poem is a "letter" in rhyme describing his day as a senator
in 1807 in thoroughly lighthearted Biddle fashion. See Appendix IV.

monument. It gives actual participant accounts of all sorts of diplomatic and political events, from chats with the czar to battles in Congress. It's a mine of information for historians. Unfortunately, though few historians seem willing to admit it, the diary is dull, dull, dull. Where the diary of the father breaks open into humor and vividness, the diary of the son is overwhelmingly dry, prosy, matter-of-fact. Here is a man who saw everything, was an actor in great scenes from 1800 on, but was usually unable or unwilling to bring any of it to life. Occasionally a page or two of the journal or of the equally monumental correspondence* does speak — a detailed description of a state banquet in Russia, a sulphurous attack on an ex-friend. He has been accused of a total lack of humor. If one means genial joking, or an appreciation of his own absurdities, that's true enough. But he can be sort of humorous in a slashing, sardonic phrase. Adams walks into the Senate on March 16, 1838, "John C. Calhoun discoursing to his own honor and glory and vituperating Henry Clay — upon which delicious topics he had already been two hours occupied." Or, at the dedication of the Bunker Hill Monument in 1843, "Daniel Webster spouting and John Tyler's nose, with a shadow outstretching that of the monumental column. . . ." †

Hate always brought out the best in John Quincy Adams.

Hatred of the slave power in the House and its arrogant undemocratic tactics brought out the best in him in those last days as representative. He was, like his father again, basing his fight on legal, not on just moral or emotional grounds. He was not an abolitionist crusader. Unlike his father, however, he did not live to see the final

---

* JQA's first letter, as a boy of 11, is to Arthur Lee thanking him for the gift of a ponderous tome on French law, in French.

† Actually, part of the dullness of the diary is due to editing. Pious Charles Francis Adams deliberately cut out all "details of common life," that is to say, everything that makes most diaries interesting. He also deliberately put in every single thing he thought might be of historic interest. Allan Nevins' one-volume abridgment relieves some of the tedium; but still, as in the case of John Adams, some final selective editorial job will eventually have to be done, reinserting the details, pruning the "historic interest," before the mass of JQA material will be generally palatable.

and ultimate victory of his cause. He toppled over at his desk in the House in 1848, and died, as he certainly would have preferred, doing his duty. The dilettante, the gentleman of leisure and letters he liked to think of himself as being, never had a chance against the ferocious political in-fighter he really was, the "bruiser," as Emerson called him.

It is as husband and father, as a man of family, that he makes his most equivocal appearance. He could be accounted, somewhat grudgingly, as a success in both areas. His wife stayed sane and stayed with him. One, at least, of his sons turned out well. Nowhere does the change of climate, the difference between the generations, show more clearly than in those marriages. The love affair of John and Abigail was a hardy one, brisk, affirmative, full of warmth and grit. The love of his son and Louisa is, by contrast, moonstruck, full of neuroses and shadows. "A more pitiable set I do not think I know than my father and mother," diarized that cold but acute prig, Charles Francis, of them. John Adams had rebounded from his previous unsuccessful pursuit of flirtatious Hannah Quincy with no psychic scars. John Quincy's affair with Mary Frazier of Newburyport was something else again. It had been a serious business. The families decided it was imprudent, they were too young. John Quincy of course acquiesced; but the breakup seemed to have had a permanently crippling effect. After this the dour, repressed, stiff man of later years takes the place of a far more active and normal boy. Then came England and Louisa. She too seems to have just recovered from a serious love disappointment. Then, shortly after they were married, Louisa's father went bankrupt. If her husband had had any Jane Austen "expectations" they were unfulfilled. This preyed much on Louisa's mind. She was in any case an introspective, rather frail Anglo-Southern blossom. She did not really like New England, or politics, or official entertaining in Washington. One feels she would have preferred to wander at twilight, or curl up with a good sad book of poetry. She often came close to nervous breakdowns, retiring for spells into solitude away from all her family. She had continued doubts about her marriage. She was overwhelmed by the suicide of her gifted and equally poetic son George. She herself wrote poetry, as well as some gloomy snatches of autobiography. Grandson Henry felt a strong kinship with her and her invalidism of spirit. "Try as she might, the Madam could never be Bostonian, and it was her cross in life, but to the boy it was her charm . . . Louisa was charming, like a Romney portrait. . . ." By the time Henry knew her she was old, "a vision of silver gray . . . an exotic, like her Sèvres china," and from her, Henry felt he was to inherit that "fall from grace, the curse of Abel, that he was not of pure New England stock, but half exotic" himself. How proud Henry was of such a "curse"! Nonetheless that frail exotic did her duty too, served as official hostess for years with success, bore her children, and also bore with the glooms and savageries of her husband. She survived.

As parents, John Quincy and Louisa were as a matter of course conscientious to extremes. She tended to be overindulgent, he oversevere. The combination killed George. John Junior and Charles lived on, though John not to much purpose. It was a grim school. A letter from his father to Charles at college shows what the children had to put up with. Charles at this time was not doing well at Harvard, and was indulging in dissipation — billiards, beer, parties, riding. His father wrote him, "If I must give up all expectation of success or distinction for you in this life, preserve me from the harrowing thought of your perdition in the next." One regrets that this kindly parental admonition seems to have had a salutary effect, like throwing the boy into cold water to teach him to swim.

Charles swam. Charles became a distinguished man, carried on the family name, established once and for all the effect of the Adamses being a dynasty. But as his father's natural bloom was destroyed by his parents' interference in his love with Mary Frazier, so any natural bloom Charles might have had was killed by such parental admonitions.

One feels that Louisa was not happy about it; not happy anyway. The marriage remained a firm bedrock to John Quincy. He expresses himself plainly enough in gratitude and affection. But Louisa was not, shall we say, well adjusted. George and John were not particularly well adjusted either, and their deaths did not make Louisa any happier. George was brilliant but thoroughly unstable, got into debt, seduced a lower-class girl, and had an illegitimate child by her (whatever happened to this twig of the family tree?). On a steamboat from Providence to New York he began to show unmistakable symptoms of insanity. He heard the engines saying, "Let it be, let it be." He woke a passenger to accuse him of circulating rumors against him. At three in the morning he asked the captain to stop and set him ashore because of a plot of the other passengers against him. An hour before sunrise his hat and cloak were found on the stern. The body was picked up later.

John had no such dramatic end. He lived in Washington, ran a mill there rather unsuccessfully, married his first cousin, had children (no Adams descendants however), declined, and died in 1834. Louisa's lines on John's grave,

> *Softly tread! For herein lies*
> *The young, the beautiful, the wise,*

remain perhaps the best in all Adams poetry. Only Charles was now left to carry on. It is not always easy to establish and maintain a Family.

4

Robert Edward Lee

Bizarre and Professional

IN GENERAL, the nineteenth century could be thought of as a period in which these families were "going up in the world." Obviously so in the case of the Roosevelts and the du Ponts, less obviously so in the case of the Biddles and the Adamses. After all, Nicholas ended as a disgraced bankrupt, which was hardly "going up." Still, the family kept Andalusia, which belonged to Nicholas's wife, and still keeps it today; and the other Biddles, the safe and sane ones and the Middle Biddles, continued in increasing prosperity and numbers. The Adamses of course were peculiar. In one sense they were going down. In each generation the incumbent loses personal stature. But historical perspective balances this out, since in each generation the family gains in dynastic value. To a lesser man accrues a greater dividend, and the prestige of the *family* keeps on increasing.

Not so the Lees. From 1800 on the Lees were definitely and precipitously going down. The great Revolutionary Lees of Stratford were dead, leaving no celebrated sons. The Leesylvania Lees were ousted from public life and poor Light-Horse Harry was beginning his course of glamour and ruin. Of course many Lees, like the Lee descendants left in Ditchley and Cobb's Hall, continued to vegetate in the obscure isolation of their ancient properties. But mostly the Lees were, or seemed to be, definitely on the descent.

Not only the Lees, but all Virginia. The crest of the wave — tobacco and tidewater affluence in the 1760's, Virginia as leader in the war and the peace afterward, the richest, brainiest, biggest, most populous state of the Union — had passed. In the new century, though the illusion carried on, though Presidents, Chief Justices and cabinet members were still as a matter of course Virginians, the basis of Virginia's pride was undermined. The planters were ruined. Already in the 1790's things were decaying. The visiting Duc de Liancourt's description of dining in mansions where the table was covered with rich silver, but where the windowpanes were broken, gives the picture of a land-poor aristocracy already living in its past. The final days of nearly all the great figures, those who lived beyond 1800, present the same picture — Jefferson in debt, having to be helped out by friends, Madison in genteel poverty; the Lees too, not just Harry, but the others who died earlier — William blind, rheumatic and in despair at Green Spring, where the water ran down the walls of the old house, ruining his French furniture; Arthur, the eccentric old bachelor, railing against democracy and the Constitution and chasing after young girls; Richard happy enough but in physical collapse, living shabbily at Chantilly with his daughters, two of whom were to marry Lees and two Washingtons.

It was in general, this period between 1790 and 1840, the Edgar Allan Poe period of Virginia. Poe was brought up in Virginia and against this background. Just because he Gothicked his work up fashionably and transposed his scenes to a Europeanized dream world does not mean he was not a realist. The goings-on in the House of Usher were no more macabre than events in many an old plantation of the time; and certainly no national figure was more straight out of Poe than John Randolph of Roanoke.

The basis of this decay was economic. Tobacco ran out. The market was destroyed by the Revolution; the soil was exhausted. The tidewater plantation was no longer a really paying proposition. From all over the southern coastline there was a migration westward to the rich bottom lands of the central states. Alabama, Mississippi,

Texas, Arkansas and Missouri were just as much pioneer states as Illinois or James Biddle's Michigan. "Go West, young man," was as much an imperative for the young Virginian as for the young Yankee; but whereas the migration of the northerners, the minor Adamses, the Lower Biddles, has been celebrated and eulogized, the parallel move West down below never seems to get talked of. Probably the emigrants wanted everyone to think they had lived in Alabama since 1600.

It was very different from the Midwest. One gets glimpses of this Hegira, seen, say, from the brand-new rough-and-ready stumps-in-the-street town of Montgomery, Alabama, as of the 1830's. Through the town would come the migrating slave owners. No covered wagons and oxen for them. Their traveling was a matter of hundreds of slaves and carriages and blooded horses with clinking bridles, camps at night in fancy tents with silver candelabra and dressed-up ladies at dinner. They were going from tobacco to cotton, and by so doing sealing the fate of the South. The owners of worn-out tobacco plantations would have been only too happy to relieve themselves of the burden of slavery. The owners of booming new cotton plantations were willing to fight to the death for the Institution. Fight to the death too for their transplanted finery and traditions, their brand-new pillared mansions, only twenty, thirty, forty years old by 1860, their brand-new status as a planters' oligarchy replacing that of the James and the Potomac.

Back on the James and the Potomac, the Mattapony and Pamunkey, the Poropotank and the Piankatank, things could get pretty awful. Has there ever been a story more phosphorescently morbid than that of John Randolph and his early family background on the plantation so aptly named Bizarre?* John Randolph was of course

---

* The story is well told by Francis Biddle in his autobiography, *A Casual Past*, and by Jay and Audrey Walz in their novel, *The Bizarre Sisters*. But why no movie?

later on the leader of Virginia and indeed the South in Congress during the Jefferson and Madison regimes, one of the nation's most prominent statesmen.

To start with, Randolph himself was physically a sort of monster. Though the Randolphs vied with the Carters in thinking themselves *the* first family of Virginia, one gets the impression that by the time of John the genes were becoming a bit specialized. Nobody, it seemed, had married outside the family in several generations, though of course the family was extensive. John Randolph's mother was a Bland, just like the grandmother of Light-Horse Harry. Of her three sons, Richard the oldest was a fine specimen, but Theodorick (this wonderfully apt and Gothic name of the Blands keeps cropping up over the Virginia landscape; one of Light-Horse Harry's brothers was a Theodorick Lee) died young of disease and dissipation. John himself, considered a beautiful boy, never really grew up. Due to either disease or glands, he remained a eunuchlike scarecrow, tall, painfully thin, with unchanged high voice, popping eyes and withered, beardless chin. He was as erratic as he was brilliant, full of all sorts of random knowledge, but not master of any one discipline. He was devoted to his animals, a reckless horseman, usually accompanied by a pack of hounds. He liked to appear in Congress in riding clothes, booted and spurred and with a whip. His eccentricities increased as he grew older. At the end of his life he was partially insane, partially alcoholic and partially a dope addict. Nonetheless his constituents kept on reelecting him. He served in Congress off and on from 1800 to 1830. When not in Congress he lived alone in a rustic remote tumbledown part-log plantation house called Roanoke, surrounded by his slaves, whom he alternately spoiled and whipped, and by his beloved animals. A visitor there would find him at death's door, lying in collapse. After saying a final fond farewell, going back down the interminable roads, a demoniac figure would tear by him on horseback, lashing his beast and screaming that he was "dying, dying!"; John Randolph recovered and out for a ride.

Beginning as a devotee to pure states' rights Jeffersonianism, he ended up as a solitary one-man band representing only himself and the whole spirit of Southern individualism, arrogance and heady intransigence. New Englanders, like Henry Adams, who wrote his biography, could make nothing of him and regarded him as simply a useless madman. To the South he obviously embodied the limits of aristocratic freedom, the runaway-horse aspect of the Southern temperament, unbreakable, irrational, that is so picturesque and so disastrous. He had a terrible tongue, and everybody was afraid of him. He actually ruined the careers of both Clay and Adams with his one speech about Puritan and blackleg. He was one of the first to create in the South that climate of insane pride and insolence that led to the Civil War.

Considering his physical defects and unstable character, it is incredible that he was able to maintain a long public career. Considering his family background it is a wonder he stayed sane as long as he did. In youth he lived with his idolized older brother Richard at Bizarre. Richard married a second cousin, Judith Randolph,* and had two sons, St. George and Tudor. St. George, otherwise perfectly handsome and healthy, was a deaf-mute. Tudor was always ailing. Into the household came Judith's pretty young sister Nancy. All the males of Bizarre courted her, the dying Theodorick, the eunuchlike John and finally her brother-in-law Richard. Richard was successful. They conceived an illegitimate child (which Nancy always liked to pretend was the son of Theodorick).

Richard, Judith and Nancy, trying to conceal her pregnancy, all went to visit more relations, the Harrisons of Glenlyvar. While there Nancy was heard to scream during the night, and next day her bed was soaked with blood. A trail of blood led down the stairs, and a slave Esau discovered the fetus of a white child buried in a pile of shingles. But nobody said anything, and the Harrisons guarded the family honor by hushing the whole thing up. Unfortunately the Harrison slaves and various Randolph relations who were

* See Appendix V.

in on the secret talked, and pretty soon the whole state of Virginia was rocking with the tale that Nancy and Richard between them had murdered and disposed of their newborn bastard. Would even the Randolphs be able to get away with that?

Things got so bad that Richard publicly and deliberately gave himself up for trial in order to vindicate his honor and bring his accusers out into the open. He hired Patrick Henry, greatest lawyer of Virginia's past, and cousin John Marshall, greatest lawyer of Virginia's future, to defend him. A daughter of cousin Thomas Jefferson was one of the witnesses. But what saved Richard and Nancy from conviction as murderers was the firm and perjured testimony of Judith. She swore that on the fatal night Nancy had had nothing more than hysterics, that she, Judith, had not slept a wink, that her husband Richard had been at her side all night, except to give Nancy some soothing medicine, and that he could not possibly have carried a dead baby downstairs. Esau could not testify because he was a slave.

Richard was cleared, on the basis of his wife's testimony, and he, Judith, Nancy and John Randolph too all went back to Bizarre. There Judith had her revenge and the really Gothic part of the story begins. The three members of the triangle lived together there consumed by guilt, passion and hatred. Judith made a slave of her sister, forcing her to do menial work, to sit at table without speaking or sharing in the coffee or wine, made her scour the chamber pots, forbade her to read, ride, play the harpsichord or appear in society. Nancy, penniless and friendless, Richard, guilty and dependent on his wife's perjury for his life, dared do nothing. Judith, nursing her deaf-mute son and gradually growing more and more unbalanced, continued to suspect her husband and sister. She feared Richard was taking legal steps to get rid of her and marry his paramour. Finally she poisoned him in such a way as to throw the blame on Nancy. Though a doctor did see the sick man, he came too late. Judith insisted on nursing him herself. He died.*

* It is characteristic of the Bizarre story that everyone on the scene should

In his will, after freeing his slaves, Richard left Bizarre to his brother John. Judith and Nancy continued to live there for years until finally Judith accused Nancy of sexual relations with a slave and had John Randolph drive her out. She had intercepted a note from Nancy directing the slave to polish the andiron and beginning "Dear Billy Ellis." This was enough for crazy Judith. Nancy somehow managed to make her way to New York, and there her years of misery were rewarded. Gouverneur Morris, in his fifties, lord of Morrisania, wit, diplomat and gallant, who was so expert at getting out of French bedchambers despite his wooden leg, met her, made her his housekeeper and then married her.

This bit of luck was more than Judith could take. In league with relations of Morris who were furious at being cut off from their inheritance,* she got half-crazy John Randolph to try to convince Gouverneur that his wife was a criminal who was trying to poison him. Morris refused to believe this. Nancy bore him a son who inherited Morrisania, and they more or less all lived happily ever after.

Not so Judith. Bizarre burnt to the ground. Her deaf-and-dumb son, St. George, always so sweet-tempered that he was nicknamed "the Saint," became violently insane. The other son, Tudor, went to Harvard, where he lived with the Josiah Quincys; but his career was cut short by consumption. John Randolph, who had transferred all this thwarted affection from his brother Richard to his nephews, never recovered from their loss. Judith lived on, declining into

---

somehow or other be of historical note. A wandering stranger passed by Bizarre and was driven to seek shelter from a dreadful storm. He departed before Richard died, and did not suspect the causes. The stranger was Benjamin Latrobe, English-born architect of the national capital, and the most distinguished of his profession in America at that time. His daughter married Nicholas Roosevelt, the inventor and steamboater.

* Here again, connections: The principal Morris kin active in this plot against Nancy were Morris's great-nephew David Ogden and his niece, Gertrude Meredith. Charles Francis Adams Jr. married an Ogden. William Shepard Biddle, son of James of Detroit also married an Ogden; and Merediths were ancestors of various Howlands, who in turn married various Roosevelts.

religious melancholia, refuge in those days for distraught widow-
hood.

   As Edgar Allan Poe has his sunnier side — visionary (*Landor's
Cottage*), straight detective-story writer (*The Gold Bug*) and hu-
morist (*The Spectacles*) — so the decadence of Virginia has cheer-
ier aspects. No family better represents them than the Tuckers, all
the more sharp a contrast to Bizarre in that they were so intimately
connected with sulphurous John Randolph. Frances Bland Randolph, John's mother, married for the second time an immigrant
from Bermuda, St. George Tucker. They had Tucker children, and
from that day to this the Tuckers have represented all that is dignified, cheerful and positive in the Virginia tradition. They lived on
plantations and were active in public affairs; but the significant difference, the saving difference, was professionalism. Instead of cling-
ing to outworn lands, like John Randolph, they rolled up their
sleeves and entered into the competition of law, medicine, engineer-
ing, the Church, where not hereditary possessions only but individual talents counted. In other words, hereditary meritocracy, not mere
hereditary aristocracy. In their various professional arenas they distinguished themselves as judges, professors of law and medicine, or
Episcopalian bishops. It was certainly this successful professionalism, which would have been beneath the contempt of someone like
pre-Revolutionary Philip Ludwell Lee, master of Stratford, that
preserved the Tuckers from disasters like those of the Randolphs.
   St. George Tucker, the founder of the family, brought up his
stepson John Randolph with care and generosity. His own sons,
Henry St. George and Beverly, admired their brilliant stepbrother
and stuck by him even after Randolph's unjustifiable break with
their father. Beverly was also a friend of Poe, and was himself poet,
novelist, editor. Yet despite these somber influences, both Tuckers
had outstanding and useful careers, and sired equally outstanding
and useful children. Indigenous Virginians though they were, the
blight of the Poe period did not descend on them.

They served again and again and in generation after generation in national Congress and state legislature, and a Tucker stands as a sort of monument over what may be the one single great turning point in the history of the South. Henry St. George Tucker in the 1820's introduced into the Virginia senate a bill for the gradual emancipation of slaves. The bill was defeated by one vote. What a load of shame, blood and guilt must rest on the shade of whatever man can be considered responsible for that single vote! If the bill had been passed, if it had become effective law, the whole history of the United States might have been different. Emancipation in Virginia would surely have led the way to emancipation in nearby states like North Carolina, Maryland, Tennessee and Kentucky. Without the border states, the irreconcilables of South Carolina and the cotton belt could hardly have dared to go it alone. If so, they would certainly have been soon defeated. A Tucker presides at the continental divide as a figure of what the South might have been. However, all this did not prevent various Tuckers from being the most violent of states' rights men and secessionists.

An equally amiable but far less consequential figure of the Virginia decadence is George Washington Parke Custis, painter, playwright, planter, builder of Arlington, stepgrandson of Washington, father-in-law of Robert E. Lee. There is something irresistibly funny about GWP, though no doubt his not-very-humorous son-in-law found his vagaries anything but amusing. He was a Gentleman Dilettante with a vengeance.

He had been brought up in Mount Vernon, and so remains the link between the greatest Virginian of the eighteenth century and the greatest Virginian of the nineteenth. He was actually George Washington's adopted son, his own father having died during the Revolution. When his grandmother Martha also died in 1802, Mount Vernon reverted to the Washingtons. Custis built himself a house called Arlington, and there brought his bride, Mary Lee Fitzhugh of Chatham. This house is probably his one notable achievement. Though as a house it was rather unsatisfactory, as a monument it was and is superb. That grand Doric pediment, à la Biddle, on its magnificent hill forms even today the culmination of one of the city of Washington's great vistas, a sort of perfect symbol, across the Potomac, of the Old South, the old plantation, the columns of romance. The other end of the vista is, appropriately enough, the Lincoln Memorial. As one of three great houses on the Potomac still preserved — Mount Vernon, Arlington, Stratford — it also aptly symbolizes the Lee-Washington connection.

Aside from the building of Arlington, G.W.P. Custis devoted his life to amusing himself. His principal amusement consisted of memorializing his stepgrandfather. Arlington was full of precious Washington relics: the china service given to Washington by the Society of the Cincinnati (probably ordered by Light-Horse Harry), Washington's bookcase and some of his clothes, the hall lantern from Mount Vernon. Every Fourth of July GWP would deliver himself of an oration, usually on Washington, and at the end of his life he devoted himself exclusively to painting lurid pictures of all Washington's battles. He was not a good painter, though faded murals about the walls of Arlington still attest to his ambitions. He was no less ambitious in other directions. He played the violin. He wrote. He wrote poetry, and especially he wrote plays. These were in fact quite successful onstage.

Most successful was a piece on that ancestress of the Randolphs, Pocahontas. It is a very silly play indeed, but in 1830, when it was produced in Philadelphia, it ran for twelve nights (one of them of course being Washington's birthday) and it was also acclaimed in New York. The style is what might be called pure mint julep. Rolfe, the future husband of Pocahontas, upon setting foot on the soil of Virginia, speaks thus: "I am completely lost amid the mazes of this interminable wood. My companions, intent on the pursuit of game, have left me to indulge in the contemplation of the sublime and beautiful, which is everywhere to be found in the wild and picturesque scenery of these interesting regions."

Our feathered friends the Indians are no less literate, and Pocahontas enters saying, "I would fain take breath awhile. Hereabouts is the shady bank and the old oak at which we us'd to rest"; or when guiding Rolfe to her father, "The paths are well known to us whose feet so often traverse them, and ere the shadows of the trees are much more aslant, we shall reach the abode of Powhatan." To what heights of rhetoric does the maiden ascend when she casts off her father, the ruthless chieftain, in favor of the prostrate John Smith! "Cruel king, the ties of blood which bound me to thee are dissever'd, as have been long those of thy sanguinary religion; for know that I have abjured thy senseless Gods and now worship the Supreme Being, the true Manitou."

In another of his plays, *The Railroad,* again of 1830, a real live locomotive crosses the stage — the first on the American boards — and whistles as it retires. Custis also wrote his recollections of Lafayette . . . and of Washington.

Though an active amateur of agriculture, like Biddle and J.Q. Adams, and interested in fancy sheep, he was a very poor practical planter. His income was derived from numerous great plantations run by overseers and tenants: White House, of four thousands acres on the Pamunkey (Martha Washington's old house), Romancock, Smith's Island and other lands. He had nearly two hundred slaves, but preferred to indulge them rather than work them. They were famous for being spoiled. Arlington itself he kept as a pleasure park, rather than a productive farm. He opened the grounds to the public, whom he welcomed personally, and even arranged for a steamer to bring over tourists from Washington city.

There is something very Russian about this feckless, happy-go-lucky semiretirement, like of that landowner described by Gogol, who liked to proclaim: "There could be nothing more gratifying than living in solitude, taking delight in beholding nature's pageantry and occasionally reading some book or other . . . if one had some scientific pursuit that would kind of stir the soul, lend one wings to kind of soar with, as it were . . ." A lazy, negligent, sunlit existence, whose reckoning in terms of debt and decline and confusion had to be paid later on by his son-in-law and executor, Robert E. Lee.

All these aspects of the Poe period were represented in the history of the Lee family — the ghoulishness of Bizarre, the dilettantism of Custis, the turn away from planting and toward professionalism of the Tuckers. In fact, the Lees make a sort of classic demonstration. Harry Lee junior, son of Harry senior and the divine Matilda, inherited Stratford and had a history just like that of Richard Randolph. The widow Ann and her brood lived in genteel poverty in Alexandria, and her children had professional careers, just like the Tuckers. The first road led to utter ruin, the second to total glory. The moral was pretty plain.

No more fortunate young man could be imagined than Henry Lee junior.* A Lee on both sides, joining the blood of Stratford and Leesylvania, he inherited the grandest plantation house on the Potomac, and then married Anne McCarty, heiress of another grand neighboring plantation. He had a respectable military career as a major in the War of 1812, for a time on the staff of wicked General Wilkinson. He had literary talent of sorts, quite enough to play the dilettante on the order of Custis, and he was famous for his hospitality, charm and conversational powers. However, unlike everyone for miles around and for generations before and after, he was ugly. Aside from this, he reminds one strongly of Richard Randolph of Bizarre, and he proceeded to do almost exactly the same thing.

His only child was killed falling down the frowning and formidable front steps of Stratford. In her grief his wife became a nervous invalid and took to dope. There was a younger sister, just as in the Bizarre case. She lived at Stratford, as Nancy had lived at Bizarre. Henry likewise seduced her, and they likewise had an illegitimate child who was stillborn. Unfortunately, as an added com-

---

* Harry junior had a sister Lucy; just to confuse things, she married Bernard Carter, brother of her stepmother Ann. They fought terribly.

plication, this sister-in-law had a fortune. Henry was her guardian and he not only took her virtue but her money. In 1828, almost exactly a hundred years after Thomas Lee built it, Stratford was seized to make up for the squandered fortunes of Harry's wife, Harry's mistress, and Harry himself. The Lees left it for good. Later, the seduced sister-in-law, now properly married, made her husband buy Stratford, and there she lived in seclusion for fifty years, dressed in black. Bizarre all over again, with a few added twists.

Black-Horse Harry, as he was derisively nicknamed after this, then made a career as a political hack. He became, in fact, a ghost writer for America's first illiterate President, Andrew Jackson, who needed help with his speeches. He lived and worked with Jackson at the Hermitage, and is usually credited with the composition of Jackson's first inaugural. As a reward, Jackson appointed him consul to Algiers. He and his reconciled wife sailed to take up the post; but the Senate by a unanimous vote refused to confirm the appointment because of Harry's moral notoriety. They were left stranded abroad, and Harry never returned. He lived on in France, a friend of Madame Mère, the mother of Napoleon. He became a violent Napoleonic partisan, and before he died in 1837, in poverty, had published one volume of a projected biography of Napoleon. The last of the Lees of Stratford lies buried in French soil along with such other moral refugees as Oscar Wilde. Forever afterward Robert would not permit his half-brother's name to be mentioned in his presence.

Great God of War

It is against the sun and shade of this decay of the Virginia plantocracy that the career and character of Robert Edward Lee must be considered. On the one side, there was the shade — the disgrace of his father and his half-brother, the more remote scandals of the cousin Randolphs. On the other side there was the example of the Tuckers. There was no longer hope for Lees to continue the role of planter, volunteer statesman, volunteer soldier that had been their birthright in the past century. It was now incumbent on the young Lees to get out and earn a living by their talents. They must support their noble but rather lachrymose and demanding and invalided mother, the widow Ann. They must refurbish that coat of arms, with its checkerboard and billets and inappropriate squirrel on top.

Duty and God, rather than Ambition and Glory were the words added to the Lee lexicon. The family in Alexandria tended to revert to religiose Richard II in its puritanical Episcopalianism. Robert E. was surrounded in his youth by a kind of Methodist sternness about frivolity — drinking, playing cards, nonobservance of the Sabbath — totally alien to the high wide days of plantation hospitality; more like Braintree than the Potomac. The genteel Victorian middle-classness of the period engulfed them. No more enlightened deism, the skepticism of Voltaire-loving Arthur Lee. No more drinkin', ridin', shootin', gamblin', seducin'. Piety, poverty, provincialism characterized these nineteenth-century Lees. No routs in Williams-burg, or schooling at Eton and Oxford, or grand tours on the conti-nent. Saturday's children, Robert and his two brothers must save their pennies and study hard and be good boys. So unlike their father.

They could not yet stoop to trade, however. Charles Carter Lee went to Harvard (the change in college from his father's Princeton may be symptomatic of the change in moral attitudes) and became a lawyer. Sydney Smith Lee went into the professional navy. Robert Edward Lee went to West Point and into the professional army. If there had been other brothers no doubt one would have been a doctor, another a clergyman (like the Tuckers). They were all three good boys, a comfort to their mother. Robert was the goodest, and the greatest comfort. The pattern of Victorianism as a moral reaction against the excesses of the Regency was never better exem-plified than by the last days of Stratford under Black-Horse Harry as opposed to the first days of Marse Robert in Alexandria. From Byron to Longfellow. Out of the wrecks of Stratford the young Lees learned patience, caution, consideration, devotion, decency; virtues by contrast and by necessity. Robert also inherited love of his native soil, pride of family and a tradition of military glory.

But what can one say of Robert E. Lee? There can be little doubt that despite all other virtues and accomplishments the fame of the Lee family rests in Robert. Without him the Lees would be a first family of Virginia along with the Randolphs and Carters; for all their services to the nation, no more than that. Robert is the apex of his family, as he is of the whole Southern tradition; a Man of Family if ever there was one.

What can one say of Robert E. Lee? He resists debunking. Military historians seem divided. Some think him among the greatest military geniuses of all time, in a bracket with Napoleon and Marlborough. Others think he lost the war for the South by failure at Gettysburg and other places. Many Northerners at the time called him a traitor to his oath of allegiance as an officer of the Army of the United States; some still do. Moderns may find the conjunction of so much Christian charity with a warrior battling to defend a cause sullied with slavery rather offensive. But no one has ever found a chink in the armor of his personal virtue. "Robert was always good," wrote his father from exile in the West Indies.

He also rather resists affection. One can worship him, and many have and do, but like Washington, unlike Adams, one cannot grow exactly fond of him. One certainly cannot laugh either with him or at him. In death as in life he forbids that familiarity. Idolatrous love, awesome respect, nothing less. One always thinks of people weeping when one thinks of Lee, as he so often wept — at the death of General Stuart, at the sermons of Bishop Meade. Like Lincoln, he carries great buckets of emotion in either hand. The dry, light wine of admiration one has for the wit, courage and spunk of the eighteenth-century Americans, for all their grandeur, is overwhelmed by the headier brew of high-tide Romanticism — orchestral waves full of nostalgia and hymn tunes. Hearts are always breaking. It's no wonder that after such a splurge America settled for Grant and materialism. One can compose cantatas for such a man, with bugles playing taps offstage; but it's hard to fit him into a family history.

His career has the classic directness of the career of Richard Henry Lee. That life leads up, in one straight line, to the motion for independence, the official bringing to birth of a nation. The career of his cousin Robert leads almost as directly to the surrender at Appomattox and the death of another nation. For a while the South thought of itself as "our country." "Our country" struggling for freedom and independence as did the rebels of 1775. It was certainly only for that "country" that Lee fought, never for secession itself or for slavery, both of which he detested.

The drama of his life falls into three distinct acts. First the long, dull pre–Civil War years of education and professional soldiering. Education at Mr. Leary's in Alexandria and play with cousins like Cassius Lee. West Point, graduating in 1829 second in his class with (of course) no demerits. Robert was always good. Marriage in 1831 to Mary Anne Randolph Custis, heiress of Arlington, whom he proposed, much to her father's disapproval, to support solely on his pay as second lieutenant. Seven children in fourteen years for Mary; posts as engineer helping to refurbish isolated forts on the southern coastline for Robert.

His first real job was an attempt at taming the Mississippi as it went by St. Louis. There, as one in that long line of army engineers who have so improved navigation and destroyed natural resources and beauties along our rivers, he roughly manhandled Bloody Island, where Thomas Biddle met his death. Fort Hamilton in New York harbor for five years. Then, at last, a war, the Mexican.

As captain, he made a reputation for his bravery, coolness and knowledge of terrain. One of his principal personal exploits was the penetration of something called the Pedegral. The Pedegral was a lava field. Three by five miles long, a horrendous mass of broken rock, it lay on the approach to Mexico City, and strategy demanded that the American forces cross through part of it to effect a surprise attack against Mexicans on the other side. Lee, under the immediate command of General Twiggs, was sent with a small force to construct a road, escorted and guarded by the rest of Twiggs' division. The roster of officers involved in this little foray reads like a Civil War memorial — Beauregard and Stonewall Jackson, McClellan and Hooker, all in junior capacities. Part of the road was built; Lee then went on ahead. The attack on the other side of the Pedegral was decided on for the next morning, but General Scott at headquarters had to be notified. Lee volunteered to walk back through the lava at night, in a violent thunderstorm, to bring the news to headquarters. In pitch-darkness and heavy rain, helped only by occasional lightning, he picked his way through the tortured landscape, found Scott, then returned after midnight to guide reinforcements; and was then present at the victorious American assault next morning without sleep or rest. Others who had tried to penetrate the Pedegral had given up. Lee's uncanny feeling for terrain and direction saw him through.

After the war he went back to various routine duties, and finally, as brevet colonel, he became superintendent of West Point. Next to his Mexican War service, this was the distinguishing effort of his prewar career. He was a very good superintendent, calm, kind, just, efficient. It was under his administration that James McNeill Whistler failed to graduate, since silicon turned out not to be a gas.

During the period from 1855 to the outbreak of war he was in command of a regiment on frontier duty in Texas. His wife stayed behind in Arlington. There her father died in 1857 and Robert became his executor. He was forced to spend much of his time in Virginia trying to untangle the mess that had been created by Custis's life of sunny skimble-scamble insouciance and by his erratic will. The will left Arlington to his daughter, various lands to the sons of Robert, instructed Robert to arrange for a fixed sum for each of his own daughters; but also manumitted all his slaves, and required Robert to pay considerable debts. Arlington was in a state of picturesque decay. It was really impossible for Robert to pay the debts, free the slaves, tidy up Arlington, turn over lands to his sons and provide stipulated legacies for his daughters all at once. He spent several miserable years doing his best. Meanwhile his wife had become, like his mother, a permanent invalid, crippled with arthritis. To add to this distress, various Northern abolitionist papers, including the *New York Tribune,* published malicious slanders accusing Lee of whipping Custis's slaves personally and preventing their manumission. Anyone who thinks that Southerners didn't have some good reasons to hate the abolitionists should read some of this lying muck. The fact that the abolitionist cause was righteous made these inflammatory untruths all the more reprehensible.

In 1859, just before the war, he was in Washington on one of his visits east. This was at the time of John Brown's raid on Harper's Ferry. Almost by chance, or by fate, it was Lee who was put in charge of capturing Brown. He executed his orders diligently, without emotion or seeming consciousness of the import of the event. He thought of Brown merely as a madman.

John Brown's body was hardly mouldering in the grave before Lee was back in Texas again, and that state seceded. Twiggs, his old superior in the Mexican War, was again in charge, and was a strong Southern states'-rights man. He surrendered the government stores to the insurgents. "Has it come so soon as this?" said Lee, and here was another occasion for weeping. Would Lee have surrendered the stores to the Texans if he had been in charge? The chances are, no. Virginia had not yet seceded. Would the Texans have fired on him? In that case Lee would have been the first to face "rebel fire" and the whole history of the war would have been different. Instead, Lee returned home.

If Lee had died at this point, his service in the Mexican War, his position as superintendent of West Point, his capture of John

Brown — and the fact that he was a Lee — would surely have earned him his modest niche in the *Dictionary of American Biography* along with all those other Lees. He would have been a successful peacetime army professional. The first fifty-four years of his life were no more than respectable. It is the last decade, half of it in war, half of it in peace again, that made him great.

There is surely no area more trampled over by lovers of American history than Lee's career as military commander in Virginia. I do not presume to trample much further. After his return from Texas to Washington, Lee was approached, through the medium of Francis Preston Blair (connected to the Lees by the marriage of his daughter to Admiral Samuel Phillips Lee), with the suggestion that he take over the command of the Union forces. He refused, resigned his commission in the army, and on April 22, 1861, a few days after Virginia had seceded, was made commander of the armed forces of his native state. He was against slavery, against secession, strongly patriotic to the Union; after all, his father had been one of the chief champions of Federalism, the family had been ever since either Federalists or Whigs. His motive was purely one of state patriotism. Virginia, rather than America, remained his "country." Later on he extended "country" to include the whole Confederacy, but his original choice was based on the impossibility of his having to fight his own Virginian "countrymen."

That sort of state patriotism is hard to understand nowadays. Regional patriotism of that intensity perhaps, but hardly for a single state. But in 1861 Virginia had been a state for less than a century. It had been Virginia for more than two. Even as a state, it had always been jealous of its independence. Many Virginians, like the obstreperous John Randolph, had always really thought of the Union as the Enemy. Still, it seems impossible nowadays not to feel that Lee's was a wrong decision. Slavery and secession were not causes to be fought for with a clear conscience, especially by one who hated both. High-minded Southerners immediately identified secession with the independence of 1775, not without some logic,

and came to identify Lee with Washington, also not without justice. The differences however were great. Should not a truly great
man have seen them? Would Washington have fought for Virginia
against America? One thinks not. And did not the presence of such
a truly good man as Lee tend to justify those things which were at
bottom not properly justifiable, making the wrong worse? What are
the limits of loyalty? Lee, once his decisions were made, never
seemed to question them.

As his life in general divides itself into three acts, so this second
act of war subdivides itself further into three scenes. The first scene
extends from his assuming command of the forces of Virginia in
April 1861 to his taking over the command of the newly-named-by-
him Army of Northern Virginia in June 1862. One of the odd, indeed "fatal" characteristics of Lee's military destiny was that, having
turned his back on his nation in favor of his state, he thereafter
usually failed in military operations outside the borders of Virginia
proper, but until the end nearly always succeeded when he fought
within them. His first success was his building up an army for Virginia from scratch. He failed in a campaign in what is now West
Virginia, and then partially failed in an effort to keep Union forces
off the shores of South Carolina and Georgia. One of his principal
antagonists down there was Admiral Samuel F. du Pont, whose capture of Port Royal in South Carolina was an early and startling amphibious victory for the Federals.

When in June of '62 General J. E. Johnston was wounded and
Lee was assigned his command, Lee was an unpopular figure,
blamed for defeats, thought of merely as an overrated favorite of
President Davis. It was in the second scene of the second act — in
the space of only one year from the Seven Days Battle in late June
'62, which drove McClellan back from Richmond, to the invasion
of Pennyslvania in late June '63, culminating in the Battle of
Gettysburg on July 2 — that Lee became the hope of the South,
"our great God of War" as the diarist Mrs. Chesnut suggested. Be-

fore this span of twelve months Lee had been comparatively un-known. Afterwards he carried the doomed hopes of the South with him in the third scene, the long retreat to Appomattox in April of '65. Out of his whole life, then, and when he was already in his mid-fifties (just having grown the characteristic beard), it was this one victorious year that established him as a contender for military glory with Napoleon and Caesar — that military glory for which his thwarted father so thirsted. The year of June to June 1862–63 was the apex of Lee family history. The ambitions of the father were realized in the son. Then the war broke in foredoomed disaster. The father had come to total personal defeat in serving a totally victori-ous cause. The son came to total personal victory in a lost one.

It was in the third and last act of the Lee drama, those five years of reconciliation, that Lee as a character, rather than as a military genius, comes to the fore. All he really did, after the ruin of the South, was to take over the presidency of a small, bankrupt educa-tional institution, Washington College, in Lexington, Virginia, and put it back on its feet. It was, like John Quincy Adams' service in the House, a comedown for the Confederacy's great God of War. But like Adams, he fulfilled himself there; as Adams showed him-self the born fighter for freedom, so Lee showed himself the born Christian aristocrat, accepting defeat with perfect calm dignity, for-giving his enemies with perfect calm charity. The glow of those last five years of Lee's life made indeed a startling contrast to the de-graded and pathetic disgrace of much of the last twenty years of his principal antagonist Grant. What price victory? One, as president of a small college, almost single-handedly redeemed his conquered country; the other, as President of the United States, did much to disgrace his. (Though Grant's wonderful courage in the face of adversity at the end of his life showed that he too was made of pretty fine stuff.)

This final victory of Lee was purely a victory of character. Yet this famous "character" has always been something of an enigma.

He has been called a Puritan misplaced on the Potomac, an eighteenth-century grandee misplaced in the democratic mid-nineteenth century. He was, I should think, an ascetic but not a Puritan; an aristocrat, but of the seventeenth, not the eighteenth century. The key to his whole nature, it would seem, is that he was a loyalist. Not a Loyalist in the narrow sense of a supporter of King George in the American Revolution, but a loyalist in the same universal sense that Lincoln was a democrat.

The only question Lee had to decide — and this of course was a terrible decision for him — was, "Where did loyalty lie?" What was his "country"? Once having decided that, there could be no further questions. Whatever his country did was right, commanded his total resources, the sacrifice of every personal ambition or attachment, commanded his life and death. This is pure, but it is not Puritan. The typical Puritan, like John Quincy Adams, has to be convinced at every individual moment of decision that he is Right, that he is on God's side, doing God's will. Since he can never really be sure what God's will is, he is always haunted by guilt. The loyalist, on the other hand, is never guilty, never troubled, so long as he remains perfectly loyal. The ultimate guilt rests with someone else, with the King or the Pope or the President. Only when loyalty conflicts with the absolutes of personal honor is there a possibility of personal guilt. If President Davis in his infinite unwisdom should choose to lose the war, that was not Lee's concern. His not to reason why, his but to do and die. Duty, not conscience; they are by no means identical. The ultimate superior, God, must ultimately decide. The conscience of the loyalist is clear, his soul at rest. John Quincy Adams found joy, if not peace, in that triumphant final battle for righteousness; Lee found peace, if not joy, in loyal defeat.

He chose his birthplace, Virginia, over his more abstract allegiances to the Constitution. Around this core of total self-giving to his Sovereign, the State of Virginia, all the other aspects of Lee's somewhat forbidding character congeal. In the end, it was the character that counted. The achievement was sizable — as his chief biographer, Douglas Southall Freeman, lists it, of ten major battles between June '62 and June '64, there were six victories, and only one sure defeat, that of Gettysburg. But still, in the end he lost. The North would at least have had victory, and the triumph of righteousness if it had not had Lincoln. What would the South have had without Lee and what he represented? Many other individuals followed the Lee pattern, but no one else, certainly not that thin-skinned neurasthenic Davis, could have served as symbolic hero; any more than cigar-and-whiskey-stained Grant would have done for the North for all his genius as a general. It is impossible to imagine the Civil War without a Lincoln balanced by a Lee, the ultimate democrat by the ultimate aristocrat.

So everything in Lee's character can be polarized around the concept of loyalty. The only professions really suitable for him were the armed services and the Church, preferably Roman. The latter was of course out of the question for a Lee. Besides, he was perfectly equipped for a military career. He was, for one thing, so handsome. Everyone always goes on about Lee's handsomeness. Why soldiers should necessarily have to be handsome is buried obscurely in psychology and sexuality, but there can be no doubt that it's part of the image. Napoleon and Frederick the Great were not notably handsome; Lee was. John Adams' unworthy and sarcastic remarks about Washington being chosen leader because he was tall apply here too. The Lee everybody knows is a rather sad old man with a gray beard. The beard was assumed only during the war. As a beardless cadet we have the glowing report of a fellow student. "His personal appearance surpassed in manly beauty that of any cadet in the corps. Though . . . perfectly erect, he had none of the stiffness [of the typical military martinet]. His limbs, beautiful and symmetrical, looked as though they had come from the turning lathe, his step was elastic as if he spurned the ground upon which he trod." He was nicknamed "The Marble Model." Not only that, but he was nice. His classmate Joe Johnston spoke of him as "full of sympathy and kindness, genial and fond of gay conversation, and even of fun, while his correctness of demeanor . . . and a dignity as much a part of himself as the elegance of his person, gave him a superiority that everyone acknowledged. . . . He was the only one of all the men I have known who could laugh at the faults and follies of his friends . . . without touching their affection for him. . . ."

Later on this elegance of person could be somewhat forbidding. Mrs. Chesnut in 1861 preferred his brother Smith Lee to Robert:

"I spoke of Rooney [Robert's son] with great praise. Mrs. Izard said, 'Don't waste your admiration on him. Wait till you see his father! He is the nearest to a perfect man I ever saw!' 'How?' 'Every way. Handsome, clever, agreeable, high bred.' Now, here in Richmond, Mrs. Stanard came for me . . . She was in an open carriage. A man riding a beautiful horse joined us. He wore a hat with somehow a military look to it. He sat his horse gracefully, and he was so distinguished at all points that I very much regretted not catching the name as Mrs. Stanard gave it to us. . . . Mrs. Stanard was in ecstasies of pleasurable excitement. I felt she had bagged a big fish. . . . As he left us I said eagerly, 'Who is he?' 'You did not know? Why that was Robert E. Lee, the first gentleman of Virginia!' All the same, I like Smith Lee better; and I like his looks too. Besides, I know him well. Can anyone say they know his brother? I doubt it! He looks so cold, quiet and grand."

All this was before he had become the South's great God of War.

This physical equipment was backed up by almost every other martial virtue — courage, coolness, ability to make the best out of a grim situation, an uncanny feel for terrain, perfect justness and firmness in disciplinary matters and, above all, the ability to inspire his troops with fanatical love — and loyalty. His greatest fault seemed to be his excess of gentlemanliness — and loyalty. He was too considerate of inferiors, too compliant to superiors, especially Davis. This gentlemanliness, noblesse oblige, was carried to the ultimate degrees of humility and democratic simplicity. As general he refused to enjoy pomp, or comfort not equally available to his troops. As teacher, later on, he was accused of being too well bred in his reprimands. He answered that if a student could not understand the mode of address proper to a gentleman, there was nothing a gentleman could do about it. "A true man of honor feels humbled himself when he cannot help humbling others." This, a succinct definition of why an aristocrat must be a democrat in manners, was written by Lee on a scrap of paper and found after his death.

That did not mean, however, that Lee felt himself one of the people, however perfect his manners. "Never marry unless you can do so into a family that will enable your children to feel proud of both sides of the house." This expresses Lee's view on alliances. It is not notably folksy. He may have despised slavery, but he was far from considering Negroes as possible equals. After the war he advised his brother Carter to employ white help on his plantation, rather than Negroes. "I have always observed that wherever you find the Negro, everything is going down around him."

As striking as the peculiar combination of pride and humility was that of ferocity and gentleness. His gentleness, the Victorian fondness for little girls and innocence, the almost sentimental, as evidenced by the famous episode of his picking up a baby sparrow and returning it to the nest right in the line of fire outside Richmond in '64 — all this is balanced by that equally famous remark about war: "It is well that war is so terrible — we should grow too fond of it." Equally grim is his bitter comment on lack of character among Southern politicians. He was speaking to his son Custis Lee in the winter of '64–'65. "Mr. Custis, when this war began I was opposed to it, bitterly opposed to it, and I told these people that unless every man should do his whole duty, they would repent it; and now — they will repent." This scorn could be turned against the North too. When Arlington was seized he considered it "degraded by the presence of those who revel in the ill they do for their own selfish purposes"; or, "these people delight to destroy the weak and those who can make no defense; it just suits them." "These people" again.

But unlike, very unlike, John Quincy Adams, he did not "revel" in reviling his enemies. Hatred did not bring out humor. Like

Adams, he too has been accused of an almost total lack of it. What humor he had was of exactly the opposite sort — a gentle sarcasm, which could be applied to himself as easily as to others. When young, he wrote, "Last night there was a cadet hop. Night before, a party at Colonel Johnston's. . . . You know how agreeable I am on such occasions, but on this, I am told, I surpassed myself." One can't imagine JQA poking even such mild fun as this at himself.

Lee, unlike Lincoln, is in no sense a literary man. He was "well educated" enough in a formal way. He admired Marcus Aurelius, whom he curiously resembles; but he was never naturally attracted to books or to the use of the language. Nothing comparable to the Gettysburg address survives him (or of course anyone else of the time). Even more curious, nothing of that time comparable to Whitman's "When Lilacs Last in the Dooryard Bloom'd" memorializes him. There is a hole here in American letters, the vacant spot one feels should have been filled by a poet equivalent to Lee, as Whitman is equivalent to Lincoln. Where was this poet? Perhaps killed in the fighting — some antebellum southern Tennysonian. The best that stars his career verbally is the small collection of quotations from himself, like that marble remark on the beauties of war. He may not have loved books, but he loved nature. He describes his lonely rides in his retirement through the Virginia wilderness on his favorite horse. "Traveler is my only companion. . . . He and I . . . wander in the mountains and enjoy sweet confidences." * That's as close to poetry as Robert E. Lee gets. Nobody in writing of him gets closer. He will have to remain his own unwritten poem.

One forgets, in the enormous shadow of Robert, that even if he had not been the great God of War, the Lees would still remain the single most prominent military family of the Civil War, as they were the single most prominent political family of the Revolution. No other family produced, besides Robert himself, three outstand-

---

* Modern poets have tried to make up for the lack; see Donald Davidson's "Lee in the Mountains," Stephen Vincent Benét, etc.

ing major generals and a well-known rear admiral. The generals were Confederates, the admiral a Federal, but they were all Lees.* They were all professional soldiers. George Washington Custis, Robert's eldest son, graduated from West Point in '54, head of his class. He was everything, as a cadet, that a Lee should be. Fitzhugh, son of Robert's naval brother Smith (whom Mrs. Chesnut preferred) was not. He kept getting into all sorts of scrapes, and was nearly expelled; but managed to graduate in '56, forty-fifth in a class of forty-nine. William Henry Fitzhugh, Robert's second son, called "Rooney" to distinguish him from cousin Fitzhugh, did not go to the Point. He was sent instead to Harvard, probably with the mistaken idea that he would turn lawyer like his uncle Carter. He didn't. He was generally a lordly misfit, though stroke of the Harvard crew. He knew Henry Adams, and Adams had much the same reaction towards him that John had towards Washington, on occasion — the irritation of the man who reads for the man who doesn't. Rooney, according to Adams, had

"changed little from the type of his grandfather, Light Horse Harry. Tall, largely built, handsome, genial, with liberal Virginian openness towards all he liked, he had also the Virginia habit of command and took leadership as his natural habit. No one cared to contest it. None of the New Englanders wanted command. For a year, at least, Lee was the most popular and prominent young man in his class, but then seemed slowly to drop into the background. The habit of command was not enough, and the Virginian had little else. He was simple beyond analysis; so simple that even the simple New England student could not realize him. No one knew enough to know how ignorant he was, how childlike, how helpless before the relative complexity of a school. As an animal, the Southerner seemed to have every advantage, but even as an animal he steadily lost ground."

Despite this blend of superiority and cattiness, which certainly reveals as much about Henry as it does about Rooney, the two actu-

---

* Just to confuse things, there was another Confederate general, Stephen Dill Lee, who was no kin.

ally remained quite good friends in college. But Rooney, thinking as little of Harvard as Harvard did of him, left in '57 to go into the army. He was a second lieutenant in the expedition against the Mormons; then resigned in '59 to settle at White House, the plantation newly left him by his grandfather Custis.

Samuel Phillips Lee, the Union admiral, was a grandson of Richard Henry. He became a midshipman when he was thirteen in 1825, and served off the east coast of Mexico while his cousin Robert was earning a reputation ashore. Samuel was still in the navy when the Civil War broke out. He stayed there, unlike Robert's brother Sydney Smith Lee, who with considerable regret went into the Confederate navy.* Samuel had a moderately distinguished career. At one time he was acting rear admiral in command of the North Atlantic Squadron blockading Virginia and North Carolina, but was removed by Secretary Welles as not being aggressive enough, the first time that had ever been thought of any Lee. His marriage to the daughter of Francis Preston Blair of Silver Spring, outside of Washington, was in its way as much of an alliance as the marriage of Robert to Mary Custis of Arlington. From him descend a line of post–Civil War worthies who remain to this day affluent and prominent in Washington, Maryland and Philadelphia.

When the war broke out, all three younger military Lees, Custis, Rooney and Fitzhugh, immediately jumped in, along with their brothers, uncles and cousins, on the Virginia side, of course.† Custis spent most of his time as aide-de-camp to President Davis. Rooney was a cavalryman. Both were captured, and Rooney severely wounded. Fitzhugh was the most prominent of the three, a "dashing" cavalryman (whereas Rooney was "cool"), generally ranked among the first dozen in America. He had a crucial role to play in Robert's great victory at Chancellorsville, and was still with Robert in his final defeat at Appomattox. He too was severely wounded,

---

* Mrs. Chesnut quotes Smith, "South Carolina be hanged! She brought us into this snarl. How I did want to stay in the old Navy. But Virginia comes first with us all, you know, so I am here."

† The family of Robert's sister's husband, however, the Marshalls, was Unionist.

and in one battle had three horses in succession shot out from under him. All three of these Confederate Lees achieved their rank as major general in spite of Robert's determined efforts not to help them in any way.

They all continued to have distinguished postwar careers too. Admiral Lee was again in command of the North Atlantic Squadron in the seventies. Custis succeeded his father as president of Washington and Lee (as it was renamed) from 1871 till he retired in 1897. He lived till 1913, unmarried; like his sisters, Daddy's girls all. Rooney was a U.S. congressman when he died in 1891.

Nephew Fitzhugh, as he was most distinguished in war, was most distinguished in peace. He was in fact the last Lee to play a conspicuous, if still minor, part on the national stage. He was governor of Virginia for four years from 1885. Then in 1896 he was named consul general for Havana, just in time to be on hand and in charge in Cuba when the trouble started there. He made himself a national hero, and when he returned to Washington in 1898 had a triumphal reception. He was commissioned a major general (of volunteers), went back to Cuba, and stayed in the army till 1901. Not many men have been generals first in the Southern and then in the Northern army. This last flare of Lee military fame crosses the first flare of Roosevelt notoriety. The last Lee to be a national figure was on the same scene in Cuba as Teddy, first famous Roosevelt. It was an appropriately significant hail and farewell as the two family fates crossed each other's passage in their opposite directions.

5

Charles Francis Adams

L EE was obviously the most important man of any of these families in the Iron Age, that period from Jackson through the Civil
War. He was indeed one of the most important men in America of
that period. Only a few, like Lincoln and Grant, could compare.
However, among the men of these five families, Charles Francis
Adams, son of John Quincy, comes closest to Lee. All the four families, aside from the Lees, were firm Unionists. The du Ponts supplied not only powder but some moderately well-known military
leaders. Various individual Biddles were active in various ways, but
not particularly notably. The Roosevelts seemed to have had no military men at all, and had close southern connections in the Oyster
Bay branch, but there is no record of really active Copperheadism
(despite Judge James J.). The only two really famous men of these
families, aside from the Lees, were Admiral Samuel Francis du
Pont and Charles Francis Adams, Lincoln's most effective diplomat.

John Adams is admirable but amiable; John Quincy Adams is
admirable but pitiable; Charles Francis Adams is admirable but
insufferable. He embodies all the dreadful virtues of Victorianism
with one salutary exception; nobody could have called him a hypo-
crite. But for sheer, calm, cool smugness, Charles is hard to beat.
The often chilly exterior of the forebears concealed eruptions of
interior lava, terrible angers and terrible self-doubts. A sort of sub-
zero gelatin seemed to ooze through the veins of Charles. Calmly he

judged his parents, that "pitiable set," calmly he judged his in-laws, "now and then a little vulgarity escapes them which annoys me exceedingly," calmly he judged his fiancée and wife-to-be, "Abby pleased me and displeased me. The fault lies so little with her I cannot blame her; it is the school she has been educated in, which is not a standard of refinement. Notwithstanding, I was gratified by her general conduct. . . ." Ah, the raptures of young love, as expressed by an Adams. Many things disgusted him besides his wife's relatives. "Infancy is a disgusting part of life," or "My disgust to politics seems to be growing." On social life in Washington: "A very crowded stupid party at Mr. Clay's in which there were many very vulgar people. I was excessively disgusted." It is only fair to add that he disgusted himself on occasion; but not so very often.

There is considerable evidence, however, in the very earliest diaries, that this aplomb was not entirely natural, but was forced on him by family pride and parental ambition, a feeling of the awful weight of Adams tradition. Even before he realized, on the death of George and John, that he was the only Adams left, any symptom of southern recklessness inherited from his mother's side was ruthlessly quenched, totally and for good, it would seem. It was obvious that he would be expected to follow the Adams schedule, and with many a groan of reluctance, he set himself to do so. Duty. The path was clearly marked: Harvard, the law, letters on political subjects to the newspapers, election to the state legislature, then to the national legislature. From there to diplomatic service culminating in the English post, the American foreign service's ripest plum. Then on to secretary of state for two terms and finally the debacle of a single term of the presidency. Charles knew exactly what he was supposed to do. To a miraculous extent he really did do it.

Harvard in 1825: he didn't distinguish himself, but at least he wasn't expelled for rioting like his brother John. The bar in 1829: he hated the law and never did well in it, though he tried. Letters to newspapers: from 1830 to 1840 and afterward he made a career as a writer of articles in magazines and newspapers. Nobody paid much attention to them. State legislature: for five years, three in the lower house, two in the upper, he had something of a success as an anti-slavery Whig. Congress: elected for two terms. Diplomacy: appointed right off the bat as wartime minister to England, a post he held for some seven years. Secretary of state and President, however, eluded him, though even here he did brush the skirts of glory. In 1848 he was the vice-presidential nominee, paired with Van Buren, of the Free Soil (antislavery) Whigs. In 1872 he was a candidate as nominee for the Liberal (anti-Grant) Republicans. He came close, but Horace Greeley won that nomination, was disastrously defeated, and went crazy.

John Quincy's heart wasn't really in it, but he *did* it. Charles Francis's heart wasn't really in it, and he just failed to do it. Although his life follows the right pattern, there is one fatal flaw: the steps do not follow at the right time. There is a curious glacial sluggishness about them. Instead of going right on enthusiastically like John, or desperately like John Quincy, there are long gaps in the Charles Francis chronicle, long gaps in which he seemed to do very little but brood. For instance, he served his last in the state senate in 1845. He wasn't elected to Congress until 1858. By the time he got back from England, presumably ready for a secretaryship of state, he was over sixty, and in fact fit to retire. The truth was that he was the first Adams who wasn't ambitious enough — for an Adams.

Part of the lack of ambition can be explained economically. Charles was also the first rich Adams. Having married into the well-heeled but vulgar Brookses, he didn't have to do anything. John and John Quincy had always been harassed financially and anxious about supporting their families. Charles Francis lived in calm security all his life after marriage. He was a good financial administrator, too, which could not be said of his forebears. Duty, and duty alone, drove him out into politics.

He had in fact three careers, in all of which he achieved a measurable success. The first was politics. He became a conservative but vocal champion of antislavery, a Conscience Whig. As such he had those five years in the Massachusetts houses and three years in Washington, his nomination as Vice President, and a fling as editor of a Conscience Whig paper in Boston. Altogether, before the war, he was a considerable, if never popular, figure in Massachusetts political circles.

It was his second career that made him memorable. As ambassador to the Court of St. James's he kept England out of the Civil War. The English upper classes and their organs of expression, such as the *Times,* were overwhelmingly pro-Southern. In the first place, they welcomed the breakup of the Union and the failure of the democratic experiment. Then, the Southerners were Gentlemen and landowners, whereas the Northerners were In Trade. Lincoln was a baboon, the Northern army would never fight, etc. Finally, much of English trade and manufacturing was based on Southern cotton. The fact that the North kept insisting, at first, that the United States was not fighting about slavery merely confirmed the English anti-Northernism. It is possible that this upper-class sympathy, combined with Northern irascibility and tactlessness, might have pushed England, against her better judgment, into some sort of active support of the South.

The crux, the kernel of Robert E. Lee's whole career, was contained in the military operations of one year. In a similar fashion, Lee's remote adversary Adams achieved his principal victories during a course of little more than two years, from his arrival in England in May of 1861, to the resolution of the conflict over the building of rams for the Confederacy, which came to a head in early September 1863. Aside from this short but intensely vital span, his life was really rather undistinguished. This however was and is enough for reputation and the continuance of family glory.

At any moment of those years a break of relations was possible and expected between the nations. On two occasions in particular,

England was almost forced into the arms of the South, first by the rash foolishness of the North, second by the dilatory foolishness of England herself.

Although Adams was appointed in March of '61, he didn't get to England till May. He delayed because of the wedding in April of his oldest son John to Fanny Crowninshield of Boston. By the time he reached London he found the government there had recognized the Southerners as belligerents, rather than merely as insurrectionists, which seemed then a step towards recognizing the Confederacy as an independent nation. The North was furious, Secretary of State Seward had the insane idea that a foreign war might resolve the problem of a domestic one, England was sure that America would never again be united. Into this unfavorable atmosphere came Adams. He was treated with punctilio but shunned socially. Other Americans might have been wounded or angered. Not Adams. He hated the English anyway, an antipathy no doubt based on a brief experience at school there when his father was ambassador. If fire can be fought by fire, so can ice by ice. No Englishman could beat Charles at cold, cautious, judicious lack of enthusiasm. It was the right weapon for the occasion. As he said himself, with that faint trace of caustic humor which is the last residue of Adams bile in him, "My practice has been never to manifest feeling of any kind. . . . Some Englishmen have taken occasion to intimate that I have been thought quite successful."

The first great crisis occurred in November '61. A hotheaded American naval officer, Captain Wilkes, stopped a ship flying the British flag, the *Trent,* and removed two Southerners, Mason and Slidell, who were being sent through the blockade as commissioners for the Confederacy. This arrest was entirely the idea of Wilkes. He had had no orders; but the North was jubilant, Wilkes was a hero. England was in a furor — insult to the flag and all that sort of thing. It was particularly aggravating since this was precisely what America had fought England about in 1812. England had repented, and now America was the culprit. Things were very tense indeed, but Americans began to have second thoughts. Charles Adams remained calm and conciliatory. Eventually the Southerners were handed back to England, and all was temporarily well.

The second crisis was created by England. In May of '62 a ship (named later on the *Alabama*) was launched from English yards, specifically designed and built as a warship to harass Northern shipping and help break the blockade. Feeble efforts were made by the English government to stop her from sailing, but she slipped out in July and proceeded to wreak havoc. Mr. Adams made it clear that his government was not pleased. His government was even less pleased when it was discovered that two more ironclad warships were being built at Laird's shipyards. Adams made it very clear indeed that if the English allowed these to escape like the *Alabama,* there would be hell to pay.

The Southerners, with the help of the French government which under Napoleon III was even more pro-Southern than England (Napoleon hoped to found a French-dominated empire in Mexico), adopted an ingenious device. A French company bought the ships, supposedly as agents for the Pasha of Egypt. It all seemed perfectly legitimate. No one could prove that the ships weren't really destined for the Nile. Actually of course they were to be resold to the Confederacy, at a nice profit, as soon as they were safely at sea; but legally the English hands were tied. They could do nothing, and did nothing. The first of the rams was actually launched on July 4 (ironic date), 1863. By early September it was ready for sea. The crisis was at hand. If the ram got loose, it would almost inevitably mean a final break between England and America. Adams sent a note to Lord John Russell, British foreign minister and his principal antagonist throughout, stating that the ram must be detained. If not, he wrote, "it would be superfluous in me to point out to your lordship that this is war." These calm words marked the closest to the point of no return achieved by England and America since 1812. Whether because of the words or independently on his own initiative (which is more likely), Russell stopped the ram from sail-

ing. The crisis was over. Adams was credited with a victory as significant as any won by a Union general. The Emancipation Procla-
mation of September '62 and the battle of Gettysburg of July '63
had already vindicated the North with the English people as a
whole and destroyed the hopes of the South. After this final diplomatic victory, the cause of the Union in England was secure.

Adams stayed on till 1868, but his work was really finished in
1863. By all rights, and following the family footsteps, he should
have been called home as secretary of state; then on to a disastrous
presidency. But not in the age of Grant. Martin B. Duberman, the
biographer of Charles, paints the picture of the homecoming hero:

"Adams' landing in New York was anything but a triumphant return.
No crowds of grateful citizens cheered from the piers . . . Instead, the
Adamses were toted to an empty dock by an inglorious revenue cutter,
and in the process were thoroughly soaked by a flash rain storm. When
Adams went ahead to scout for rooms in the city, it was only to discover
that all the hotels were either full or undesirable. On trying to return,
he then found his way to the cutter blocked by a stubborn gatekeeper
who stoutly refused him admission. Only intervention by officials of the
line . . . put an end to the comic opera."

This unseemly incident could be thought of as the finale in the
public career of the Adams family. So on a note of minor frustration, ludicrous inconvenience and general neglect, the saga of three
generations of service concluded. As no Lee ever again, after
Appomattox, achieved true national significance, so after this ig-
noble debarkation no Adams ever again held really important elective, diplomatic or even appointive office. This tradition ended not
with a bang, but a whimper, as a later New England relative put
it.

There were of course other public events in family history.
Charles himself went to Geneva in 1871 as American delegate to a
conference on the adjustment of American claims against England
for damages caused by the *Alabama*. It was a significant conference,
and it was satisfactory from the American point of view. England

paid America fifteen and a half million dollars' indemnity. The credit for the success of the negotiations went to Adams. This is not, however, the Treaty of Ghent.

Much later, in the 1920's, a grandson, Charles Francis Adams, was secretary of the navy under Hoover, not a thrilling period in American naval history. Whatever reputation came to later Adamses came in other fields. Public life on the national scene was more or less closed to them. It has been often customary to blame the country, rather than the Adamses, for this failure of continuity; but surely the presidential and political careers of John and John Quincy were not calculated to inspire confidence and fervor in the hearts of the electorate. The Adamses were really not much good as political executives, no matter how high-minded. Nothing in the character of Charles Adams suggests that he would have been any better. Even his supporters backed him out of duty, not emotion; one such described him as "the greatest iceberg in the northern hemisphere."

Charles Francis, however, had that third career, which came to fruition after the war, and in which he was also successful; successful in the same way as in politics or diplomacy: limited goals securely achieved. He had none of the futile poetic aspirations of his father, none of the real if dispersed verbal felicity of his grandfather. His articles do not seem to be much worth rereading. But as an editor and biographer he succeeded in building a monument, a granite mausoleum of words in which his ancestors were suitably embalmed, and the Family, once and for all, immortalized.

Also, he kept a diary.

As early as 1840 he began to edit and print family letters, Abigail's to John (1840), John's to Abigail (1841). In the fifties he edited and published a monumental edition of the papers of John Adams, with a full-length biography as preface. The first chapters of the biography had already been written by John Quincy Adams. Then, after the war, he performed the same services for his father.

He was a conscientious and honest editor, far above the low standards of his time. His changes were minor, his deletions not serious. Still, he did alter and delete, all with a Victorian emphasis on propriety. Ribald stories were overlooked, or the too frank details of barnyard life. Crudenesses of grammar, or of spelling (such as "Canady" for Canada) were smoothed out. A good deal of the salt of John got filtered. Perhaps more disastrous was his handling of the John Quincy diaries. In his ruthless intention to present only the historically important and to avoid the trivial, most of the personal and topical and family items that make any diary interesting were omitted. The result is admirable enough. For a hundred years the words of the two statesmen have been available in print to students of American history. But it is all rather insufferable. Dullness, a large solid dung-colored Victorian dullness hangs over the volumes, dimming the verve of John, almost totally obscuring the humanity of John Quincy, poet and psychopath. It was a meritorious service, well done. It founded the fame of the family. Now it all has to be done over again in modern terms. Charles' biography of John is not lively or up-to-date, the edition of the works neither truly complete or authentic on the one hand, nor condensed, edited and readable on the other.

And then, Charles Francis Adams kept that diary.

As his son Charles Francis junior said of him — and seldom has a son seemed so publicly to dislike a father — "He took to diary writing early, and he took to it bad." His son found that he displayed no humor, no picturesqueness, no imagination, no love of nature or of sports or even of gossip, "no eye to the dramatic . . . no touches of sympathy or fun. . . . He studied the classics and read Clarissa Harlowe to his young wife, who evidently was bored to extinction." He went to church because it was the right thing to do, but even though he was in turn bored "to extinction" by the sermons, he epitomized them in his journal. No one who has dared to peruse the two first volumes of this diary as now printed in the new edition of the Adams Papers will equally dare to argue with the diarist's son.

And yet, and yet . . . is there a nicer description of a giddy collegiate weekend in New York (believe it or not) than those entries for June 1826? Or a more revealing picture of a young prig, self-made out of rather recalcitrant material? Then there is that dreary, funny and pathetic chronicle of frustration, the long engagement of a haughty poor boy to a stuffy rich girl; or, later on in England, as quoted by his son, that vivid comparison between the funerals of Cobden and Palmerston. Much of the diary is unreadable, most of it is unimportant, but the stuff of life is there to be mined and sifted. When all sixteen or so volumes are at last printed, and the record goes up to 1880, it will really be an awe-inspiring panorama: John's diaries from 1753 to 1804, John Quincy's from 1779 to 1848, Charles' from 1820 to 1880. Is there anything else in the world quite like it? Charles Francis junior wrote, perhaps unwillingly, a biography of his hated father, printed in 1900. So we have here too something of a family record: John Quincy writes a bit of biography of his father; Charles Francis writes a piece of memoir of his father, as well as a full biography of his grandfather; Charles Francis junior writes a full biography of his father; Abigail Adams Homans writes a biographical memoir of her father and uncles (including Charles Francis junior); her son Robert Homans writes a charming short reminiscence of his uncle, Charles Francis Adams III. Is there anything else in the world like *that*? John Adams wrote his autobiography; Louisa Adams wrote bits of her autobiography; skipping a generation, both Charles Francis junior and Henry Adams wrote their autobiographies; Abigail Homans' book is also an autobiographical memoir. Where will it end? Is there anything else in the world . . . ?

The mass of Adams writings, above all of Adams diaries, is so crushing as to defeat most possible human purposes. Will anyone, aside from the editors, ever really read all of it? Dreadful thought. In the middle of this black thundercloud of words, the diary of Charles Francis Adams stands central. It has never been printed before. How will it stand up against such born diarists as George

Templeton Strong or Sidney Fisher? Adams seems to lack all the natural gifts of these latter men; those gifts so aptly enumerated by his son. Still, judgment must wait. It is possible, indeed probable, that his fame in the end will be that of a diarist.

6

Du Ponts

FROM 1800 on, the story of the du Ponts becomes increasingly a Family story, less and less a story of individuals. In fact, of all these Family stories, none is quite so overwhelmingly Family as this one. Even the Adamses, Family-hounded as they were, remain always individuals. With the du Ponts, it's the family, as embedded in the Company, that counts.

To tell the truth, the actual people seem to become more and more anonymous throughout the nineteenth century as the Company becomes more and more prominent. Nobody among his immediate descendants approaches Pierre Samuel in originality and foolishness. The sons, Irénée and Victor, have more color than their children. In mid-twentieth century the individual du Pont is quite obliterated in the bulk of the institution. Still, there are sports; and the story of the Company has its own color and originality.

No one of course was more conscious of founding a family, and a noble family too, than Messire Pierre Samuel du Pont de Nemours, Chevalier of the Order of Vasa. There is the record of an absurd and charming quasi-masonic ceremony called "The Investiture" or "The Accolade," which Pierre imposed upon his sons. Their mother had died in 1784. A few days after her funeral, Pierre summoned the boys into his presence. He was sitting on a high-backed chair, to one side of him a bust of his dead wife, to the other a bench holding a sword and a hat. In front of him was a cushion. Irénée knelt. Pierre exhorted him to honor, reverence, loyalty to France and his parents, and then dubbed him by striking him with his sword and proclaiming "No privilege exists which is not inseparably bound to a duty." He then made both boys promise always to stand together in danger and difficulty, and gave them his paternal blessing. This ritual, with its mixture of the sublime and the ridiculous so characteristic of the time, the place and the person, seems to have had the desired effect. The boys did not forget either the incident or the advice. A modern diorama in the Hagley Museum in Wilmington depicts the scene; and the boys and their descendants certainly did stick together.

Victor was handsome, social, inclined to stoutness, improvident. Irénée was intellectual, gloomy, practical and meager. Victor's milieu was diplomacy and high life. Irénée took to chemistry. It is to Victor and his line, on the whole, that the so-to-speak extracurricular or non-Company glamour and distinction adhere. The fate and future of the family was bound up in Irénée's chemistry.

They were both, of course, grown married men with several children apiece before they settled in America, and had already had active if abortive careers. Victor had married a noblewoman, much to his father's satisfaction, Gabrielle Josephine de la Fite de Pelleport, daughter of a marquis (Victor's godfather had also been a nobleman, the Marquis de Mirabeau). Irénée, on the other hand, had married plain Sophie Dalmas. Pierre was bitterly opposed. What, the son of a nobleman, of a du Pont, marry a tradesman's daughter? Fortunately, Irénée married her anyway. She was a brave, sensible girl, and the family needed just those qualities in those times. Popular too; Irénée had to fight two duels with a rival suitor to get her. Victor ran up debts and led the life of fashion. He had experience in the foreign service, all in the United States, first as attaché before the French Revolution in the first French legation, then again after the Revolution, and finally, after his marriage, as consul in Charleston, South Carolina. There, two of his children were born. In 1798 he was appointed consul general to the whole United States. But when he got to Philadelphia, President John Adams refused to accept him. Relations with France were just about at the breaking point; and besides John Adams and all good Federalists knew that the du Ponts were nothing but subversives. "We have had too many French philosophers already and I really begin . . . to suspect that learned academies not under the . . . control of the government have disorganized the world and are incompatible with social order."

Victor returned to France again just in time to get ready for the final emigration back to America. Meanwhile, he reported in to Talleyrand on the state of feeling toward France there, and that canny statesman immediately began to change his policies, so that war was avoided.

Irénée had been adopted by France's great chemist Lavoisier as his pupil and possible prospective successor in charge of the Royal Powder Works. But the Revolution put an end to that when Lavoisier lost his job and his head. Irénée joined his father in his post-Revolutionary publishing ventures. His heart remained in the powder works.

As soon as the du Ponts settled in America, in a house they christened "Good Stay" (*Bon Séjour*) in New Jersey, across the river near Manhattan, grandiose and chimerical schemes were hatched by Pierre to make a fortune. There were lands in the West, where a Utopian community called Pontiania was to flourish. The new du Pont Company was to handle rich cargoes between France, the United States and the West Indies. Victor was his father's chief assistant in these doomed enterprises. Pierre got in touch with his old friend President Jefferson as soon as they settled. Jefferson advised him not to indulge in land speculations. The two kept on writing till du Pont died; a most instructive exchange, which brings out so clearly the impractical and fanciful nature of the Frenchman, the more canny idealism of the American. Some of the best statements of both men are embalmed in this correspondence.

One effective result of the interchange was the Louisiana Purchase. Pierre and Thomas discussed the whole business, and then when Pierre went back to France in 1802 to raise money for his new company, he served as an intermediary between Jefferson and the French government. Less effective were the attempts of Pierre and Victor to get the new du Pont enterprise operating. Pierre had managed to raise some capital, at least in the form of promises from Swiss financiers like Bidermann and Necker (Madame de Staël's uncle) and from Frenchmen sympathetic to America, like Lafayette and his son-in-law de La Tour-Maubourg (kin no doubt of that lady with the fairy-tale name who married a Montchanin). Even old Beaumarchais showed interest. Victor was active in America, but unfortunately his activities did more harm than good. Thinking he might win favor with Napoleon, Victor helped Napoleon's younger brother Jerome in his American escapades. In fact, this so infuriated Napoleon that Victor's name was added to a list of those who were not to be mentioned in Bonaparte's presence. Hopes of rich cargoes evaporated. The company in fact never did any profitable business at all.

What saved the family was of course Irénée's American powder works. But for him they would all have died in poverty. The story is that Irénée went out shooting one day in 1800 with a French friend. They ran out of powder. When they bought new powder of native American manufacture, they were appalled by its worthlessness. This naturally gave the former pupil of Lavoisier the idea of starting a powder works in America. By the spring of 1802 Irénée and his family had settled on the Brandywine, near Wilmington, Delaware, and the industrial saga had begun. Powder is no longer made at the old site on the Brandywine, and most du Ponts live far out in the surrounding country, but the city of Wilmington remains to this day the heart and center of their enormous, far-flung empire.

The history of any great industrial enterprise begins with the lonely struggles of a hardy, energetic, persevering pioneer. The du Pont Company is certainly no exception. However, the career of Irénée does differ a bit from that of many company founders. The emergent rugged enterpriser usually sheds his obscure parentage at an early age, leaving illiterate forebears behind in some humble cot. Irénée, on the contrary, had to carry his famous father around on his back, like an Old Man of the Sea. The burden nearly killed him.

The du Pont group returned to France, Irénée and Victor temporarily, Pierre more or less permanently. Irénée succeeded in not only raising capital but in getting all sorts of technical help from the French government, pleased with the thought of a good powder works in America as a rival to the British. Pierre continued to propagandize his grandiose schemes. The only collateral he had, besides his well-known name, was the powder company. When Victor at last went bankrupt in 1805 and took refuge in New York State for a while as a storekeeper, when Pierre himself liquidated his company in 1811, the whole gaggle of creditors and investors descended on Irénée. The future of the powder company had been mortgaged to the hilt, and demanding and meddlesome shareholders made life miserable for Irénée throughout the rest of his life.

Pierre, when he wasn't mortgaging away his son's future, was as usual busy in politics and economics. Napoleon would have little to do with him, so his career under the Empire was perforce rather obscure. He spent his time editing and publishing the works of his master Turgot in nine volumes. Despite defects, these volumes remained the only collection of the master's works till mid-nineteenth century, and the edition is in fact probably du Pont's most significant literary contribution. He was also a member of something called the Paris Chamber of Commerce, not a voluntary association of businessmen, but a government agency. As such he was indefatigable as ever. But on the whole it was more busywork than accomplishment. His last chance at glory occurred in 1814. When Napoleon fell and the allies entered Paris, a rump Senate, a provisional government, was created by Talleyrand (who always managed to land on his feet). Talleyrand had remained friendly to du Pont, and appointed him secretary general of this government. The post was more ornamental than powerful. Talleyrand dictated its policies, du Pont signed the official papers. Still, some of these were fairly important, such as the Senate decree deposing Napoleon, and Napoleon's Act of Abdication in April 1814.

Naturally when Napoleon came back from Elba next year, du Pont was a conspicuously marked man. Just a few hours before the ex-emperor reentered Paris, Pierre left for Le Havre to escape to America. Under a false passport, arranged by the American minister, he got away safely.

He spent the last years before his death in 1817 with Irénée along the Brandywine. It was a happy retirement, a final reaching of harbor. He kept up his correspondence with Jefferson, now also in retirement, but missed seeing him at Monticello. Finally, Pierre died as he would have preferred, as the result of action on behalf of the common good. In July of 1817 a fire broke out in the charcoal shed of the powder works. Despite his age, Pierre joined a bucket brigade that got the fire under control before it reached the powder stores. Due to the exertion, the soaking and the singeing, he took to his bed and in a matter of weeks was gone. His wife, still left behind in Paris as the result of an injury, did not hear of his death for several months. He was buried in Wilmington in the graveyard that has become the resting place of so many du Ponts; Irénée is buried to his left, Victor, as firstborn, to his right.

He wrote his epitaph in one of his letters to Jefferson. "Poor ants, let us be satisfied with bringing our grain of millet to the ant hill, and let us die while looking for another one!" The worth of du Pont's particular grains of millet may be doubtful, but no one can dispute his eagerness in bringing them to the ant hill.

By the time of Pierre's death, the powder company was firmly established, helped along first by Jefferson's presidency, then by Madison's war. Wars naturally were always good for the powder business; it is ironic that a company bearing the name Irénée (*irene* means "peace" in Greek) should have been largely successful because of wars. Pierre was not unaware of this potential discrepancy. He wrote to Jefferson, "This *peaceful friend of liberty,* although he manufactures gunpowder, hopes it will not be used for war." His hopes were doomed to profitable disappointment.

The history of the du Pont Company in its first phase spans almost exactly a century. In this phase, the Company was wholly owned and controlled not so much by any individual as by the Family itself. Production did not really get going till 1804. In this year E. I. du Pont de Nemours and Company sold ten thousand dollars worth of new powder. In 1902, after Eugene, the last of the direct presidential heirs of Irénée, died, the Company was offered for sale for fifteen million dollars. In 1970 the Company's annual sales alone amount to over three *billion* dollars. This represents a tidy increase on the original investment. Since the investors have been predominantly du Ponts, and since the presidency has never wandered further from the family than a brother-in-law (William S. Carpenter, ninth president, was the brother of R. R. M. Carpenter, who married a Margaretta du Pont, great-granddaughter of Irénée) or a father-in-law (present President McCoy has two children married to family members, one of them a Carpenter), one can easily see that the family fortunes have improved since that impromptu meal in Newport on New Year's Day.

How does it happen that the family still hangs on so tenaciously to its company? A hundred and fifty, sixty, seventy years is a long time, even in the histories of royal successions. The Tudors and Stuarts did not wear as well. The present chairman of the board, Lammot du Pont Copeland, eleventh president, is a great-great-grandson of Irénée. Such continuity through five generations would seem the exception rather than the rule in American industry. The continuity and the family cohesion were forged during the nineteenth century.

The reigns of Irénée and his descendants during this first century of Company history are as follows:

Irénée	1802–1834
The Bidermann Regency	1834–1837
Eldest Son Alfred V.	1837–1850
Second Son Henry	1850–1889
Grandson (son of Third Son Alexis) Eugene	1889–1902

Third son Alexis himself never got to be president, but was killed in a powder explosion in 1857, first but not last of family martyrs to powder making.

Under Irénée the Company was an autocracy, in which nonfamily partners such as Pierre Bauduy were driven out, foreign investors, such as widowed Madame de Pusy staved off and eventually paid off. All family members, such as improvident Victor, were somehow supported. Since he was obviously not a person useful in powder making, Victor was, so to speak, given a woolen mill to play with. He and Pierre Bauduy ran this, but it was never a very flourishing enterprise. However, it kept Victor busy and on the Brandywine. The powder mills meanwhile, after precarious early years, prospered. Marred by disasters, the explosions and fires which were always the built-in hazards of the enterprise, and helped by disasters, the various wars of America or others, the du Pont powder gradually came to be acknowledged as the best in America.

Victor died in Philadelphia of a heart attack in 1827. Irénée died in Philadelphia of a heart attack or stroke in 1834. The business was left not to any one individual, but as indicated, to the whole family. Each one of the seven children had a partnership, but the active running partners were a triumvirate of Irénée's three sons: Alfred Victor, thirty-six at the time of his father's death; Henry, twenty-two, a cadet at West Point, who regretfully left his military career for the mills; and Alexis, only eighteen at the time, but already an active powderman. Alfred was not really fit for the presidency. He was an introspective person, never robust, more interested in his grandfather's essays and in his own inventions and chemistry than in actual powder making. The second in command for years had been not a son but a son-in-law, Antoine Bidermann. His father Jacques had been the largest of the original Company's Swiss backers. Young Antoine was sent over to see just what were the prospects of the powder company, the only asset salvaged from the debacle of Pierre's illusory projects. Antoine found the prospects good and the scenery delightful. He married Irénée's daughter Evalina and stayed on to help Irénée. When Irénée died, it was Antoine who took over for a few years, a sort of regency, during which he straightened out the Company's affairs, went back to France to clean up the last of the firm's foreign indebtedness, and then gracefully retired. All of his descendants seem to have lived in Europe. They form a rather shadowy penumbra of continental du Ponts, under such fancy names as Aliette Antoinette Gabrielle Amélie Aubert de Trégomain or Loïc Phillippe George Jean-Brice de Barry.

When finally in 1837 Alfred did take over, the most odd and characteristic period of family history began, a sort of communism much like that of those religious enclaves then so popular all over America, or a socialist Fourierism — the colonies at New Harmony or Oneida, for instance. The Family owned the Company, and the Company owned the Family. Nobody was paid a salary. Nobody owned a house or even evidently a horse. Members of the family lived in company houses; when a new one was needed, the Company built one. There is a famous chit which reveals to what extent the Family was dependent on the Company. As late as 1850 Alfred, then just retired, wrote to Henry: "I must go to Philadelphia. . . . My object is to pay off every small debt I owe. To do this I wish you to send me a check on the Phil. Bank for $100. . . . I should wish to have the carriage at 11 oclock . . ." Evidently both petty cash and transportation had to be thus requisitioned.

There was of course a hierarchy within the Family: Alfred (1798–1856) as senior, then Henry (1812–1889), and then Alexis (1816–1857), and finally the girls. Of the four females, all partners in their own right, one had married active Antoine Bidermann, who was thus only a partner through his wife, though a working one. Another girl married a local doctor called Smith, who seems to have had no Company interest; Alexis married Smith's sister, a continuing family pattern of such brother-sister marriages. Sophie married her first cousin Samuel, an even more persistent pattern, and thus brought the Victor line into the company partnership for the first time. The eldest daughter, Victorine, was a blossom early blighted.

Indeed, the chronicles of the third generation begin in both branches with love tragedies. Victorine, oldest child of Irénée, married Ferdinand, the son of obstreperous, early nonfamily partner Pierre Bauduy. Since it was Bauduy who had originally brought Irénée to the Brandywine, where he was already settled as a Haitian refugee, and had been one of the few early hard-cash backers, he did deserve some credit and recognition. The marriage of his son to Victorine, though a true love match, was also an alliance, cementing the fortunes of the two antagonistic houses. If it had lasted, it might well have blended the blood of the Bauduys into the great river of du Pont, where so many other tributaries have mingled. But after only eleven weeks, young Ferdinand died. The du Ponts and Bauduys, brought together briefly by sorrow, split apart again. Bauduy eventually broke with the family altogether, sued them for various reasons, and even started a rival powder factory which kept going up to the time of the Civil War. He was the first and last nonfamily-connected partner in this early phase of Company history.

The story of Amelia, oldest child of Victor, was equally sad but more bizarre. An Englishman called Clifford took over the management of Victor's woolen mill. He soon took over Amelia, who was the family ugly duckling. After a brief spell of married life, it was revealed that Clifford was a bigamist, with a wife in England.

Clifford disappeared from the Brandywine. Amelia never married again, broken-hearted like her cousin Victorine; but a daughter Gabrielle grew up to wed respectably and leave many descendants.

Otherwise the marriages of all the second generation seemed to turn out well; and at this point the distinct differences between the lines begin to be manifest. The differences should have resulted in a split as conscious as that between the Hyde Park and Oyster Bay Roosevelts; certainly as great as that between the branches of Biddles. This split, however, does not seem to have occurred. In the first place, the Company kept them all together, economically and physically. Irénée built Victor a house called Louviers (after a French city famous for its woolen manufactures) on company land. The woolen mill, after all, was a subsidiary of the Company. Despite political activities in the Delaware state capital, Dover, the descendants of Victor kept right on living by the Brandywine, alongside the descendants of Irénée. And then they kept marrying one another. In each of four generations down from Victor and Irénée there was at least one cross-branch du Pont–du Pont marriage; sometimes more than one. The result is a great intertwining homogeneity, despite contrasting heredities.

The nineteenth-century differences can best be labeled as the contrasts between, say, plain and fancy, or high-toned versus down-to-earth. The marriages along the main line of Irénée, hardworking, misanthropic, were definitely plain. First there was Sophie Dalmas, daughter of a tradesman, of whom Pierre so disapproved socially. Then Alfred, Irénée's oldest son, married a plain Lammot, anglicization of the French La Motte, a Huguenot name so like those that weave through the annals of the family back in Rouen. Then, in the third generation, Alfred's son Lammot married a Belin, again French, again plain. Mary Belin's father was a bookkeeper at the works. The only disturbing element here was that back a generation one grandparent had been of Jewish origin. It is this line of plain stock, French stock (with a Jewish tinge), that has kept its hands on the Company. With three exceptions, all the presidents of the

Company down to the present have been associated with this particular bloodstream.

A completely different pattern, equally hereditary, is exemplified by the main line down from Victor. Victor himself having married the daughter of a marquis, as he spent the early part of his life in diplomacy, spent the latter part, from 1815 to 1824, in state politics. He was for many years a state senator of Delaware. His older son, Charles I, followed this pattern by being not only the most enlightened du Pont of his period, but also a state senator of Delaware. He married well; not one, but two heiresses of Delaware's most prominent legal-political families. His oldest son Victor in turn took Charles' place in the state senate, and then two of this Victor's sons-in-law became United States senators. So from Pierre, senator (Council of Elders) of the French Directory, through Victor, Charles, Victor and then his sons-in-law Saulsbury and T. Coleman du Pont (of the Irénée branch), there were five successive generations of senators of one kind or another.

The first marriage of Charles Irénée, to Dorcas Van Dyke, was by far the most glittering social event in the family's early history. It occurred when Lafayette was on his grand triumphal visit in 1824, and Lafayette himself gave the bride away. The Van Dykes were as important as anyone in Delaware could be. Dorcas' grandfather, Nicholas Van Dyke senior, of St. George's Hundred near Newcastle, had been one of the scanty score of Delaware delegates to the Continental Congress, and then first president (governor) of the state after the Revolution.* His son, Nicholas junior, the father of Dorcas, had run the gauntlet of office from state representative to U.S. Representative, and from state senator to U.S. Senator. The Van Dykes were important, and by marrying into them, the du

---

* Another odd pattern in these families is a connection with early governorship of their respective states. Samuel Adams was one of the first governors of Massachusetts. Archibald Bulloch, ancestor of Theodore Roosevelt, was first governor of Georgia. Charles Biddle was one of the first vice presidents and then acting president of Pennsylvania. Thomas Johnson, uncle of Louisa Adams, was first governor of Maryland, and was succeeded by Thomas Sim Lee. Harry Lee was one of the early governors of the state of Virginia.

Ponts, somewhat shady and subversive furriners as they were, became accepted into the local stability and aristocracy of a high legal and political, as opposed to a low commercial, sort.

Then Charles, finding himself in middle life a widower, compounded his good fortune by marrying for his second wife Ann Ridgely, of an even more prominent Delaware family, if possible, than the Van Dykes. So what with the Montchanins, de Pelleports, Van Dykes and Ridgelys, the veins of the Victor line were adequately infused with blue. The fact that Charles' only brother Samuel married a du Pont and two of his children, Charles junior and Amelia, also married du Ponts, blended this blue with the soberer strains of the powder making side of the family.

Charles' sister Amelia was of course the heartbroken bride of bigamist Mr. Clifford, but his other sister Julia married into a family as distinguished as the Van Dykes. Her husband, Irvine Shubrick, was a South Carolinian and a commander in the navy. Some seven Shubricks, all told, were naval officers; Irvine's brother William, later a rear admiral like Samuel du Pont, took over command of the Pacific squadron in the Mexican War from James Biddle.

A son of Irvine, Thomas B., was one of the very few naval casualties in that war. He was about to be engaged to his cousin Mary, the daughter of Charles; to carry on another du Pont tradition, that of the blighted romance of the eldest child, Mary too was brokenhearted and never married.

So on the one hand you get the descendants of Irénée, working hard, marrying plain, getting rich and blown up; and on the other hand the descendants of Victor, marrying heiresses and indulging in senatorial politics. And both branches incessantly marrying one another.

Alfred retired from the Company management in 1850 and his place was eagerly taken by aggressive brother Henry. Till his death in 1889, Henry ran the community and the Company with an iron hand — the beneficent Stalin of this particular bit of communism.

He had been forced out of West Point by his father's death, but retained military ambitions. During the Civil War he was made commanding major general of the state militia, and of course was ever afterward known as the General; and he sent his son Henry to carry on for him at West Point. During the Civil War the du Ponts and their Company were uncompromisingly Unionists. Various attempts were made to sabotage the works, but none succeeded. As in any and every war, the powder works prospered. The transition from Wilmington family firm to national big business took place under Henry.

After the war, the commercial chaos, in which speculators were selling army-surplus powder at cut-rate prices and causing confusion, forced the old-line big powder companies to get together for self-protection. A group calling itself the Gunpowder Trade Association was formed in 1872. This was the nucleus of a Powder Trust that paralleled the various other trusts of the Gilded Age. It too practiced price-fixing, ruining smaller competitors, and all the other unsavory shenanigans of the age of the robber barons. Pretty soon, by acquiring companies or stock, the du Ponts under Henry owned or controlled the majority of America's powder production.

Still, during all this time, the Company supposedly remained the same curious communal affair. Henry did take the largest share of the profits for himself, du Ponts were becoming famously rich, new and more sumptuous houses were being built; but E. I. du Pont de Nemours stayed a close-held family partnership, not a corporation with stock, officers and directors. Henry ran this increasingly tremendous show himself. Henry was boss. From his tiny, old-fashioned, candle-lit office (he never even permitted gaslight to be installed), into which modern inventions such as the typewriter were admitted only with the greatest reluctance, he supervised an empire with new mills built or bought all over the country, and in which, again over the reactionary objections of Henry, new methods were being applied to the making of explosives.

Henry was never one for new methods. Even after that

typewriter was at last insinuated into his office, he refused to use it or to dictate to a secretary. He continued to write out all his letters longhand. He was sure that Nobel's newfangled discoveries involving nitroglycerin were no good and refused to let the Company experiment with dynamite until nephew Lammot, the du Pont inventive genius of that period, threatened to leave and start manufacturing it on his own.

Henry always appeared in a high silk hat. He would stalk about on inspection tours so adorned, and on one occasion thus saved the works from disaster. He discovered an overheated shaft which might have set off a series of explosions. He rushed to the creek, filled his top hat and cooled off the inflammation by pouring water over it. He was land-hungry, buying acres and acres up the Brandywine and fencing them with well-constructed stone walls. In fact he kept a special force of masons busy with nothing but wall building. They were known as the "never sweats" from their leisurely work methods. It is these lands, then owned by the Company, which now form the basis of the du Pont estates, which stretch for miles north and east of Wilmington. Many of the family resented his dictatorship, his insistence on keeping things just as they had always been, including Company control of their houses, possessions, incomes and lives. They resented his totally autocratic ways and whims, and his allocation to himself of the largest share of Company earnings. But it was Henry who transformed the Company from a successful local to *the* successful national powder-making outfit; and like his methods or not, the family could hardly complain that they were being ruined.

Boss Henry is the great representative du Pont of the Iron Age. When he died in 1889, dressed, one feels sure, to the very last in stiff collar and high top hat, the Company may have been the greatest of its kind in the country, but its management structure was completely out-of-date. That such an unwieldy affair could continue to be run as a one-man-ruled, family partnership was impossible. Eugene, Henry's nephew and Alexis' son, attempted to do so. He did introduce some modernisms — a large new office adequately housed and staffed — but he was no Henry. In 1899 the Company, much to the regret of many older du Ponts, was incorporated, and the peculiar family control officially ended. Of course all the new officers were du Ponts,* but still, the Company had become just a company like others. Only a few years afterward Eugene died; with his passing in 1902 the old era, and the nineteenth century, officially ended for E. I. du Pont de Nemours & Co.

All three of the sons of Irénée — Alfred, Henry and Alexis — married and had children, and it is among these descendants that the continuing control of the Company has rested. None of the marriages — Lammot, Gerhard, Smith — could be called brilliant. Gerhard and Smith were both respectable but not upper-class Philadelphia families. The Philadelphia diarist Sidney Fisher knew Louisa Gerhard, Henry's wife, and commented in his usual forthrightly class-conscious way. He had been an old friend of her brother Ben, whom he regarded generally as a likable-but-boorish parvenu lawyer. In 1860 he took a train trip with Louisa from Wilmington to Philadelphia.

"She is a very charming woman, still handsome, very intelligent, soft, gentle, feminine, and her manners thoroughly ladylike and refined. I was surprised and highly pleased. The du Ponts are an old family and have been settled on the Brandywine for two or three generations, where they have extensive powder mills. They own a very large landed estate there and are very rich. The different families of them, eight in number, all live on the property and have handsome establishments, forming a little community, and all share in the business and its profits which are held in common."

The "surprise" was occasioned by Louisa's being so well-bred, considering her low origins and uncouth brother. He seemed to feel

---

* Eugene was president; Francis Gurney, Alexis, Col. Henry A., vice presidents; Charles Irénée III, secretary and treasurer. The first four were allotted 20 percent of the stock shares apiece. Charles and Alfred I. were each given 10 percent.

no such reservations about the du Ponts themselves. They were evidently thoroughly established by that time.

It is at this point, from the fourth generation down from Pierre Samuel and on, that the family begins to spread and proliferate almost beyond human comprehension. Alfred had seven children, Henry had nine, and Alexis had eight. Naturally all did not live and breed; but enough did. There was no question here of splitting into further "branches." All du Ponts seemed as one. The forty years of domination by Henry tended to put most of the other du Pont males into something of a shade. Lammot was the most distinguished of the sons of Alfred, a chemist and very active in promoting new methods and new companies, mostly over the objections of boss Henry. Like his uncle Alexis, he too gave his life to his company. He was killed in an explosion in 1884. It was he who married the Belin and so added a faint Jewish tinge to the du Pont main line.

General Henry himself had only two sons, Henry Algernon and William, separated by nearly twenty years and by seven sisters. Neither distinguished himself particularly in the Company, though Henry A. was one of the three vice presidents in 1899; but to put it poetically, Henry won laurels on the field of Mars, and William on the field of Venus — that is, Henry was a hero in the Civil War, and William, later on, the hero of the first really shattering family scandal. Of the seven sisters, only one has descendants. She married a New York Irving, kin of author Washington Irving, proprietors of the Irving Trust Company. Her descendants have followed the matrimonial advice of Robert E. Lee by being exceedingly proud of "both sides of the house."

As for the children of Alexis, the third son of Irénée: Eugene became president of the Company and married his cousin Amelia du Pont. Francis Gurney was also active in powder making, and was another of those first vice presidents. Otherwise this group was distinguished by various incredibly complex multiple marriages into the Bradford, Dimmick and Coleman families. These cross-connections are known as "keeping the family together." * Like the Lees and the Biddles, and the Adamses in their Johnson-Smith reaches, nineteenth-century people just naturally seemed to prefer marrying cousins.

All this making of powder and of money, all this marrying and crossbreeding, characteristic activities of nineteenth-century du Ponts, has been enlivened by two military sports. Samuel Francis du Pont can be thought of as America's first admiral. Henry Algernon du Pont is one of the first to be awarded the Congressional Medal of Honor, then as now America's most distinguished decoration.

They were both professionals. In the du Pont–Jefferson correspondence we have Pierre asking Thomas to assure the appointment of Samuel, son of Victor, as midshipman in 1815, and Jefferson congratulating Pierre on that appointment. "I hope your grandson will have become one of our High-admirables," he wrote, better prophet than speller; for in fact du Pont did become one of our rear, if not high, "admirables." He served gallantly in the Mexican War alongside and under his various Shubrick in-laws and Biddle contemporaries. Then, in the Civil War, he achieved the Union's first naval victory, when by superior strategy he captured the crucial harbor of Port Royal, South Carolina, and went on to take other secessionist installations in Georgia and Florida.

Eighteen sixty-one was a bad year all round for the Union, so this naval victory was received with ecstasy. Du Pont was a hero, and Congress in 1862 promoted him to the brand-new rank of rear admiral.† Nobody had ever risen higher than commodore in previous American naval history. The climax and key of the Southern offshore campaign however must be the capture of Charleston, where

* See Appendix IV.
† However, several other officers were simultaneously created rear admiral; including Commodore William Shubrick.

the war had originated. Here du Pont failed. The blame is generally put upon Secretary Welles, whose obstinate faith in the invincibility of the newfangled ironclads forced du Pont, against his better judgment, into using them for the assault. The assault failed, du Pont was the scapegoat, and from being a hero he was now a villain. He was replaced as commander of the blockade by his friend Dahlgren, and retired disgruntled to du Pontland on the Brandywine. There he died in 1865. Posthumous honor was done him by the naming of du Pont Circle in Washington, for years the center of that city's fashionable life.

Henry Algernon, son of General Henry, graduated first in his class at West Point in 1861, just in time for action. As an artillery officer in the Shenandoah Valley, and as assistant to notorious General Hunter, he has been falsely credited with refusing to shell the buildings of VMI. He shelled VMI; it was White Sulphur Springs that he spared. He received a brevet commission as lieutenant colonel and his medal for gallant action at the battle of Cedar Creek, still in the Shenandoah campaign.

Finding the peacetime army boring, he resigned in 1875 and returned to Wilmington, where he ended as president of a local railroad, a vice president of the Company, and, later on, a crusty politician and senator. These two belligerents are the only du Ponts, since Pierre, who have really distinguished themselves away from the aura and area of the Brandywine and the Company.

For the rest, the family moves like a slow flood, increasing in numbers and wealth. By the last quarter of the nineteenth century, the "eight families" of Sidney Fisher had increased to some 125 du Ponts still living in that home area on those lands foresightedly acquired by Henry, in houses either built by the Company or, increasingly, by the increasingly rich individual families themselves.

Not until the *fin de siècle,* or the new century, did the du Ponts begin to be spectacular. But that story of palaces, politics, and problems belongs, strictly speaking, in tone if not always in time, to a new and later chapter of family history, the era of plutocracy for which the family is now most famous. It was, however, the curious tightness of the communal arrangement that held them together and kept them on the Brandywine during the Iron Age, the period of the Company's growth. Though later generations were the most flamboyant of individualists and rabid defenders of Private Enterprise, the foundation of their good fortunes is this special brand of family cooperation, which reminds one so of the cohesion of the great Jewish families like the Rothschilds or Guggenheims. For all the Enlightenment of Pierre and his sons, for all the coats of arms and "time immemorial" of the Montchanins or de Pelleports, it was the residual bourgeois and Old Testament character of the Huguenot Duponts of Rouen that has molded the family character. Blood will tell.

7

The Four Adams Brothers

THE FATE of the Adams had pursued her victims relentlessly for three generations: two out of three sons coming to bad ends, and even the one who came to a good end, following the exact footsteps of his father, always ousted from his career just at its summit. Finally in the fourth generation one can think of the Fate of the Adams, her grim visage twisted in an ironic smile, as relaxing her grip. There were four sons — John, Charles Francis junior, Henry and Brooks — not three. No one of them died young and disgraced, like Charles or George Washington, a drunkard or suicide or sire of illegitimate children. No one of them even declined into nondescript middle age, a quarrelsome alcoholic like Thomas Boylston, or a mediocre business failure like John Quincy junior. They all lived to a respectable age, they all had money, they all made a reputation and a position for themselves. But on the other hand, no one of them was able to make a career in politics and diplomacy, to follow those paternal footsteps. For three generations the Adams had been not just meritorious but *famous*. As far as fame is concerned, what the four men of the fourth generation did achieve in the end was — one book. A book recounting just how the Fate of the Adams brought this generation to its "failure." The book was famous, though its author never lived to see that fame.

Superficially none of the four brothers followed the Adams pattern to its conclusions: Harvard, the bar, letters to newspapers, state legislature, U.S. legislature, diplomacy (minister to England), second in command as Vice President or secretary of state, then one fatal term as President; after that a bitter, useful quarter-century of quasi-retirement. Nobody came close to being minister to England or secretary of state or President. Already in the third generation Charles Francis, though following the pattern in general, followed it only at a distance and partway. In the fourth generation it was as though the electric force, the energy, instead of being channeled into one person, had been dissipated, parceled out among the four; each one getting a part, but none getting the whole (a simile of which Henry and Brooks would have approved).

The first steps were followed by all of them: Harvard, then the law. Though none was a successful practicing lawyer, all tried. John really made it his profession, but he was, of all things for an Adams, lazy about it. Charles Francis tried but failed. Henry studied but never really tried. Brooks practiced and then taught in law school, but could hardly be called a successful practicing lawyer. All, even John, wrote for newspapers and magazines — letters, articles, correspondence. Beyond this initial stage, however, their careers split: John into politics, Charles into business, Henry into teaching and history, Brooks into the writing of theoretical polemics. They all had a certain success, and a certain distinction in these careers; and yet, especially by Adams standards, they were all failures. They were none of them, during their lifetimes, important public figures. For the first time the Adams family had sunk below the national into the private, local and professional level.

Of all the family, John (1833–94) the oldest was the most unusual Adams; that is to say, most like a normal, pleasant, human being. He was that incredible phenomenon, a *nice* Adams. Everybody loved him, he was fun and could make people laugh, he was gregarious. He was happily married and his children loved him and he failed to ruin their lives by good advice. He hated writing and refused to keep a diary or preserve letters (a "vile family habit" he thought). Once, when asked by his daughter why Uncle Charles and Uncle Henry and Uncle Brooks spent all their time writing, he replied, "I suppose it amuses them." As though any Adams ever did anything just because it amused him! Fishing, however, amused John more than the law; on one occasion, when called to attend court on a case, he refused to come because the smelts were "biting like thunder."

John did, though, betray one fatal Adams inclination, the love of reform. Reform led him into politics, as it led Charles into railroads. And in fact, reform in various ways dominated the lives of all four of the brothers, as it had that of their father. "Reform" before the Civil War was of course the reform of slavery and its abuses, a reform in which both John Quincy I and Charles Francis I had been most active. The Civil War put an end to slavery. The issue that had polarized American politics from 1840 on was gone. There were a few years of aftermath, from 1865, say, to the death of Lee in 1870; years of bitterness or reconciliation in the South, of return to the fleshpots in the North. Then, beginning definitely in 1872 with the abortive attempt to nominate Charles Francis Adams as a reform candidate against Grant, and with Greeley's defeat, America once more began to be polarized about a fundamental issue.

This new polarization, which has dominated America's domestic history for a century, could be, and was, labeled in various ways. Whatever the labels, one side usually represented Reform. The other side, whether its labels were Grant or Gold, usually represented Riches. This great American confrontation of Reform versus Riches culminated in the Roosevelts and the political victory of Reform. During most of the Gilded Age, that third and last phase of the nineteenth century, the battles all seemed to go in favor of Riches.

Reform began first not so much as an attack on Riches as upon political and financial corruption, the low politics of the Grant administration, the devious doings of Jay Gould. Honest government, regulation of railroads, civil-service reform were the first objectives of the reformers. Only gradually did Americans in any numbers begin to feel menaced by the basic power of capital itself. In these early stages of reform the three older Adams brothers were active. In election after election it was reform and redress on one side, prosperity and protection on the other. First the mismanaged nomination and campaign of Greeley against Grant; then Tilden against Hayes, in which Tilden really won but was defrauded of his victory; then the unexpected civil-service reforms of Arthur, after Garfield's assassination; and finally, in the person of Cleveland as a Democrat, the triumph of virtue over the dubious Blaine. After that followed the continual seesaw of what came eventually to be considered "liberal" versus "conservative" — Harrison, back to Cleveland, back again to McKinley, then the first age of Roosevelt, marked by the relapses of Taft; Wilson, and the reaction against him in the twenties; finally FDR. The pattern still persists, emerges clearly over the century of conflict as a gradual taming of raw and irresponsible but productive and dynamic American capitalism in the interests of the general populace through the medium of the central government — that odd blend of Hamilton-Biddle centralism and Jefferson-Jackson populism known as the New Deal.

All the attitudes of the Adamses of the Gilded Age, their failures and successes, are intimately bound up with this struggle and with the Adamses' own rather ambivalent attitudes towards both Reform and Riches. John's attitude was most forthright and consistent; and least effective. He gave up the Republican party in disgust and became a Democrat. He ran as Democratic candidate for governor of Massachusetts again and again and again, and was always defeated. He even was an unwilling candidate for Vice President on a sort of renegade "regular Democratic" ticket split off from the Greeley reformers in 1872. If his father had been nominated instead of Greeley, father and son would have been electioneering against each other. In any case, Grant won. When Cleveland and the Democrats finally came in, John was offered the position of secretary of the navy (a position his son held later on as a Republican). But by then he was no longer interested. His health was poor, he declined the office, and in 1894 at the age of only a bit over sixty, much too young for an Adams, he died. If he had lived, he might have been the one to carry on the Adams tradition. He did after all run for Vice President, like his father. He was in the state legislature, like all his forebears. He could have been a cabinet officer, if not secretary of state. But somehow one feels, given his curiously un-Adams personality, he would have been more surprised than pleased to be on the winning side. "I like a minority," he said. It was the fun of being a loser that amused John.

Charles Francis came much closer to following in the footsteps, and indeed he did follow the family schedule to an amazing extent; not in politics, but in business. Here too, after Harvard and the law, we have letters to newspapers, then office in Massachusetts followed by national office, and finally a presidency, which like all the family presidencies, ended in disaster; and then the usual bitterly fruitful quarter-century of retirement. In outline it is exactly the Adams Fate. In content, however, it is nowhere diplomatic or political. Instead of foreign service, we have war service. Charles was the first Adams to be a real warrior. He fought four long, hard years as a cavalry officer, emerging with broken health and a fine record as a brevet brigadier general. His letters to his family remain one of the better glimpses of war seen from inside the fighting.

Then, after the war, he deliberately chose not law and politics, but railroads as his field of endeavor. Railroads, stimulated phenomenally by the war, dominated the country economically and politically. Charles set himself up as an expert on them. He wrote articles (*Chapters of Erie,* etc.) exposing the manipulations of railroad financiers like Jay Gould, suggested remedies, and was a member of the first effective railroad commission of the country, that of Massachusetts, set up largely to order by him. Finally he moved on to become chairman of the government directors of the floundering Union Pacific. In 1884 he became president of that railroad. Here, like his ancestors, he came to grief through treachery from within. As John was defeated by Hamilton, so Charles was by Jay Gould. Gould took over the railroad. Charles retired to Quincy, there to settle into a comfortable routine of town government, along with brother John, conservation in the form of city parks, and a mass of local historical writing, full of tart Adams asides.* He became president of the Massachusetts Historical Society and an overseer of Harvard. At the same time, he remained head of the Kansas City stockyards. He had built them into a flourishing company from almost nothing. Railroads and reform ceased to concern him. The happiness of his retirement was spoiled by the depression of 1893, which caught him financially overextended, and nearly ruined him and the whole Adams family. It was half a dozen years before he could restabilize the family fortunes. By then he felt himself an old man; and though he lived many years longer, not dying until 1915, he never was active again beyond the boundaries of his native region.

So the Adams design of success and failure was repeated in commercial terms and worked itself out for the same reason: as Adamses

---

* As historian, one of his most conspicuous efforts was a speech at Washington and Lee during the Robert E. Lee Centennial. Adams said Lee was "the highest type of human development." This was popular in Virginia and did much to conciliate North and South.

had been successful in politics because of merit, intelligence, integrity, industry, but failures because they essentially despised people, notably their political supporters, so in railroads Charles succeeded as a reformer, but failed because he despised businessmen. Two contradictory statements, both of course designed to contradict, stand out in his autobiography. One is his famous estimate of his financial confreres: "I have known . . . a good many 'successful men' . . . and a less interesting crowd I do not care to encounter. Not one that I have ever known would I care to meet again, either in this world or the next. . . . A set of mere money getters and traders, they were essentially unattractive and uninteresting." And yet, in this summing up of his life, he rejects professional, military, political and literary success, in favor of — money: "What I now find I would really have liked is something quite different. I would like to have accumulated . . . one of those vast fortunes of the present day . . . 'money to burn.'" Not of course for amusement, heaven forbid! "I do not want it for myself," but to give to Harvard. "I would like to be the nineteenth century John Harvard — the John-Harvard-of-the-Money-Bags. I would rather be that than be Historian or General or President."

Both these statements were designed to shock; nothing Charles enjoyed more than playing Adams to the hilt. It was he who quoted with so much glee Charles Eliot Norton's saying that the "Adamses have a genius for saying even a gracious thing in an ungracious way!" "So keen and true!" chortled Charles. He was certainly not going to let tradition down. He conscientiously devotes the first, and best, chapters of his autobiography to excoriating his Boston childhood and his Boston education. He makes plain his dislike of his sacred father, his hatred of the Boston Latin School and of church observances, and even though he has to admit he liked Harvard, he makes it equally plain that it was a poor sort of place educationally in his day, and that his class, 1856, was chiefly distinguished for "contributing two inmates to the State's prison." It amused Charles to pose as an iconoclast. Yet in the end he winds up as the crustiest of conservatives, a man interested in provincial security and folkways, local history and the local historical society, Harvard and Quincy. He becomes in fact a sort of model of the New England "character": the man who complains, for instance, that he found difficulty in learning to ride a bicycle when over sixty, blaming his lack of early education in sports for this; or the man who could not be prevented by September northeasters from taking his daily swim off the Cohasset rocks, but stood "gazing out at a gray sea while pensively rubbing his bald head and happily murmuring 'My God, how dreary.'" *

As in all his generation of Adamses, there exists the same ambivalence. He hated his father, yet wrote a judicious biography of him and spent the end of his life amassing materials for another, greater one. He hated business and businessmen, the corruption of the railroad world, yet devoted his life to it, tried to make a fortune himself and become the "John Harvard Moneybags."

The key to the ambivalence is essentially Family. To the Adamses, as to all those who had arrived before the Civil War, there was something gross and terrible about the thunderous rise of wealth afterward. The new plutocracy, the parvenu ostentation, were offensive to taste and conscience. It was inevitable that an Adams would begin as a reformer. But in every case the Adamses failed as reformers, for equally hereditary reasons. Only by joining the disgust of the superior classes with the resentment of the inferior classes could the reform hope to be effective. That kind of junction an Adams could not and would not make. He might despise businessmen, but he despised the democracy more. The crude East of New York and Newport might be loathsome, but the crude West, as eventually personified in Bryan, was worse. John kept on fighting, defeated, till he dropped. But for Charles the motto of "if you can't lick 'em, join 'em" became more and more apropos. He tried to lick them, then tried to join them, failed in both, and then retreated miffed into the safe shell of New England, where an Adams could

* Quoted from Abigail Adams Homans' delightful *Education by Uncles*.

always play Adams, and where Harvard stood ready to forgive and embrace, perpetual alma mater.

Still, in the end, Charles Francis had to confess he had had what his forebears hadn't: "I have perhaps accomplished nothing considerable, compared to what my three immediate ancestors accomplished; but on the other hand . . . I have had a much better time in life — got more enjoyment out of it. In this respect I would not change with any of them."

The road from simple postwar, anti-Grant, upper-class disdain and reform was more complicated and led in more terrible directions for the two younger sons, Henry and Brooks. They too failed to lick or join, they too were repelled by both Newport and Bryan; but for neither of them was the shell of New England enough — Harvard, the Massachusetts Historical Society, Quincy town meetings, daily sea-bathing at the Adams summer group-establishment, The Glades. Their eccentric courses took them both away from not only New England, but America, and headed them into the outer spaces of politics and philosophy to circle the dark sun of what we would now call fascism.

Henry's was the more interesting journey, and justified itself, to the extent that it can be justified, in that book, the book that remains the most memorable monument in act or word of this fourth-generation of the Adams family. The book is of course *The Education of Henry Adams*, which describes that "interesting journey" from New England certainty to modern uncertainty, from Puritanism to perplexity. The book is, in a curious way, a sort of capstone and keystone of the whole family history.

In the first place, of all the incredible welter of Adams words — the letters, the diaries, the speeches, the articles, the pamphlets, the poetry, the constitutions, the theories, the dispatches, the legal briefs — it is the *only* Adams book that can be called popular, that has been really read, that *is* really read, that has achieved the status not of a special work (like, say, *Mont-Saint-Michel and Chartres*),

but of a general classic. Yet it is, in a way, a rejection of all the
Adams words that preceded it, including those of Henry himself.
This irony is only a culmination of many ironies. The whole tone of
the book is deliberately ironic, a bitter amusement at the inability of
an Adams to cope with the Gilded Age. Then there is the irony of its
history as a book — written in 1905, printed in 1906 for private circulation only, but building up a sort of hidden notoriety, then finally
published publicly in 1918 after the death of its author — and immediately becoming famous. The dead Henry won the Pulitzer Prize
in 1919, an honor he surely would have disdained. Striking exactly
the right note of disillusioned pessimism hatched by the First World
War among intellectuals, this entirely nineteenth-century, *fin-de-
siècle* book has become a twentieth-century favorite. The subtle-
ties, the perplexities, the ironies, all appeal to the particular taste of
an epoch that, like the Pulitzer Prize, Henry would also surely have
despised. No story of a "failure" has ever been such a success among
the Americans to whom it was not addressed.

The success of this book has helped to redeem and save from
oblivion a whole world, a generation of Adamses, a tangle of other
books. It is certainly safe to say that without the *Education* the
other works of Henry, as well as those of Brooks and Charles Francis, would be of scholarly interest only. Not that these other works
are not in their way admirable. Henry's *History of the United
States,* a nine-volume coverage of the country under the four administrations of Jefferson and Madison, 1800–1816 (that *one* gap
in earlier American history during which neither John nor John
Quincy were importantly active in domestic affairs), is generally
credited as a monument. Historians rate it as one of the best, probably the best of the scientific, as opposed to the romantic, American
histories published in the nineteenth century.* But it is pretty special after all. A closely packed nine-volume work covering such a

---

* The judgment of America's foremost Jefferson authority is that, like Gibbon's
Decline and Fall of the Roman Empire, the Adams history is *sui generis* for the
Jeffersonian period; but that as Gibbon totally fails to understand the chief pro-
tagonist of his history, Christianity, so Adams fails to understand Jefferson.

narrow range of political time is hardly going to have many nonspecialist readers. It would always be reputable among the learned; but if it hadn't been written by the famous author of the *Education,* would anyone except the learned have heard of it? Even more obscure would be his excellent biography of Gallatin, or his anonymously published and witty novel *Democracy* or his somewhat precious adulation of twelfth-century architecture, *Mont-Saint-Michel and Chartres.* All these books have had and would have admirers; but it is most certainly the fame of the *Education* that keeps them alive today. If they had been written by a John Smith, who wasn't an Adams and who hadn't written his autobiography, it is pretty certain that a meritorious neglect is all they would receive from moderns.

It may well be the fame of the *Education* that has kept the popular reputation of the whole family alive since the 1920's, and that the present postwar Adams boom, as represented by *Those Who Love* and the Adams Papers, and above all the Pulitzer Prize biographies — Bemis' of John Quincy (1950) and Samuels' of Henry (1965) — depend pretty much on the stimulus given to interest in the Adamses by interest in the *Education.**

Yet the whole point of the *Education* is the often quoted "unimportance of being an Adams." It is a minutely detailed bad example, a specimen of one way in which families can go down hill; the Decline and Fall of the Adams Empire.

Henry's "failure" of course was only relative. Quite aside from the *Education,* he was perhaps the most distinguished American professional historian of his time, a position recognized by his confreres with his election in 1894 as president of the American Historical Society. He of course refused to attend any of their meetings,

---

* Perhaps I have here overestimated the impact of the *Education* and underestimated his other books. Perhaps the "Adams boom" was inevitable. Perhaps as in the case, say, of FDR, it is hard to say what *might* have happened. Actually I myself think the *Education* a bit overrated, fascinating as it is, reflecting a pessimism as much fashionable and personal as truly profound. However . . .

but the recognition remained. It was based not only on his *History* and his *Gallatin,* but also on his seven years of teaching at Harvard, during which his influence and example were important both for his pupils and the university.

True, it took him a long time to get started. Graduating from Harvard in 1858 (in the same class as the nongraduating Rooney Lee) two years after his brother Charles, he was aimed uncertainly and unwillingly towards the law when war came. He was taken to England as his father's secretary, just as Charles Francis went with John Quincy, and John Quincy with John. His schoolboy brother Brooks went too. John stayed in Boston to manage the family affairs; Charles Francis fought.

Henry never had any official position in England, but he was useful and became much at home there. He wrote letters for the newspapers, as an Adams should, and even some general and historical articles.* When he arrived back in the country in 1868, he was a man of thirty and really had no occupation or profession. As an unmarried son of a rich family, his problems were not really pressing. He settled in Washington and for a couple of years tried to make his way as a political journalist. But journalism seemed a failure, and his real career began only in 1870 when he was asked to become a member of Harvard's newly revitalized three-man department of history and simultaneously editor of the powerful but hardly popular *North American Review* (circulation between three and four hundred). That a perfect amateur, with no training in either academic history or professional editing should have been offered such positions on the basis of a few articles is rather startling. Being an Adams certainly had something to do with it; just as Charles Francis senior, the year before in 1869, had been offered the presidency of Harvard, just because he was who he was. (He declined.)

As an historian, Henry was put in charge of the Middle Ages — everything between Ancient and Modern. He was by all accounts a

* His first was a piece debunking the Smith-Pocahontas myth. Shades of George Washington Parke Custis!

thorough and inspiring teacher, both deeply scholarly and deeply stimulating. As an editor he tried to make of the *Review* an engine of Reform. There he was defeated by reactionary trustees. He got bored with Cambridge and teaching. He hankered after Washington and politics. Even though he knew he could probably never at such a late date hope for elective office, nor even for a good diplomatic post (he was eventually offered a post in Costa Rica; he declined), he felt he could work behind the scenes, or at least observe.

His marriage in 1872 to Marian Hooper of Boston marked the beginning of a new life — one of the few truly happy spans of life for any Adams. They settled in Washington in 1877, they became social arbiters, they created there an exclusive, powerful nucleus of friends, and Henry settled down to the creation of the monumental *History*. The Fate of the Adamses however was not going to be *that* lenient. When his brother Charles heard he was going to marry a Hooper, he went even beyond the bounds of Adams ungraciousness. He said to Henry, "No! They're all crazy as coots. She'll kill herself, just like her aunt." Charles was quite right, as other ungracious Adamses have been before (*vide* Samuel Eliot Morison's dictum that the Adamses were usually right, but they were unnecessarily disagreeable about it). In 1885, swallowing some photographic solution, Marian Hooper also committed suicide, as did her brother and sister.

The Adamses were just completing a new house, designed by their friend Richardson in vaguely Romanesque style and built simultaneously side by side with that of Henry's bosom friend John Hay.* Mrs. Adams never lived to move in; but Henry did, and it remained his headquarters for the rest of his long, wandering life. But his wife's suicide broke his mainspring. In his own heartbroken words, "As long as I could make life work, I stood by it," but, "fate at last has smashed the life out of me."

He still had his friends — a charmed circle of intellectual statesmen, scientists, artists — John Hay, poet, journalist, diplomat, finally

---

* Hence the name Hay-Adams for the hotel that now stands on the site.

secretary of state under two Presidents; Theodore Roosevelt, author, cattleman, President; diplomats and cabinet members like Wayne McVeagh and Henry White, and the Englishman Cecil Spring Rice; the strange, ebullient geologist Clarence King, who mapped the minerals of the West and made part of that innermost circle of Adams friends, before Marian's suicide, the Five of Hearts, along with the Hayses (King's secret marriage to a Negro woman was no bar to Henry's friendship); artist John Lafarge, with whom Henry took a memorable tour of the South Pacific; sculptor Augustus St. Gaudens, who did the somber memorial at his wife's grave in Rock Creek Park; the James brothers, positive William and evasive Henry; George Santayana; and Bernard Berenson, who for all his Jewishness became a later confessional for the anti-Semite Henry; and the ladies — Edith Wharton; Elizabeth Cameron, wife of the boss of Pennsylvania, Senator James Donald Cameron; a whole gallery of nieces in fact or by adoption who provided Henry with the kind of young, adulatory, female society he preferred. Never in fact has American history known, since the days of the Founding Fathers, a group of intellectuals and aesthetes who were so close to the throne. This whole refined, perhaps overrefined, and rich, perhaps overrich, world of sophisticated *fin-de-siècle* America touches the supposedly reclusive Henry at every point. He wrote letters to these people and they wrote him. He took trips with them and showed them those privately printed copies of his last works. As the reputations of Henry James, Edith Wharton and Henry Adams himself continue to grow, the whole elaborate social continent, obscure during the antagonistic years of boom, depression and war, begins to emerge. Henry is at the center of it.

But that last period of Henry's life, from the final publication of his *history* in 1892 to his death in 1918 — that typical bitter Adams postcareer — was not devoted only to grief and trips, to friends or to the writing of his most famous books, *Mont-Saint-Michel* and the *Education*. He also spent his time, "amused himself" as John would have said and Henry would have admitted, with trying to evolve a "theory of history." Theories of history are now regarded by professional historians with justified suspicion. Anybody can prove anything by history, so long as the proper illustrations are selected. That does not alter the terrible fact that theories of history have taken the place of theories of religion in modern life, and that whereas wars were once fought under banners of opposing theology, they are now being fought under banners of economics and history. A theory of history is after all the firm basis for the faith of Marxists, the belief in an inevitable course of events leading to victory, as proved by history, and so justifying every act, no matter how violent or underhanded. Similarly, theories of history helped justify fascism, notably Spengler's visions of the "Decline of the West," with its bias against democracy and towards an "inevitable" Caesarism.

Both Henry and Brooks Adams promulgated such theories of history. Fortunately, America has never taken them seriously. Both theories were totally pessimistic. Henry seemed to allow humanity no choice or chance. Brooks, like Spengler, seemed to permit a choice between total collapse and dictatorship. The basis of the systems of both Henry and Brooks was the same: it wasn't the Adams' fault that their fourth generation had "failed," it was the fault of the world. Brooks in fact says this, in no uncertain terms. In his preface to his most famous book, *The Law of Civilization and Decay,* he writes, "Nothing is commoner . . . than to find families who have been famous in one century sinking into obscurity in the next, not because the children have degenerated, but because a certain field of activity which afforded the ancestor full scope, has been closed against his offspring." That is to say, the failure of the four brothers to fulfill the Fate of the Adamses was not their fault; it was not even the fault of the time, the Gilded Age. It was nothing less than the fault of the universe, the inevitable decline of the whole history of man. Never has a family worked so hard to give its comedown a cosmic setting.

What these theories are is hardly the concern of a family historian. Henry's theory, presented in three longish papers,* tried to answer the question "What is the nature of history? If history is a science, then what is its nature?" The same, thought Henry, as the nature of physical science. Scientific laws of energy must also be valid for history, since man, after all, is a part of nature and subject to natural laws. Therefore the Second Law of Thermodynamics must be just as applicable to history as to physics. "Dissipation of energy" characterizes evolution. The planet is cooling off, the sun is shrinking; mankind is dissipating his energies too, like an exploding galaxy, degenerating from the vibrant unity of the twelfth century towards the pointless dynamism and multiplicity of the twentieth. There was nothing mankind could do about this except, like Henry himself, face the scientific facts as he must face any facts. The inscrutable resignation of the St. Gaudens statue in Rock Creek Park over Marian's grave best symbolizes humanity's proper attitude.

Brooks also based his theories on the same "scientific principle" that "animal life is one of the outlets through which solar energy is dissipated." But he ends up more in the realm of economics than of physics. Civilizations, like that of Rome, first rise as they concentrate their energies, then decline as concentration becomes the death grip of capitalism and of the hoarders of gold. From "disintegration, wherein the imagination kindles," i.e., the Middle Ages, we pass to "consolidation whose pressure ends in death," i.e., modern monopolies and Jewish International Finance. Nathan Rothschild became the representative modern villain, a new aristocracy of the Gold Bug (as opposed to an older aristocracy of people of merit like the Adamses).

The end result of both theories, however, is much the same, as is their basic premise ("dissipation of solar energy"). It is Fascism, the salvation of the rentier who equally despises dynamic capitalism, the aristocracy of the Gold Bugs, and the dynamic proletariat, the masses of Socialism. A military leader, a strong man, backed by an

* *The Tendency of History* (1895), *The Rule of Phase Applied to History* (1909), *A Letter to American Teachers of History* (1910).

elite of people like Brooks and Henry, can control the capitalist and the mob, channel the energies of a dying civilization at least towards order and stability. Eventually of course, this too will run down. Then the only hope is "infusion of barbarian blood." In the present, however, the chaos created by the rule of capitalist over proletariat can only be resolved by an Augustus. In 1896, for instance, Brooks was reading Caesar in the original to learn how a strong man could break the banker's stranglehold on society. Legal or democratic means were useless; might makes right. "There is but one moral, the moral of success," he liked to say, or "We are rapidly approaching the moment when we shall be reorganized by soldiers." Or more prophetically, "We must have a new deal . . . we must suppress the states . . . centralize."

Who was to be Caesar? Brooks Adams thought friend and fellow Harvard man Theodore Roosevelt would do very nicely. Brooks spent much time in the White House working on Theodore, and Theodore was not totally unresponsive. Who knows how much of the bigness of the Big Stick may be traced to Brooks? Henry of course would have nothing to do with this. He tended to despise Roosevelt as politician and preferred to coddle his despair uncontaminated by action. He couldn't stand Brooks' preaching and argumentativeness, and in later years used a good deal of ingenuity in trying to avoid his brother.

And in fact Brooks was pretty awful. He had been a difficult child. Twitchy. His mother complained in desperation, "Papa reads aloud . . . and poor Brooks screams and laughs and rants and twists and jumps and worries about so." His two oldest brothers teased him cruelly and laughed and laughed at him when he fell off horses. Henry was nice to him, and so Brooks (Peter Chardon Brooks was his real full name) grew up to idolize Henry as Henry had idolized Charles.

In college Brooks suddenly blossomed, joined the most socially august of Harvard's clubs, Porcellian (none of his brothers made it), and was something of a dude. Afterwards he too, of course, tried the law, he too wrote for newspapers.* But something went wrong. Collegiate flowering gave way again to twitchiness. He remained always a semi-invalid, beset by neurasthenic collapses. Even his marriage, a fairly cold-blooded affair by some accounts, did not do much to help him. He had, supposedly, proposed to a girl who turned him down. "Why you perfect damned fool!" he said, incredulous that anyone should turn down an Adams. He took his neurasthenics to the wife of his friend, Henry Cabot Lodge. If she could find somebody just like herself, he would marry her. Mrs. Lodge had a sister. Brooks married her. She too, like his mother, found Brooks hard to take, and eventually declined into the twilight of "nervous breakdowns."

Despite these neurotic handicaps, Brooks had a career. He taught brilliantly and provocatively at the law school of Boston University. (He alone of the Adamses seemed to dislike Harvard, despite his earlier social success there.) He wrote incessantly, his bibliography coming to well over a hundred titles; he argued with everyone who would listen to him; he tried to convert people to his theories. But in the end he too was forced into an Adams retirement. He was ousted from his law-school job when a new dean was appointed there. Nobody listened to him at the White House after Theodore left. Nobody paid any attention to him when, as a member of the Massachusetts Constitutional Convention of 1917–18, he publicly advocated a system of state socialism. More and more, as Charles became the stock character of the crusty Boston Brahmin, so Brooks took on the role of the New England village agnostic, a local eccentric. Nobody really took his books and theories seriously. Perhaps the most acute and important review he ever got was a piece, early in his career in 1897, appraising the *Law of Civilization and Decay*, and written by prepresidential Theodore Roosevelt. Before he died he had been largely forgotten, his fame obscured by that of brother Henry.

---

* He even tried politics. He failed to win nomination for the Massachusetts legislature by two votes — those of his uncles Chardon and Shepard Brooks.

To the end, he kept up the family tradition for crotchetiness. On his deathbed his nurse kept telling him, "Lay down, Mr. Adams." Finally he couldn't stand it any longer. He reached up, grabbed her by her side hair and screamed, "How many times have I told you to say 'lie'?" With his death in 1927, the last of the brothers, the last Adams to live in the Old House, the last of nineteenth-century males of the family had gone. Of the two sisters, brilliant, gay Louisa, who married a Philadelphia Kuhn,* died early. Quieter Mary, who married one of the last of the Quincys, lived on till 1928.

Charles as a Bostonian, Henry as a writer, Brooks as a theoretician, all achieved their real stature in this new century. But they were essentially figures of the Gilded Age. Confronted with the rise of Plutocracy, they took refuge in Reform — until it became clear that reform could not be managed by gentlemen only. America was not going to return to the ideals of John Quincy Adams and Nicholas Biddle, was not going to let itself be represented by liberal Gentlemen of Leisure, amateurs who would know what was best for their constituents. Reform, to be effective, was going to need professional help from below. But this was just what the Adams brothers refused to acknowledge. Henry specifically rejects just the very joining of forces that made for the triumph of Franklin Roosevelt. In the *Education* he says that although of all forms of society capitalism is the one he likes least, still "a capitalist system . . . must be run by capital and capitalist methods . . . nothing could surpass the nonsensity of trying to run so complex and so concentrated a machine by Southern and Western farmers in grotesque alliance with city day-laborers." Most present-day capitalists might still agree. Nonetheless it was just this grotesque alliance, led by Harvard-educated rentiers like the Adamses and staffed by reformist intellectuals (like Francis and George Biddle) that did wrest the running of the "system" from Henry's hated Gold Bugs.

* For a bit of background on the Kuhns, see *The Perennial Philadelphians* by N. Burt.

The real tragedy, the real failure of the fourth generation was not in their blighted personal success. Actually, they achieved considerable personal success. It lay in their failure to follow through with the reform, on which they had staked their sacred honor, because of their refusal to recognize popular democracy. Of the four, John actually achieved less personally, but came closest to success as a reformer. At least he was following the right path. Charles left reform and in fact joined the enemy. His failure was a failure to become a thorough Gold Bug. It is the failure of Brooks and, above all, Henry to see the future, and to follow the positive and affirmative and democratic path, the path of the Roosevelts, that turned them off into fascism. The first John Adams was falsely accused of monarchism. He was a republican, if not a democrat. But in his republicanism may have lain the seed of a different sort of monarchism. Distrust and fear of the people, of the mob, must inevitably turn towards rule by strength, rule by an elite, rule by a Caesar. The seed finally flowered in the pernicious historical heresies of the fourth generation of the Adams family.

The theories themselves had no political effect. It is the stance, the attitudes, the tastes that have been effective. There is no party bearing the slogan "dissipation of solar energy," and advocating, as Brooks did, that all schools be turned over to military direction. The descendants of Henry and Brooks have been not politicians but poets. From Henry, particularly the Henry of *Chartres*, are obviously derived both the wasteland postures and medievalist theocratic reaction of T. S. Eliot. He is, incidentally, a distant relative through Mary Smith Cranch, sister of Abigail Adams. More tenuous but not less striking is the descent of Ezra Pound's anticapitalist fascism from Brooks. A whole big section of Pound's *Cantos* (nos. LXII–LXXI and elsewhere) is, after all, devoted to the Adamses. His ranting about Usura (Canto XLV), his admiration for simple societies free of bankers and dominated by warriors, priests and artists, his violent anti-Semitism — all these came from Brooks, either directly or secondhand. From Eliot and Pound in turn spring a whole race of Treasonable Clerks, haters of democracy, betrayers of their country, apostates to the faith of their fathers. These are the seeds of the fall of the Adamses. The Adamses failed because in the end they could not take democracy (and indeed it is hard to take, especially for intellectual aristocrats — unless one happens to be as natively aristocratic as Jefferson). They could not trust their compatriots. They believed it was because their morals were too high. It was really because their sympathies were too thin. They were too proud to "play politics," which was virtuous. They were too haughty to understand other people, which was ruinous.

8

Roosevelts

THE FATE of the Roosevelts was quite different from the Fate of the Adamses. Nothing could present a more dramatic contrast than the history of the two families during the nineteenth century. Whereas the Adamses decline conspicuously into private life and Boston, quarreling all the time in public with their destiny, the Roosevelts thoughtlessly and privately, with full bellies and cheerful faces, gradually rise in riches, New York social position and sheer numbers towards their twentieth-century apotheosis. The Adamses were going down in a most interesting way. The Roosevelts were going up in a most conventional fashion.

Between Isaac the Patriot and Teddy the President, the two main branches of the family show nothing that could not be duplicated by hundreds of other families of their kind, class and period. If it weren't for a rather peculiar variety of minor exploits — steamboats, sainthood — on the part of numerous offshoots, the family chronicle would be one of type, not of individuals. As such the two stories, Oyster Bay and Hyde Park, are merely representative, specimens of the kind. As background, however, these chronicles do become important; it was thanks to these backgrounds that the political character of America is what it is today.

Among our five families then, the Roosevelts best offer something average: a model of post-Revolutionary, pre-Civil War moneyed family establishment. They were, more than the other families, purely moneyed. The Adams were political, the Biddles professional, the du Ponts manufacturing, the Lees ex-planters and military. The Roosevelts, as appropriate perhaps to New York, were almost purely financial. Different kinds of finance however. The Hyde Parkers were rentiers who lived off their incomes in the country and kept it fresh by marrying well. The Oyster Bayers were active businessmen who moved up from hardware to investment banking, lived primarily in the city, and married for use rather than for advantage.

The younger branch, the descendants of Jacobus, grandson of the original Claes, was first to establish itself. Isaac the Patriot was, after all, a pretty distinguished man locally, and a rich one. Mayor Philip Hone, as ubiquitous diarist of New York's earlier nineteenth century, gives the best picture of his position. He speaks memorially of "Isaac Roosevelt, the first president of the first bank of New York at a time when the president and directors of a bank . . . were the only nobility we had. . . . Men could not stand straight in their presence, and woe to them who bowed not down. . . ." Although his description of Isaac as first banker is factually inaccurate, it is practically true. Isaac's predecessor, the good General McDougall, only lasted about two years and was hardly a professional financier.

For the next three generations of the Hyde Park Line — James, Isaac, James — these Jacobite Roosevelts maintained themselves. They were typical of that kind of aristocracy which is quite opposed to the meritocracy of the Adamses — the aristocracy of maintenance and tenure, not of achievement. They did nothing to add to the luster of the family name except hang onto what they already had. This in general has always been the norm of any oligarchy. Prestige accrues to any family that simply keeps going. The psychology of whole communities, like that of Philadelphia, is based on the assumption that this kind of family continuity is the best and safest sort of continuity. Stay put is better than get ahead. It is a psychology that does have many merits. It makes for a sort of simple, secure, restful good breeding quite alien to the world of striving, pushing success. It avoids extravagance, ostentation and vulgarity. It can afford to be nice, and despise and avoid those who are not nice. (The adage that nice guys finish last can be read, in this context, two ways.) It is not very characteristic of New York, the water hole par excellence of achievers. Those New Yorkers who want to be maintainers of this sort tend to leave the city for quieter refuges. The Jacobite Roosevelts went up the Hudson into patroonland, where their Hoffman ancestors had originally settled.

Isaac, the self-made man, the achiever, stayed in town; it was his son James, the inheritor, who moved out and up. This James was not an interesting man. One of the first Roosevelts to go to college, as befitted a rich man's son (Princeton, 1780), he kept on with his father's sugar refining business, the true basis of Roosevelt fortunes; he married three times and had ten children; he wore spectacles. He even carried on his father's political activities as a state assembly-man (Federalist for one term in 1796–97). As far as Roosevelt family history is concerned, however, his principal contribution was his retirement to Poughkeepsie. There in 1819, outside the town and not far from the hamlet of Hyde Park, John built himself a mansion called Mount Hope. As a latter-day minor patroon he lived in commodious seclusion. When he died in 1847 at the age of eighty-eight he had earned that sobriquet of all good maintainers, again in the dairy of Philip Hone, a "gentleman of the old school."

Nothing is more important for maintenance than good marriages.

All of James' three were good. They were all into families of a certain kind — not maintainers, not patroons, but from the circle of what were always referred to in the earlier nineteenth century as "merchant princes." That is, rich people who were not actually in business or trade, like hardware, nor in banking or manufacturing, nor successful, professionals, but people engaged in foreign trade and shipping abroad and in real estate and investments at home. The marriages of the Hyde Park branch of the Roosevelt family for the next three generations were of this sort and in fact they concentrated on one particular family of merchant princes, the Howland-Aspinwall complex. James' first wife, and ancestress of Franklin, was however not a Howland but an Eliza Walton. Her grandmother had been a Beekman, thus tying her into the patroonship. Her great-grandfather had been the richest of New York's early-eighteenth-century merchant princes, the non-Dutch and pro-English William Walton, nonetheless known in the colloquial Dutch of New Amsterdam as the *Baas,* or Boss. In the magnificent Walton mansion on Queen Street was first housed Isaac's Bank of New York. The Waltons, however, were ruined by taking the wrong side in the Revolution. Eliza died, James Roosevelt married a Barclay, of a family also Tory; and finally, at the age of sixty-one, he married Harriet Howland. Though he had no children by Harriet, he certainly established a family pattern.

Like the Waltons, the Howlands and Aspinwalls were very much merchant princes; achievers, not maintainers. Both families had come down from New England to New York after generations of life at sea (a Howland fell off the *Mayflower* and nearly drowned). Together they founded one of New York's principal pre-Civil War importing firms and fortunes. As partners in the firm, Aspinwalls and Howlands were of course related by marriage. Typical Yankee traders, they sent their ships all over, but in particular to Central America and the Pacific. One of the partners, William Henry Aspinwall, built a railroad across the Isthmus of Panama, which came in mighty handy when gold was discovered in California. The present town of Colon at the end of the present Panama Canal was originally named Aspinwall.

Of all Howlands and Aspinwalls, the most magnificent was this William Henry Aspinwall. Both Philip Hone and later George Strong, who like Sidney Fisher in Philadelphia left the most vivid and complete of mid-nineteenth-century diaries, acknowledged that Aspinwall's house on University Place was, in the Little Old New York of the 1830's and 40's, the most magnificent in the city. "One can't make a satisfactory guess at the amount he's invested in rosewood and satin, mirrors, cabinets and vertu," chronicled George Strong after his New Year's call in 1846. Aspinwall became a partner in the firm of his uncles, G. G. and S. S. Howland. His only rival as magnifico was his contemporary, William Backhouse Astor, son of the great John Jacob. All these — Aspinwall, both Howlands and Astor — were dinner companions of Hone's, as their descendants were of George Strong.

The Roosevelts did not dine with Hone. The Oyster Bay Roosevelts had not yet made the grade. The Hyde Park Roosevelts lived in comparative seclusion up the river. They let the Howlands and Aspinwalls do the hustling and town-house furnishing and simply married their money. As a result we have one of those admirable genealogical tangles so characteristic of the nineteenth century: Harriet Howland, who married James Roosevelt (son of Isaac the Patriot), was a sister of G. G. and S. S., and an aunt of splendid William Aspinwall. Splendid William's sister Mary then married James' son, Dr. Isaac (i.e., her Aunt Rebecca's stepson). Then, in the third generation of Roosevelts, Isaac and Mary's son James married Rebecca Howland, daughter of G. G. (Rebecca being first cousin of James' own mother Mary Aspinwall), this Rebecca being in turn the stepmother of Franklin Delano Roosevelt.

Meanwhile, besides marrying Howlands, what did these Roosevelts do? They lived on their estates. James of Mount Hope spent his earlier years as an active businessman of course, and even held those few minor offices, city and state. He retired only in his maturity. Son Isaac, however, was the most flawless specimen of a Gentleman of Leisure, a man of the Silver Age. After Princeton, he studied medicine at Columbia and was ever thereafter known as Doctor. But the bloody business of actual practice disgusted him, and his only medical interest after graduation was in his own health, of which he was so careful that he seldom dared go beyond the boundaries of his properties. The very thought of his son's European trip was enough to prostrate him. He devoted his energies, such as they were, to farming and to botanical experiments. A recessive bachelor, he suddenly, at the age of thirty-seven, decided to do the conventional thing and marry an Aspinwall. He created an estate of his own, Rosedale, near Mount Hope, and there produced his two sons, James and John Aspinwall, who also both settled on neighboring estates and in turn lived on their incomes.

Nothing could provide a more striking contrast to this life of elegantly idle country seclusion than the career of the contemporary Roosevelt of the other, older, Johannes branch. The son and grandson of Johannes, founder of the Oyster Bay line — a Jacobus, just to confuse things, born in 1724, and a James J. born in 1759 — were totally inconspicuous. They were hardworking, Dutch-speaking, Dutch-marrying, prosperous lower middle-class burghers, involved in hardware. They had nothing to do with merchant princes or patroons like the Waltons and the Hoffmans. The man who established the fortunes of this branch was the great-grandson of Johannes, Cornelius van Schaack Roosevelt, of the same generation as Dr. Isaac. He was born in 1794 (Dr. Isaac in 1790) and determined to make a fortune. While Isaac botanized, Cornelius slaved. He couldn't tear himself away from business, even to make love, and sent rather piteous letters to his Philadelphia fiancée, Margaret Barnhill, complaining of his obsession. "Business calls me with its imperious beckoning," he wrote her. "Oh could I tear myself from that absorber of every gentle feeling . . . and fly away and be at rest in the midst of the more enchanting pursuits of the mind." He used the prosperous hardware business inherited from his father to build himself a fortune in real estate. During the depression of 1837, caused by the ruckus between Biddle and Jackson, he had the means and foresight to buy depressed Manhattan property. He was also one of the founders and directors of the Chemical National Bank. In 1868, a few years before he died, he was listed as one of the ten largest holders of real estate in the city along with Astors, Rhinelanders, Goelets, Lenoxes and Lorillards. All told, he was considered to be the town's fifth-richest man. Strong memorialized him as "a highly respectable old landmark and millionaire" (which is not quite a "gentleman of the old school") and remarked that he always thought of him as looking like a "Hindoo idol." Cornelius was as definitely a family founder as Isaac the Patriot. His cousin Dr. Isaac, resting so comfortably in the midst of the enchanting pursuits of the mind, as represented by greenhouses, no doubt would have considered him a rather crude fellow. His marriage did nothing to help. Though Margaret Barnhill was a beloved and admirable wife and mother, the Barnhills, in Philadelphia parlance, were nobody in particular, any more than had been the Sjoerts, Bogards and van Schaacks in the maternal line of Cornelius; very different from the minor patroons and merchant princes represented by Hardenbroecks, Hoffmans, Waltons, Howlands and Aspinwalls in that of the Jacobus branch (though there were collateral marriages along the way to De Peysters, Schuylers, etc. in the Oyster Bay branch too).

But by the time of the Civil War generation, the generation of Theodore Senior and James, the fathers of the two Presidents, the branches were pretty much neck and neck, all part of the same general area of the pre-Civil War gentry that, like the Adamses, was inclined to look down on the post-Civil War plutocracy as Gold Bugs and ostentatious parvenus. Cornelius was richer, but Dr. Isaac was socially superior. Their children were all about on the same level and moved in the same circles, and in this generation the two branches were intimate with each other. Unlike every other family

of the kind, there had been no cross-fertilization. The seclusion of
the Hudson River dwellers and comparative obscurity of the pre-
Cornelius hardware-store city dwellers may have kept the branches
apart socially. The gap between the Roosevelts in trade and the
country gentlemen was erased by the success of Cornelius' real
estate.

James, son of Dr. Isaac and father of Franklin, was brought up
under the influence of his hypochondriac old father in what must
have been the rather odd and melancholy world of Rosedale: a remote atmosphere, full of country pleasures and confined to the
society of other river folk, the Indian Summer of the patroonship.
James, perhaps spurred on by his firm-minded mother and the adventurous Aspinwalls, reacted against his upbringing and became
very much the extrovert, an active, late-Victorian sportsman, investor, traveler and social figure on two continents. He took the grand
tour, after schooling at Union College and Harvard Law School,
and fought with Garibaldi's Red Shirts in Italy, *pour le sport.*
Though the Hudson River remained his home, he did not seclude
himself there as his father had. He too bought himself a Hudson
River estate, Springwood, near Mount Hope and Rosedale, and
moved there with his Howland bride in 1867. They had a son,
James Roosevelt Roosevelt (known as Rosy). Father James was patron of good works and civic betterment in the hamlet of Hyde
Park, active in local politics as a Democrat, busy with his farming,
and also involved in industry — railroads, as director and later vice
president of the Delaware and Hudson, which brought coal from
Pennsylvania — in real estate in the Lake Superior region and a
steamboat company on Lake Champlain. James drove a four-in-
hand and bred horses and was much involved with the Dutchess
County Hunt. James traveled abroad and visited great houses in
England and rode with the Belvoir hounds there. He cultivated
sideburns and, according to an ill-wisher, tried to look like Lord
Landsdowne but succeeded in looking like his coachman. The face

is certainly that of a bland Englishman of the period, whether lord or coachman. He filled his world with ease and aplomb; only his Democratic politics, which had wavered during the war and his pro-Union sympathies, separated him from most of his society. This particular kind of Democratic politics, however, was by no means a sign of revolt and advanced tendencies. On the contrary, it was more likely to be a sign of antique, landowning, conservative reaction against the businessman Whigs and the radical abolitionist Republicans. It was very common in Philadelphia among Biddles and Cadwaladers, who also retained their allegiance after the war.

In the mid-seventies James' wife Rebecca died. Then his son James married Helen Astor, granddaughter of William Backhouse, and daughter of *the* Mrs. Astor, hostess to the Four Hundred (the number of people she could accommodate in her ballroom). The Roosevelts, however, drew the line at Vanderbilts, and refused to dine. James existed for a few years as a gay widower. Then, according to family legend, at a dinner in 1880 at the house of his cousin-by-marriage Mrs. Theodore Roosevelt senior he met a young, a much younger, Hudson River dweller, Sara Delano. There were all sorts of connections. For instance, Sara's uncle, Franklin Delano, had married an Astor too, an aunt of Rosy's wife Helen, and they too lived on the river at Steen Valletje. Sara's parents lived across the water at Algonac, near Newburgh.

When Sara married James in the fall of that year 1880, the bride hardly left home. Springwood was the same sort of place as Algonac, though not as large. From the point of view of James, the Delanos were just like the Howlands. They too were Yankees, merchant princes, involved with shipping. Like Howland and Aspinwall, the great Boston firm of Russell and Company, with which the Delanos were connected, also did business in the Pacific. Sara had spent part of her girlhood in Hong Kong. Very little adjustment was required on the part of either the bride in her twenties or the groom in his fifties. In 1882 their only child, named Franklin Delano after

Sara's childless, Astor-marrying uncle, was born. The children of Franklin's stepbrother Rosy, a James (Tad) and a Helen, were Franklin's contemporaries and playmates.

In a world much like that of the Virginia plantation, but based on city incomes rather than agriculture, in estates overlooking the Hudson as Arlington and Stratford overlooked the Potomac, the Hyde Park Roosevelts lived in genial affluence, first at Mount Hope (which burned in 1866; the land was sold to the state for an insane asylum), then in Rosedale, Springwood and the Red House, where James Roosevelt Roosevelt lived. There were Algonac of the Delanos and Steen Valletje; Rokeby, and Oak Terrace at Tivoli, Livingston houses lived in by Astors and Halls (Eleanor Roosevelt's mother was a Hall). There were friends and neighbors, the Maturin Livingstons of Staatsburgh, where the newly married Sara went for her first dinner party; the Dinsmores at The Locusts; the Bigelows of Malden; the Archie Rogers in their fabulously expensive imitation castle. In such places up and down the Hudson lived the "river people," feudally patronizing the villagers with good works and social condescension, visiting each other at leisurely intervals by horseback and carriage, proud of whatever traces of Dutchness and patroonship they could claim; marrying each other.

The sons of Cornelius were also on their way to landowning and estates, not up the Hudson but out on Long Island. There were five surviving sons: Silas Weir, James Alfred, Cornelius junior, Robert Barnhill and Theodore; but for some obscure reason, Cornelius junior, though he married and lived on, seems to drop out of the family reckoning, whereas the other four are remembered in one way or another as integral parts of the first generation of the family to really settle on Long Island. Of these four, Robert was the most interesting and significant as a person; but it was from the three others, S. Weir, James and Theodore that the Oyster Bay part of the family descends.

They were all three men of business, though Silas from the basis of the law. Roosevelt and Sons, that had been a hardware-and-glass-importing business, became investment banking. James took over from Cornelius, then his handsome son William Emlen, who died as late as 1930. His son in turn, a George Emlen (born in 1887), was the grand old man of the firm in modern times. All three of the businessman brothers married southwards, as their father had done. The Philadelphia influence was already fairly strong. Silas Weir, like his kinsman S. Weir Mitchell, Philadelphia's famous man of letters and medicine, was named after a prominent Philadelphia businessman married to a Barnhill. Robert got the "Barnhill" as middle name. Both Silas and James then compounded the taint by in turn marrying Philadelphians, Mary West and Elizabeth Norris Emlen. The Wests' most distinguished representative was Benjamin, the painter. Otherwise they seem to have been respectable if not exciting Quakers. The Emlens, unlike the Barnhills, could never be described as "nobody in particular." They were weighty Friends and medical people and, as Mrs. Roosevelt's middle name indicated, connected with the august family of Norris, more weighty, more Friendly, more medical; just as Old Philadelphian indeed as the Cadwaladers, but eschewing the worldly pomp of plumed beds.

Theodore went farther afield. Introduced by the brother of Silas' wife, Hilborne West, he wooed and won a Georgian, Martha Bulloch (West married her half-sister). The Bullochs were plantation owners, descendants of the state's first governor, and violent secessionists during the war. Martha's half-brother James became the almost personal antagonist of Charles Francis Adams when, as Confederate naval agent in England, he supervised the building and launching of that *Alabama* whose career involved Adams in so much difficulty. His brother, as a naval officer, fired the last shots off that same *Alabama*. After the war James Bulloch and his brother were among the few Confederates not included in the general amnesty. They settled in Liverpool, and when they did dare to visit their native country and their Roosevelt sister they had to travel under assumed names.

The household of Cornelius must have been very different from that of his reclusive cousin Dr. Isaac. He had a big luxurious house on Union Square, filled with servants and furniture and children, and there the family romped and argued and quarreled and enjoyed each other in a frenzy of vitality. The Roosevelt family habit of all talking at the same time seems to have been established then and there. Beginning after the Civil War they took summer refuge out on the north shore of Long Island. Cornelius rented a house after the Civil War; then his descendants followed suit, first renting, and then finally buying or building. Gradually this particular part of Oyster Bay, Cove Neck, became as much of a Roosevelt colony as Hyde Park. In places ancient and modern, named Yellowbanks, Waldeck, Sagamore Hill, Old Orchard, Gracewood, Dolonor, Tranquillity, Mohannas, lived and live the descendants of Cornelius, cheek by jowl, childhood playmates along the water and in the woods. In the winter they returned to substantial brownstone houses in New York. Against this background of Oyster Bay summers and brownstone winters, of connections southward to Quakers and the Confederacy, of a noisy, close-knit, proliferating group of cousins, most of whom became proper bankers and members of the best clubs (all five sons of Cornelius were members of The Century), was born Theodore junior, almost alone of this group, it would seem, sickly and at a physical disadvantage.

Theodore senior, though his son idolized him and thought him the finest man he knew, was of this group of four perhaps the least interesting and important. As a businessman he never achieved the successes of S. Weir and James A., nor as a politician and crusader was he as distinguished as Robert B. He was, however, successful enough in both roles, and generally respected and beloved by all and sundry. As a pleasing combination of kindness, liveliness, practical energy and effective civic conscience he was a proper inspiration to his President son.

The real political background of Theodore and hence Franklin, comes not by direct descent, but indirectly by uncle and great-uncle. The other odd and distinguished persons who add what spice the family history has in the nineteenth century were also none of them direct ancestors of the Presidents.

Most odd and interesting was Nicholas, uncle of Cornelius, born in 1767; another sport off the main branches somewhat like Nicholas the goldsmith in the eighteenth century. He too was a craftsman, and he too left his mark in an area quite divorced from politics or money. His chief claim to fame is that he was the first person to take a steamboat down the Mississippi. That whole glamorous tradition of the riverboat, of the *Robert E. Lee* (for which one waited) and of Mark Twain begins with a Roosevelt. The actual trip itself was pretty glamorous.

Nicholas was what would now be called an industrial engineer. As a precocious mechanic he fooled about with steam engines and paddle wheels at the turn of the century, when it was still experimental to do so, but made his living first as manager of a copper foundry in New Jersey under the auspices of the Schuylers, then as assistant to Benjamin Latrobe in setting up the waterworks for the city of Philadelphia.* In 1809, already over forty, he married Latrobe's daughter Lydia. He had had various dealings along the way with Chancellor Livingston and his protégé Robert Fulton. In 1798, for instance, he built a steam engine for a projected Livingston-Fulton steamboat, and in the process urged Fulton to put his paddle wheels on each side rather than in the stern. This seems to be the first recorded suggestion of that idea, which was to make steamboats generally practicable during the nineteenth century. Livingston rejected the idea of side wheels, and then the whole plan for the steamboat fell through.

Finally in 1807 Livingston and Fulton got together again and without any help from Roosevelt produced the famous *Clermont*

---

* The same Latrobe who appeared briefly at Bizarre during the climax of that Poe-like story.

(named after Livingston's Hudson River estate). Nicholas was more surprised than pleased to note that his idea of side paddle wheels had been adopted, without any thanks to Nicholas. This, however, did not prevent him from doing business with the gentlemen. In 1809 they hired the newly married Roosevelt to explore the possibilities of running a steamboat down the Ohio and Mississippi from Pittsburgh to New Orleans. First, accompanied by his intrepid bride, he went down the river system on a flatboat. The trip took six months; they stopped off at the only notable towns en route, Cincinnati, Louisville and Natchez, advertising their steamboat plan, and had the foresight to buy and open various small coal mines, piling depots along the banks for the forthcoming steamboat trip.

They reached New Orleans and sailed back towards New York (a far more desperate trip than the run down the river; yellow fever broke out on board, killing a passenger, nephew to wicked General James Wilkinson). Roosevelt convinced Livingston and Fulton that the steamboat scheme was practicable and returned to Pittsburgh in 1811. There on the banks of the Monongahela he constructed a boat and engine, to Fulton's design with, incidentally, the paddle wheel at the stern. The boat, called the *New Orleans,* some 116 feet long and 20 wide, contained two cabins, one for Roosevelt and his wife aft, and one for the crew forward. Mrs. Roosevelt, though expecting her second child, insisted on going along as she had on the flatboat trip. There was a captain, an engineer, a pilot, six hands, two maidservants, a waiter, a cook and a big Newfoundland dog called Tiger.

The first part of the trip was a triumph. Both Cincinnati and Louisville turned out en masse to greet them, and they were entertained at the latter place by a public dinner with many a toast. The Kentuckians' only regret was that they would never see the *New Orleans* again, since obviously once on its way the ship would not be able to come back upstream. To repay hospitality, Roosevelt asked his hosts to dinner on board. During the middle of the meal there were rumblings, the ship began to move. The guests, afraid they would be wrecked on the Falls of the Ohio below town, rushed on deck, where they were astounded to see that they had traveled upstream almost out of sight of Louisville.

Roosevelt found he couldn't proceed because of low water over those dangerous Falls of the Ohio. So to rub the point in, he took a trip back to Cincinnati and proved once and for all that the *New Orleans* could indeed go upstream. Eventually the river water rose enough to permit the boat to ride the rapids. Meanwhile Lydia had her child. But she insisted on continuing the trip, baby and all.

Supposedly the voyage from this point on should have been easy. Instead, they were plagued by a series of thoroughly sinister phenomena. There had already been a comet, which led Indians and others along the banks to confuse the effects of the steamboat — steam, whistles, fire and noise — with the effects of the comet. In the spring there had been disastrous floods, then followed a mysterious and equally sinister migration of squirrels, invading southward by the tens of thousands, drowning in the Ohio like lemmings as they passed. Finally, during a spell of terribly oppressive weather, windless, the sun a red disk by day, the nights starless, a terrific earthquake shook the Mississippi. The tremors evidently continued for days, rocked the *New Orleans* at her moorings until the passengers became nauseated, caved in the riverbanks, altered all the channels, and filled them with fallen trees. The little frontier settlement of New Madrid was destroyed, whole houses and their inhabitants being engulfed. Even an island to which the *New Orleans* had been tied up overnight was completely submerged and obliterated. Tiger, more sensitive to the tremors than humans, who couldn't really recognize them when the boat was in motion on the water, prowled about moaning. When he came to Mrs. Roosevelt and placed his head on her lap, it was apt to be a sign that the earth was quaking with more than usual violence.

Indians, who were still the principal inhabitants of riverside Tennessee at the time, called the ship the "fire canoe" and thought it, as an extension of the comet, the causer of the earthquake. They considered the thing an omen of disaster, and on one occasion a large party of them raced alongside in a war canoe, whether for sport or vengeance the *New Orleans* did not stop to find out. The local Indians retained their prejudice against fire canoes for a generation, and when at last their prophecies of misfortune were fulfilled in the 1830's and they were kicked off their homelands, many of them refused to use steamboats for transportation and went into exile on foot.

A blaze broke out on board, almost destroying the forward cabin. The pilot spent most of his time telling the captain that he was lost, since all the old channels had disappeared. Refugees from New Madrid and other stricken settlements kept begging to be taken aboard and were refused. Altogether the trip (though it took only fourteen days of steaming as opposed to the six months by flatboat) was one of "anxiety and terror."

At last they reached Natchez. They were again greeted by festivities; to provide the proper Technicolor ending, the captain and the Roosevelt's maid got married. Another Livingston, Edward, emigrant to Louisiana and future secretary of state, greeted them in Natchez and took up the cause of steamboating on the Mississippi from his older brother in New York. The rest of the voyage from Natchez to New Orleans was uneventful.

It would be nice to record that Nicholas made himself rich and famous from his pioneering, but as in the case of many precursors, he didn't. Everything got entangled in troubles and lawsuits about patents. Though he lived on till 1854, he retired from the whole business of steamboats to a place in Skaneateles, New York, and there founded a third, Latrobe Roosevelt, branch of the family, quite divorced from the other New York branches. His descendants made a reputation for themselves in the navy. A marine, Colonel Henry Latrobe Roosevelt, great-grandson of Nicholas, became one of the innumerable members of the Roosevelt family circle, and fourth of the name, to occupy the almost hereditary post of assistant secretary of the navy. There was even a cross-branch marriage here — a

Montgomery Roosevelt Schuyler, grandson of Nicholas, married a daughter of one of the Oyster Bay brothers, James Alfred. They had an early and rather scandalous divorce.

Of all the doings of all the pre-Teddy Roosevelts, certainly the omen-attended ride down the river was the most significant and striking. Who can say the omens and the Indians weren't right? Nothing of greater importance happened to the river valley before or after. The advent of the steamboat opened the whole vast region to settlement and commerce. Without the steamboat the cultivation of cotton on a great scale would hardly have been practicable; the growth of cities like Cincinnati and St. Louis was almost entirely founded on river trade. It was this prosperity that eventually forced the Indians off their lands, that revivified slavery, that shifted the balance of political and economic power westward to Jackson-Lincoln-Bryanland. The constellation of Roosevelt, Fulton and Livingston was more fateful for the country than any number of squirrel migrations, earthquakes or comets.

Nicholas was the most interesting of the Roosevelt offshoots, but there were lots of others of some note. The tradition of mechanic-craftsman derived from Nicholas the goldsmith and Nicholas the steamboater was carried on by a Hilborne Roosevelt, son of Silas Weir. He made revolutionary electrical improvements on the pipe organ and even, unlike Nicholas, a fortune. His brother Cornelius on the other hand was a black sheep. He lived in Paris, married a French woman of dubious repute, and subsisted off other people's money. He had a son André who did more or less the same. Teddy did not approve. There was a Clinton Roosevelt, also a Johannite, who was a radical nineteenth-century writer on economics. He hated bankers, like the Adams, and has had a slight comeback in modern times.

Then there are the Roosevelt saints, the doers of good works, the religious. They are Jacobites. The word saint, incidentally, is no exaggeration. Mother Seton, a descendant of a sister of Isaac the

Patriot, has been a candidate for Roman Catholic sainthood, the first such born in America, as founder in 1809 of the order of the Sisters of Charity.* Her nephew John Roosevelt Bayley preceded Cardinal Gibbons as archbishop of Baltimore. James H. Roosevelt, another of the Hyde Park branch, is memorialized in Roosevelt Hospital. An early romance was blighted when he was crippled by polio. Neither he nor his fiancée ever married, but devoted themselves to charity — James to the building up of a million-dollar fund to found a hospital. Roosevelt Hospital, which has usually had a Roosevelt on the board, remains his monument.

Far more crucial for family history, however, was a succession of politicians. First of course, aside from those early aldermen, was Isaac the Patriot. None of his descendants sullied their hands with more than an occasional dabbling in minor state, city, or local Hyde Park affairs. Not so the Oyster Bay branch. James J., a brother of millionaire Cornelius, was a flamboyant political personage in mid-nineteenth century. He was an uncompromising Tammany man, and something of a show-off. One pictures him strolling down Broadway in flowery waistcoat with big cigar and top hat rakishly askew. As such he was despised by both Philip Hone and George Strong, in whose diaries he makes various uncomplimentary appearances. He occurs, for instance, in Hone's diary as creator of a fancy visiting card. While attaché at the French legation in the 1830's he presented himself as "Membre du Conseil du New York et Attaché, l'embassade des États Unis." "This," wrote Hone, "is one way of bringing a New York assistant alderman into notice and transforming a minister plenipotentiary into an ambassador."

Later references are no more flattering. When James was a member of the state legislature in 1840, and a defender of Tammany against attempts at voting reform, Hone describes him as "the leader of the blackguards in whose person, as its representative, our

---

* The Biddles have a similar remote connection: Mother Katharine Drexel founded the order of the Sisters of the Blessed Sacrament and is also a candidate for sainthood.

poor city is disgraced." And again, "James J. Roosevelt, the chief of a most unworthy delegation . . . a small man and very conceited." After a spell in the U.S. Congress, he ended up a judge and a U.S. District Attorney. Strong had legal dealings with him and no kinder feelings than Hone. "Judge Roosevelt is making a special ass of himself in the matter of Central Park." That is, James was opposing the creation of the park in the interests no doubt of sound Tammany real estate. Unlike all his five nephews, Judge John failed of election to the Century Association, and when he died at the age of eighty in 1875, Strong wrote, "His gross personal prejudices and partialities spoiled him for a judge. . . . He was too servile a white nigger [i.e., a pre-Civil War pro-Southerner] not to disgrace the U.S. District Attorneyship even in the days of Buchanan and the plantation whip." His death was caused by a fall with attendant broken bones. This so affected his stomach that it refused all food and he starved to death.

He had many years of high living before this, and not only seemed to have plenty of money himself, but married a glamorous heiress, Cornelia Van Ness. She was the daughter of a governor and senator of Vermont, minister to Spain, justice of the New York Supreme Court. Cornelia spent time in her youth being a Federal belle in the Latrobe-built Washington house of her uncle General Van Ness, whose wife was also a Queen of Society. James met and married Cornelia in Paris, and, like Dorcas Van Dyke in Delaware, she was given away by General Lafayette, who evidently enjoyed giving away brides. She was in later years considered, like her aunt, one of America's Queens of Society, holding court at home and abroad. President Tyler played cards at the Roosevelt house when James was in Congress, and John Quincy Adams contributed to her guest album. Victor Hugo had written a poem there in 1831:

> *La Poésie, inspiré lorsque la terre ignore,*
> *Ressemble à les grands monts que la nouvelle aurore*
> *Dore avant nous à son reveille.*

John brought the sonorities down to the scale of Quincy, Massachusetts, reducing Hugo's mountain to a hill, when he translated it thus:

> *The bard is like yon hilltop high,*
> *At sunrise shining to the sky*
> *While darkness reigns below.*

Which gives some idea of why his poetic reputation has not been higher. Of James' eleven children only four grew up, and their descendants seem to have gone to Europe and married various noble remnants.

No one can honestly say that James J. (this seemed to just stand for "junior" or "son of James," a Dutch custom) leaves a very fragrant memory; though of course the Whig-Republican bias of Hone and Strong is partly to blame for this. However, he was a conspicuous enough figure in New York and is part of a tradition of political activism that was carried on by his nephew Robert, fourth son of Cornelius. Robert was also a Democrat, but unlike his uncle James very much a post–Civil War reformer. In fact, except for party affiliation, the general outlines and directions of nephew Theodore's career are obviously foreshadowed. Reform, conservation of natural resources, writing ability, a general individualistic rambunctiousness were all part of Uncle Robert's essence.

Robert B.* began, like Teddy, as an outdoorsy writer. He was a naturalist, sportsman, hunter, and sailor, who published books on game fish and game birds during the 1860's. He even wrote a novel. He was a leader of the pro-Union Democrats in New York (unlike the judge, that "pernicious old Copperhead," as Strong called him),

---

* An odd facet of his career, never adequately explained, was his change of middle name from Barnhill, his mother's name, to Barnwell. Barnhills were connected with Barnwells, who were prominent South Carolina secessionists; and there were also old New Yorker Barnwells, but neither seemed to have close personal relationship to Robert. One story is that a newspaper got it wrong and he just failed to correct it, and so got stuck with it.

and was a founder of the Union League. He was by profession a successful lawyer, but inherited lots of money and retired to his avocations — reform politics, where he was one of those most instrumental in routing Boss Tweed, and conservation, where for twenty years as chairman of America's pioneer State Fishing Commission he defended wildlife. Like his uncle, Judge James, he also served his term in the U.S. Congress (1871–73). Writing, sporting, conservation, reform — all completely in the style of Teddy. His ambition, again like Teddy, was to be reform mayor of New York, but here Tammany was too much for him as corresponding bosses were too much for Theodore. When Cleveland came in, however, he had his reward, as John Adams, brother of Henry, might have had, and James (Hyde Park) Roosevelt too. He was given, as a faithful Democrat during the years in exile, the post of minister to the Netherlands, where he could brag that his father spoke Dutch as a boy, though perhaps not quite the same kind as spoken in Holland. He did not summer in Oyster Bay, but across the island in Sayville, where he died in 1906, having seen his reforms initiated on a national scale by his nephew; but unfortunately under the protection of the Republican party, an apostasy to family tradition that Robert never quite forgave. The Roosevelts in both branches, during the nineteenth century, had been *Democrats*.

IV

The Age of the Roosevelts

1900–1945

1

Theodore

As the nineteenth century in America was marked off most distinctively by the political career of a member of one of these five families, so was the twentieth. Indeed the parallels are so many and so peculiar that it all seems rather contrived. The eighteenth century officially ended with the defeat of John Adams for the Presidency and his angry departure from the White House in 1801. The nineteenth century officially ended with the assassination of newly elected McKinley and the swearing in of His Accidency Theodore Roosevelt in 1901. A Harvard man left Washington in 1801, a Harvard man arrived there in 1901. The last Harvard man, the last true Man of Family and member of the meritocracy to reign there was John Quincy Adams. He was separated from his father's presidency by a twenty-four-year gap, as Franklin Delano's first incumbency was separated from that of his uncle-in-law by a twenty-four-year gap. The "coincidences" — or the fatalities — pile up.

As for the other families: the death of Eugene in 1902 marked the end of absolute family control, the emergence of the du Pont Company into modern times. Fitzhugh Lee, as consul in Havana in 1898, seems to have played the last prominent public part any Lee was to play. Nothing very special seems to mark the century's beginning for Adamses or Biddles. But the twentieth century was not an Adams or a Lee or a Biddle or even a du Pont century, as the eighteenth and nineteenth centuries had been. The twentieth was overwhelmingly a Roosevelt century. No other name, even Adams, of any kind at any time in American history has so dominated such a long period as the name of Roosevelt has. Theodore Roosevelt was unquestionably the most conspicuous American of pre–World War I America, Franklin of pre–World War II America. The entire fabric of American political life has been molded by the leadership of these two men. Everyone else fits in as friend or enemy.

It is with the two Adamses of course that the Roosevelts most obviously compare. In this comparison, a central conundrum intrudes. Just how seriously *is* one to take this business of family "fate"? It is amusing of course to compare the beyond-coincidental patterning of Adams lives. When one begins to strike the same thing in Roosevelt lives, and even in the comparison of Adamses with Roosevelts, it becomes a bit spooky. It's as though some hand more aesthetic than moral, that preferred tasteful arrangements, had been busy placing events in order. Whatever attitudes can be taken, the patterns remain.

For instance: There is the curious "Collegiate Pattern" that spans the presidential years of the early nineteenth and of the early twentieth centuries. These have been the only periods in America's history when graduates of the four oldest colleges (Harvard, William and Mary, Yale, Princeton) have been prominently President; Ivy League years. Perhaps the pattern can be best shown diagrammatically (see page 305).

Such other Presidents as did go to college tended to be graduates of smaller places like Dickinson (Buchanan), Bowdoin (Pierce) and Kenyon (Hayes).

After Series I there were no more prominent Ivy League Presidents (William and Mary included here by courtesy of seniority).*

Well, these are *facts*. (But *why?*) From the Ivy League point of

---

* There *was* one more Ivy Leaguer. Tyler, elected Vice President in 1840, was another graduate of William and Mary. He was of course the first Vice President to succeed a deceased President. John Kennedy, also an Ivy Leaguer, also comes along at an interval after such a Collegiate Sequence. Both Tyler and Kennedy followed generals in office, and both were involved in that most ominous of sequences, the twenty-year Fatality (See later footnote).

*Series I:	HARVARD	*J. Adams* (1796–1800)
	WILLIAM AND MARY	Jefferson
	PRINCETON	Madison (1808–1812; 1812–1816)
	†x——	Monroe
	HARVARD	J. Q. *Adams* (1824–1828)
*Series II:	HARVARD	T. *Roosevelt* (1901–1908)
	YALE	Taft
	PRINCETON	Wilson (1912–1916; 1916–1920)
	‡x——	Harding, Coolidge, Hoover
	HARVARD	F. D. *Roosevelt* (1932–1945)

* It is superfluous to point out that each sequence is balanced by a repetition of family names, A-A, R-R, and that a gap of twenty-four years separates each repetition; and that Princeton comes neatly in the middle with Madison and Wilson.

† X: Monroe failed to graduate from William and Mary.

‡ Ohio Central, Amherst, Stanford, respectively.

view the culmination was the election of 1912, a Big Three HYP championship, in which, due to the bitter animosity of Yaleman Taft and Harvardman Roosevelt, the Tigers triumphed.* Will such things ever happen again — say between 2000 and 2030? The only major difference between the two sequences was that there were three terms between Wilson and Roosevelt, only two between Madison and JQA.†

* Another similar contest was the Adams-Jefferson-Burr runoff (H-WM-P). William and Mary won that one. Both Princetonians won presidential victories in '12; Stevenson of course lost, since he picked the wrong date. The numerology piles up; childish perhaps — but there it is.

† Equally curious and more sinister is the involvement of both Roosevelts in the Twenty-Year Fatality. That is, every President since William Henry Harrison elected on the twentieth year of a century — 1840, 1860, 1880, etc. — has died in office. Not necessarily during the twentieth-year term (Lincoln 1865, FDR 1945), but still, in office. The first Roosevelt was a beneficiary, the second a

Comparisons between John Quincy Adams and Theodore Roosevelt have often been made — breadth of intellectual interest in literature and science, educational background. Comparison between the twoness of Adamses and Roosevelts is also obvious. The full coincidence of pattern however is certainly — well, odd.

There's more to it than that. As one can set up a parallel chronology between the careers of the two Adams Presidents, a step-by-step, beyond-coincidence chronology, so one can do the same for the two Roosevelt Presidents. It's not quite so detailed and neat, but the beyond-coincidence aspect of it is about as conspicuous. They both show, for instance: birth in New York, graduation from Harvard, early death of father while there, engagement and marriage immediately on graduation, an older daughter followed by four surviving sons (in each case the namesake son ran for governor of New York and was defeated), an undistinguished pursuit of the law after study at Columbia, an early career in the state legislature followed by a period of appointive office culminating in the position of assistant secretary of the navy, election as governor of New York, nomination as Vice President, finally the presidency and reelection as President. As in the case of the Adamses one can, by straining at the meaning of the words, credit this to ambition, inheritance, or luck. But again, in the case of both families, the intervention of disaster can't be so easily "explained." As the end of the presidency of both John and John Quincy was attended by personal sorrow — the death of a favorite son in disgrace — so in the career of both Roosevelts there is a lacuna, a time of troubles in which both per-

---

victim, as were respectively Tyler and Kennedy. Theodore compounds this sort of thing by being involved in another one, the Vice-Presidential Fatality. No Vice President succeeding as President has ever had two terms entirely on his own. The four of the nineteenth century (Tyler, Fillmore, Johnson, Arthur) did not even succeed themselves once. The four of the twentieth century, so far, have all had one term on their own (Roosevelt, Coolidge, Truman, Johnson), but then have voluntarily refused a second ("I do not choose to run"); so we all should have known that Johnson would pull out. We can of course then expect that in 2060 a President will be elected who will die in office, and be succeeded by a Johnson (like Lincoln and Kennedy), and that this Johnson will at some point choose not to run. Wait and see.

sonal misfortune and political eclipse coincide, intervening between early promise and later triumph. This again, as in the case of the Adamses, is a bit more than "ambition," "inheritance" or even "luck" can be made to bear.

There is, however, one big chronological discrepancy. The assistant secretaryship and the vice-presidential nomination come at different places in the two Roosevelt careers. For Theodore they lead direct to the White House. For Franklin they occur before the "eclipse." Otherwise one can follow along side-by-side, if not quite evenly date-by-date.

1858; 1882: Born in New York State (New York City; Hyde Park). Another rather strained comparison: Theodore was one of three younger children, along with sister Corinne and brother Elliott, who were intimates and called themselves "we three" as separated from the older sister Bamie (Anna). Franklin, though he had no brothers or sisters, had that much older stepbrother, James Roosevelt Roosevelt, who in turn had two children. These half-siblings (when is the English language going to get a decent word for "brother-sister"?) were contemporaries and playmates of Franklin's, almost as the "we three" were of Theodore's childhood. Elliott, Theodore's brother, died a black-sheep alcoholic. Tad, the nephew of Franklin's three, disgraced himself by marrying a whore and was also a black sheep. Corinne, the sister of Theodore's three, married a Douglas Robinson; Helen, the niece of Franklin's three, also married a Douglas Robinson — Theodore Douglas Robinson, the son of Corinne. It's a bit like the "three-brother" fatality that went down through the Adams generations.

1878; 1900: Father died early in son's career.

1880; 1904: Left Harvard. (Franklin actually graduated in 1903, but stayed on an extra year.)

1880; 1905: Engaged immediately, married soon after graduation.

Children: An older daughter of rather conspicuous independence (Alice; Anna), and Four Brothers: Theodore junior, Kermit,

Archibald, Quentin; and James, Elliott, Franklin junior, John Aspinwall. Theodore also had another daughter, Ethel; Franklin, a son, another Franklin junior, who died in infancy.

1880 —; 1904 —: Undistinguished career at Columbia Law School and law practice in New York.

1881–84; 1910–13: New York State Legislature (TR in assembly; FDR in senate).

1889–98; 1913–20: Appointive office. Theodore: 1889–95, civil service commissioner in Washington, D.C.; 1895–97, police commissioner in New York City; 1897–98, assistant secretary of the navy. Franklin: assistant secretary of the navy only. Other family members holding the job were Theodore Roosevelt Jr., Theodore Douglas Robinson, and Henry Latrobe Roosevelt, descendant of Nicholas the steamboater.

1884–89; 1920–28: Eclipse. In 1884 both Theodore's mother and wife died simultaneously. He was not reelected to the assembly, was not eligible for appointment as a Republican in Cleveland's first administration, and was badly defeated for mayor of New York in 1886. His world brightened in 1886, however, with his second marriage to Edith Carow and with his appointment in 1889 under Harrison as civil service commissioner. From then on his ascent to President was uninterrupted. Franklin's eclipse was longer, and occurred after his appointive career, not before. In 1920 he was nominated as Vice President with Cox, and defeated. In 1921 he was stricken with polio and it was several years before he was able to bring himself back into active political life. The light began to show for him in 1924, when he appeared in public to propose Al Smith as Democratic nominee for President. Smith was not nominated, but Roosevelt was in the news again.

1899; 1928: Elected governor of New York.

1901: 1932: Becomes President, Theodore of course through the assassination of McKinley.

1904; 1936: Reelected.

1912; 1933: Assassination attempt, in both cases close but unsuccessful.

1919; 1945: Death, just at the end of a great war, when comparatively young (sixty-one, sixty-three).

The comparison of course is by no means quite as fascinatingly detailed as that between Adamses. Still, it is striking enough. Certainly in both cases the junior deliberately imitated the senior, even down to flashing teeth and sparkling eyeglasses; but it's not easy to follow a career step-by-step, as the unfortunate sons of both Theodore and Franklin found out. As for the arrangement of personal disasters at parallel points — this is indeed a special sort of emulation and heredity.

In many ways the two Adamses and the two Roosevelts compare. In other ways they violently contrast. One way in which they contrast is a Family way. The Roosevelts are at the culmination of their tradition, the Adamses at the beginning. The presidential Adamses founded their political dynasty, the Roosevelts merely elevated theirs. True, elder Adamses had been busy about Braintree as surveyors and even moderators, but John's career was a most sudden jump upward. The older Roosevelts had not been great figures politically, but still they had held office, and up to the grand climax of governor and President, the two descendants were more or less just following their footsteps.

The Adams family tradition is rigidly hereditary from father to son, the other branches round about dying off as if smitten by a plague. The Roosevelt tradition skips blithely from branch to branch, and in general is an uncle to nephew, not a father to son, succession. For eight successive generations some Roosevelt has held some public office; pretty undistinguished, these public offices might be, but the line has not been broken except for the very present generation, that of the presidential grandchildren.

The tradition begins with (1) Nicholas, son of the original

Claes. He was an alderman of New York in 1700. His son (2) Johannes, founder of the Oyster Bay line, was an assistant alderman c. 1717 and thereafter. Not much, but something. Skipping across to the other branch, the nephew of Johannes, (3) Isaac the Patriot, was of course conspicuous in state politics as state senator, etc. (1777 on). His son, the bespectacled (4) James, first Hyde Park dweller up the Hudson, was at least a state assemblyman (1796) and an alderman (1809). Again switching branches, we have flamboyant (5) James J., that "old Copperhead," as assistant alderman, state legislator and U.S. Congressman (1841–3). His nephew (6) Robert B. was also alderman (1882) and U.S. Congressman (1871). His nephew (7) Theodore was President, as was Theodore's nephew-in-law (7) Franklin of the same generation. (8) Theodore junior was in the New York Assembly in 1920, and both (8) Franklin and (8) brother James have been U.S. congressmen. Like the record of the Victor du Ponts as senators, it is a continuous, if sometimes obscure, tradition.

So much for the patterns. What of the persons? What can one say of Teddy Roosevelt (teeth and glasses, "bully" and "*delighted*," Rough Riders and Big Stick, Panama Canal and Trust Busting)? Was ever any American public figure less after a familiar pattern, more individually patterned? And yet, in examining that individual pattern, the elements of it do invite comparisons. As man of action, intellectual, gentleman, reformer, moralist, politician, world figure, he inevitably makes one think back to predecessors, particularly John Quincy Adams and Andrew Jackson. As the first* Man of Family in the White House since the last Adams he is a most striking figure in the history of American hereditary meritocracy.

It is particularly as man of action that he is so striking. America has had vigorous Presidents before him. Some of the greatest — Washington, Jackson, Lincoln — have been famous for their strength and vigor; but not in the same way as Theodore. These

* Those Harrisons, of course . . .

others were born active and were developed in rugged careers as surveyor, military man, frontiersman. They came by their ruggedness naturally. Theodore of course did not. He was, in the first place, a sickly child (asthma) who deliberately built himself up over tremendous handicaps. Then, in the second place, his ruggedness was that of the aristocratic sportsman on the English pattern who deliberately courts hardship and danger in hunting field and jungle. As opposed, say, to the calm and easy physical mastery of a Lee or the maritime gumption of a Biddle, the vigor of Theodore seems forced. He achieved remarkable feats, but it was will power, effort. He discovered, only at the age of thirteen, that he was almost totally nearsighted. He had to wear glasses ever afterward. On his expedition to Cuba he carried along more than half a dozen extra pairs, just in case. Yet his favorite avocations were bird watching and big-game hunting, both of which require the keenest eyesight, and at both of which he excelled. At any point in his life and character one strikes these contradictions. He was a "self-made man" to a most special extent.

"I was a 97-pound weakling," an advertisement for physical culture used to read. Theodore as a boy was everything that a sickly, bookish, timid, pampered, rich child should be. His adored father, himself a hearty, sporting fellow, encouraged him to exercise. An experience of being bullied by two bigger boys, again at the crucial age of thirteen, brought the lesson of his weakness home to him. From then on, by deliberate overexertion, he gradually conquered his asthma and became in fact the athletic phenomenon he wanted to be.

It is easy to understand why he thought this aspect of his life so important. Still, it is rather odd, from an objective point of view, to read the autobiography of a major American statesman and find the whole second chapter of it, a long one, devoted entirely to physical exploits. The one thing the office of the President of the United States does *not* require is muscle. "How I was almost killed by a grizzly," "How I stopped a rhinoceros in the charge," etc. etc. Roosevelt cultivated this picture of daring, what he called the "strenuous life," for all it was worth. Actually, as a writer his most vivid passages are liable to be accounts of such exploits either by himself, in his autobiography and his *Hunting Trips of a Ranchman,* or by others (like James Biddle) in his *Naval War of 1812* or the *Winning of the West.*

He was not a fake or poseur. We have ample testimony to his skill in bronco busting and roping out West, his cheerful intrepidity in danger and discomfort. As a weakling in a sporting family, he had had examples. His father drove a reckless four-in-hand, as did cousin James of Hyde Park. Uncle Bob was an all-round outdoorsman, hunter, fisherman, sailer, rider. Theodore's southern mother, aunt and grandmother brought him up on tales of Georgia derring-do among the males of the Bulloch family. Before he went West he had ridden, driven, boxed, rowed. He mentions a day of ninety-one games of tennis while visiting his first wife's family in Chestnut Hill, Massachusetts. Later on, he recounts with relish a bloody day in the field with the Meadowbrook Hunt on Long Island. He was thrown going over a fence ("My face will not be scarred except across the nose") and broke his arm. "The accident did not keep me . . . five minutes. I rode straight through the rest of the hunt. . . . I did not know it was actually broken until . . . the bones slipped up past each other — went out to dinner that night. I don't grudge the broken arm a bit; I would willingly pay it for the fun I have had. . . . I like to drink the wine of life with brandy in it."

When he was President, the strenuous life continued unabated. He kept up with his boxing and as a result lost the sight of his left eye when a sparring partner injured it. Much publicity was given to his "Tennis Cabinet," friends who played the game with him in the court behind the White House. One of these, the French ambassador Jules Jusserand, has left a wonderful tongue-in-cheek account of the desperate "walks" on which Roosevelt forced his guests. No one was allowed to protest as TR led terrified and perspiring senators and generals on cross-country obstacle courses;

rivers were forded, cliffs were scaled. On one such walk in February 1908 with Fitz Lee II (his aide, a son of General Fitzhugh), he took a Colonel Lyon of Texas through Rock Creek Park. Colonel Lyon balked at swimming the icy creek. "Or rather," wrote TR, "I was afraid to let him when I found he was doubtful as to his ability to get over; for I did not want a guest to drown on one of my walks." The walk Jusserand describes so inimitably was a bit milder but still involved swimming.

"President Roosevelt invited me to take a promenade with him this afternoon at three. I arrived at the White House punctually, in afternoon dress and silk hat, as if we were to stroll in the Tuileries Garden. . . . To my surprise, the President soon joined me in tramping suit, with knickerbockers and thick boots and soft felt hat, much worn. Two or three other gentlemen came, and we started off at what seemed to me a breakneck pace, which soon brought us out of the city.

"On reaching the country, the President went pell-mell over the fields, following neither road nor path, always on, on, straight ahead! I was much winded, but I would not give in, nor ask him to slow up, because I had the honor of la belle France in my heart. At last we came to the bank of a stream, rather wide and too deep to be forded. I sighed relief, because I thought that now we had reached our goal and would rest a moment and catch our breath before turning homeward.

"But judge of my horror when I saw the President unbutton his clothes and hear him say 'We had better strip, so as not to wet our things in the Creek.' Then I, too, for the honor of France, removed my apparel, everything except my lavender kid gloves. The President cast an inquiring look at these as if they, too, must come off, but I quickly forestalled any remark by saying, 'With your permission, Mr. President, I will keep these on; otherwise it would be embarrassing if we should meet ladies.' And so we jumped into the water and swam across." *

Things were just as strenuous in the bosom of the family. The introduction of young Eleanor Alexander, wife of Theodore junior (The *other* Eleanor Roosevelt), to life at Oyster Bay was equally

---

* Since Jusserand was an expert mountain climber and outdoorsman, as well as a good friend of TR, this must be taken as pure spoof.

devastating. On her first real visit there in 1912, when the whole family was at home, she was much shaken. The Roosevelts never went to bed before midnight. Then they were up by six, all in full cry.

"One day Colonel Roosevelt [after Cuba he was usually called 'Colonel'] announced he would take the day off and we would all go on a picnic. . . . I liked picnics . . . lettuce sandwiches in waxed paper, chicken salad. . . . It would be pleasant on such a blistering day to have lunch outdoors in the cool shade. . . . Before we were well underway I realized . . . that this was not going to be that sort of picnic. Our provisions . . . consisted of a large basket of clams, another of thick ham sandwiches, and a demijohn of water. . . . By ten o'clock a dozen people had gathered. . . . We headed for the beach, walking the half mile through the woods as fast as we could. . . . At first I could see no reason for such haste. . . . Then I understood. The mosquitoes in those woods seemed as big as bats. . . . Soon I was running ahead of everybody.

"On the beach were five rowboats, two of which had comfortable chairs in the stern. I waited, thinking someone would suggest that I sit in one. . . . I had the wrong idea. I should have run ahead, seized one, and held it against all comers. By the time everyone else was settled there was nowhere for me but a small space between the basket of clams and the demijohn of water.

"Under the blazing sun we rowed and rowed. There was no breeze. . . . Two hours later we landed on a beach precisely like the one we had started from. . . . We settled ourselves at the water's edge, unable to go near the trees because of poison ivy. The provisions were spread out and a kettle filled to make tea. The thought of hot tea was depressing enough, but it was worse to see the roaring fire built over the clams. When they were judged ready, Colonel Roosevelt selected one, opened it, sprinkled it with salt and pepper and handed it to me. It was large, with a long black neck. I managed to get it all in my mouth, burning myself quite badly. . . . Soon it became a piece of old rubber hose. Finally I slipped it under a log.

"As we packed to go home a head wind started to blow. It took four hours to get back. My father-in-law had a difficult time reaching shore, as the boat in which he was rowing . . . was leaking badly. This was called 'one of the best picnics we ever had' and everyone else was delighted with it."

During her visit she lost twenty-six pounds, which she never regained.

The most significant aspect of the Strenuous Life was Roosevelt's brief but action-packed experience as a cattleman in North Dakota. His career as a true rancher was very short. It began with his first visit to the valley of the Little Missouri in the fall of 1883 and ended in the fall of 1886. The great blizzard of 1886–87 wiped out his operation as it did that of many of the ranchers of the Northwest. Afterwards he returned to his ranch only for annual fall hunting trips. Nonetheless, this short, much-interrupted span of three years was crucial in his development and really meant more to him personally than any other single aspect of his early career. It was "the romance of my life," he liked to say later on.

From a practical point of view it was a disaster. He invested at the top of a boom and never recouped his losses when the boom broke. He bought and stocked two ranches, the Maltese Cross and the Elkhorn, both along the Little Missouri River in the North Dakota Badlands. He built his living cabin at the latter, northernmost location. He ran altogether about three thousand head, before the blizzard wiped him out. But it was obviously not the business that meant so much to him, but the life. He took active and exhausting part in the physical labor. In between, he went on epic hunting trips, which he then described in books. Not only did the western experience transform him physically from the slender, reedy-voiced, rather affected but always energetic Manhattan-cum-Harvard dude* to a rugged outdoorsman; it also saved him psychologically from what might have been a fatal blow.

Returning in February 1884 to New York from Albany to see his

* Newspaper reporters loved to dwell on his foppish manner, voice — "exasperating drawl" — and appearance. One of the most damning signs of dudishness was his "hair parted in the middle."

wife and newborn child, he was greeted at the door by his brother Elliott, who proclaimed melodramatically, "There is a curse on this house!" Inside he found both his wife and mother dying simultaneously. A few days later there was a double funeral. Theodore, like Henry Adams at almost the same time (1885), felt his life was over; the "light went from my life forever." Whereas Henry retired into a long career of profitable disillusion, Theodore threw himself back into politics. But politics also failed him. In the election of 1884, which saw the triumph of Cleveland, the first Democrat to sit in the White House since the Civil War, Roosevelt and his newly intimate friend Henry Cabot Lodge tried to prevent the nomination of Blaine, the tarnished Plumed Knight of Maine. When nonetheless Blaine was nominated, Roosevelt and Lodge decided to stick with the party. All their reformer friends, those who had originally backed them, those of their own social class, deserted Blaine and voted for Cleveland and honesty. Roosevelt and Lodge were ostracized, and excoriated by the liberal press. Roosevelt justified himself on the basis of party loyalty, but his conscience obviously hurt him. He never forgave the Mugwumps, those like the Adams brothers, led by Charles Francis junior, who turned Democrat. His political career was temporarily destroyed.

He found refuge in the West, and in hard physical exercise — cutting down seventeen cottonwoods to help build his cabin at the Elkhorn, days and even nights in the saddle in all weathers on roundups and hunting trips. The "romance of his life" with the Wild West, the Old West, is so crammed with color and incident and anecdote that it could only be properly covered by a separate book of its own, and indeed has been in Hermann Hagedorn's *Roosevelt in the Badlands*. In his own books he described much of it. In other books, notably those of his college friend Owen Wister, there is more. Still, the exact importance of this "romance" for American life and letters has never been quite properly appreciated.* One

---

* But see G. Edward White, *The Eastern Establishment and the Western Experience*, New Haven, 1968.

could almost say that the West, as we know it in fact and in fiction, was the creation of that triumvirate of Eastern intellectuals, Roosevelt, Wister and the painter Remington, all friends, all closely and consciously motivated by a burning desire to memorialize a region and a period. As Jackson personified the frontier of the early nineteenth century, that of the Mississippi Valley, so Roosevelt personified, or at least represented, the frontier of the cowboy West. It would be hard to say whether the West was more important to Roosevelt or Roosevelt to the West.

One must remember that, as Jackson's Hermitage was a brand-new plantation in a brand-new world of such Mississippi river valley plantations, so the Elkhorn was a brand-new ranch in a brand-new Northwestern ranching empire. When Roosevelt first arrived in the Badlands in 1883, the last buffalo herd, representing the previous Old West of Indians and trappers and soldiers, had just been slaughtered. Custer had made his last stand only seven years before, in 1876. In 1887, when TR quit ranching, this second Old West of the open range, new as it was, was also wiped out. The cattle business goes on today, as it did then, with cowboys, horses, ropes, roundups and drives. What has changed is that cattle ranchers now like to have their ranges under fences and under control. In Roosevelt's time all you needed to start an outfit was some cattle, some horses, unbroken and unshod, and some cowboys. Around was an unlimited supply of grass. The cattle were turned out in it all year round with everybody else's cattle. There they bred and grew fat; or died. The great fall roundups with dozens of ranches participating and hundreds of cowboys, the great cattle drives of hundreds of miles, were all part of this particular phase of the business. It was a brief phase in the Northwest, beginning not much earlier than 1870, ending pretty much for good in 1886. The unlimited horizons and total freedoms — and total irresponsibilities — of this phase of cattle raising never returned.

When Roosevelt and Wister wrote about the life, they always wrote of it as something past or passing. The whole tone of the

Virginian is one of nostalgia. Although 1870 was about the earliest possible date at which a "horseman of the plains" would have worked at his trade in Wyoming or the Dakotas, by 1900, thirty years later, their world had become to those who knew it in the 80's something romantic, glamorous and done for. The Old West as created by Roosevelt and Wister was already "mythical" by the time they created it, and by the *way* they created it. They were beglamorized easterners, gentlemen, Men of Family, escaping from an industrialized world that did not suit Men of Family. Henry Adams, scorning the crude West, turned towards Gothic Europe. Wister and Roosevelt, both of them half-southern, found in the cowboy West an antique chivalry, a physical aristocracy that was bleached out in the East, whether grimy proletarian or gilded plutocratic. Physical daring and physical grace, the scorn of the horseman for the pedestrian, the feudalism of the cattle baron and his loyal band of reckless riders — here was a re-creation of plantation virtues and southern swagger, or of olde English country life, without the stain of slavery or the curse of caste. Here at last they found a combination of aristocratic ideals of gallantry combined with a total democracy. A man was a man; yet he was still a horseman in a feudal organization. Between them as writer and publicizer, Wister and Roosevelt gave the world the most potent single dream-protagonist of modern times. Others aided and abetted, but they were first and foremost.

Roosevelt used his identification with the cowboy to vault into the seats of power. His Rough Riders were inspired by his western experiences. He'd already had the idea of creating such a corps back in 1886, hoping for a war with Mexico. From bellicose assistant secretary in 1898, to Cuba for a few months of fighting in the summer of that year, then back to New York and election to the governorship that fall, where his popularity was based entirely on his reputation as a soldier (as he campaigned, trumpeters blew "charge" from the back of the train platform); Vice President in 1900 and

President in 1901 — that breathtaking rise to power was propelled by the glamor of his identification with the West. After that he could claim solid accomplishments as a reformer; but he got there, so to speak, on horseback. The image of the cowboy made Roosevelt; Roosevelt and his circle made the image of the cowboy. Without this dash of frontier excitement and virility, of "romance," the great reform, the really important political domestic achievement of twentieth-century America, might never have got started. When that handsome Lone Stranger rides into town on TV to right wrongs and foil nasty bankers, it is Theodore Roosevelt riding into Washington to punish malefactors of great wealth. Never, since Jackson or since Lincoln-and-Lee, have American myth and man been so identified.

Actually, as man of action, his cowboy and fox-hunting days did not compare to the time he spent big-game hunting. It was as big-game hunter that he really expressed himself. Three especially noteworthy game-hunting and exploration adventures emphasize three separate phases of his life. The first was the period in the '80's in Dakota, which marked the break between his ruined earlier career and his return to politics. The second was his triumphal trip to Africa in 1909–10. This was the crest of the wave. He voluntarily renounced the presidency, handed over the reins to his friend Taft, and sailed to the land of the lion. The safari was followed by an almost equally fabulous European progress: a fight with the Pope in Rome, visiting and condescending to the kaiser in Germany, as a recipient of the Nobel Peace Prize preaching a League of Nations in Scandinavia, and finally the climax, the funeral of Edward VII in England, Europe's last panorama of royal pageantry, where Roosevelt in civilian clothes among all the uniformed cousins represented Democracy and the future — and of course stole the show.

Everything from here on was downhill. First came the return to America and the gradual disillusionment with Taft, then the breakup of the Republican party and the triumph of Wilson and his foul Democrats. The last great trip was the nearly fatal one in 1914 with his son Kermit to the Amazon to explore the sinisterly named River of Doubt. This was a gesture of despair, of death wish and last chance. He was not well when he left, and he nearly died en route, largely due to a leg injury he sustained in the jungle. At one point he tried to get the expedition to leave him behind as a useless burden. From the effects of this last adventure he never really recovered. When his youngest son Quentin was killed in the First World War, and Wilson coldly turned down his futile offer to raise another group of Rough Riders for France, the "strenuous life" collapsed. His final illness began the day of the Armistice, November 11, 1918. He rallied, only to succumb on January 6, 1919.

Roosevelt made himself a man of action. By nature he was a man of books. As a child, before he started his career of self-improvement, he was already a reader and a naturalist. Roosevelt may have been the first gentleman sportsman in the White House; he was also the first professional writer. It is doubtful that any of his work would survive on its own merits — the prosy but praiseworthy *Naval War of 1812,* or the later, more lively and monumental *Winning of the West,* the various books on hunting. But still, before he was President, he was historian. He was president of the American Historical Society in 1912, just like Henry Adams. He was one of the original members of the American Institute of Arts and Letters, beginning in 1898 before he was President, and he was also a member of its august, fifty-member offshoot, the Academy. He was prodigiously widely read, according to all contemporaries, though there were doubts about the depths of this reading. He valued the political boss Matthew Quay, for instance, for introducing him to the works of the Finnish novelist Topelius. He impressed others with his grasp of Romanian and Icelandic literature. However, he was not a classical scholar like John Quincy Adams, and his languages were more inclined to be fluent than accurate. Writers were always friends: Wister from college days, Stewart Edward White as a marksman and member of the Tennis Cabinet, John Burroughs as naturalist, Kipling as Imperialist. Richard Harding Davis, original Gibson Man, first of the glamorous war correspondents, made him the hero of Cuba. All sorts of intellectuals were entertained at the White House and never before or since, even under an Adams or a Kennedy, did they find a more sympathetic and responsive appreciation. "I never can like and never will like . . . that enormous proportion of sentient beings who are respectable but dull," he said. His patronage of Edwin Arlington Robinson, whose pessimism he surely could not have found attractive, is a famous and indeed perhaps unique case of an American President's saving from starvation a later important but then obscure American poet. While President he wrote a review of one of Robinson's books; that surely is unique in the annals of the presidency. JQA wrote poetry, but he did not review it.

For the first time, perhaps, since Jefferson, the White House took on the quality of a salon. Roosevelt was very much part of the Hay-Adams charmed circle. The Englishman Spring Rice, Henry's close diplomatic friend, had been best man at Theodore's second wedding in London in '86. John Hay, poet, novelist, historian and best friend of historian Henry Adams, was his secretary of state. Theodore listened to Brooks Adams and his theories with mixed apprehension and excitement. In 1897, for instance, Theodore speaks of the Russian as "the one man with enough barbarian blood in him to be the hope of a world that is growing effete." The source of that kind of thing is easy to trace. Henry, for all his sneers, remained always a close friend.

There were women too, though never quasi-romances like that of the widower Henry and Elizabeth Cameron. Theodore was ferociously strict in his moral attitudes. But socially the background of life during the Roosevelt incumbency was embroidered with witty and beautiful ladies of the same charmed circle — Mmes. Cameron and Lodge, Mrs. Oliver Wendell Holmes, Mrs. Grant La Farge, whose husband helped design Sagamore Hill, Mrs. Cowles, Theodore's older sister Bamie, and many others. They gave to the dinners and balls of his administration an elegance quite different from, say, the soirees of prohibitionist Mrs. Hayes, where "water flowed like champagne." Comparing these ladies with those of the 1920's, Wister said, "To the society of the present day, they seem to bear the same relation that Gobelin tapestry does to linoleum."

As Roosevelt had been a bookworm before he was a cowboy, so he was a snob before he was a liberal. As a young man his class bias was automatic. When cousin Cornelius married a French actress he commented, "He is a disgrace to the family — the vulgar brute." On his first hunting trip with brother Elliott to the prairies, before he went further west, his letters reveal touches of this unconscious arrogance. Speaking of his stay with Illinois farmers, he says, "I don't wonder at their thinking us their equals, for we are dressed . . . as badly as mortals can be." And of Chicago, "there are a great many fine houses; but I should rather doubt the quality of the society." He never would have been guilty of this kind of thing after the Badlands. But class and kind remained with him. His dislike of "respectables" was after all nothing but the common disdain of liberated upper-class people for the conventional middle class, the "Duke or dustman" kind of attitude common to dashing Englishmen. There is a lot of this in his feeling for the cowboy, as opposed to others. He thought them "much better fellows . . . than small farmers or agricultural laborers; nor are the mechanics and workmen of a great city to be mentioned in the same breath" — a feeling of innate cowpoke superiority that persists in the West to this day.

Despite his best efforts, his strong racist bias does keep cropping up. In his *Naval War of 1812* he celebrates the native virtues of Anglo-Saxon seamen as opposed to tricky Latins, "treacherous, fond of the knife . . . likely to lose their wits . . . in a tight place." Greasers. Belief in "blood," preferably Nordic, is never far from his thought. His attitude towards minorities in America was tinged by these beliefs and was certainly ambivalent. He frankly despised Indians as treacherous, cruel and unworthy of occupying the land; in fact he came close to subscribing to the "best Indian is a dead Indian" proposition. The particular emigrant groups that loomed large in political life were the Irish and (rather strangely) the Germans. To the extent that they were assimilable into Anglo-Saxon culture and accepted its values, he approved. But he makes it quite clear that he considers them generally inferior to "natives." No one of course was more conspicuous as a champion of the Negro. That great scandal of his first administration, the dinner with Booker T. Washington that so infuriated the then totally unenlightened South ("the most damnable outrage") became a sort of milestone in Negro history. Roosevelt, however, did not really intend it as such, was surprised at the uproar, and if anything, rather sorry about the incident. It was justice, not sympathy, that guided him.

It is certainly an irony that the winner of the Nobel Peace Prize of 1906, the first American Nobel Prize, should have been the most militarist President since Jackson. "Carry a big stick" became identified with him perhaps more than the corollary "speak softly." His talk to the officers of the Naval War College in 1897 gives the idea. He spoke of "the most valuable of all qualities, the soldierly virtues." "Peace is a goddess only when she comes with sword girt on thigh." Only cowards evade the cost of just war. Build up the navy. He could be even more bellicose. "The victories of peace are great; but the victories of war are greater," and "Every man who has in him . . . joy of battle . . . does not shrink from blood and sweat . . . he revels in them. . . ."

Yet he acted as successful peacemaker between Japan and Russia, Germany and France, coal miners and employers; and avoided a showdown with Japan over restrictive immigration to California and with England over the Alaska-Canada boundary. Among all the contradictions of his character, cowboy-intellectual, gentleman-populist, moralist-politician, the contradictions of jingo-pacifier are among the more peculiar.

Most of these contradictions of personality can be traced to class, to his inheritance as Man of Family. The whole business of the

Strenuous Life, from hunting to cattle raising, from admiration of barbaric virtues to jingoism, is rooted in upper-class, Anglo-oriented emphasis on sport and the somewhat artificial hardihood of the fox-hunting gentleman, the feudal loyalties to "King and country." Sport and war, horsemanship and seamanship had always been the arenas of a gentleman's best efforts (in America, seamanship to the North, horsemanship to the South). It is obvious that in the Roosevelt family these attitudes were more recently acquired than in the Lee or the Biddle families. Cornelius, so wedded to that imperious muse, Business, did not have time for fox-hunting and war. The Hyde Parkers were already country gentlemen, so at least involved in horses. Still, no Roosevelt had ever distinguished himself as a soldier or sailor. Even the bookish Adamses had Brigadier General Charles.

In other words, the transition from peace-loving, city-dwelling Dutch petty bourgeois to war-loving, landowning, upper-class Anglo-Saxon gentry was pretty recent. Theodore longed to confirm the status, to get in on a war, to prove his "gallantry," as a gentleman should. He did his best; there was an element of strain about it.

His role as reformer and moralist was equally class-based, the revolt of an "honorable gentleman" against the gross corruption of post–Civil War industrialism. It was not identification with the workers, but scorn of the employers that motivated him. He was for the proletariat only in the role of the schoolboy hero who defends the underdog against the bully. He had been an underdog himself, as a weakling boy, and then as a member of a displaced aristocracy.

One can't help feeling that Theodore was more important for what he was than for what he did. He is first of all a wonderfully picturesque President, after a long succession of gray ones. He gave a cachet and excitement to the office that it desperately needed if it were to play the role demanded of it during the twentieth century. Competent mediocrity was no longer enough. It was his presidency as a whole, not individual incidents such as the Panama Canal or Trust Busting or Conservation, that counted. Quite apart from such incidents, his presidency was surely just in itself a turning point in American history.

Actually as a politician, he was, like the Adamses, in the end a rather disastrous failure. By the close of his presidency he had lost control of Congress and his reforms had come to a standstill. Under Taft, despite much real reform accomplishment, the Grand Old Party drifted back towards an elephantine standpat. When Roosevelt broke with Taft in 1912 he sealed the fate of his brand of liberal Republicanism. From that point on, the party of reform was the Democratic party, and Republicans stood for "normalcy," money, prosperity — Big Business. Everything Theodore Roosevelt fought against.

The nature of Roosevelt's failure is compound. First of all, Fatality: why did he refuse to run in 1908? It was his own doing, based on a feeling of traditional respect for the third-term prohibition. Still, it wasn't really a third term, and he most surely would have been reelected. Yet he stepped down as all Vice Presidents since have stepped down, and so cut off his career in the middle. He lost his power and then ruined his party. Yet surely a feeling of such "fatality" could not have been conscious.

Then there is the feeling that he was in the wrong party all along anyway. Why was he a Republican? He says in his autobiography, "At that day, in 1880, a young man of my bringing up . . . could join only the Republican party." But all the Roosevelts had been Democrats, Uncle Bob was active all through Roosevelt's early career, all the Bullochs were Democrats, his first Lee father-in-law, a Boston Brahmin, was a Mugwumpy Democrat, the Adamses shifted to Democrat at that time. Uncle Bob is particularly mysterious. He is only mentioned once in Theodore's autobiography, and then in a rather condescending way. Yet he is so patently the model for his nephew as sportsman, writer, conservationist, politician. Even the detailed Putnam biography cites him only in a footnote. Why? Uncle Bob was a Democrat, he did not live in Oyster Bay, there was family disapproval of aspects of his personal life — but still, the silence seems odd. Cleveland was far closer to Roosevelt's ethos than Blaine. Harrison, who grudgingly appointed him as Civil Service commissioner, never even asked the Roosevelts to the White House. Cleveland did. Roosevelt hated Jefferson, hated Mugwumps, loathed Southern secessionists; yet who was more like Jefferson in interests, more naturally a Mugwump, and half Southern? Above all, Roosevelt hated Wilson; yet it was Wilson who carried on the Square *Deal* in his *New* Freedom, which in turn merged into the *New Deal*.

As a Republican and a politician Roosevelt was a failure. As a person and a reformer he was a success. Above all, as a John the Baptist of a new order, the control of the American economy by the people through their President, he is significant. The direct line from Roosevelt through Wilson to Roosevelt is clear. We still live in the world that Teddy was the first to proclaim.

Women

There's another parallel between the Adamses and the Roosevelts: both families are conspicuous for their women. The women of the Biddle and du Pont families, for instance, never seem to step beyond their portraits and genealogies. They represent names — Cadwalader or Van Dyke — not people. But the Adamses are different. Tart Abigail, as revealed in her letters, is one of America's historical heroines. Frail Louisa, though scarcely a heroine, lives in her grandson's memories.

Theodore was surrounded by women and nearly all of them have character; but only two, his daughter Princess Alice and his niece Queen Eleanor, really played prominent roles onstage. In striking contrast to Franklin, neither the mother nor the wife (or wives) of Theodore is very conspicuous. He was a father's boy, as Franklin was a mother's boy. He idolized genial, upright, vigorous, all-around Theodore senior. Though he did love his mother, he also seemed to rather despise her. She was in fact odd, a spoiled, whimsical, Southern belle who must have suffered a good deal in her transplantation north. She remained, for instance, an ardent secessionist all through the Civil War, backed up by her refugee mother and sister, cheering for her brothers while her husband and all his kin cheered (but, notably, did not fight) for the Union. It must have been trying for Theodore senior.

Martha Roosevelt was evidently a hopeless housekeeper, and the older daughter Anna took over in her early teens. Martha had the vapors and the sulks. She would order the carriage for an afternoon drive and then not take it. She would refuse to go out to a dinner party at the last minute for no reason. She had been beautiful, reckoned in her earlier days as one of the Queens of New York society, a throne she shared only with that connection of the Hyde Park Roosevelts, Mrs. Gardiner Howland. Her influence on her son seems to have been negative rather than positive, a hatred on his part of secession and of recessiveness.

Of his first wife Alice Lee almost nothing survives, even pictures. She was pretty, lively, very young. Her family was an integral part of that Essex Junto of Salem families that took over Boston after 1800, superseding the Braintree Faction of Adamses and Hancocks. This Junto was always the Adamses' enemy. Cabot-and-Lowell are the most famous of Junto names in Boston, corresponding to Cadwalader-and-Biddle in Philadelphia; but Higginson, Jackson and Lee are equally representative. After Alice died, Theodore refused to talk about her. She is not mentioned in his autobiography (like Henry Adams' wife). He never mentioned her even to her daughter Alice. Peculiar.

This may have been partly the work of his second wife, Edith Carow. Edith was a New Yorker. She had evidently known and loved Theodore before he married Alice, had made up her mind to get him, and got him. She makes an ambivalent impression. She was beautiful in a somewhat formal way; she was charming in a somewhat cool fashion. She occupies that favorite role in American folklore, the sensible, pretty, humorous wife-and-mother who appears in *Life with Father* or *Father Knows Best* or *The Happiest Millionaire*. One pictures the scene: Theodore on a particularly outrageous rampage, Edith (perhaps knitting by the fireside) saying calmly, "Now, Theodore!" and Theodore, collapsed, spluttering, "But . . . but . . . but." This is *not* the role played by Eleanor with Franklin. It's all rather patly lovable. Edith was an excellent President's wife. As hostess and mother of an unruly family she is admirable. Much better probably than pretty Alice could have been. But there is certainly something a bit chilling about such excellence. A person who never makes mistakes may require our respect, but not often our affection.

Theodore's sisters also were minor personages: poetic Corinne, who rather slavishly worshiped him and wrote verse, achieving something of a semiprofessional reputation (she was vice president of the Poetry Society of America at one time); and Anna — Aunt Bamie or Auntie Bye to all younger generations of both branches of Roosevelts. Like others of the family, she had her physical troubles. She was a sort of semihunchback, but her beautiful eyes and charming ways made everyone forget her disabilities. It was she who formed the link between Hyde Park and Oyster Bay. She was always "taking over" in emergencies. When Alice died she took over the care of little Alice. Franklin's half brother James was in London as first secretary of the American Embassy when his wife, the former Helen Astor, died. Bamie took over in her place as hostess. All through her life she helped and advised Eleanor, especially when Eleanor moved to Washington as awkward young wife of the assistant secretary of the navy. Young Alice always turned to her with devotion.

But it was young Alice herself who emerged as the true child of her father and the true personage among the women of his family. There was nothing cool, collected or canny about Alice. From her teens on she did and said what she wanted and everybody, or nearly everybody, loved it. "I can be President of the United States — or — I can attend to Alice" is the most famous of her father's estimates of her. She lived at a happy time for nonconformists, the beginning of the twentieth century, when one could pleasantly upset the public by doing very innocent things — smoking a cigarette not only in private, which was bad enough but even, oh horrors, in public; driving a motorcar unchaperoned with friend Ellen Drexel Paul from Newport to Boston at a reckless twenty-four miles an hour; carrying a pet green snake named Emily Spinach around to house parties. High-spirited and individualistic without ever being really outrageous, pretty and indefatigable, she shocked the people everyone likes to have shocked — the prissy and prudish — and delighted the newspapers. As the first presidential daughter in the White House since Nellie Grant, her debut and then her marriage to Nicholas Longworth of Cincinnati (a member of Porcellian at Harvard, like her father) were news. It was as though she were a female Prince of Wales. Her spectacular preengagement trip to the Orient with the semiofficial Taft party, her future husband being along on the trip too, was followed with breathless interest and publicity, step by step. The value of her wedding presents was vastly exaggerated; but, still, they were flamboyant enough — a string of pearls from Cuba, presents from the Kaiser and other royalty, including the Empress Dowager of China. "Alice blue" was her color and "Alice Blue Gown" one of her songs (the first popular song I remember hearing on records). Never before or since has there been anything quite like Princess Alice in American public life.

If she had died young or retired from the limelight like her sister Ethel, who also got married in the White House, though nobody seemed to care, she would still remain one of the more charming and piquant memories of the Confident Age. But she didn't. Her husband served almost perennially in Congress, Speaker of the House under Coolidge and Hoover, and Alice stayed in Washington as its wittiest and most acidulous commentator. Perhaps she didn't actually invent all the things that are attributed to her — the famous demolitions of public characters such as Harding ("He wasn't a bad man. He was just a slob"), Coolidge ("He looks as if he'd been weaned on a pickle" — Alice said she picked that one up from her dentist), Dewey ("The bridegroom on top of the wedding cake"). But like Oscar Wilde, she earned the right to appropriate them. One can dislike her political stances: the isolationism that killed Wilson's League of Nations and Wilson; her protest against entering the war against Hitler; her biting Republican comments on her cousins Franklin and Eleanor, full of real meanness. One can admit that she didn't do anything very much. Even her writings fail to reproduce her personality. Her rather scandalous teacup battles with people like the newspaper heiress Eleanor Patterson or the Vice President's sister Mrs. Gann are more amusing than edifying. Nonetheless, charm and person triumph over time and faction, and, intact through the administrations of Kennedy and Johnson, she has still been Princess Alice, one of the more delightful figures of Washington and the country, a caustic watcher of Washington from the sidelines like Henry Adams, still witty, still elegant, still vigorous, still pleasantly shocking and malicious.* Saintly Eleanor and naughty Alice, the salt of the earth and its pepper, make an amusing contrast in first cousins.

Sons

It is not enough that one Roosevelt should follow right in the path of another; their sons also follow a pattern. Here again we have, like the Adamses, a branch of a family splitting into four. Of all these family patterns, this one of the Four Brothers is one of the most curious and baffling. Does it really mean something genetically, the dispersal of energy acquired in four generations down from a John Adams or from a Cornelius Roosevelt? Or, again, coincidence? Four bright and active brothers succeed to an important father without ever quite equaling him. Each one assumes some facet, some aspect of the parental character, but no one matches the

---

* "If you haven't anything nice to say about anybody, come sit here by me" is a quotation of which Mrs. Longworth must be getting tired.

whole. Thus of the Adamses, nice John took to politics, Charles Francis paralleled the presidential career, but in business; Henry and Brooks took over literature and contrariness. Almost the same thing happened to the four sons of Theodore; but none of them has written an *Education*. Just to rub it in, the same pattern is being repeated among the four sons of Franklin. So we have in *both* Roosevelt families: one son, a namesake (Theodore junior; Franklin junior) taking over the parental political pattern, but just like young John Adams, failing; another son (Archibald; John) retreating into business, retiring into the semi-anonymity of private life; another son (Kermit; Elliott) taking over the role of sportsman-adventurer, big-game hunter, aviator. The favorite son of Theodore, Quentin, did not live to fulfill his fate. He remains the glamorous, predestined, hero-victim aviator of World War I. James, among the sons of Franklin, remains the "sport."

Of the four sons of Theodore, Theodore junior was by far the most conspicuous. He obviously should have made his career in the army. All the sons followed up their father's militarism with outstanding military careers. Theodore junior was a hero, twice wounded in the First World War, ending as a brigadier general in the second, a casualty during the invasion of Normandy. He wanted to go to West Point, but his father, who probably hoped he might follow his footsteps in politics, dissuaded him. So, like any good Man of Family, in a thoroughly Adams fashion, he gave up the army and tried to follow those paternal footsteps — *exactly*. First Harvard,* then just like Dad, a session in the state legislature; then just like Dad again, assistant secretary of the navy succeeding cousin Franklin. But here fate intervened; a later, less complacent Roosevelt Fate. He was caught in the unseemly mess of the Har-

---

* The Roosevelt family tradition at Harvard only begins of course with President Theodore. Before that the Oyster Bay branch had been more or less identified with Columbia; Uncle Silas was an active alumnus. Hyde Park was equally more or less identified with Princeton; James, son of Patriot Isaac, and Isaac, son of James, both went there. James, father of Franklin went to Harvard Law School after graduating from Union. Franklin's half brother James Roosevelt Roosevelt went to Columbia, Class of '77.

ding administration. Though perfectly innocent himself of the doings involving the Navy Department and Secretary of the Interior Fall, he nonetheless resigned. When he took the next step, running for governorship of New York in 1924, he was defeated by Al Smith. That ended the footsteps. He served with merit as governor of Puerto Rico and the Philippines. When cousin Franklin came in, Theodore junior went out. He never again held public office.

It is with Theodore and his blighted political career that the rift between Hyde Park and Oyster Bay began. Before that they had continued close friends and cousins. When Franklin was campaigning for Vice President in 1920, Theodore junior went around speaking against him. In Sheridan, Wyoming, trying to be real Western, he disowned Franklin's Rooseveltism. "He's a maverick, he does not have the brand of our family." Then, when Theodore in turn was campaigning for governor, Eleanor rigged up a tea kettle on a car to symbolize the Teapot Dome scandals. This was, as Eleanor later on admitted herself, pretty low. It may however have been effective. From then on, Oyster Bay and Hyde Park were political enemies. Alice's remarks didn't help either. Oyster Bay continued to drift to the right as Hyde Park drifted to the left.

Kermit never entered politics, but he did carry on his father's tradition, inherited from Uncle Bob, as writer-sportsman. While still a college boy, he accompanied his father on the triumphal safari to Africa in 1909–10; then later on he took the despairingly dangerous trip up the River of Doubt. He was a banker in South America, and in both wars jumped the gun to serve in the British army in far off places like Mesopotamia and Egypt. He too collected wounds and medals (including one from Montenegro). He wrote half a dozen books, most of them about hunting adventures in remote, romantic lands: *East of the Sun and West of the Moon, Cleared for Strange Ports*. He died during the Second World War on a mission to Alaska. Glamorous.

Archibald, though he too was wounded in the First World War

and went to New Guinea in the Second, is the only one to survive into the post–World War II era. He joined the enemy, so to speak, the side of those "malefactors of great wealth" against whom his father fought. His Republicanism, like that of most post-Theodore Oyster Bayers, has been definitely that of the Elephant, not of the Bull Moose.

But especially the sons fulfilled their father's military ambitions. After all, Teddy was a summer soldier, who actually fought only a few months in Cuba. Here first, and on a grand scale, the Roosevelts *did* fight. The list of their collective battles and wounds and medals is almost oppressive. Medals in both wars from America: Distinguished Service Cross, Purple Heart, Silver Star. Medals from France: Legion of Honor, Croix de Guerre. Medals from Belgium and Britain and Montenegro and even China (Theodore junior acquired the Grand Blue Cordon of the Order of the Jade). Three Roosevelts, Quentin, Kermit, and Theodore junior died as war casualties, Theodore being awarded posthumously the Congressional Medal of Honor and the Bronze Star, thus acquiring *every* U.S. combat medal. The survivor, Archibald, is perhaps the only U.S. officer who was discharged from *both* wars as totally disabled; the Strenuous Life with a heroic vengeance. In that way, at least, the sons fulfilled the dreams of glory of their somewhat frustrated father, and made up in gallantry for the somewhat ungallant Dutch-burgher past of the Roosevelts.

Others

Du Ponts

Meanwhile, other families besides the Roosevelts were surviving, and during the reigns of both Theodore and Franklin produced noteworthy characteristic specimens of their kind and their period. One thing distinguished all these families in this period: they were rich. In the twentieth century, for the first time, though these families may retrogress from the point of view of national service, they prospered economically. Even some Lees were rich.

Richest of all of course — rich, rich, rich — were the du Ponts. As Sidney Fisher noted in mid-nineteenth century, the family already had a reputation for wealth, even in its communal phase. It was not till after the turn of the century, however, that there began to be something stupendous about it. In 1902, when the three first cousins, Alfred I., T. Coleman, and Pierre S., bought the Company from their elders for some fifteen million, the family and the Company may have been affluent; but after all, fifteen million is hardly a staggering sum, even for that comparatively deflated period. Du Pont may have had a monopoly control of powder, but that was not the same thing as a monopoly of oil or sugar. It was after that that the orgiastic flow of gold began.

The death of Eugene marked a low ebb in the Company and family fortunes. Henry the Great had built the Company into a national giant. Eugene tried to carry on his one-man rule, though after 1899 over an incorporation, not a family partnership. However, he was simply not the man to do it. When he died, the family leadership was shared by a group of rather tired men, all but one of them sons of Henry or Alexis, who, either like Colonel Henry of Civil War fame were not very interested in powder manufacturing, or who did not have the strength of character and the stamina to keep the family control going. Above all, no one of them seemed to emerge as a natural leader. It seemed as though perhaps at last the du Pont family merit was giving out.

It was not. The management decided to sell the Company on the open market. To avoid this disaster, the three young first cousins, all descendants of Irénée, all in their thirties, got together and decided to buy it themselves. These were Alfred Irénée, orphaned oldest son of an E. I. who was oldest son of Alfred Victor (oldest son of Irénée); Pierre Samuel, oldest son of Lammot, who was second son of Alfred Victor; and Thomas Coleman, oldest son of Antoine Bidermann, who was youngest son of Alfred Victor.

These three cousins managed to scrape up enough credit to take over the management from the somewhat feeble hands of their elders. Helped largely by the enormous profits of World War I, they between them lifted the family fortunes to the plateau where it still continues — the largest combined family fortune in America. It is this period of Company history and these members of the family who have made the modern reputation of the name "du Pont."

Of the three, only Alfred I. was already prominently connected with the Company. As oldest son of the oldest son of the oldest son, he by rights should have been the natural heir. He was the only one really fitted for the job. But he was not popular with his elders. He had forced them to admit him to partnership by sheer aggressive energy and talent. When the ailing seniors, more or less behind Alfred's back, decided to sell the Company, Alfred behind *their* backs, made his hurried financial arrangements.

The new triumvirate took over and revolutionized the Company's operations: Alfred the manufacturing, Coleman the financing, Pierre the administration. The trend toward monopoly continued. Other lesser powder firms were gobbled up by the scores, including the chief rival, Laflin and Rand. By 1906, du Pont was responsible for as much as three quarters of the national output of most types of powder. In 1907, the government, in full Teddy trust-busting form, attacked the powder trust, as it had others. Du Pont was found guilty under the antitrust laws; but how to re-create a situation of fair competition in powder making when all du Pont's old rivals had been absorbed and liquidated? The government told the Company to find its own solution, a rather odd way to punish a malefactor of great wealth. The Company was split into three — du Pont, Atlas, Hercules; but due to impassioned military pleas du Pont still retained a 100 percent monopoly of military smokeless powder. Nothing much could be done about private family ownership of stock in

Atlas and Hercules. By 1942 the three companies were under suit again for breaking those same antitrust laws.

However, the general result of the breakup of monopoly was beneficial for the Company. It tended to force du Pont away from powder into chemicals, from war to peace; and it established the principle of family control by stock ownership and holding companies rather than directly through the Company, a process which has made the total family, rather than just those associated with E. I. du Pont de Nemours, so inordinately prosperous. World War I, in which du Pont supplied a lion's share of all the powder used by the Allies and the Americans, enriched the Company and the family beyond reasonable dimensions. Called "patriots" while the fighting was going on, they were called "merchants of death" in the reaction afterward. During the war the Company's gross income totaled a billion dollars.

Then, almost simultaneously, came the take-over of the lead in chemicals from the war-liquidated Germans. This, plus the war profits, established du Pont as one of the great corporations of the world. From rayon to nylon, from cellophane to neoprene (artificial rubber), du Pont as a producer of synthetics went on from glory to glory. Powder became a sideline, and the merchants of death changed to merchants of plastic. On the basis then of these two developments, near monopoly of powder in the war and near American monopoly of synthetics afterward, the du Ponts began to emerge during this period as "America's richest family."

The swelling industrial progress commenced under this triumvirate of cousins; but the overindividualistic personalities of the three men soon led to friction and finally to feud. Of the three, Alfred was the most unpredictable and peculiar. Years of being snubbed by the elders of his family bred a sort of pugnacious perverseness. Of the three he was the only real powderman. He had himself worked in the plant along the Brandywine and was idolized by the workmen.

His very faults of character made him popular there, his brusqueness and combativeness. He had few outside intellectual interests, except for an amateur love of music expressed by his activities in a semihumorous local musical association called the Tankopanicum Club. The qualities that made him popular with the hands made him unpopular with the family. He compounded this unpopularity by a scandal so flagrant that he was eventually ostracized.

The breath of scandal, since the days of bigamist Clifford and his marriage with Amelia, had never touched the family name; at least in public. Then suddenly in the eighties and nineties, under the loosening influence of increasing prosperity and increasing numbers, the control of the tight-knit family began to break up. First and mildest of these scandals was the marriage of Maurice du Pont, brother of Alfred I., to an Irish barmaid he had picked up stopping off in Queenstown for a drink on a trip to Europe. Newspapers got hold of the story, but the turmoil and family outrage subsided when they found her attractive and acceptable, and when Maurice more or less permanently moved away from Wilmington.

The next scandal was not so easy to take. It resulted in the first sensational divorce in the family annals. William, second son of Henry the Great, nearly twenty years younger than his brother Colonel Henry, had been dynastically wed in 1878 to his cousin Mary of the Victor branch, daughter of the state senator of that name. She had already fallen in love with a young law associate of her father, Willard Saulsbury; but the match went through on schedule, another exemplary du Pont–du Pont branch graft. The mismatched couple took it for years. Then suddenly in 1892, William went to South Dakota and there divorced his wife. The first divorce in the family. When Mary shortly married Saulsbury and William shortly married a divorced Mrs. Zinn, all hell broke loose. William was exiled, forced to sever connections with the Company and retire into affluent seclusion on a plantation in Virginia (Montpelier, Madison's old house). Saulsbury, as lawyer and Democratic politician, spent his life hating and badgering his new in-laws. Alfred I., just to be contrary, stuck by William when everyone else deserted him.

One reason why Alfred stuck by William was that he too was unhappily married; and he too shook up the proprieties by an even more scandalous divorce, the family's second such. He had been married in 1887 to a cousin, Bessie Gardner.* There were all sorts of sinister omens surrounding both the cousinship and the marriage. Bessie was related by way of one of those wonderful mix-ups of interconnection so delightful to amateurs of pure genealogy, a complex of five different stocks, the du Ponts, the Gardners of Rhode Island, the Cazenoves of Switzerland, the Hendersons of Virginia, and, finally, and most satisfactorily, the Lees of both Stratford and Leesylvania.† The particular connection with the du Ponts was through a Charlotte Henderson. Charlotte's father, an integral member of the Virginia planter oligarchy, was Archibald, first general of the Marine Corps. Married to a son of Alfred Victor before the Civil War, Charlotte found herself, like Martha Bullock amid Roosevelts, a rebel among Unionists. Mother-in-law trouble loomed large. Instead of adjusting, as did Martha, poor Charlotte died insane. Alfred I. was her son.

Bessie Gardner, before marrying Alfred, had been loved by Alfred's brilliant brother Louis. Shortly after her marriage, Louis committed suicide. Bessie and Alfred had little in common: she was interested in intellectual matters; he was interested only in powder and the Tankopanicum Club. They grew more and more estranged, despite the birth of four children. Alfred found consolation with another kinswoman, connected even more closely than Bessie through another elaborate crisscross. She was Alicia Bradford, daughter of a Judge Bradford who had married a du Pont and whose half sister had married a du Pont. Alfred, rather than face a

---

* All three of the triumvirate married cousins, Pierre a Belin, T. Coleman another du Pont.
† See Appendix V.

divorce, effected a most curious compromise. He arranged for Alicia, evidently quite willing, to marry one of his employees, a handsome nondescript called George Maddox. Maddox was sent off on increasingly long tours of duty to far places; Alicia and Alfred spent increasingly intimate hours together. A child was born to Alicia Maddox with overwhelmingly du Pont characteristics. Finally in 1904 Bessie walked out. In 1906 Alfred, like William, went to South Dakota for his divorce; Maddox conveniently and mysteriously disappeared and was never heard of again. A divorce was granted on the basis of abandonment. Alfred married Alicia. There were rumors that Maddox had been rewarded with a million dollars.

This scandal was of real dynastic importance, and the resultant feud, when almost all the family except William turned against Alfred, threatened to break up the solidarity of both family and Company. Alfred, Alicia, Bessie and the children, the Bradfords, all continued to live right there in du Pontland and the social turmoil among cousins can well be imagined. As a gesture of pride and defiance, Alfred in 1910 built the first of the du Pont palaces to house his new bride and offend Wilmington. Called "Nemours," it was a grand marble affair of seventy-some rooms set amid formal gardens and surrounded by a great wall capped with broken glass — to keep the family out. No du Ponts, except the renegade William and one other, were allowed to cross its threshold; at least till time began to heal the breaches. Alicia only enjoyed the splendor for a decade. She died in 1920 and Alfred remarried the next year.

Besides splitting the family socially (there were others besides William who sided with Alfred and Alicia, notably Madeleine, his daughter by Bessie), the scandal affected the operation of E. I. du Pont de Nemours, Inc. Alfred was first pushed out of his control over production; then, through a bit of secret double-dealing on the part of Pierre, deprived of his position as one of the majority stockholders.

T. Coleman, at about the same time as Alfred's scandal, began to get bored with Wilmington and powder making and to look for more adventurous fields of enterprise. He was, in contrast to brusque Alfred and mild Pierre, the epitome of the genial, glad-handed robber baron. He came not from Wilmington, but from Kentucky, where his father and an uncle had emigrated to found a prosperous paper mill. He went to a small midwestern college where he played football, then to the du Pont's favorite, M.I.T. After that he was involved in coal mining in Pennsylvania. A genius at financial combinations and sleight of hand, it was he who increased du Pont's monopoly position to the point of government suspicion. Perhaps feeling that he'd had all the fun he could possibly extract from powder mergers, he descended on New York and became involved in huge real estate and insurance deals, built a hotel, the McAlpin, with a lush apartment where he entertained many a chorus girl, and in general lived it up away from family scrutiny. He was the kind of man who passed trick cigars out to his friends and roared with delight when they exploded. He exercised his sleight of hand not only on their finances but on their watches.

Finally, needing capital for one of his New York ventures, he decided to sell his du Pont stock. This was in 1914 when the war in Europe was making du Pont stock increasingly valuable. He offered it to the Company. The directors, under the leadership of the estranged Alfred, quoted him an absurdly low price for it. Meanwhile, Pierre, on his own, borrowed money from J. P. Morgan, ironically almost the same amount, fourteen million, that Alfred had originally borrowed to buy the whole Company in 1902, and bought Coleman's stock for himself and friends. This was the final outrage. Alfred and his friends sued Pierre; but nothing really came of it except bitterness and Alfred's final separation from all aspects of the Company's management. Alfred's third marriage was to Jessie Ball of Virginia (George Washington's mother was a Ball; Balls of course connected with Lees). He removed his operations largely to

Florida, where du Pont has become almost as important a financial name as it is in Delaware.*

Pierre, from the time of the First World War, took over the Company.

Pierre could not have been a greater contrast to both rugged, cantankerous Alfred and genial, roguish T. Coleman. He was everything that was mild, discreet, polite, sensitive. He did not lose his temper, he did not hand out loaded cigars. He loved flowers. No breath of scandal touched him. Under this deceptive exterior, however, he concealed an executive genius that came near to making du Pont the one single most powerful economic unit in the world. His talent seemed to lie not in a knowledge of manufacturing processes or financial combinations, but in men and administration, in choosing the right person for the right job at the right time, in knowing when and how to extend the Company's control.

His greatest coup was the take-over in the twenties of General Motors and the building of it from a bankrupt collection of mergers into the greatest single manufacturing concern in the U.S.A. With the aid of his faithful henchman, John Jacob Raskob, and close to one hundred million dollars, he bought control of the stock of what was in 1920 a ramshackle collection of twenty-one automobile companies — Cadillac, Buick, Oldsmobile — that had been put together by one William Crapo Durant. Durant was an enterprising entrepreneur, without much staying power. Durant was pushed out; Pierre became president himself for a few years, then turned the works over to his hand-picked successors, Alfred Sloan and Donaldson Brown (a cousin). The company lost thirty-eight million dollars during its first year of operation under Pierre, but thereafter has showed a tidy profit. Until another antitrust suit in 1957 forced a separation, the du Ponts controlled General Motors as absentee landlords.

* Jessie's brother Edward Ball now seems to own most of Miami, etc.

Pierre's particular personal monument was the second of the du Pont palaces, Longwood. This, a garden rather than a house, is an incredible Versailles of hothouses, rose gardens, fountains and one of the world's largest pipe organs. It is now open to the public. It's a Sight of America like Niagara and the Empire State Building.

Spectacle of another and less exalted kind was provided by the du Ponts' excursions into national politics. Members of the Victor branch may have been senators of Delaware, but none had been senators of the United States. The first of these was Colonel Henry, hero of the Civil War. His entry into politics, at an advanced age, was as champion of decency against a most indecent opponent, one John Edward O'Sullivan Addicks.

Of all the flamboyant and disreputable products of the Gilded Age, certainly Addicks was one of the most. From humble beginnings in Philadelphia, "Gas" Addicks, as he was called, had made a fortune in manipulating gas companies. He had a country place in Delaware, and suddenly and rather whimsically decided he would like to crown his career by a seat in the Senate. Since at the time, of course, senators were elected not by the people but by the state legislatures, his plan was simple: bribe the legislators of Delaware to elect him. This in such a small state was not unfeasible. He nearly did it. He moved in on Delaware in 1889. Year by year, election by election, he bought his way toward success. The Family and honest Republicans of the state in desperation put up Colonel Henry as an impeccably distinguished opponent to Addicks. Since when Addicks began there were only 30-some members of the Delaware legislature, 16 were all that he needed for election. Beginning with only one supporter in 1889, he had gradually built up his votes, 6 votes in '95, 18 in '99, 20 in '01. But, most unfortunately for Addicks, the population of the state kept increasing too, and hence the number of state legislators. He was never quite able to catch up with a clear majority. The result was a series of compromises and deadlocks in the election of senators from that state.

The dignity and medals of Colonel Henry obviously were not enough. He called in cousin T. Coleman to help him out. T. Coleman had none of the scruples of Henry. He outbought Addicks. As their Democratic opponent, none other than cousin-in-law Willard Saulsbury, liked to suggest, Coleman, as opposed to Addicks, knew how to buy votes like a gentleman.

For several years, between 1901 and 1903, due to this deadlock created by Addicks and his efforts, Delaware had no senators at all. The scandal became national. Teddy Roosevelt, fearful of upsetting Republican balances in the state, was afraid to interfere.* But in 1906, finally, Colonel Henry was victorious. Addicks gave up and left the state. Personal scandals and personal bankruptcy destroyed him. He ended up a bum in New York, forgotten and penniless. As a result of Delaware's scandals, the election of senators by popular vote was confirmed by the Seventeenth Amendment.

Coleman, having tasted blood in helping cousin Henry to the Senate, decided he would like to try for it himself. Despite his gay life in New York, he had always carefully maintained Delaware residence. He managed, after years of frustration due largely to the political opposition of cousin Alfred, to get himself appointed by the governor to an incompleted term in 1921; but in the following election of 1922 he was narrowly defeated by another cousin-in-law, the Democrat Thomas Bayard, who was supported by Alfred. However, he made it on his own during the Coolidge landslide of 1924. His enjoyment was short-lived. Progressive cancer of the larynx forced him to retire in 1928. In 1930 he died, leaving an estate of only seventeen million, paltry by du Pont standards.

Alfred, enormously rich in his own right, but almost totally separated from the Company, lived on till 1935. His assets in 1930, compared to Coleman's, were reputed to be a comfortable sixty-eight million. For years the bitterness with his ex-wife Bessie and his family persisted. One of the strangest incidents was his effort to have the name of his own son, whom he had not seen since early

* Wister has a long story about this.

childhood, changed by the state legislature. This perversely vindictive eccentricity nearly succeeded, since the legislature of Delaware was inclined to do what du Ponts asked of it, and Bessie and son knew nothing of the maneuver. They discovered it just in time to stop it; and so Alfred Victor kept his du Pontish name and failed to assume that of Dorsey Cazenove, surnames prominent in his mother's background. (See Appendix V.)

Toward the end of his life, however, Alfred began to mellow. He and Coleman were reconciled before Coleman died; and even son Alfred Victor and his wife were actually invited to Nemours. They were among the very first du Ponts thus honored. The reunion was so successful that young Alfred, a prominent architect, was asked to design sunken gardens for Nemours itself and various other commissions for old Alfred. Jessie Ball, Alfred's third wife, had no stigma in du Pont circles, and as a spectacularly able manager of her late husband's enterprises has been a power in her own right, even in Delaware.

Pierre, who was never reconciled with Alfred and refused to attend his funeral, substituted a triumvirate of brothers for the triumvirate of cousins. After the death of Eugene, Coleman had become president of the Company. Alfred was never more than vice president. In 1915 Pierre became president himself, followed by his brothers Irénée (1919–1926) and Lammot (1926–1940). These were the last men actually surnamed du Pont who ran the Company. Though it is still a family corporation, it is "family" in a somewhat broader sense. The history of this later period and its aftermath is linked not with Theodore, but with Franklin Roosevelt.

Biddles

Aside from the Roosevelts, the du Ponts were the most flamboyantly conspicuous of the men of these particular families in the twentieth century. Some Biddles came fairly close, however; at least one man of one branch of them. The Drexel-Biddle union demonstrated a problem involved in marriages of old names to new money. Nobody doubted, for instance, that Abbie Brooks had married into the Adams family. Edward Biddle was surprised and evidently not pleased to find he had married into the Drexels. Edward, grandson of Nicholas, had Spanish blood on his mother's side and expressed his lineage with haughty demeanor, a cape-wearing swagger and a life of determined dilettantism. He wrote articles about art, helped to compile the still recognized authoritative catalogue of the paintings of Thomas Sully, and played tennis till he was eighty. He insisted on doing the marketing himself, striding down with a basket to make sure his chickens were properly plump. When he married Emily Drexel he found he was expected to live in West Philadelphia near a complex of great, hideous Drexel mansions and to take a job in Drexel and Company. He was not happy there. He was fired from the company when he complained of the manners of another more valuable employee; and when his wife died, fairly young (as a result of trying to lift a piano, of all things), he severed relations with the Drexels and married again — a Lillian Lee from Salem, of the same Essex Junto family as Alice Lee Roosevelt. By her he had a second, non-Drexel and definitely Biddle family. Lillian married into the *Biddles*.

As a result, his Drexel children were brought up under Drexel influences and endowed by Drexel trusts. One son, Livingston Ludlow,* was a quiet, gentlemanly fellow, with literary tastes and conventional sporting and financial affiliations. The other brother, Craig, was a playboy. Not so the oldest brother, Anthony Joseph Drexel Biddle. Though born in 1874 and thus more a contemporary of Franklin than Theodore, he followed almost slavishly the latter's life patterns, not of course on purpose or politically, but simply coincidentally and in character, as part of the Spirit of the Times perhaps. Just like Theodore, he was a sickly, pampered, rich boy, with bookish leanings and asthma. Just like Theodore, he realized his

* Both these names are prominent in the ancestry of Eleanor Roosevelt.

deficiencies and overcompensated. He was taken to the island of Madeira for his health (on his father's second honeymoon), then off to Switzerland for schooling. There he was introduced to boxing by various English classmates. From that time on he devoted himself to the Teddyish pursuits of literature and mayhem. He never went to college, but married a sensible heiress from Pittsburgh named Cordelia Bradley, acquired a grand mansion on Walnut Street in the fashionable part of Philadelphia, and proceeded to indulge himself furiously in his hobbies. One was a publishing company, which concentrated on the writings of A. J. D. Biddle: *The Froggy Fairy Book, Shantytown Sketches,* and other not very memorable productions. The most popular of Drexel Biddle Publishing Company's books was a life of the boxer Gentleman Jim Corbett; the most valuable, Biddle's own descriptive history of Madeira, quoted by an earlier edition of the *Encyclopaedia Britannica* as one of the authoritative sources. Meanwhile he occupied his time giving elaborate parties, boxing with anyone who would take him on, learning savate and judo, keeping alligators as pets, and attempting to sing in grand opera.

As to many Biddles, war offered him opportunities. In the spirit of Theodore's preparedness, he organized a training corps which in 1917 involved twelve thousand men. This had begun as a Bible class, with boxing attached, very much in the spirit of Teddy; it was easy to develop this kind of muscular Christianity into soldiering. In fact, he became quite intimate with Teddy himself in the process. People always wondered who outtalked whom. Biddle enlisted as a private in the Marine Corps and emerged a captain.* He spent the war training marines in bayonet drill and hand-to-hand combat. Champion Gene Tunney was one of his pupils, and Tunney always credited Biddle with giving him his first boxing lessons. They remained firm friends and mutual admirers.

When the next war came along, Biddle, though now in his late

* AJDB was not the only Marine Biddle. A General William P., nephew of George Washington Biddle, born in 1853, was commandant of the corps, 1911–14.

sixties, was ready. He was put in charge of the marine's judo program, which after Pearl Harbor suddenly became crucial. He continued his bayonet drills, urging his students to kill him. They tried
but failed. He had the reputation of knowing more ways to commit
murder with bare hands than anyone alive.

He outlived both Roosevelts, dying in 1948, bellicose to the last,
famous in Philadelphia and among marines for his energy and eccentricities.

As though the Drexel-Biddle match had not been enough, a
Biddle-Duke marriage compounded the connections of this branch
of the Biddles to great wealth. The Dukes, starting from scratch
after the Civil War, had cornered tobacco as Rockefeller cornered
oil — or du Ponts powder. By the time Anthony's daughter Cordelia
married the Duke heir, Angier, the Dukes were ostentatiously multimillionaires. The Duke-Biddle wedding was one of the sensations
of 1915. Thousands crushed about Trinity Church on Rittenhouse
Square and had to be held back by policemen. Almost as many attended the reception and were awed by the Stotesbury gift of an
enormous sapphire. This alliance was no more stable than the
Drexel-Biddle one. It ended in divorce. The bride remarried, then
went on to help create one of America's oddest postwar myths, the
Happiest Millionaire. In an uninhibited and affectionate memoir,
written skillfully for the box office by Kyle Crichton, an image of
an amiably offbeat parent was manufactured called *My Philadelphia Father*. Turned into a Broadway farce, *The Happiest Millionaire*, and then into a movie, it gathered strands of *You Can't Take It
With You*, *Life with Father*, and *Auntie Mame* to present a sympathetic but synthetic character with little resemblance to the original.
The real Anthony was, after all, a fairly tough character, whose
reputation in the Marine Corps was solidly based on his extreme
physical skill and durability. His neck muscles were so strong that
he was literally unchokable. Surrounded by the palaces, conserva-
tories, yachts and lavish parties of the Gilded Age (Uncle Tony
Drexel's *hôtel* in Paris, with the best chef in Europe; brother Craig

Biddle's marble mansion Lorento on the Main Line, where gaiety ran around the clock; George W. C. Drexel's massively gabled monument Wootton in Bryn Mawr, where famous guests planted trees), AJDB remained devoted to simple morality, physical energy and uncritical literary efforts. He makes a nice illustration of the Spirit of Teddy carried out in purely private, nonpolitical terms.

Lees and Adamses

The other two families, Lees and Adamses, were represented less spectacularly, if perhaps really more considerably, in the years before Franklin, by Senator Blair Lee and Secretary Charles Francis Adams (the third). Francis Preston Blair Lee was like Anthony Joseph Drexel Biddle, the result of an "alliance." He was the son of that apostate to Virginia, Admiral Samuel Phillips Lee USN and his wife, the daughter of Jackson's crony, Frank Blair. Daughter Elizabeth Blair was such a pet of Jackson's that he took her to live at the White House to protect her from the damp cellars of Blair House. The admiral was a grandson of Richard Henry Lee. His only son Blair was brought up at Silver Spring, the Blair estate in Maryland, and in Blair House in Washington, now the President's guesthouse. As in the case of AJDB, influences were Blair-maternal rather than Lee-paternal. He was not so much interesting in himself, though certainly a worthy fellow, as in being the last Congressional Lee — the ninth to serve there, the last to sit in that Senate where his great-grandfather Richard Henry had been one of the first. His marriage, like that of his father, helped to keep this particular branch of the Lees prosperous. His wife, Anne Clymer Brooke, belonged to one of the best established of the semifeudal ironmaster families who flourished in eastern Pennsylvania during the eighteenth and nineteenth centuries. The Brookes of Birdsboro, like other such families, lived in a sort of baronial isolation in big houses on the hill, actually often called "manors," dominating their workers' cottages and their mills down by the river; very much like the du Ponts on the Brandywine. Anne's great-great-uncle George Clymer had signed the Declaration along with her husband's great-grandfather. A supporter of Wilson for President, Wilson in turn supported Lee for the Senate in 1913. William Jennings Bryan even came east to speak for him.

There is something satisfactorily symbolic about the fact that this last of the political Lees also happens to be, due to his off-year election to fill a vacancy, the very first senator elected by popular vote "pursuant to the seventeenth amendment to the Constitution" —and as a result, in part, of the Addicks scandals in next-door Delaware. (At that time, 1913, the Delaware senators were Colonel Henry and Willard Saulsbury, second husband of his divorced brother William's first du Pont wife. Henry so despised Willard for this misalliance that he refused to grant him the customary senatorial courtesy of escorting him to his chair when he first appeared in the chamber.) Senator Blair served his term as a liberal and popular politician without making any notable contributions to statesmanship. He retired to remain, so unlike most of his relations, very comfortably fixed. His son, P. Blair, as one of Philadelphia's foremost bankers, has fixed this branch of the Lees even more comfortably.

Financial stability also characterized the Adamses, as embodied in a third Charles Francis. He was the son of nice John, the Democrat. Like any good Adams, son Charles switched parties in mid-life and became a Republican. He was not, like his father, an unsuccessful politician. He was instead a very successful businessman; really the first in Adams history, since his uncle and namesake, though he did well in the end for himself and the Adams estate, was a conspicuous failure as a railroad man.

Charles III took care that no such misadventures befell him and came close to being the John Harvard Moneybags that uncle Charles *said* he had wanted to be. He was treasurer of Harvard for thirty years, and became in fact the epitome of the cautious, canny, clam-mouthed Boston Brahmin; the first prominent Adams to keep his mouth shut and his pen idle. He did not keep a diary or make speeches; a man, so very, very unlike other Adamses, of few words. He represents a curious sort of turnabout tale, the final victory of State Street and the Gold Bugs over Quincy and Adams intransigence. This Charles generally eschewed national public life, concentrated on Boston and money, and ended up as a father figure in his city, but more or less unknown outside of it. He might just as well have been a Cabot. For an Adams to say, even in jest, as Charles III is reported to have said, that because he got only one thousand dollars a year for being mayor of Quincy he "couldn't afford politics" is indeed apostasy.

In return for throwing in the sponge, Boston made the Deacon (as he was nicknamed) its unofficial First Citizen. He rose at 6:45, like a good Adams; but then, so unlike an Adams, went to an office. On State Street even, at one time. He began as a lawyer but devoted his efforts to the affairs of Harvard and to his investments. He was an officer or director of some forty corporations, including such echt Boston affairs as the Boston Ground Rent Trust Co., the Old Colony Railroad, the Fifty Associates, and so many others. A daughter even married a son of J. P. Morgan — Morgan, that Gold Bug of Gold Bugs, that leader of the International Jewish Capitalistic Conspiracy! Enough to make great-uncle Brooks froth at the mouth. How have the mighty fallen.

Charles also expressed New England's special sporting bias by becoming one of the best saltwater sailors in the world (best in Boston, hence best in New England, hence best in world). His nephew George Homans has vividly described his experiences sailing with Uncle Charlie; especially the somewhat Spartan journeys from The Glades at Cohasset across to the races at Marblehead and back, unfortified by the comforts of life. An uncanny sense of wind and weather, which his rivals believed a form of black magic, and an attention to the tiniest details of equipment, combined with a ruthless Adams will to win ("I like to win bot [sic] races"), made him the terror of the sporting seas. His great particular triumph occurred in 1920 when the *Resolute* defeated Sir Thomas Lipton for the *America's* Cup. The appointment as secretary of the navy was partly in recognition of his seamanship, partly a reward for his having joined the right, or Republican side. He had fallen first from his father's party by voting for Harding. Can one conceive of any previous Adams voting for a Harding? He served in the cabinet under Hoover. It was a bad time for the navy, since Congress cut appropriations to the bone. Charles' farsighted plans to build up forces against a Japanese threat did not have a chance. Only one story seems to have survived about his public service. When he was appointed, photographers and reporters made an occasion of it. After all, John Adams had usually been considered the Father of the Navy. The newsmen asked him to pose at his desk writing something. He wrote, "this is hell this is hell." He was later on a firm though comparatively temperate anti–New Dealer; FDR *was* a Harvard man. One Adams tradition at least he did maintain, that of longevity. He died in 1954 at eighty-seven.

2

Franklin

O F ALL the great men sprung from all these families, Franklin Delano Roosevelt is by far the most famous. Though one may hesitate about using the word "great," since time has not done its proper work of embalming, there can be no question about "famous." John Adams, Robert E. Lee fit prominently into that imaginary Pantheon of the Republic, purely American. FDR has one of the very most prominent places in another imaginary monument, the Chamber of Heroes and Horrors of the Twentieth Century. This monstrous edifice memorializes not just American but world history. And surely if human history has any future at all, this complex will attract visitors for the next millennium.

What a fantastic pile! Looming, dazzling, lurid, built on the blood and bones of millions and millions of victims, clumped in a Kremlin-like, pinnacled, gargoyled assortment of shrines to that queer assemblage of Great Leaders, friends, allies, enemies, who dominated the period of the Second World War: the Baddies, Hitler and Mussolini, the Bad Goodies, Stalin and Chiang Kai-shek, and the Goodies, Churchill and Roosevelt. What company for a gentleman of Family to keep — the abysmal horrors that underlie the reigns of friend Stalin and foe Hitler, Uncle Joe and Little Adolf, humanity revealed once and for all as demonic; the gallantry and traditional guts and pomp of a Churchill, with Blenheim back of him; Madame Chiang and her silk sheets and her Dragon Lady suavities; the sinister buffooneries of Mussolini; the mechanized medievalist samurai of Japan. It was a world incredibly remote from the securities of the Hudson and the pieties of Groton. Yet in that monstrous world the son of Hyde Park and Harvard triumphed. In fact, of all those world figures, he is the only one who did wholly triumph, for Stalin has been violently repudiated after his death, and even Churchill lived to be rejected domestically, to see the crumbling of the empire he was so determined to preserve.

Franklin Roosevelt's greatest triumph was his death just before the final crest of victory. Perhaps if he had lived on he too would have been personally repudiated. Still, for all the flaws and anxieties and legitimate criticisms, the Pax Americana of the following two decades has been firmly based on the domestic and foreign policies he established — welfare at home, internationalism abroad; as opposed to laissez-faire and isolationism, the two shibboleths of his enemies.

In fact, what does distinguish Franklin Delano Roosevelt from all the great men of all these families before him is precisely this triumph. Every single one of the other important figures we have considered ended in some way as a definite failure. The one exception is perhaps Richard Henry Lee, and he never has been given his historical due. A posthumous failure, so to speak. All the Adams were political disasters. Henry's greatest success, which of course was posthumous too, was a study in Adams failure. The defeats of Arthur, Light-Horse Harry and Robert E. Lee were spectacular. Theodore Roosevelt pulled down his career and his party about him like Samson. One Nicholas Biddle blew up, the other went bankrupt. The steamboating Nicholas Roosevelt got nothing out of his pioneering genius. Only the snug lesser men, Isaac the Patriot or rich Cornelius V, that "Hindoo idol"; old Thomas Lee of Stratford or later Senator Blair; Chancellor George Washington Biddle or doughty Commodore James could be described as living "happily ever after."

And also FDR. Though of course he did not live ever after, he certainly was a success. Luck? Fate? Character? All three certainly. Yet of all the important men of all these families he seems the most unlikely to succeed. In every other case it is possible to observe how the great man emerged from the person — Robert E. Lee's pious determination to redeem his ruined family name, to justify his father's military ambitions; Theodore Roosevelt's energetic battle against childhood weaknesses. The personality and background of Franklin offer no handholds: a smooth, slippery, shiny, round mold, to which he was perfectly adjusted, without showing the slightest sign of originality or rebellion or leadership. There really is no accounting for FDR on the basis of origins and childhood. He remains a biographical enigma. He is just pure Man of Family raised by circumstances to an nth degree; a force rather than a character.

Comparisons with Cousin Theodore are particularly revealing. For instance, whatever else he might be, Theodore was a character. Nothing he touched or did or said was unpicturesque; except perhaps his own writings. Any example will do, almost at random; like the whole business of the Panama Canal. Item: When the two cloak-and-dagger agents, Bunau-Varilla and the somewhat mysterious lawyer Cromwell, were working to persuade the Senate not to approve a Nicaraguan canal route, they distributed Nicaraguan stamps to the Solons, picturing volcanoes. One of those very volcanoes, Mount Monotombo, obligingly blew up; obviously very bad for canals. The Senate switched its allegiance to a canal across the Isthmus. Item: Whoever actually got the forty million dollars the U.S. paid over to the French company representing rights in the defunct de Lesseps operations? It remains a secret to this day.

Or: When TR was police commissioner he would leave a formal dinner and, still in evening clothes, with a broadbrimmed hat and wrapped in a black cloak, cruise the streets at midnight like Harun-al-Rashid, flashing his teeth at evil doers surprised at work. Toy sets of teeth were sold as crook-catchers.

Or: How he took on the English language and its spelling and actually succeeded in banishing the "u" from "honour" (where it's rather appropriate) but not from "through" (where it's a damn nuisance). Or his assault on naturalists who falsified their accounts of wildlife. One account that particularly irked him had a fox running along the railroad tracks and thus luring hounds to their death by train. It so happens that this really and truly does in fact occur. Theodore was wrong; but what other President in all American history would be involved in a controversy about foxes on railroad tracks! That's the kind of thing you get into with Theodore.

It is not the kind of thing you get into with Franklin. Crucial events, not picturesque incidents, mark his life. Theodore is interesting because of what he was. Franklin is important because of what he did. Yet in many ways the two were so alike. The parallels of their careers have already been indicated. There is a story, perhaps after the fact, that as early as 1907 Franklin predicted to fellow law clerks just how his career would follow that of his uncle-in-law: Assistant secretary, governor, President. One can be skeptical; still, there is no question that Franklin consciously modeled himself on the older Roosevelt. Henry Adams, referring to his own studies of medieval theologians, said that Theodore was like the church fathers' idea of God, "pure act." Theodore in fact was much too full of crotchets to be pure anything. The description fits Franklin better. Still, they were both dynamos of energy. Franklin played his fifty-six holes of golf in one day to match Theodore's ninety-one games of tennis. The awe-inspiring fact that Franklin almost never had insomnia, never lost any sleep during depression or war — there's something almost inhuman in that. They shared extroversion and overwhelming love of people and infallible charm. They were interested in *you*. But here again Theodore was certainly far more of an inner man, a thinker and intellectual than Franklin and seems to have come by his gifts as a mixer later and harder. Franklin was not the most popular man in Harvard; just average. But Theodore was downright unpopular: a loud talker, an interrupter of teachers, something of a crank. Not cool. Franklin has been described again and again by contemporaries, including himself, as the least introspective of men. Like Theodore, he seems to combine a positive anti-intellectualism, a real distaste for theorizing, with an omnivorous, if perhaps superficial, ability to read everything, remember everything, quote everything. Franklin's knowledge, for instance, of geography and terrain (like Robert E. Lee's) was considered astounding by military men (like Eisenhower). He could cite, and cite accurately, an immense wealth of statistics or items of natural or American history.

At the same time, Franklin shared Theodore's curious simple-minded, closed-minded religious primitivism — if that is the word — a moralistic firmness and faith quite opposed to the Adams' constant, tortured self-flagellation. Good was good and God was God and that was that. Neither of them was loyalist in his attachment to a church, both being rather vague upper-class Episcopalians, Theodore from a Dutch Reformed background (Theodore senior was an active Presbyterian). Nothing reveals Franklin Roosevelt's state of mind better than two often-quoted statements. He said to Eleanor once, apropos some religious doubt, "I think it is just as well not to think about things like that." In answer to a query as to "what he was," "I am a Christian and a Democrat, that's all." This complete moral certitude contributed to force and efficiency in leadership. It does not endear the Roosevelts to intellectuals, who much prefer Henry Adams' sophisticated and subtle wrongness to Franklin's almost mindless rightness.

Yet it was certainly this instinctive moralism that made both Roosevelts reformers. Not elaborate Utopian fantasies, but a plain bias in favor of "decency" put them into their particular positions. Americans should be able to lead "decent lives." Whatever interfered with that decency was wrong. Roosevelts would right these wrongs. What turned out to be mostly wrong was not, as both of them originally presumed, wicked politicians, but "malefactors of great wealth" and "economic royalists" whose selfish greed controlled and then wrecked the American economy, in particular the multimillionaires of later origin than Roosevelts. Neither Roosevelt thought that people should be *"too* rich," as FDR once said. Just rich enough, like the Roosevelts, to be free from having to think much about money.

Neither man possessed a construct of philosophy and theory back of him, such as communism or fascism might have provided, nor did either of them evolve any integrated plan. Intellectuals, like Braintruster. Rexford Tugwell, could never really forgive Franklin for his failure to impose some sort of dogmatic straitjacket on the country when he had the chance. Instead, both Roosevelts improvised to meet crises. In the end — luck? leadership? — the crises were met. Love of people, love of "decency" seemed to be enough as motive and theory.

Combined with this simpleminded emphasis on "decency" was also a special but fundamental strain of conservationism, love of the land. In both cases, by family tradition from Uncle Bob on one side and the Hudson River landowners on the other, each Roosevelt inherited a country gentleman's feeling for orderly, useful, beautiful landscape. The vandalism committed on this landscape in America by entrepreneurs outraged them, as all country gentlemen should be outraged. Stupid farmers or greedy lumbermen both must be taught soil manners and soil morals. If the Square Deal and the New Deal have any common core it is certainly this vivid feeling for the protection of natural resources. Decent people living in a decent landscape. The battle is still being fought along Roosevelt lines.

Back of all their policies, both Roosevelts shared the conventions and convictions of the pre-Civil War gentleman, the Man of Family. Unlike so many of their class contemporaries, but like their Democratic predecessor Jefferson, they were gentlemen first and landowners or rentiers second. They took their class codes literally — *noblesse oblige,* defense of the weak against the bully, scorn of ostentatious luxury, that "decency" in manners and morals; honesty, gallantry, courage. They understood, instinctively at least, that democracy is the distillation of the kind of good manners of a Robert E. Lee, who felt ashamed if he had to "humble" others.

And yet, in both cases, the touch that so strikingly distinguishes Roosevelts from Adamses, and in fact most gentlemen in politics. is that contradictory, rather ungentlemanly genius for sheer politics — compromise, intrigue, handling people, the ability to keep the ends in mind while traveling to them by the most circuitous ways. No Presidents have been better at this sort of political maneuvering than both Theodore and Franklin.

At about this point the likenesses end and the contrasts begin. There is first of all a fundamental contrast in quality of personality, more easily sensed than defined, perhaps a "dog" versus "cat" comparison — Theodore so affectionate, noisy, all-over-the-place, his bark always worse than his bite; Franklin (*The Lion and the Fox,* as one of the more subtle studies of him is entitled) so indirect, so essentially secretive and solitary, so given to cruelly affectionate teasing. Despite the fact that they were of the same family and from the same region, both well-off and pushed down similar educational grooves, their backgrounds and upbringings were very different. Theodore was a weakling, an inhibited child surrounded by a great gang of cousinly competition, a hurly-burly of relations of whom he was runt of the litter. Everyone has always remarked on the noisy, clannish, exuberant family life of the Oyster Bay branch, even before Oyster Bay.

Franklin's boyhood was different. He was the only child of his old father's late marriage, idolized, doted upon, carefully tended and coddled, the single twig on the tree. No runt of the litter, he was from the very beginning a Golden Boy. Theodore was a city child and, despite Oyster Bay summers, a brownstone boy. His father and uncles were all busy in business. Franklin was a country child, and his father and uncles carried on the tradition of their father as rentier landed gentry. James did choose to interest himself actively in railroads and coal and other enterprises, but always as a capitalist investor, never as one who made his living or profession in business. Affairs never kept him in town from country pleasures or trips abroad.

Theodore's family all looked southward to Philadelphia and Georgia for their brides, the land of the horse. Theodore expressed himself in horsemanship. Franklin's family looked northward for alliances, Yankee traders like the Howlands, Aspinwalls, and Delanos, the land of sail. Franklin expressed himself in boats.

Even in schooling there were strong contrasts. Though they both began in the sheltered world of family tutoring, Franklin was exposed to Groton and Doctor Peabody. It is hard to say what Groton did for and meant to Franklin Roosevelt. The best picture of what Groton was like at the time can be found not in any works of or about the Roosevelts, but in the works of Biddles, the autobiographies of Francis (*A Casual Past*) and George (*An American Artist's Story*). Neither Francis nor George liked Groton, though they respected it. Certainly neither of them conformed as successfully as Franklin. Biographers, desperately searching for clues to Franklin's character, try to pretend he was haunted by failures and inadequacies there, and so learned to feel for the forgotten man. Even Eleanor thought so; but there is not the slightest inkling of this to be found, at least, in his schoolboy correspondence or in later remarks of his. He seemed to have admired headmaster Endicott Peabody; Endicott Peabody admired him. The rather appalling, yet truly virtuous, rigors and dogmas he imbibed there seem to have been the foundations of his morality. Yet no one could pretend that Groton was a seedbed of radical reformation. Francis and George Biddle saw through to the contradictions of worldliness and money values that lay behind the pieties of Peabody. Not so Franklin.

Similarly of Harvard. Franklin was not an overwhelming success there. He did not make the social ultimate of Porcellian, like Theodore, contenting himself with respectable Fly. Here again biographers try to make much of this. It is very doubtful that Franklin really cared. He failed to make varsity teams, though he played football and rowed. This did not seem to upset him much. He edited the *Crimson* and so became a sufficiently big man on campus (or Yard), but revealed no special gift at unearthing causes or scandals. He was an appallingly ordinary nice schoolboy and collegian. There seemed to be no flaws of adjustment, no secret yearnings, no frustrations, no dissipations, no problems. Conventional is the word for young Franklin. Who could suppose him taking on the massed forces of first finance and then fascism? And coming out winner?

His personality, if not his character, was formed early in life — Golden Boy. Everyone, as in the case of Robert E. Lee, goes on about his handsomeness (which for modern tastes is marred by those pince-nez glasses and that high stiff collar). Especially in early maturity, before polio, we have encomiums from Walter Camp, the physical fitness expert of World War I, who describes him as "a beautifully built man, with the long muscles of the athlete" and Woodrow Wilson who described him as "the handsomest young giant I have ever seen." His gaiety and frankness, on the other hand, though pleasing, made people think him a lightweight. Even later on he liked to pretend that he was a "frivolous fellow" who made important decisions whimsically and could not take things solemnly. Roosevelt gaiety, Roosevelt gallantry, reflected earlier in Theodore's "bully" and teeth, were reflected in Franklin's cocky cigarette holder and grin. His telegram to Winston Churchill, "It is fun being in the same decade with you," reflects that quality in an epic frame. This jauntiness was birthright to him, however, not the result of deliberate effort, at least not until he had to reachieve vigor in his conquest of polio.

What FDR did, as opposed to what he was, is of course the history of America in the most crucial decades of the twentieth century. As Doctor New Deal (his own phrase), he cured the patient of the most dangerous internal disorder; as Doctor Win-the-War, he cured the patient of the most dangerous external attack. Perhaps it wasn't really his doing that the depression was licked and then the Axis. But they were licked, and as Quentin Reynolds said of the war effort, "This enormous program must have been thought out and planned by someone. Could it have been the President?" The fact of success is the best of arguments. The patient survived, and it's hard to say the Doctor was wrong. Somebody licked the depression; somebody led the country to victory. Who but Roosevelt?

Women

Like Theodore, like the Adamses, Franklin also has his women. Not his daughter, though Anna, eldest of her brood as was Alice of hers, is like Alice a person of charm and character and of all the children most like her father. It is his mother, formidable Sara, and above all his wife who are memorable.

One of the things that differentiates Theodore from Franklin is this emphasis on mother rather than father. Though in both cases the father died when the sons were still in college, though in both cases the fathers were loved and admired, Franklin's father was always distant, at one remove from his son behind the figure of the mother. Certainly Franklin's relationship to this prominent maternal dominance is one of the most important aspects of his personal life; bond and conflict. Franklin looked like her, was brought up by her, depended on her, even financially, even after marriage. Until her dying day she would not let him leave the house, when she was present, without checking to see if he was wearing his rubbers. Yet his whole presidential career, beginning with his determination to overcome the ravages of polio by reentering politics, was a repudiation of her. She took it, she was proud of him, but she could never have really approved of either his policies or the career itself.

Her husband may have been an old-fashioned pre–Civil War Democrat, of the kind whose party affiliation was originally determined by sympathy for Southern landowners, not by liberalism of any kind; her own family, the Delanos, were rock-ribbed Republicans, and Sara's father was surprised to find that his son-in-law James could be a Democrat and a gentleman at the same time. Sara had no doubts about the total unassailability of her own class position, and tried to keep her son true to the faith, as her correspondence with him occasionally demonstrates.

In the end, she failed. Eleanor and circumstances were too much for her. Sara held on hard. When she moved to Boston as a recent widow to be near her boy in college, when she took him on a cruise during his last year at Harvard (he had actually graduated the year before, scholastically) to try to break up his engagement to Eleanor, finally when she tried to persuade him as polio victim to retire permanently to the Hudson and private life, his career shows evidences of that hold. But he married Eleanor, he went into public life. Sara found herself gallantly entertaining his peculiar political guests at Hyde Park. Occasionally she permitted her distaste for them to show through; as when Huey Long, seated by Franklin at dinner, could hardly have missed Sara's penetrating whisper, "Who is that dreadful person sitting next to my son?" If Franklin had given in to her, he would have been the nice, conventional, crippled gentleman of law and leisure she probably hoped he would be; and whom anyone studying his youth would have expected him to be. There was more in him than that. It took another woman, Eleanor, to bring it out.

Eleanor was a long time coming out herself. She too had been dominated in a far more terrible way by the women of her family: mother, grandmother and even great-grandmother. She was the childhood victim of a pathological matriarchy, taking refuge in fantasies and dreams about her adored but mostly absent father.

She was, of course, Theodore's niece; and despite her shyness and timidity, especially in the romping rowdiness of Sagamore Hill, she was his "favorite niece." She was not pretty. "Her mouth and teeth seem to have no future," wrote cool Edith to Bamie. She was not athletic. She was as different from cousin Alice as it is possible to be. Yet Theodore evidently saw in her some spark of Roosevelt character not visible to others.

She had a dreadful childhood and adolescence. While Alice was growing up in the center of the spotlight and responding to it as only a Roosevelt could, Eleanor was growing up in the shadows of her mother's family. Her father Elliott, once the leader of "we three," healthy, handsome, loved by all, had his weaknesses too, not so much physical like Bamie's or Teddy's, but psychological. He had some sort of breakdown at school, and like all boys of the period when they had breakdowns, was sent West where he mastered riding and shooting. He was never able to settle successfully to a profession. He became instead an alcoholic. Eleanor was brought up by her mother. Her mother was a Hall whose mother was a Ludlow whose mother was a Livingston. She was thus related to the whole world of the patroons in a much more definite way than other Roosevelts. As seemed to be the case with many people who married Livingstons, this tied the family umbilically to the Hudson, so that Eleanor's background was much closer to Franklin's than to Theodore's. Grandfather Hall, who did nothing, just like Franklin's grandfather Isaac, lived near Tivoli in a big, gloomy, mansarded house called Oak Terrace.* There he collected religious books and had a sort of chaplain, a clergyman called W. C. P. Rhodes, who lived with him so he would have someone to talk to about theology. He never permitted his wife to trouble her pretty head about business or her children. When he suddenly died, without leaving a will, the whole responsibility of six offspring was thrust on her. She was not able to handle the responsibility. Her two sons became charming ne'er-do-well alcoholics like Elliott. (Since Eleanor's own brother Hall also became an alcoholic like her two uncles and her father, it's no wonder that she never liked to serve cocktails, though Franklin insisted on his.)

Two of Eleanor's aunts, also of the household when she was a girl, the lively Maude and the artistic Pussie, led lives of emotional and financial disorder, ending in marital separation or divorce. A third daughter, Anna, was Eleanor's mother. She was a belle. All the women of her family had been belles. Her only interest was in an elaborately busy New York social life appropriate to a belle. Eleanor was a disappointment to her; she was obviously not going to be a belle. Anna teased her daughter, called her "granny" before guests — "Such a funny child, so old-fashioned" — and generally made her disappointment clear even to an infant. "I was always disgracing my mother," wrote Eleanor. When Eleanor was about eight, her mother died. Her father by this time was far gone, sent off to sanatoriums. Eleanor was adopted by her Grandmother Hall and lived alternately in a gloomy brownstone on West Thirty-seventh Street in the city or in equally gloomy Oak Terrace. The household, with its drunken uncles and neurotic aunts, was positively Gothic. Since the Halls disapproved of the raucous Roosevelts, almost all communication with her father's family was prohibited, especially after her father died when she was nearly ten.

Her grandmother, in turn, had been the victim of a mother. There's a glimpse of this terrible old woman, née Livingston, in Eleanor's autobiography. She remembers stopping at her great-

* But not often. It was usually referred to as Tivoli.

grandmother's house with Aunt Maude to explain that Mrs. Hall had a cold and could not visit her mother as usual. "The old lady . . . shook her stick at us and told us to go straight home and send Molly down immediately. We went home, and I think my grandmother got out of bed and went to see her."

In the summer glooms and glades of Tivoli, Eleanor had no playmates. During the course of each summer little Carola De Peyster came to spend a day. Little Eleanor returned the visit. That was it. Otherwise she read, explored the grounds, was fitfully taken up and dropped by temperamental Aunt Pussie, learned to bear the outrages committed by drunken Uncle Val. As time went by, guests were few, since the embarrassments created by his behavior made ordinary entertaining impossible. Her grandmother spent most of her time, especially in winter, up in her bedroom. Having been an impossibly indulgent mother, and in consequence having ruined her children, she compensated by saying "No" to Eleanor on every possible occasion.

This Cinderella regime was finally broken by several years in an English boarding school under a French headmistress. Eleanor was sent there because her grandmother thought the household in New York was "too gay" for an adolescent girl. Though this school was physically as depressing as Oak Terrace and far more uncomfortable, intellectually and emotionally it brought Eleanor to life. At last she had companions and friends of her own age, and found in Mlle. Souvestre someone older in whom she could confide, someone real, not merely the dream presence of a dead father.

When she came back she was faced with the only two possibilities open to young ladies of her kind: a debut and charitable work. Coming out was an agony. She went through it, and grew to know Cousin Franklin. Shy, tall, and with her futureless mouth and chin, she was still obviously not a belle, as Franklin was obviously a beau. They had of course met before, since the two Roosevelt families were still intimate at that time, and Elliott Roosevelt had even met Anna Hall at Algonac, Sara's father's house. Elliott was Franklin's godfather. Franklin, in a letter to his mother, apropos of a schoolboy house party planned for Hyde Park, wrote that Eleanor and Cousin Teddy Robinson would "go well and fill out chinks." Not a rapturous endorsement.

However, when they met again later on, Franklin thought her beautiful where others did not. He always spoke of her eyes and hair, and though photographs did her cruel injustice, early pictures confirm his complimentary impression — eyes and hair. Golden Boy as he was — rich, handsome, full of bounce and charm and ease of manner, socially more than secure — he could have chosen anyone. He chose Eleanor. One gathers his mother was disappointed. She thought he might have done so much better.

They were married on St. Patrick's Day, 1905. President Theodore, standing in for his dead brother, gave his favorite niece away, and of course stole the show. Everyone congregated in the far room around Theodore, who liked to be "the bride at every wedding, the corpse at every funeral," and left the newlyweds standing alone. Theodore congratulated the couple. "There's nothing like keeping the name in the family."

For this was the first Roosevelt-Roosevelt wedding. Every one of our other families had been cross-breeding for generations. Though no Adams actually married an Adams (what other Adamses were there, after all? Surely not those of Sempronius, New York, and Blue Mound, Kansas), there was that incredible tangle of one kind of Adams, two kinds of Smith and two kinds of Johnsons (Maryland and Utica). Of the Biddle-Biddle, du Pont–du Pont and Lee-Lee marriages no mention need be made. This was *the* Roosevelt-Roosevelt marriage — the end, the climax, the last word in such branch mergers.*

The bride found herself escaping from one matriarchy to another. Sara assumed command, taking over from Grandmother Hall. She built two houses side by side on East Sixty-fifth Street.

---

* There is another modern one within the Oyster Bay branch. Mrs. Philip J. Roosevelt was also née Roosevelt.

Sara lived in one, Franklin and Eleanor in the other. The furnishing and decoration had been done by Sara. Once Franklin found Eleanor in tears at her dressing table. She was crying because she'd never had a home really all her own.

The first break came when Franklin entered politics and went to Albany. Eleanor did have a house of her own there, though it was only rented. But mostly she lived in the family circle. In Washington, when Franklin was assistant secretary, they took over Aunt Bamie's house. In the summers they went to Campobello Island — right alongside Sara.

It was only in the epic struggle over Franklin's polio and its aftermath that Eleanor finally emerged victorious from the shades of martyrdom by matriarchy. As Theodore's time of troubles — the death of Alice Lee, his political eclipse in the Blaine campaign, and his flight out West — was the crucial turning point in his life, so Franklin's attack of polio was the crucial turning point for him. His defeat as Vice President, and the Republican take-over, put a temporary end to political life for him, but he was not unduly disturbed. He had made a good personal showing, and nobody really expected him to win. Polio was something else again. It was here that wife and mother-in-law finally met head-on, and we develop that favorite surefire dramatic scene so capably handled by Jane Austen in *Pride and Prejudice,* the young woman defying the old dragon in the interests of her man.

The battle over Franklin lasted for a good year at least. Sara thought she had him at last. He could be taken back to Hyde Park to be cherished as an invalid — *her* invalid. Eleanor knew better. The fight was waged by all sorts of female stratagems. One little incident, a nasty skirmish: released from the hospital, Franklin returned to the house on Sixty-fifth Street, Sara next door. The house was full of children and also contained that mysterious kingmaker, Louis Howe, the shriveled newspaperman who was determined to make Franklin President and who successfully devoted his life to the project.

Howe had been given a big front bedroom, supposedly adolescent daughter Anna's room. Anna had been moved upstairs. Sara (it was no doubt she; Eleanor in her biography just discreetly says "someone") influenced Anna to make a scene demanding back her room. Sara hoped of course that Franklin would be afraid of hurting Anna, Howe would be insulted and ousted, perhaps deserting FDR for good. Then Franklin might give up politics. The stratagem failed, but the strain of this kind of thing told. As a result of this incident, Eleanor had a queer sort of breakdown, the only one she ever had. She was reading to the children and suddenly began crying. She couldn't stop. She shut herself up in a deserted room in Sara's house and at last got control of herself.

Repudiating his mother and urged on by his wife, Franklin went back to business in the fall of '22 and then to public life. He presented to the world the same robustness, gaiety and "frivolity," optimism and charm. Nothing seemed changed except that he could not use his legs. He would never mention the word "golf" again. Some, like his critical biographer Burns, believe he was not fundamentally changed by polio, that he was already the champion of the people. Others, like Frances Perkins (one of the two cabinet members along with Harold Ickes who served through his entire administration), believe his disease made a permanent difference, marked a watershed. Ordinary common sense would agree that an eight-year battle with polio would certainly tend to give a Golden Boy his first real understanding of what it was to be "underprivileged," and of what surmounting adversity really meant. He certainly had not had it before. This particular drama of disease and recovery, of battle between mother and wife, is the core of Roosevelt's personal story, the *Sunrise at Campobello* story.

At the end of it all, Eleanor emerges at last as true First Lady and begins to take up her special role in the world. Ridiculed by her enemies, including Cousin Alice, adored by millions, she too, like her husband, has her shrine. As he is memorialized in the Pantheon of Leaders, so his wife has been canonized as one of those strange, modern Saints of Humanity — a secular hagiography that includes women like Helen Keller and Marian Anderson, men like Albert Einstein and Albert Schweitzer, who have embodied for moderns a triumph over disaster and discrimination combined with a reaching out for the human heart.

To the hard-boiled and humorous, to the world of Princess Alice, there is undoubtedly a good deal of mush about this idealistic humanitarianism. Early in the game, Edith Carow Roosevelt is said to have said, though it sounds more like Alice, that Franklin was nine-tenths mush and one-tenth Eleanor. Perhaps in turn Eleanor might have been characterized as nine-tenths Franklin and one-tenth mush. But Franklin had practically no mush in him, as it turned out, and Eleanor's somewhat naïve-seeming love of mankind concealed a hard core of realism. Her later autobiographies, so full of tiresome accolades to the worthy, have also some nice glimpses of the less worthy, all handled so gently, so kindly. Of Madame Chiang Kai-shek:

"A certain casualness about cruelty, which was always a surprise to me, emerged sometimes in her conversations with the men, though never with me. I had painted for Franklin such a sweet, gentle and pathetic figure that, as he came to recognize the other side of the lady, it gave him keen pleasure to tease me about my lack of perception. I remember an incident at a dinner party. . . . John Lewis was acting up at the time, and Franklin turned to Madame Chiang and asked, 'What would you do in China about a labor leader like John Lewis?' She never said a word, but the beautiful, small hand came up very quietly and slid across her throat."

Not so much mush there. She certainly got involved with groups like the Youth Congress that might have made others more wary. But as emissary and publicizer and woman representative of the New Deal she played a role new to the White House and American history.

As a footnote to Franklin's women there is of course the somewhat shadowed and mysterious career of Lucy Mercer Rutherford.

Was she or was she not in fact his mistress? The evidence that Eleanor was afraid of her, did not want to recognize her existence, is plain. What could be more suggestive than the fact that though Mrs. Rutherford, along with Cousin Laura Delano and another woman, was in Warm Springs at the time of Franklin Roosevelt's death, and in fact actually in the room facing him when he collapsed, Eleanor fails to mention her name in writing of the event? The silence here is deafening.

The story has been largely the private-public property of Jonathan Daniels, son of that Josephus who was Franklin's boss as secretary of the navy. Jonathan himself was FDR's press secretary. Except for the rather damning absence of her name in Eleanor's memoirs — she appeared first as a social secretary when the Roosevelts moved to Washington, but here too is not named — the rest is a ripple in that vast sea of Washington gossip that washes at the feet of every public figure. There is so much of it that no one can ever be sure that some of it is not true. There's been singularly little of that sort of gossip about most of these men — or women — of Family. Assertions by his enemies that Nicholas Biddle consorted brazenly with the Italian adventuress Signora Vespucci, or that hint in the diary of Charles Francis Adams that he put away a mistress when he became engaged to Abby. The truly scandalous stories of stray sheep like George Adams or Black-Horse Harry Lee. The gay life of T. Coleman du Pont and the other du Pont scandals. But the evidence in the case of Lucy Mercer seems to be largely circumstantial or negative — her absence from the official and public record. She was charming, she was a lady, she married well, she is dead. Perhaps, unless more specific proof comes up, it might be well to leave it at that.

Sons

Since Fate loves symmetry — once again, four sons. One followed his father's footsteps, one was an adventurer, off to far places, one relapsed into the family background of conservative finance. The record differs only in that a fourth son of Franklin, James, who does not fit the pattern, is perhaps the most important of them.

Any other family group of brothers would be considered pretty satisfactory if it contained two congressmen, an assistant cabinet member, a representative to the United Nations, a mayor of a large American city, candidates for governor of both New York and California, a general, one winner of the Purple Heart and of the Navy Cross, two winners of the Silver Star, also a vice president of Bache and Co., one of the more substantial investment banking firms of Wall Street. Not to mention the authorship of two best-selling books, one printed in seventeen languages. When these various activities cover New York, Florida, California and what have you, the national spread of such meritocracy appears even more unusual. The bearer of such a brood might well be elected Mother of some year on the basis of this multifarious accomplishment alone. Nonetheless the children of FDR have earned the reputation of failures. The average person persists in thinking and saying that they "haven't amounted to much." Exactly the same oppressive cloud of expectation has blighted their lives as blighted the life of Theodore junior. They are not Daddy. This fatality of the four sons of a distinguished father is a naked demonstration of the worst side of hereditary meritocracy — the inferiority complex so galling to Henry Adams and *his* brothers. Despite the honors and medals and offices, one cannot avoid observing a kind of frenetic, desperate, hurtling quality about the lives of all these sons of FDR, evidenced mostly in geographic and marital dispersion. None of them seem to be able to settle down to permanent careers or householding.

The eldest of them, James, has done best: proper educational pattern, Groton, Harvard 1930, a mixed-up business career beginning in Boston insurance and going on to movies and once more insurance in Los Angeles. Then, following that, a really substantial service for six terms as a congressman from Los Angeles, and resignation followed by his appointment as representative to UNESCO in 1965, a position once held by his mother. (Has a son ever succeeded a *mother* in an important American post before?) It was James who was candidate for governor of California and author of one of the books — about his father of course, called *Affectionately, F.D.R.* Though he has now retired from the nation's service into finance, it has certainly been a respectable public career.

Elliott, the next brother, corresponds roughly to Kermit — the adventurous one. He refused to go to Harvard, after a restless school career at Groton. Instead he went West and into all sorts of colorful but not very successful enterprises — newspapers (working for Hearst, archenemy of Roosevelts), radio, advertising, uranium, airplanes. He lists one residence as a ranch in Colorado, another in Phoenix, Arizona; he lived for a spell in Texas and emerged in 1965 as mayor of Miami Beach, Florida. It was Elliott whose book, *As He Saw It* (about Father of course), was so widely translated. Of all the brothers, he had the most newsworthy war service, beginning with his extremely controversial appointment as a fledgling captain in the Army Air Corps in 1940. At thirty-four he became a brigadier general, on the basis largely of his activity as a photographic pilot all over the war-torn globe. He got the Distinguished Flying Cross, Legion of Merit, Air Medal, Order of the British Empire, Legion of Honor and Croix de Guerre, and is a Commander of the Order of Assoum Alaouite. Sounds like one of TR's sons. James was a colonel in the marines (Navy Cross, Silver Star) despite ulcers acquired during an unfortunate spell as his father's presidential secretary. Franklin junior collected the Legion of Merit, Silver Star, and Purple Heart as lieutenant commander in the navy on destroyers. John was a lieutenant commander on carriers.

It is Franklin of course who tried footstep-following. A U.S. congressman from New York beginning in 1949 (rather than state legislator), he took the next step as U.S. undersecretary of commerce (rather than assistant secretary of the navy). Then, just like TR junior he tried for the crucial way station, the governorship of New

York. A candidate not of the Democratic but of the splinter third Liberal Party, he was thoroughly defeated in 1966. Is that the end for Franklin junior as it was for Theodore junior? Fate, family fate, national fate, likes its patterns tidy and repetitious.

John is the businessman; but even he did not stay put, beginning in Boston working in the financial end of Filene's department stores, then going on to Los Angeles like James, and finally returning to New York and Bache and Company. He is the only one to stay up the Hudson, at Val-Kill Farms, the house next to Springwood at Hyde Park, built by his parents. He has even reacted so far as to become a Republican, to the extent of actually campaigning for Eisenhower.

No single aspect of the careers of Franklin's children has been more of a contrast to the careers of Theodore's children, or has emphasized the restless quality of their lives, that desperate attempt to find themselves in the family limelight, than their remarkable marital liquidity. Just for the record (figures in parentheses are number of children):

Anna:	Dall (2), Boettiger (1), Halstead.
James:	Cushing (2), Schneider (3), Owens.
Elliott:	Donner (1), Googins (3), Emerson, Ross, Whitbread.
Franklin:	du Pont (2), Perrin (2).
John:	Clark (4), McAlpin.

Fifteen spouses in all; since some of these have been married before and again, sometimes to people who have been married before, etc. etc., the web stretches out into infinity. This may well be some sort of family record, like the number of Biddles in the Philadelphia Club, or the number of du Pont–du Pont marriages. The not very edifying spectacle has been of course a windfall to Republicans who know just where to put the blame. If it had been a record of alcoholism, one might deduce the hereditary causes. The White House won't do as an excuse; the children were not, like Theodore's, a

White House Gang. They were out from under by 1932. In fact, Anna and her two children, Buzzie and Sistie, took refuge there while she was getting one of the first of the family divorces. The tearing up of family roots from Hyde Park because of politics may be a much more convincing explanation for it all. Of course, divorce has been epidemic among American upper echelons anyway. Theodore's grandchildren of the same generation have done their bit, as have various Biddles and du Ponts. But still . . .

These younger Roosevelts are all very much alive. It would be foolish to write them up and write them off at this point. Because Theodore junior was a political failure, this does not really mean that Franklin junior *must* be a political failure too. Unfortunately Republicans have come in at just about the same point in his career as Democrats intruded upon Theodore junior, thus blasting hopes of appointive office. We shall see. Perhaps James, odd man out and consequently less fate-ridden, has the best chance of beating the Four Brothers jinx that has characterized the Roosevelt family as it did the Adams.

Others

Du Ponts

To the extent that Adamses, Biddles, du Ponts and Lees were involved in public life from 1930 to 1945, they were involved in the wake of Franklin Roosevelt. Charles Francis Adams, as a Republican cabinet member, lost his job. Like Blair Lee, he was the last of his family onstage. Neither Lees nor Adamses played any particular political role in the consultations of Doctor New Deal or Doctor Win-the-War. Not so the du Ponts and the Biddles, who found themselves polarized by events. Du Ponts emerged as leaders of the opposition; Biddles as among Roosevelt's most active supporters. Again, as so very often in the case of these families, it took a period of national emergency to bring them out. The slack interlude of normalcy, though it did see an Adams in the cabinet, was more concerned with business as usual.

Business was, as usual, notoriously good for the du Ponts. Unfortunately for symmetry, the history of the Company during the period between the wars is dominated not by four, but by only three brothers: Pierre, Irénée and Lammot, sons of the chemist Lammot who married the part-Jewish Mary Belin and was blown up in 1884. These three succeeded each other in the presidency. There were actually five brothers altogether — Pierre, Henry Belin, William Kemble, Irénée and Lammot. No less than three of these married kin. Beside Pierre and his Belin cousin, Henry married a Bradford cousin and Irénée du Pont married an Irene du Pont; almost incestuous, orthographically. When you consider that the previous triumvirate of Alfred, T. Coleman and Pierre (again) had also all married cousins, it really does begin to seem a small world there on the Brandywine.

Pierre, the oldest of them, lived till 1954, and since it was he who wrested the control of the Company away from Alfred by buying out Coleman in 1915, it was he who was really the Grand Old Man for the next four decades, its most prosperous years. During the interregnum between Roosevelts, General Motors, Pierre's acquisition, began to emerge as the greatest industrial enterprise in the country and the du Pont Company expanded as one of the greatest, king of synthetics and chemicals. Yet this empire was still run not only by the family, but by one family within the family, descendants of the original Irénée's oldest son Alfred Victor. (Pierre, Irénée, Alfred V., Lammot, Pierre and his brothers in a fifth generation). It is perhaps nicely symbolic that the last of the du Ponts to be a great power in the Company was named Pierre after the founder of the family.

What first brought du Ponts and Roosevelts together was Prohibition. It is impossible for anyone not alive at that time to appreciate how vital an issue Prohibition seemed from 1928 to 1932. Before the crash, in fact, it was *the* issue. Passions ran high. On one side were small-town, middle-class morality, the law and reform. As Hoover said, mincing his words, it was an "experiment noble in motive." The Demon Rum, blighter of lives and homes, was to be finally expelled from society. Generations of women, backed by their Protestant clergymen, had fought for this. Incredibly, an amendment to the sacred Constitution embodied this idealistic attempt at moral control. In arms against the reformers were two main groups, the upper classes, particularly those of the eastern seaboard, who liked their wines and fiercely resented anyone's telling them they could not drink them, and the urban lower classes, those to whom the saloon was a club and the bucket of beer a staff of life. The Catholic clergy, as opposed to many Protestants, were not interested in Prohibition. Al Smith, easterner, Catholic, cockney, had been the first presidential candidate who had dared to stand up against teetotalism in favor of repeal. The du Ponts had been traditionally Republican since the Civil War, as represented by Senators Henry and Coleman; but John Jacob Raskob, Pierre du Pont's right-hand man, was a Catholic and a fervent admirer of Al Smith.

Raskob had been picked up by Pierre during Pierre's period of exile from Wilmington. Pierre had felt, like Alfred, that under Eugene younger members of the tribe were being ignored, and in disgust he quit the Company and went west. While running a steel plant in Lorain, Ohio, Raskob became his right-hand man. Pierre took him back to Wilmington with him. Raskob was concerned principally with Pierre's General Motors interests, but was also busy with the Company.

In the mid-twenties Raskob met Al Smith, then governor of New York. As fellow Catholic and fellow wet, Raskob became an admirer, and when Smith ran for President, Raskob left his job as chairman of the finance committee of General Motors to become chairman of the Democratic National Committee and run Smith's campaign. Money ceased to be Smith's major problem; but Raskob's

support merely emphasized his other problems. Rum and Roman-
ism, his Catholicism and his anti-Prohibitionism both helped to defeat him in the formerly solid-Democratic South. The fact that
Raskob was a millionaire and connected with the du Ponts didn't
help either.

An American Anti-Prohibition Association (AAPA) had been
formed, and it continued the battle. John Raskob and Pierre du Pont
were among its most important backers. When Roosevelt became
the Democratic nominee in 1932, nobody really knew too much
about him, or exactly where he stood on most issues; but they did
know he was against Prohibition. The Anti-Prohibitionists voted for
him, including Pierre and Raskob.

Already, however, the rift between Al Smith and Roosevelt,
which had begun when Roosevelt, as Smith's handpicked nominee
for governor, refused to let Smith interfere in the governorship,
yawned to a chasm in the early days of the New Deal. At first,
during the upsurge of optimism created by Franklin's first efforts —
his "We have nothing to fear but fear itself," the Bank Holiday, the
exciting turmoil of the Hundred Days with its legislation and pro-
liferation of alphabetic agencies — du Pont and Raskob, like other
businessmen, supported the administration. Pierre was a member of
the Labor Advisory Board of the NRA. Soon ardor began to cool.
By 1934 the reaction had set in strongly. Pierre's friendly correspondence with the President ceased.

Meanwhile, Prohibition had been repealed. The AAPA was no
longer necessary. The idea occurred to Raskob and others of turning
it into something else, an organization now to be used to fight rather
than support Roosevelt. The new organization was called the Liberty League and was backed by Raskob, Pierre du Pont and Al
Smith. It was going to defend the rights of business against the
attacks of the New Deal and finance the defeat of Roosevelt in
1936.

Raskob indicated where the support for the Liberty League was
to come from. The du Pont family controlled, he said, "a larger

share of industry through common stockholdings than any other group, including the Rockefellers, the Morgans, the Mellons" or anyone else. Actually, not Pierre but his pipe-smoking and rough-hewn brother Irénée was the ardent and active champion of the Liberty League. The climax of the League's drive was a great dinner given in Washington early in 1936. A representative assemblage of business leaders, dressed to the gills, applauded Al Smith's attack on his former friend and protégé, FDR. "There can be only one capital, Washington or Moscow," bellowed Al. His inference was of course that Stalin controlled Washington through Roosevelt.

Nothing could have been better propaganda for Roosevelt than this dinner. Here were all the malefactors of great wealth and economic royalists gathered together in their evening clothes, while millions were still unemployed and starving, to attack the champion of the common man. Roosevelt's overwhelming victory in '36 finished off the Liberty League, and the du Ponts' active personal connections with national politics and Franklin Delano Roosevelt.

Come the war, the hatchet was more or less buried, and no industry participated more actively in war production, including the new FDR-sponsored field of atomic energy — or made more money — than E. I. du Pont de Nemours, Inc.

It was during this period, beginning in the mid-twenties and carrying on till the mid-fifties, that the third and most spectacular of the du Pont palaces was created. First had been Alfred's spite-dream Nemours, surrounded by walls topped with broken glass. Then had come Pierre's fantasy, the gardens of Longwood. Finally came Winterthur, the creation of a Henry du Pont, son of Colonel Henry and grandson of Henry the Great. Winterthur had been built originally by Irénée's son-in-law Antoine Bidermann, and named after the Bidermann's native city in Switzerland. A square, white, neoclassic box, it had acquired Victorian excrescences and a collection of fine old furniture when, on the last day of 1926, Henry junior inherited it. He decided to devote his energies to collecting

Americana from the seventeenth century through about 1820. Eventually over a hundred period rooms filled the house and an immense new wing. The du Ponts lived in the house itself up till 1951, and very spooky it must have been, from all accounts, a sort of deserted palace of room after room of flawless decor with nobody there except guides and visitors during the day. Eventually the family moved out, building other, more convenient quarters nearby, and the house and its gardens are now a public display like Longwood. The gardens are as famous as the furniture, not formal like Longwood with its fountains and greenhouse, but "natural."

It takes a full day to see the whole museum. You are taken around in groups of four by appointment, and a staff of guides, many of them local housewives with a passion for furniture, educate you in finials and drawer pulls. Each room is completely furnished (curtains, upholstery, rugs, pictures, knickknacks — all *original,* not reproductions — acres of rugs, tons of china, thousands of chairs). It's as awe-inspiring and beautiful in its own very different way as the Grand Canyon. Many family items are tucked into the vast collection. Together with Longwood and such other attractions as the Hagley Museum (history of the powder mills) and the Eleutherian Mills–Hagley Foundation Library (industrial history), it makes of du Pontland a tourist-and-research center comparable to Williamsburg — and all, of course, a memorial to du Pont taste and money.

Biddles

The effect of Roosevelt on the Biddles was diametrically opposed to his effect on the du Ponts. Whereas some du Ponts became representative enemies, leaders of the economic royalists, some Biddles became representative Roosevelt supporters; three of them in particular — Francis, his last attorney general; George, one of the principal instigators of the artists' section of the WPA; and Tony, ambassador to Poland and the governments in exile. They were of course all Democrats, though that was not necessarily the party of choice for the majority of Philadelphia Biddles during this period.

Anthony Joseph Drexel Biddle Jr. was the antithesis of his father. Nobody could have called him "eccentric." He was the very model of fashionable suavity and glamorous high living. Of all the members of all these families, he seems to be the only one who has cut a swathe in the tarnished chambers of Society and yet continued a family record of accomplishment. He married Mary Duke, sister of his sister's husband Angier. His new mother-in-law, disliking the flatness of Somerville, New Jersey, where the wedding was to be held, ordered a mountain, studded with large trees, to be erected for the occasion.

Floated on a flood tide of the twenties with Duke and Drexel (but not much Biddle) money, he cavorted about from palace to palace being snapped by photographers. Glossy magazines of the time, like the now-defunct *Spur*, that devoted themselves to the now equally defunct plutocratic glories of the era, loved to give full-page spreads to the top-hatted Tony Biddle strolling near his residence in New York at 1009 Fifth Avenue, or stepping off the plane at Palm Beach, in days when just stepping off a plane meant something, to take up residence at Villa Sarmiento (named in honor of his Spanish ancestors), or roughing it at Chetwode on Bellevue Avenue in Newport. In Palm Beach in particular, Tony epitomized everything in the way of elegance, gaiety and aplomb that such a resort could hope for — a founder of the Bath and Tennis Club, where charter membership cost ten thousand dollars, and a member of a group called the Coconuts, who gave an annual lavish ball.

This late-Cleveland-Amoryish style of life lasted through the boom and the Republican administrations. Come the Democrats, Biddle's active career in the diplomatic service began. He ended up in a most crucial post as ambassador to Poland. He was there when Hitler invaded in September 1939, and in fact Roosevelt heard of the event through all Philadelphia channels, Biddle calling to Bullitt, Philadelphian ambassador to France, Bullitt calling to Roosevelt in the White House. Seldom has disaster been announced under such respectable auspices.

Biddle followed the Polish government into exile and London, and there became a sort of diplomatic storage warehouse for refugee governments, ambassador extraordinary and plenipotentiary to Poland, Belgium, Netherlands, Norway, Greece, Yugoslavia, Czechoslovakia and Luxembourg (he was only minister to the last). Through this comprehensive position — Biddle must surely hold the American record for number of ambassadorships — he served a vital function in helping natives of all these countries to escape the Nazis. Naturally these governments gave him medals, so that his list of decorations makes those of the combined sons of Theodore look skimpy. He even got the Order of St. Charles from Monaco; but not the Order of the Jade from China, or that Assoum Alaouite. He belonged to the best clubs of course, and even won the court-tennis championship of France, a high-toned thing to do. (Court tennis is that original form of tennis played in a big thing like a basketball court with all sorts of queer projections, Renaissance rules and regal traditions. There are only about twenty or thirty courts now active in the world, most of them in England.) In semiretirement under Eisenhower as adjutant general of Pennsylvania, he died with his diplomatic boots on as ambassador to Spain in 1961, where he was shortly thereafter succeeded by his nephew Angier Biddle Duke. Needless to say, Biddle too divorced his Duke and married several other times thereafter, the last being a lady whose previous married name had been Loughborough-Loughborough.

Nothing could have been more of a contrast to this giddy whirl of fashion and conspicuous consumption than the childhood of Francis and George Biddle. They belonged to the other, or Solid, branch, grandchildren of august Chancellor George Washington Biddle, translator of Demosthenes. Here again, four brothers. All of them made successful careers for themselves, the oldest, Moncure, as an investment banker in Philadelphia; the youngest, Sydney, as one of the country's earliest practicing psychoanalysts. He had been a pupil of Freud's daughter Anna. Francis and George were the two who achieved national prominence.

AJDB senior represented the world of Theodore Roosevelt, as written up, say, by Richard Harding Davis. AJDB junior represented that of Scott Fitzgerald. The four brothers were brought up almost literally in the world of Henry James. Their father, Algernon, was a brilliant but too ambitious lawyer who more or less killed himself by overwork. He left his four young sons in the charge of their fascinating but thoroughly neurotic mother, Frances. She was not a Philadelphian, but by descent a Randolph of Virginia, and seemed to carry on many of the exotically perverse traits of that ill-starred clan. She was a great-granddaughter through her mother of Edmund Jennings Randolph, first attorney general of the United States under Washington, who was forced to retire under suspicion of being in treasonable correspondence with the revolutionary French (i.e., a "Communist agent"). He was a second cousin of wizened John Randolph of Roanoke and Bizarre; and there was certainly something of the Bizarre in Mrs. Biddle. Her father, Moncure Robinson, had been a great engineer and builder of railroads, also a Virginian moved to Philadelphia. He had surveyed one of America's very first commercial railroads, the Pottsville and Danville in 1829, then in the 1830's he built the Reading. His daughter Fanny, though she idolized her husband, and was never consoled after his premature death, nonetheless went right home after her wedding ceremony and locked herself up in her room, refusing to attend her own wedding reception and staying in bed for a week. Hardly the normal reaction of a rapturous bride. Her best friend was Mrs. Owen Wister, daughter of actress Fanny Kemble (best friend of Henry James) and mother of the writer Owen Wister, best friend of TR. There Fanny Biddle was introduced to Henry James himself. He found her "elusive"; no accolade could, as it were, have been higher. She was so afraid of destroying the initial impression that she refused to let him call on her.

After an idyllic country-suburban Philadelphia childhood dominated by a formidable nursery governess called Annie Deane and enlivened by fantastic games of knights and battles invented by the imaginative brothers, they were one by one thrown into the cold tank of Groton.

Moncure was there first and suffered most. Smug Franklin Roosevelt in his correspondence thoroughly approved of the punishments with which Moncure was menaced by his schoolmates for being so brash, pumping (held upside down under a jet of ice-cold water) or boot-boxing (shut up in a shoe chest). "The Biddle boy is quite crazy, fresh and stupid, he has been boot-boxed once and threatened to be pumped several times." And again, "Poor Biddle has been sent to bed for being saucy to one of the masters. . . . I found it necessary to chastise him yesterday." George and Francis were less saucy, but they did not particularly like the regime, of which they both give such vivid pictures in their respective autobiographies. It is odd that of the four, the greatest rebel in school, Moncure, became the greatest conformist in later life, whereas George, who tried hardest to conform, became an out-and-out rebel as an adult.

Henry Adams may have been an artist in his inclinations and sensibilities, as his two novels and his two famous books, the *Chartres* and the *Education* indicate; but he could not be called an "artist" professionally. For the first time in all these particular family chronicles, we do finally strike such a professional artist in George Biddle. He was a long time getting started, after Harvard and a try at law school. At last, prodded by William James Jr., artist son of the philosopher and nephew of Henry, he went to France, studied painting and bohemianism, and began a career that extends from the twenties to the present.

The details and evaluations of such a career are no more family history than the battles of the Lees or the politics of the Roosevelts.

His strongest early influences seemed to be a Gauguin-like spell of native living in Tahiti and the style of the French-Bulgarian painter Jules Pascin. He combined these exotic influences with the kind of social consciousness prevalent in the thirties to produce an odd style, now of course very much out of fashion, which combined somewhat primitivistic, quirky realist forms and very individual mannerisms, with liberal social messages. Much smitten with the success of Mexican muralists like Rivera, he hoped to achieve something of the same sort of revival of serious mural painting in the service of humanity and the government here in the United States. To that end he stirred up artistic and New Deal agencies, and the result was the WPA mural that still decorates many a post office. The idea of paying unemployed artists day-laborer wages as a form of relief was certainly a shock to many in both artistic and antiartistic circles; but it was one of the projects that personally intrigued schoolmate FDR, and though Roosevelt was numb to all art except pictures of ships, he became thus indirectly the greatest patron of painting in American history.

Biddle's own best-known murals are in the Department of Justice Building in Washington. He shook the dust of Philadelphia and eventually settled with his sculptress third wife in a handmade stone house up the Hudson. No one was a more vitriolic New Dealer critic of his own class and kind. Francis, on the other hand, moved more slowly towards his New Dealism. During the twenties he was a successful Philadelphia lawyer, whose restiveness was expressed only in a rather Henry Jamesy novel of disillusion on the Main Line called *The Llanfear Pattern*. Public Service, however, called. He found private life and professional success unsatisfactory personally, and perhaps from a Family point of view too. In his autobiography he presents the state of mind, more vividly than perhaps accurately:

"When I was at college, Dr. Weir Mitchell [Silas Weir Mitchell, writer, doctor and kin of the Roosevelts] the most venerable and august (and egotistic) representative of [the Philadelphia] past . . . reminded me that for the first time in the history of Philadelphia there was no one of my name who was contributing anything of leadership or service to the community. There were plenty of them, but what were they doing? — pleasure seekers, sportsmen, play boys [this obviously in reference to the Drexel Biddles] whose names were constantly in the illustrated journals, who could lead cotillions and were prominent in clubs, but nothing more, nothing virtuous in the true sense of that word. What, was the question with which he left me . . . was I going to do about it?

"It was true, I thought, my Biddle relations were not doing anything, hardly even a lawyer or a doctor among them, few who were making a living. I wondered if the family was petering out, like all families in our country which had once upon a time counted. Of course there were still the Adamses — and then one paused. The Randolphs . . . were contributing little more, if even as much as the Biddles, to the public welfare."

This was of course before the Roosevelts could claim to be a "dynasty," and before the New Deal Biddles had contributed to the public welfare.

It would be hard to say, given this somewhat perverse and supercilious Biddley attitude, just to what extent family consciousness forced Francis into "public welfare." He had been a violent supporter of Theodore Roosevelt as Bull Moose candidate. Though of course he had known Franklin Roosevelt in school and followed him at Harvard, he had no particular impression of him as a liberal leader. However, when in 1934 he was asked to head the newly created Labor Relations Board (Pierre du Pont had served on its predecessor, the Labor Advisory Board) he accepted, and from then on his career was that of a confirmed Roosevelt henchman. First as solicitor general, and then as wartime attorney general, he was an undeviating though certainly not an uncritical supporter of the President.

His job during the war involved dealing with enemy aliens. On the whole, the government's war record was humane and in salutary contrast to the anti-German mania of the First World War. The great blot on the record, the internment of the West Coast Japanese, Biddle could not prevent, though he tried to. This received all the publicity that the tactful handling of such matters elsewhere did not. After the war he was one of the judges at the Nuremberg trials of Nazi leaders. His wife, Katharine Chapin, was a much published and praised poet. Like Corinne Roosevelt Robinson, she too was a vice president of the Poetry Society of America. The Mexican government at one point asked the whole family group down as guests — Francis as lawyer, cabinet member and litterateur (not only was his novel a modest success, but his personal reminiscences of Justice Holmes were the basis of a very successful play and a bad movie); his wife as poetess, several of whose patriotic poems had been set to music and performed by important musical groups like the New York Philharmonic; his brother George as one of America's foremost mural artists; and George's wife as a distinguished sculptor. Few family groups could have been put to more varied intellectual uses. Actually, none of the performances or commissions came through at the time, but it is doubtful if supporters of the Harding administration could have fielded a team of kinfolk as sympathetic to intellectual Latin Americans.

Summary

What Franklin did as President, as opposed to what he was, is simply American history. To those who lived through it, that history would hardly seem to need retelling. To the millions born since, many now mature, it is already antiquity. Nonetheless, nothing since has been as shattering and triumphant an experience as the Roosevelt years, those two decades beginning in 1932 and really prolonged in aftermath, through Truman's administrations, to 1952. The history of the earlier twentieth century, Theodore Roosevelt, Woodrow Wilson, the Republican interregnum, leads up to this crest. The history of the century since simply remains on a plateau, as a sequel — the follow-through of Roosevelt's New Deal at home and his internationalism abroad. Laissez-faire capitalism of the Liberty League sort and antiliberal isolationism of the America First sort have been lost causes whose last stand in their old forms would seem to have been the Goldwater campaign. Only perhaps now as we go into the Seventies is there a real change of climate and the emergence of really new alignments among members of a generation born beyond the shadow of the Great War. Criticism among younger historians and the breakup of the alliance of minorities has dissolved some of the charisma of both New Deal and FDR. But to a greater extent than one can say of any other American President, Washington, Jackson and Lincoln included, the before-and-after shadow of Franklin Roosevelt has dominated seven decades.

The total Roosevelt family tenure of more or less continuous public office has been matched only by that of the Adamses from 1765 to 1848: Samuel Adams' election to the Massachusetts legislature to John Quincy's death in the House. There are really no significant gaps in this sequence of offices. Samuel served almost continuously to the Revolution and the Continental Congress and beyond, John till 1800, his son till his death. The gaps were very short. The Roosevelt record begins to run almost continuously from 1882, when Theodore strode into the New York Assembly, till 1966 when James left his post in the United Nations. There are more sizable gaps here than in the span of the Adamses. There was, for instance, a five-year period, 1884–89, when Theodore was in limbo, and a two-year gap, 1908–10, between Theodore's stepping down from the throne and FDR's election to the state senate. Franklin was out of politics from 1920 to 1928, but Theodore junior served as assistant secretary of the navy, succeeding Franklin, until 1924, and then as colonial governor 1929–33; so there is only a four-year gap there, 1924–28. From 1945 to 1951, Eleanor was the American representative to the United Nations; Franklin junior was in Congress 1949–55; James likewise 1955–65 and he then served with UNESCO till 1966. In 1965 Elliott was elected mayor of Miami Beach, which is, after all, public office. He would, incidentally, seem to be the first mayor in the family, despite all those aldermen, though Theodore tried and failed in 1886. If, however, one counts 1966 as the closing date of the Roosevelt span, the Adams and the Roosevelt dynasties reign over almost identical periods, eighty-three years (1765–1848) for one, eighty-four years (1882–1966) for the other.*

Franklin's personal career from 1910 to 1945 covers a longer period than that of John Adams. No one before has had a longer presidential career, nor will again as long as the Republican-inspired Twenty-Second Amendment, which is designed specifically to prevent another FDR, stands on the books. Of the crucial events that happened in America during those fateful fifteen years from 1930 through 1945, none happened outside the Roosevelt orbit. Some Presidents do little more than preside. Not FDR. Even the barest recapitulation of these events shows him active and influential, and usually successful in every direction. First there was Prohibition, which was repealed in his first term. Then there was the depression, which as governor of New York, then as President, he attacked by all sorts of vigorous pump-priming projects. In 1933 came the Bank Holiday and the Hundred Days, which thawed the deepfreeze of inertia and despair and started American life moving again; then followed the tumultuous years of alphabetic agencies and experimentation — AAA, CCC, TVA, WPA — each a revolution in government manipulation of national resources and the economy. Already in his first term began the secession of the business community, led by the du Ponts and the Liberty League. Restored prosperity and his overwhelming victory in 1936 confounded his critics and liquidated the Liberty League. This led him in his elation into the few blunders and defeats of his career, the attempt to "pack" the

---

* This leaves a vacuum of some thirty-four years, 1848–82. Even then, Charles Francis was a congressman (1858–61) and then ambassador till 1868. John Quincy Adams II, his son, was elected to the Massachusetts legislature in 1869 and served there as late as 1874. Robert B. Roosevelt was in Congress 1871–73. So, except for a ten-year gap, 1848–58, and a similar seven-year gap, 1874–81, the Roosevelt-Adams public careers between them have blanketed the entire span of the history of the United States as an independent nation.

Supreme Court by adding new liberal justices to outvote old reactionary ones, and the attempt to purge Congress of reactionary Democrats. He failed; but though he lost those battles, he won this war. The old reactionary justices soon left the bench, dead or retired, and he was able to appoint his own men; as the exigencies of the war increased, opposition to his policies in Congress evaporated.

Perhaps his greatest mistake in this period, and his greatest near-defeat, was the recession in the economy in 1937–38, which seemed to indicate a failure of his experiments, but which may have been rather the result of an attempt to curtail them in the interests of balancing the budget. If the war had not happened when it did, it is possible that Franklin, like Theodore, might have faced hardening opposition to his reforms in Congress and the failure of his whole New Deal.

From 1938 on, however, America was forced, unwillingly, to turn outward. Japan's conquests in China, Hitler's advance in Europe, posed a global threat America had never thought of facing before. Many, a majority at first, refused to face these threats. The country still remained overwhelmingly determined not to repeat 1917–18. Roosevelt, conscious now of Woodrow Wilson as he had been before of Theodore Roosevelt, obviously committed from the start of the war to the cause of England and to the defeat of Hitler, almost by instinct rather than willpower, nudged and pushed, leading only as far as the populace would be led, away from neutrality, towards preparedness, aid to Britain and then Russia, everything short of an actual declaration of war. Isolationists, as embodied in the America First organization, were as outraged as the conservatives of the Liberty League had been during the New Deal. As the war in Europe rescued him and the American economy from the quandaries of 1938 (although not until we were actually at war in 1943 did unemployment vanish), so the Japanese attack on Pearl Harbor rescued him from the quandaries of an increasingly false neutrality. The Japanese bombs blew up isolationism along with the fleet; blew up the depression too.

Following the pattern of both the American Revolution and the Civil War, first came the long, desperate period of continuous defeat, Japan overrunning the Pacific, threatening to walk through neutralist India to join forces with Germans coming down through Russia and the Middle East. Then gradually, in 1942, came the turn of the tide which began with the battles of the Coral Sea and Midway in the Pacific and the bogging down of the German advance in Russia. In all the strategy of the war, Roosevelt, Churchill and to a lesser extent Stalin, kept in constant personal touch, were actively concerned in every phase of combat. With the crossing of the Rhine into Germany in February 1945 and the dropping of the atom bombs on Japan after Roosevelt's death in August 1945, the two events that definitely signalized the end of the war in East and West, Roosevelt's plans came to their successful conclusion. He was as much author of the Second Front as anyone else, and he seized on the idea of the atom bomb, when it was first projected, as one of his foremost concerns. He realized more keenly than many others before (or since) just what it would have meant if the Axis, not the Allies, had been first to develop it.

This has all become ancient history at last. A whole huge generation has grown up since these events. What seems to their elders so vivid is dusty to them. Most of the contemporaries who so hated Roosevelt are dead, like most of his advisers and supporters. As one recedes from a mountain, the details blur, the mountain rises higher. Unless events as cataclysmic engulf the country during the next thirty years, producing a crop of competing prominences, the stature of FDR is liable to become more and more elevated. He may well turn out to be the great American of the twentieth as Lincoln was of the nineteenth and Washington of the eighteenth century.

George Washington was a man of family, and an idolized leader, but no one could have applied to him the Lincoln label of "The Great Commoner." No one could have called Lincoln a Man of Family. It was Roosevelt's ambivalent role to be both a man of family and a "great commoner." Many felt and feel a certain falsity in this. How could his understanding of the common man have been real, anything but a demagogic vote-getting pose? How could he have known anything about "commonness"? Certainly no President has ever combined the two roles more exaggeratedly. Not even John Quincy Adams followed family patterns more consciously; and the Adamses were, after all, only in their second generation of establishment. Hyde Park Roosevelts were in their fifth down from Isaac the Patriot. It is the blend of the traditions of Washington and the Adamses, of gentlemen in the country's service, combined with the traditions of Jackson and Lincoln as tribunes of the people, foreshadowed by Theodore Roosevelt and Wilson, that makes Franklin Roosevelt such a special and enigmatic figure. There is no real doubt that his convictions were totally sincere, though his cordial manner may not always have been. The adoration he aroused among the forgotten men he was remembering was equally sincere. Yet socially he continued to feel most at home with people like Vincent Astor, who represented his own background, and at the same time everything he was fighting. He was never, like George Biddle, a self-conscious rebel; the quarrel with his own class was picked by them, not by him. He remains a man of contradictions. No one then or since has ever quite penetrated his genial but opaque and opalescent personality, or really explored what Robert Sherwood called his "heavily forested interior." Some still hate his politics, others dislike and distrust his personality. Many leftists believe he failed to take the opportunity to really reform American life. Perhaps as Theodore was eclipsed by Franklin, Franklin will be eclipsed in history by someone in the future. Certainly not by anybody before 1970, however. No one else at this point looms larger in the American twentieth century than that cocky sphinx.

V

Epilogue

1945–1970

1

Grand Old People

With the death of Franklin Delano Roosevelt, this particular family chronicle closes, or seems to close; that is, no member of any of these families born in a later generation has outstandingly distinguished himself on the national scene in the quarter century since 1945. There has been no dearth of merit; but there has not been the kind of national reputation that distinguishes these particular families from many other meritorious ones.

This of course does not mean much. Who, looking about between, say, 1840 and 1860, or between 1870 and 1890, would have been able to spot anyone of outstanding "national reputation" emerging into visibility from any of these families? In 1850, Charles Adams was an unsuccessful pamphleteer and politician, Lee an ordinary army career officer; in 1880 Henry Adams had not yet written his history, nor Theodore Roosevelt entered politics. These low ebbs in the family chronicles, usually coincidental with low ebbs in the national chronicle (that is, peace and prosperity), have occurred before and will again. The period between 1950 and 1970 appears to be another such low ebb. On the other hand, it may really be that these particular five names have exhausted their vitality, used up their fates, and sunk back into the multitude of the excellent but not "fated." Perhaps the sap no longer runs in the family trees, and they can no longer send out branches conspicuous enough to be seen all over the U.S.A. On the other hand it is possible that another period of turmoil will again thrust up some Lee or

Adams into leadership. Meanwhile, though younger people do not hold the limelight, some older ones have carried on from 1945 right through to the present, continuing to keep their families in the public eye.

In particular, three women have survived into the post-Eisenhower era to keep at least two of the names green. Eleanor Roosevelt "on her own," till she died in 1962, unquestionably continued to be First Lady of America if not the world. Indefatigable as champion of humanitarianism (she is to a large extent the inspirer of that idealistic Declaration of Human Rights promulgated by the United Nations), she continued to travel and speak and investigate and write almost to the day she died. Her enemies continued to regard her as a fuzzy-minded pinko busybody, her idolators continued to beatify her as a secular saint; meritorious and nationally conspicuous at least she certainly was. Nobody could say the name of Roosevelt had retired from action as long as she was about. She has one of the very few personal memorials in that rather austere riverside garden in front of the UN buildings in her native New York City — a chaste marble bench with her name, Anna Eleanor Roosevelt, on it and her dates, 1884–1962; opposite, an equally chaste marble shaft carved with those words of Adlai Stevenson, "She would rather light a candle than curse the darkness."

The name Roosevelt in any case would still be newsworthy in Alice Roosevelt Longworth. She has survived her first cousin, and if not exactly First Lady of the country, is certainly unofficial First Lady of Washington. Living in her house on Massachusetts Avenue crowded with old and new mementos,* but certainly not in retirement, she keeps up with the very latest in political and social rumor. No party is an event without her presence and comment,

* One of the most striking of these mementos is what appears to be a hideous family daguerreotype of 1860: father in frock coat, wizened mother in poke bonnet, nasty baby. This, according to Mrs. Longworth herself, is the Republican Holy Trinity of the 1950's — Father Joseph McCarthy, Mother Robert Taft, Baby Ike Eisenhower.

usually caustic. The feuds of the past are now good anecdotes. If only she could or would write down in her own inimitable conversational style everything she has seen, just as she really saw it! (How many reputations would be singed?)

Eleanor was First Lady of America as long as she lived. Alice lives to be First Lady of America's capital. First Lady of Boston (Hub of the Universe) is Abigail Adams Homans, daughter of John, niece of CFA^2, Henry and Brooks, sister of CFA^3. Some of her ancestors, like JQA and CFA^1, were not notable for their sense of humor. Others, like CFA^2, were famous for being difficult.* Mrs. Homans preserves Adams independence along with a notable sense of humor and a minimum of social intransigence. Still, as a member of her family, she does maintain some of the family reputation. As she says of herself, "I could stand on my head on Boston Common and people would just say, 'Oh, it's only Abigail Adams.'" Her son, George Homans, has broken all traditions by becoming of all things a prominent sociologist at Harvard. As he likes to boast, a self-made man (of a rather special sort), and another good demonstration of surviving hereditary meritocracy.

It is rather odd that this span of family history should end in three such conspicuous women; for in fact these Family histories are not conspicuous for conspicuous women. Most of the hereditary merit, or at least the national reputation, has been male, not female. Yet it is obvious that the feminine influence on hereditary meritocracy must be enormous, and that the truism that back of every great man is a great woman is true here as elsewhere. There are

---

* One of the most difficult moments in the life of CFA^2 occurred in the early days of the Chilton Club, then as now Boston's best for women. When Charles first went there he was refused admittance through the front door, reserved for the ladies, and told to go around to the men's door at the side. "I never enter by a side door," he said, and pushed his way in. Boston was, as usual, properly outraged. As one Boston historian wrote to another, "You can't spell gentleman with two A's, one d, one m, and one s." Henry objected to a third historian who was proposed as author of a biography of Gallatin, a subject already sufficiently covered by Henry himself, or so he thought. "I regret that such an indescribable brute and ass . . . should do Gallatin." Henry's friends who most loved him liked to call him "Porcupinus Angelicus" — angelic porcupine.

certainly examples — noble Ann Carter Lee and her beloved Robert, romantic Anne de Montchanin Dupont and her beloved Pierre. Still, in a chronicle concerned with war and peace, battle and politics, it is hard to give these women their just due. They remain a faint, backstage fragrance, with their sons and husbands bustling about in the foreground.

The exceptions are few: Abigail Adams as a personage in her own right, Eleanor and Alice Roosevelt. A few others emerge strongly as influential characters, Louisa Johnson Adams, Sara Delano Roosevelt. But on the whole the women have to be inferred. Nicole-Charlotte-Marie-Louise Le Dée de Raucourt du Pont was obviously a remarkable woman, whose influence on the founding of the du Pont family must have been profound. Yet what can one really say of her except that she was a fine manager of Bois-des-Fossés and a good wife and mother? Only at the beginnings of the chronicle, with one Abigail, and at the end with another do we have personalities strong enough to stand on their own (or on their heads). Perhaps the times, Revolutionary stress, modern emancipation, with Victorian repression in between, have something to do with it.

In any case these three splendid specimens of female character do bring to a close the annals of an era in their particular families. Abigail is the last of her generation of Adamses alive, the generation succeeding to the Four Brothers, fifth in establishment from and including founder John the President.

Alice is not the last of her generation. A Grand Old Man, her half brother Archibald Roosevelt, is still alive, and still summers at Oyster Bay. But though sufficiently prominent as a financial figure, titular head of Roosevelt and Sons, as a writer of articles and as an ardent Republican, he does not share the Roosevelt spotlight with Alice. Even more secluded is sister Ethel Derby, who sees to it that, like the Edwardian lady-of-the-old-school, her name will appear in the papers only at birth, marriage or death, with the exception of a gathering of Roosevelts to dedicate something. Her daughter, Mrs.

Andrew M. Williams of Seattle, however is active in West Coast Republican politics, and hence more liable to be publicly noticed. Otherwise one doesn't hear much of the Derbys, of Archibald Roosevelt or, in fact, of any of the Oyster Bay Branch.

Besides the Grand Old Women, there have been a few other Grand Old Men besides Archibald Roosevelt, survivors of two wars and the great depression. Most prominent of these have been the two surviving Biddle brothers, Francis (who just died in 1968 at eighty-two) and George. George still lives up the Hudson, still paints and still writes; at least his book, *The Yes and No of Modern Art,* a quizzical query on the progress of modern painting in late years by one of the pioneers of American modernism, appeared as recently as 1957. Francis, though not active legally, was godfather to every liberal movement, as chairman or member of a board — ADA, ACLU, anything of that sort, including the still abortive attempt to raise a monument to FDR in Washington equivalent to those of other famous Presidents. His wife Katharine survives, but again is no longer active in literature. She still remains, of all this span of family literary history, the one member of any of these clans (though of course by marriage) who has achieved a really respectable public-professional literary reputation as a "creative artist," under the name of Katharine Garrison Chapin.* Henry Adams was of course professional as an historian. As a novelist and belletrist he never really trusted himself to the marketplace. Mrs. Biddle's few books of verse were "trade books," not like Henry's far more famous works, either anonymous, or printed privately for circulation among the elite. She does not seem to be much regarded nowadays, but in

---

* A measure of her reputation was her inclusion in 1948 on the jury to award the first Bollingen prize for literature, along with such poetic bigwigs as T. S. Eliot and W. H. Auden. The jury awarded the prize to Ezra Pound (disciple of Brooks Adams), then incarcerated for profascist broadcasts during the war. There was such a furor that the prize was not awarded again for several years, and then under different auspices. Another professional literary Biddle has been Livingston Jr., nephew of Mad Anthony, who has published four novels with considerable success. A Roosevelt, Theodora Roosevelt Keogh, has also published novels.

the 20's and 30's she was certainly a modestly distinguished figure as a poetess of taste, skill and sensitivity.

The du Ponts' Grand Old Men have been legion, but grandest and oldest have been the three president brothers, Pierre (died 1954), Lammot (died 1952) and Irénée, who lived on till 1963. As the last men actually named du Pont who have been presidents of the Company, their shadows, first as successive chairmen of the board, then as simply presences, must have been enormous. As father figures, if not active industrialists, their influence has continued almost up to the present.

None of the later presidents of E. I. du Pont de Nemours has in fact been surnamed du Pont, and only one of them, Lammot du Pont Copeland, has been a genuine blood relative of the family. As the reign of the three cousins was succeeded by the reign of the three brothers, so in turn we have had the reign of the three in-laws. William Carpenter (president from 1940 to 1948) was not himself related or connected, but his big-game-hunting brother, R. Rudilph Morgan Carpenter, married Margaretta, sister of Pierre, Irénée and Lammot. Next came Crawford Greenewalt (president 1948–62), who also married a Margaretta, daughter of Irénée. He is incidentally a well-known and much-published ornithologist; one wonders how he had time to run the Company. He was succeeded by Copeland, whose mother was Louisa, sister of Pierre, Irénée and Lammot.

Now Copeland has moved up to chairman, as of December 1967, and his place has been taken by Charles Brelsford McCoy. He is the first president of the Company who has no real family connection, not even that of an in-law. However, two of his children married into the family; but not du Ponts.*

McCoy links, however tenuously, the du Ponts to one of the Brandywine's other most famous dynasties, that of the Wyeths. The

---

* McCoy's kinships: Charles Brelsford McCoy Jr., married Carol Kitchell, daughter of Irene du Pont Carpenter Kitchell, daughter of R. Rudilph and Margaretta du Pont Carpenter. Ann Brelsford McCoy married George Weymouth, son of Dulcinea Ophelia du Pont, daughter of Eugene, son of Alexis. See Appendix V.

Wyeths of course are not Delawarians and do not live in Delaware but in Chadds Ford, Pennsylvania. However, this is right up the Brandywine, and is within the region of du Pont estates, which extend up across the Pennsylvania border to join the estates of Philadelphia's best fox hunters moving down through Chester County. In the middle of one of America's highest concentrations of rural opulence, the Wyeths carry on one of America's longest and most opulent artistic continuities, a dynasty which began in Wilmington.

Howard Pyle (1853–1911), who was so famous as an illustrator of children's books (Robin Hood, pirates), was a native of Wilmington who moved north, made good, and moved back. The most famous of many famous pupils and in turn an illustrator of children's books was a New Englander named Newell C. Wyeth (1882–1945) who settled in Chadds Ford to be near his master Pyle. N.C.'s son Andrew has in turn become perhaps America's most beloved, most highly paid and, in advanced New York critical circles, most unacceptable painter. In a thoroughly Robert Frost vein of bleak but sturdy realism, he presents a world of spare, wintry handicraft derived from Chester County and seacoast Maine — those two landscapes so familiar to America's most discreetly luxurious people, du Ponts and fox-hunting Philadelphians. He Quakerizes the kind of pastoral view available from the windows of any of the neighboring du Pont châteaux or lavishly remodeled farmhouses (or from their summer "cottages" in Maine); omitting of course the sunken gardens and the swimming pools. In nearly all of these same châteaux there will usually be found a Wyeth portrait of a member of the family, or a Wyeth sketch in the bathroom. Though no one member of the family seems to be a notable Wyeth collector, there are certainly lots of individual Wyeths scattered about the neighborhood. There is a certain irony in such aesthetic agrarian-austerity hidden in the midst of a surrounding lavishness produced by immense incomes derived from industrialism.

The Wyeths continue as a dynasty of hereditary merit like those neighboring du Ponts. Wyeth's son James is carrying on his father's tradition as a painter in a third generation. One of Wyeth's sisters, herself a painter, is married to the most famous native painter of New Mexico, that Peter Hurd who had so much trouble with Lyndon Johnson over his presidential portrait. Another Wyeth sister, a musical composer, is married to John McCoy, a painter in a delicate Wyeth-like vein of flowers and still lifes, who also lives in the Chadds Ford area. John McCoy is the brother of Charles McCoy, the present president of E. I. du Pont de Nemours.

Still another of the more conspicuous older du Ponts has been Henry of Winterthur, born in 1880 as son of Colonel Henry A. and grandson of Henry the Great. This third Henry just died in 1969 at the age of eighty-eight, his museum-monument completed, but still most active personally in everything involving historic preservation, on various worthwhile museum or horticultural boards. The du Ponts, as opposed to their peers the Mellons and the Rockefellers, have contributed little to the arts,* at least comparatively, and that mostly locally. But thanks to Pierre's Longwood and Henry's Winterthur, they stand preeminent in the area of what might be called "house and garden." There are few horticultural displays equal to Longwood in America, and no displays of furniture equal to Winterthur. These two remain the du Pont family's major contributions to American culture.

No Lees of this particular generation and kind have survived. Senator Blair died way back in 1944. Perhaps closest to "grand old man" was George Bolling Lee, grandson of Robert E., son of Rooney, who until his death in 1948 was one of New York's foremost gynecologists. An Edmund Jennings Lee (Leesylvania branch, born 1877), headmaster of a distinguished girls' school, Chatham Hall in Virginia, who was still alive into the 1950's, seems to have been the last Lee who could be called prominent as a resident of the

---

* For instance, a Paul Mellon established the Bollingen Foundation, which gave the controversial poetry prize in 1948, and the Mellons have contributed enormously to the National Gallery, whereas the Delaware Art Center in Wilmington gets along without a permanent gallery to show its permanent collection (of Pyles, Wyeths, etc.) despite so many surrounding du Ponts.

Old Dominion. Most other well-known Lees have been either rov-
ing servicemen, or have lived northward in Washington, Maryland
or Pennsylvania.

2

Families

Adams

UNDER the shadow of these various patriarchs and matriarchs,
the five Families have continued in peace and prosperity, in
merit and social position — but just not *famous*. No shirt-sleeves to
shirt-sleeves for them even in their sixth and seventh generation of
gentility; much worthwhile personal success. No national greatness.

With the exception of the Lees, all these families continue to be
umbilically attached to their native centers, Boston (if not Braintree), New York and environs, Philadelphia — and Washington.
Washington has captured some of all of them but notably Lees.
Others are off in San Francisco, Seattle, Miami, Texas, and what
have you. Also, most of these families, far from dying out, have bred
like rabbits. The descendants of Pierre Samuel, either du Ponts or
others, are surely by now close to the thousand mark. The Lee family association numbers over four hundred members, though not
many of them are surnamed Lee; yet some of the more prominent
Lees don't belong to it. Biddles abound, as do Roosevelts, especially
of the Oyster Bay variety.

Only the Adamses of the Royal Line remain, as they have always
remained, a select group. Of course descendants of Henry Adams of
Braintree are in multitudes all over the country, moving on from

Sempronius and Blue Mound upwards and outwards. Even in Boston itself there are eminently proper Adamses who are sure-enough Braintree Adamses, but still not of the Royal Line. The Royal Line itself has finally done what all these other families did long ago — split into two branches. These are the descendants of nice John, the elder branch; and the descendants of railroader CFA[2], the younger branch. Just to make things contrary and confusing, the John branch has been best represented by two CFA's in turn, who have forcefully embodied all the characteristics of previous CFA's.

Secretary of the Navy CFA[3] remains to this day in Boston a sort of symbol of quintessential Bostonianism, both as a strong and prickly person ("that wonderful old bastard") admired by many, loved by some, and as a formidable financial power. Above all, he is still revered as a superlative "gentleman sailor." To be this kind of gentleman sailor in Boston is of course like being the best gentleman rider in Philadelphia or Virginia, an achievement in physical skill and courage which can only be truly appreciated by other sailors. In a way he had a "national reputation" as elevated as any of his ancestors, Henry's books or John's presidency. However, there are not quite as many sailors as readers or voters.*

To have to succeed to this reputation as seaman and financier would be enough to break the psyche of anyone but an Adams. Nonetheless son CFA[4] has done it. He has succeeded to his father in precisely the way one Adams always succeeds to the prominent forebear in the generation before him — high achievement on a slightly lower level, just one step down (the jet of water falling from granite basin to granite basin). As the most prominent living male Adams, the present Charles Francis (Harvard '32) is also a financial power and a sailor. Starting from a beginning as trustee and broker, he took over the business management of Raytheon,

---

* The other Families have not been idle in the world of sport either. The du Ponts are famous in horse-racing circles, not only because of the thoroughbred Kelso. And a Blair Lee was on the champion 1965 Princeton football team.

was for years its president (without the disasters of other Adams presidencies), and has now moved up to the chairmanship. Raytheon is one of the largest of the electronic firms that have sparked the present industrial renaissance of Boston with laboratories and factories around in a circle along the new belt expressway. Raytheon employs about fifty thousand workers and has numerous branches elsewhere; as the man who has led it to its present eminence, Adams can certainly consider himself thoroughly successful. True, this is not quite the same as being First Citizen of Boston and secretary of the navy (or president of the Union Pacific or wartime ambassador to Great Britain or President of the U.S.A.) but still . . .

CFA⁴ has also inherited his father's skill as a sailor, though not his national reputation. One nice Adams incident: while beating across Buzzards Bay in a fresh sou'wester, Adams' fifty-foot cutter, *Auk III,* was observed by its passengers to be on a direct collision course with a five-hundred-foot American Export Line freighter. As skipper of *Auk III,* CFA⁴ continued imperturbably to hold his course, despite increasing hysteria among his crew. Finally, perhaps twenty yards from a fatal conjunction, the freighter, engines rung up to full-speed astern, boiled to a stop. An infuriated officer on the bridge shouted down: "Who the hell are you and what the hell do you think you're doing?" "I am C. F. Adams, and I have the right of way." Adamses so often have had, and have kept to their collision courses.

CFA⁴ thus remains the sixth consecutive man of outstanding merit in his family; not quite in direct line of course, due to that sudden genetic shift in the fourth generation. From the first John (of whom Benjamin Franklin so damningly said, "Always an honest man, often a wise one, but sometimes, and in some things, absolutely out of his senses"), through John Quincy (Emerson's "bruiser") and Charles Francis Adams ("the greatest iceberg in the Northern Hemisphere"), through CFA², who refused to go through side doors, through another CFA and then still another (this one referred to on occasion as "the rudest man in the Somerset

Club," which is going some), the Adamses have continued to be right and ungracious. Adamses.

A John Quincy Adams (Harvard '45) of this branch, first cousin of CFA[4] through an Arthur, is a vice president of the John Hancock Insurance Company (whose "old building," a sizable modern skyscraper, is about to be superseded by an even bigger one. The "old building" contains a Dorothy Quincy suite). There's something nicely apposite about an Adams being a vice president to a Hancock. All in the family.

In the other Charles Francis branch, a Thomas Boylston Adams, whose mother came from Kansas City, where his father, a twin son John of CFA[2], lived for a spell and where his grandfather owned the stockyards, has become the chief tender of the shrine — president of the Massachusetts Historical Society, like both grandfather and father; president of the board of the Boston Athenaeum, whose largest early gift of books came from JQA. A "retired innkeeper" as he has been known to describe himself (that is, formerly associated with the Sheraton Hotel corporation), he is now known for witty speeches, historical lore and running for various minor political offices, unsuccessfully.

There are some other Royal Adamses; another JQA, for instance. But not many. Almost all of them live around Boston, several in a beautiful exurb called Dover, southwestwards from the Hub. None still live in modern Quincy, though in fact it is not as drab as one might suspect from the fact that the Adamses won't live there anymore. Some Adamses still dive and sail off "Cohasset Rocks" at the Glades. None of them are nationally famous, but they have pretty well consolidated their primary position in Boston, despite keen Cabot-Lowell competition. They remain, of these five families, certainly the most continuously distinguished. Probably in their sixth generation, still the most distinguished example of direct hereditary merit in America.

Roosevelts

The Roosevelts are different. Having exploded in the two deto-
natingly colorful careers of Theodore and Franklin (the rockets' red
glare, the bombs bursting in air), the two branches seem to be dis-
persing and dissipating like the aftermath of fireworks. The sons of
Franklin are of course still much in the news; but not always fortunately. For instance, one of the latest headline appearances could
not have been more unfortunate. James' latest wife, while they were
resident in otherwise placid Switzerland, tried to stab him to death
in a fit of insanity. The "national reputation" of the Hyde Parkers
has been much too full of this sort of thing. The sons' real if modest
accomplishments have been obscured either by scandals and notoriety, or by too much publicity based purely upon their parents' fame.
The next generation is on the whole still too young to have done
much except graduate from college and marry. One exception is
Curtis Dall ("Buzzie"), son of Anna, who has changed his name to
Roosevelt, married several times, and works with his grandmother's
old firm, the United Nations.

 Meanwhile, after suffering somewhat the same general kind of
false publicity, without the marital scandal, the children of Theodore have left grandchildren and great-grandchildren who have
tended to merge, like du Ponts, into a sort of family mass — "Oyster
Bay Roosevelts"; although in fact not so many live in Oyster Bay
now, even in summer. It still remains, in a residual way, a Roosevelt center, but obviously a dying one. Sagamore Hill and next-door
Old Orchard, the house of Theodore junior, both belong to the
National Park Service. Yellowbanks, oldest of the lot, is still
owned by a Roosevelt, but not very actively used it would seem.
There are other Roosevelt houses tucked away in the oak woods
out there, but most younger males have moved out, either to con-
tiguous Long Island suburbs like Syosset or altogether away. Cove

Neck itself seems to be a somewhat nostalgically romantic place of elders and widows.

A representative specimen of modern Oyster Bay Roosevelt might be Theodore Roosevelt III (Harvard '36). He, however, lives not on Long Island but in Philadelphia, married to a native there, and a successful partner of the Philadelphia investment brokerage firm of Montgomery, Scott (after a brief period with du Pont). He is an accepted member of the same essential Philadelphia clubs that cherish Charles J. Biddle or P. Blair Lee. He has a son, Theodore IV, just out of Harvard, and seems to be a universally liked and respected figure of private, not public, reputation. If he gets into the papers (and nearly everybody in Philadelphia sooner or later gets into the two local papers), it is on the financial and social, not the front, pages. The fact that he has made his secure but modest upper-class niche in Philadelphia, rather than the more Roosevelt-oriented New York or Washington, is in itself a sort of sign of merit. The name Roosevelt can't have been much help in the particular circles in which he has been moving, since both Theodore and Franklin were violently unpopular there; more the occasion for groans and hisses than cheers. Though the name may be a handicap on the Main Line, it remains famous among slum dwellers and sharecroppers, Russians and Africans. The Roosevelts are still certainly the most famous of American families.

Self-Made Men?

What has been most characteristic of these families these late years has been just this kind of Theodore III merit and success, that of the ordinary professional and business "self-made man" — of Family. Many examples could be cited parallel or equal to CFA[4] and Theodore III. This kind of success is meritorious all right, but it is not usually conducive to national fame unless very spectacular; or even notorious like the reputation of Jay Gould, that enemy of CFA[2].

Among Biddles and Lees, those two other somewhat older Phila-delphians, C. J. Biddle (Princeton '11) and P. Blair Lee (Princeton '18), are equally representative of this sort of merit and success as lawyer and banker respectively. Charles John Biddle, just recently retired as a senior partner of Drinker, Biddle and Reath, is the pres-ent incumbent of beautifully classic Andalusia. He inherited it from his father, who in turn got it from Judge Craig, a childless son of Nicholas the Great. Judge Craig, who lived on until 1910, spent his summers there with his unmarried sisters. They existed in al-most Bostonian simplicity without central heating or plumbing, and it is only in comparatively recent times that the house has been habit-able all year long. The Judge, famous as a wit and character, used to commute to Philadelphia by boat down the Delaware River. The house also used to have its own railroad station called Andalusia (now demolished of course) and a small town of that name has grown up about it (as has the big Washington suburb of Arlington around that house). The present Charles J.'s other claim to fame, besides the law, is as an aviator in World War I. An ace of the Red Baron period, along with Quentin Roosevelt, he wrote a book of experiences, *The Way of the Eagle,* recently republished as a "clas-sic of aviation."

Similarly, P. Blair, son of Senator Blair, grandson of Admiral Samuel, great-great-grandson of Richard Henry, son of Thomas of Stratford, has occupied the same sort of comfortable, elevated, se-cure and, outside of Philadelphia, inconspicuous niche. He is the retired president of a famous old bank formerly called the Western Saving Fund Society (once usually abbreviated, like the PSFS, to WSFS and now shortened to just the Western) and was, as chair-man of the Philadelphia Housing Authority, involved in the up-heaval known as the Philadelphia Renaissance, a sort of belated local New Deal which has been remodeling the city politically and architecturally. When Philadelphians make the kind of list of City Fathers, in newspapers or elsewhere, that they like to make, the name of P. Blair Lee is always included, usually along with that of C. J. Biddle. Like CFA⁴ of Raytheon, they are local establishers of their families' primacy, carriers of the strain of hereditary merit — but still *not* nationally famous.*

It would be boring and superfluous to continue to list the many others, young and old, who as members of these families continue to maintain said families in prosperity and respectability: army and navy (General William Shepard Biddle III of the Detroit branch, and Admiral Fitzhugh Lee, grandnephew of Robert E., at one time commandant of the Naval War College — both now retired); diplomacy (Angier Biddle Duke, grandson of Mad Anthony, former chief of protocol, then ambassador to Spain, and Armistead Lee, son of Edmund J. of Chatham, foreign service officer); learning (George Homans at Harvard, Maurice du Pont Lee as professor of history at Princeton, Illinois and Rutgers); and numberless men of finance and business. This kind of thing shows continuing merit, all right, but not much in the way of journalistic excitement.

Biddles

Actually, as noticed previously, it is by now, at this time of history, the Family itself that looms as important rather than individuals. As just families, the Adams are still prominent despite their few numbers, and still Bostonians; the Roosevelts are more in numbers, but less distinguished individually in a younger generation. They make up a nucleus of some score of different family groups, mostly still resident in or around New York, of social and financial authority and aplomb. The situation with the Biddles and du Ponts is a bit different. Here the Family-ness is rather staggering. In a city like Philadelphia, which is inordinately Family-conscious, the Biddles continue to have a kind of position which is, like the Order of the Garter, rather aside from mere damn merit.

---

* This business of "fame" and "merit" poses problems. Secretary CFA³ was surely more meritorious than notorious. The opposite is true of AJDB Sr. Everybody's heard of *The Happiest Millionaire*. But how many of Secretary Adams?

Part of this is numbers. There are still more Biddles in Philadelphia (and more du Ponts in Wilmington) than there are anything else of this particular sort. Upper Biddles, Middle Biddles, Solid Biddles, Romantic Biddles, rich and poor, well known and obscure, socially flamboyant, recessively eccentric, Biddles are all over the place. No one would pretend that the Roosevelts, despite their worldwide fame, are Family Number One, as such, in New York. The grudgingly-granted number oneness of the Adamses in Boston is obviously based on continuing individual get-up and grit. The du Ponts dominate Wilmington by sheer weight of power and prestige and money, huge frogs in a smallish puddle. The Lees no longer have a home state (Virginia) nor a hometown (Alexandria) which they can dominate, since most of them live elsewhere. No one in Philadelphia, least of all descendants of Cadwaladers, Shippens, Willings, Morrisses or Norrises, is going to admit that Biddles are Number One. No Biddle is going to *say* so. Nonetheless, they have certain claims. There are so many of them (almost forty family listings in the *Social Register*), they have persisted steadily in numbers, position, board and club membership and social activity continuously from the Revolution to the present, and — a special, but in Philadelphia rather extraneous, grace note — they do have all that merit.

"Everybody" (that is, upper-class Philadelphians) says Biddles of course aren't *really* Old Philadelphians. After all, the Revolution is only just over. Everybody says they are dying out and not amounting to much these days (like S. Weir Mitchell). Of course there's still one on every board, but that's just tradition. Everybody in fact would sooner die than admit them as a family to the sort of social presidency in Philadelphia that the Adams have forced upon Boston. Still, the Biddles and their in-laws and their cousins and their cousins' in-laws are stuck all around through the Philadelphia suburbs like raisins in a plum cake. A vast root system of kinship connects them with the well placed in what is still America's fourth largest and one of its richest cities. Though without an historical patina equivalent to the Adamses or Lees, or the economic force of the du Ponts, they sit on a kind of massed basic social position that it would be hard to parallel or duplicate (or even quite describe) — tenure-cum-money-cum-merit diffused among half a hundred individual representatives for a hundred and a half years. In this vague area of "social prestige," the Biddles are certainly more thoroughly embedded in a specific large community than any other of these five families; and perhaps, though one certainly would not care to debate the question, are presently more purely "socially preeminent" than any other American family in numbers, wealth, length of continuity, local prestige, and accrued accomplishment all *combined*.*

Du Ponts

The exact relative present position of Biddles to other similar families may be ambiguous. There is nothing ambiguous about the present position of the du Ponts. They are America's oldest-richest family, and that is that. Other families (all other four of these five) are older in America. Other equivalent superrich families like the Mellons of Pittsburgh, the Rockefellers of Cleveland and New York, the Fords of Detroit, may possibly be richer, or have more easily ascertainable concentrated-in-family-hands private wealth. But these are all so much more recent. As rich *families*, they exist only in the twentieth century since the deaths of Andrew Mellon, John D. Rockefeller Sr. and Henry Ford Sr. The du Ponts, thanks to their early communism, were already established as a rich *family* by mid-nineteenth century, as Sidney Fisher intimates. They are still famous as a rich family in mid-twentieth century. Unlike some other rich families this richness is not in a few identifiable hands. There are not dozens and dozens of Rockefellers, Mellons and Fords. There are dozens and dozens of du Ponts. They occupy just about the same amount of space in the same *Social Register* as the Biddles (almost forty listings in the Philadelphia book; Wilmington

* The Tafts are more recent, the Cabot-Lowells less numerous, various Southern clans less rich, etc.

is included because it's so small and so close). Though not all the du Ponts there listed have shares in the Company or the various holding companies like Christiana Securities, or in the inherited complex of trusts and estates, most of them probably do have *some* financial connection with the cloud of gold that hovers rather ominously over the Brandywine (the du Ponts and their in-laws and their cousins and their cousins' in-laws). Some members of the family, like Lammot du Pont Copeland, or moribund Mrs. Alfred (Jessie Ball) are obviously enormously rich, live in great palaces; Copeland in a blown-up Virginia plantation house called Mount Cuba, built all of rosy, handmade bricks; Mrs. Alfred still in walled-in Nemours. These are known to have wide financial connections. Others live in charmingly secluded Andrew Wyeth–cum–swimming pool farmhouses and hunt things and are merely "comfortable." Some are connected with the Company; others have made it in other fields on their own. Lairds, Carpenters, Bissells, Bucks, Bredins, and dozens of others, all kin, fill the country around Wilmington with their houses, horses, and children; fill the du Pont–built business offices in downtown Wilmington with their various professions and affairs.

According to Ferdinand Lundberg, that egregious muckraker, in his best-selling *The Rich and the Super-Rich,* the du Ponts as a collective entity, a combination, are still the richest family in America. Just how rich he thinks they are is a bit hard to determine, a matter of some seven billions. And a very bad thing it is too, according to Mr. Lundberg, since those superrich are engaged in a conspiracy to defraud starveling morons like you and me of our few miserable pennies in order to buy up Congress, the army, the navy, and the Post Office Department for their own sinister ends. In real fact it would be almost impossible to determine (a) who "the du Ponts" actually are (Lundberg estimates there are "250 big du Ponts"), (b) how rich these du Ponts are, (c) to what extent they are a combination, sinister or otherwise. In the days of Pierre the Magnificent, Sieur de Longwood, Chevalier of the Order of Chevrolet, who actually himself ran and controlled both General Motors and the then totally triumphant E. I. du Pont de Nemours Company, not to mention all sorts of subsidiaries, holding companies, trusts and directorships, the family fortune might perhaps have been computed, using Pierre as a center, his brothers (and some others) as allies, with Coleman a bit to one side and Alfred's great fortune lying out beyond, segregated, but still indisputably du Pont. Nowadays who can tell? Is Ed Ball's stranglehold on Florida real estate and southern railroads to be counted as "du Pont money" because it originated with his brother-in-law Alfred? Is the famous New York brokerage firm of Francis I. du Pont, started in the thirties with branches in every city, and still run and owned by sure-enough genuine ex-Wilmington du Ponts, but having no direct connections with either the Company or Wilmington, to be included here? How about the varying fortunes of in-laws like the Bayards (Delaware's first family politically for five generations, related to the Bayards of patroon New York, connected now for two generations to the comparatively parvenu du Ponts) or the Irvings of New York; or the Peytons of Princeton, New Jersey, who once quarreled with du Ponts over powder mills in California, but now sit on du Pont boards? Are all these part of the superrich du Pont conspiracy? There certainly exists that "cloud of gold," that great floating mass of capital, which could be labeled "du Pont money," and which seems to have a separate Frankenstein-monster life of its own.

Perhaps. Perhaps every single living descendant of Pierre Samuel has to consider himself, no matter what his last name may be, "part of the family." And hence part of the conspiracy. Certainly few other American families go to such lengths to keep themselves together. For instance: 1) Some rather obscure gland of the Company, in charge of a Laird cousin, secretes genealogy and produces at intervals an extraordinary family tree, which is sent gratis to any head of family recorded in it. The book is almost as massive as the latest coffee-table book of Wyeth reproductions. In it, on separate spiral-bound charts, the complete descent of every single twig of the family down from Pierre of Paris is displayed, up-to-date now as of about 1963. It is a model of genealogical research and production. No one escapes. 2) A companion publication, unfortunately complete only up as far as about 1936, is a set of thick books of pictures (paintings or photographs) of every single one of these descendants. A blank space is left for the few who have no surviving likenesses. This marvelous panorama of physiognomies sure enough reveals the stamp of family likeness. One face in particular occurs and reoccurs — an unmistakably French, square face with strong black eyebrows, piercing black eyes, short nose, handsome firm mouth and a chin with that dimple which was part of the charm of Anne de Montchanin. Edmond du Pont, president of the brokerage firm of F.L. is a good sample (but no dimple). 3) Every New Year's Day a great circumambulatory family reception is held in Wilmington. Ladies of the family within geographical reach (as far as New York at least) are sent a mimeographed sheet ordering them to be at a certain specific locale, a country club or a château, at such and such a time to receive the hordes of husbands who drive about from one of these depots to another, like an all-male garden tour. Some designated women accept and stand, others throw the sheet into the wastebasket with a ladylike curse. But they all keep right on getting their orders every year. 4) Occasionally a great reunion takes place, to which anybody who can go goes. Such things, according to even noncooperative family members, are not to be missed. The grandest was on January 1, 1950, and over six hundred people attended. It celebrated the one hundred and fiftieth anniversary of the landing of the family at Newport, and some of the menu attempted to duplicate that of the impromptu party of 1800 (johnnycake, game pies). Other items, like champagne, were added. Dinner was served at Pierre's Longwood, and everyone was assessed fifty cents for each year of his age. Pierre paid forty dollars. Other families have reunions and bulletins and associations (notably Lees and Howlands), but none that I know of is organized in quite such a well-subsidized and efficient way. A conspiracy?

As for the Company itself, one gets an impression (really nothing more) that perhaps family control *is* relaxing, and even that the Company itself isn't quite what it was. However, the various boards of directors remain weighted with du Ponts and cousins and in-laws. Of the twenty-six directors of the Company nominated in 1969, only four are actually named du Pont, but thirteen (including Mc-Coy) are "kin." Of the nine members of the powerful Finance Committee, eight are family. Back of this are the foundations and trusts and holding companies that control stock and wield influence. These are certainly in family hands. One supposes, it remains safe to say (this is not the kind of thing that is made easily available), that directly or indirectly the family controls the lion's share of the Company and the Company still controls the lion's share, no longer so much of powder making as of chemical synthetics. Whether or not through back-door residual control of General Motors and U.S. Rubber, *et al.,* the family and the Company control a lion's share of the American economy, knows God; and perhaps one or two key du Ponts.

Still, it is notable that of the ten du Ponts, as opposed of course to plain Duponts* listed in *Who's Who* for 1968–69, only five have a present direct connection with the Company as officers or employees; and of these, some (Henry of Winterthur for instance) are superannuated. The record of the Company in *Fortune's* annual survey has been steadily downwards in relative national position, in some areas at least, since the first one in 1954. Though its rank remains in the first dozen as to sales, the Company was number four in assets in 1954; it rated number eighteen in assets in 1967, with a

---

* There are at least five different ways of writing the name now in use in America: Dupont, Du Pont, DuPont, du Pont and duPont. "du Pont" is the official family version, used by both the Company and by the brokerage house; but alas not by every genuine member of the family. In general, one can say that a Dupont is definitely not of the Family, that a du Pont pretty definitely is, and that other variants might or might not be. The name is really common only in places with a background of French settlement. There are some four columns in the Montreal telephone book — Duponts of course; some fifty Duponts in New Orleans. In Wilmington the half-hundred listings are all du Pont or Du Pont. No Duponts. Elsewhere in the nation, a mishmash.

similar decline in net profits and capital investments. Du Ponts no longer, since the antitrust suit of 1957, officially control General Motors.* Perhaps behind the scenes another great dynastic battle is brewing, in which the Family will either lose control of the Company altogether, or sending up new men of merit will once more firmly reassert itself, as in the days of the Triumvirate of Cousins. Meanwhile, no one disputes the du Pont's position as oldest-richest family in America; and perhaps still oldest-richest-most-powerful.

Lees

And then there are the Lees. They certainly are not America's richest or most powerful family, and indeed would probably be disdainful of these particular honors. They are not, however, notably poor. The ancient division into a Stratford branch and a Leesylvania branch, which split the more active members of the family at the time of the Revolution, was dissolved in the next generation by that frenzy of intermarriage, mostly on the part of the children of Richard Henry; none of whom, incidentally, was particularly distinguished. As a result, many Lees are now both Stratford and Leesylvania, and the branch divisions are different. One can make out at least three groups, out of many, who best represent the family nowadays.

First and still foremost in prestige are the Confederate Lees — the descendants of Robert E. or his brothers. Robert's own family was almost liquidated by father worship, that is, the spinsterhood of his daughters, and the bachelorhood of Custis. Rooney's children by his second wife, a Bolling (Bollings related to Tabbs, Tabbs to Barksdales, Barksdales to du Ponts) survived, however, and in turn reproduced. Dr. George Bolling Lee of New York was one of these distinguished reproductions. Having married westward, his family

---

* This absentee landlordship of du Ponts over Detroit seems to have had its effect. Whereas the Fords are indisputably First Family there financially, socially and culturally, no comparable General Motors dynasty has emerged. The gap is striking.

has moved all the way out to San Francisco, far from the Lee Society and all that. A Robert E. Lee IV now lives in California, and probably must be considered the "titular Lee" of the family for the present day. He is a businessman.

Another Lee of this branch is Admiral Fitzhugh, son of army officer George Mason, son of cavalryman Fitzhugh, son of Robert's naval brother Smith, whom Mrs. Chesnut preferred. These Lees are strictly Leesylvania Lees.

Then there's the Union branch — the Blair Lees. Their marital alliances northward to the Blairs of Missouri and Maryland, and to the Brookes of Birdsboro, have turned them into Mugwup Northerners (though still Democrats). However, Maryland is not far from Virginia, and P. Blair's brother Colonel Brooke still lives at Silver Spring. He and his family have been active, but not very successfully, in local Maryland politics. These Lees are strictly Stratford Lees, down from Richard Henry.

In between, neither identifiably Union or Confederate, are the Cazenove Lees. They are the ones who are so mixed up with the du Ponts. A Cazenove Gardner Lee Jr. (1882–1945) lived in Washington and, like Thomas Boylston Adams in Boston, was the principal tender of the shrine while he lived. He did all sorts of useful research into the origins of the Lees in England and into their ancient properties in Virginia. In his widow's house in Washington are now kept most of the original Lee portraits; and there lives a present-day Richard Henry Lee, their son, who devotes himself to Christian Science activities. Cazenove's brother, Maurice du Pont Lee Sr., lives in Wilmington, retired after years with the Company. The descendants of these two are scattered about the country, male and female. One daughter is married to a senior editor of the *Reader's Digest*. One son is married to a New Zealander, lives in Connecticut, and works with a big chemical company. This branch is descended from both Stratford and Leesylvania Lees, and from Alfred V. and Irénée du Pont; not to mention Gardners, Cazenoves, and Hendersons. In the Great Feud, they sided with Alfred against Pierre and were among the few du Ponts mentioned in Alfred's will. There are other branches of course, but these three now seem to be the most evident. Of these five families, the Lees are the most anciently established, the most obviously aristocratic.

No Lee has been great and famous lately, but a member of the Family — kin in the broadest sense, that of the interrelated planter aristocracy of Virginia — has been at least one of the very greatest American soldiers, if not the greatest, of his century: George Catlin Marshall. He is of the same family as the Chief Justice (who was related to the Randolphs, and hence to everybody), and seems to have inherited many of the characteristics of both George Washington and Robert E. Lee (whose sister married a Marshall). He too was rather austere, rather impassive, a model of courtesy, formality, fortitude and probity. He too added that extra dimension of service after war to his reputation, exemplified by Washington's Presidency, Lee's work of reconciliation at Washington College, and by the Marshall Plan in Europe. Evidently we can hope for one of this kind, from the same hereditary source, every hundred years or so.

Tenure

The Lees are the only one of these Families who were well established before the Revolution; and who are not, now at least, a social and financial power in their original homeland. There are Lees and Lee descendants in Virginia, but the basis of their original prosperity, tobacco planting, has long been liquidated there, and their shift from landowning to the services and professions has scattered them about to the centers where such professions succeed. It is a question whether a Family can eventually survive as a Family in exile, uprooted from its soil. The fact, at least, is that the four other families have retained prestige just by being so rooted. This rooting, however, is *not* hereditary meritocracy, but something quite different.

To use (once and once only) an even more fearsome neologism, it is that "hereditary tenurocracy" already discussed in connection with the immediate ancestors of FDR.

It is very hard to draw a strict line between the inheritance of merit, of which in general democratic Americans tend to approve — generation after generation of what are in fact self-made men — and this contradictory sort of inheritance by tenure. The former presupposes the handing down of character, genes, energy, a tradition of accomplishment, a duty to the Family of bestirring oneself to some purpose. The latter presupposes the handing down of tangible property, privileges, tradition and the ability to hold onto them. This is much closer to the tradition of European aristocracy, those six hundred years of Shropshire Lees at Coton Hall. This kind of heredity is not popular among democratic Americans and has always been looked on with suspicion and no little contempt. It is around this conception of class inheritance that the "shirt-sleeves to shirt-sleeves" mythology has been developed; not without reason of course, especially when families rise too fast too soon. Families of pure tenure go to seed like others, but in fact many of them go on and on, in America as well as in Shropshire. They do it by being careful, by marrying well, and by engaging in the safe guardianships of capital and land on which their security rests. And this all does take merit, hereditary merit. But one can say that the kind of merit displayed by Secretary Charles Francis Adams, by lawyer Charles John Biddle or by banker P. Blair Lee comes perhaps closer to that of tenure than does, for instance, the risky business of American politics or diplomacy or high finance as indulged in by their ancestors.

In general one could presume that the tendency of later generations of meritocracy is to relapse into tenure — to become "nice," guarding what one has (like Richard Lee II or William Biddle II), rather than going in for pioneering individual achievement. The basic history of the Roosevelts and the Biddles, as families, the soil from which their men of merit are to some extent exotic growths, is hereditary tenure. Dr. Isaac of Mount Hope, botanizer and marrier of Aspinwalls, is really more representative of Roosevelts as a whole than Theodore and Franklin.

So in a way these families and all Families are a mixture — some merit, some tenure, some failure. The Lees have avoided shirt-sleeves and demonstrated successful merit of either achievement or tenure in eight straight generations, beginning with Richard I (achievement), Richard II (tenure), Thomas (achievement), Richard Henry (achievement), his son Francis (minimum tenure), Admiral Samuel Phillips (modest achievement), Senator Blair and son P. Blair (a mixture of modest achievement and tenure). The other Lees, those of Leesylvania, one generation more advanced at the time of the Revolution, show tenure rather than achievement until one gets to Harry in the fifth and Robert in the sixth generation.

With the du Ponts one can trace at least one continuous span of five generations leading from achievement to tenure (but always successful), through Pierre, Irénée, Henry the Great, Colonel Henry, to Henry of Winterthur. Of all du Ponts this might possibly be the most unbroken and directly meritorious line. With the Adamses one bowls right down the hereditary alley, except for that odd jog through nice John (President John, JQA, CFA[1], CFA[2], CFA[3], CFA[4]), moving always tenure-ward, yet never losing a strong emphasis on personal achievement. Odd but sad that all these three particular lines now seem to be broken. No descendants of P. Blair Lee have distinguished themselves. Henry of Winterthur had no sons; and the sons of CFA[4] are semi-invalids. The case of the Biddles and Roosevelts is different. Here one has spasms of tenure (those Hudson River country gentlemen, James, Dr. Isaac, James) interrupted by somewhat sporadic displays of talent (Nicholas the goldsmith; Nicholas the steamboater; in the present generation, a Nicholas who is a well-known foreign correspondent and former minister to Hungary, brought up in Oyster Bay but now living in California). It might be possible to say that the Adamses are basically a family of achievement, increasingly buttressed by tenure, and the Biddles are basically a family of tenure, ornamented by achievement. The other three families range on some scale in between, a blend of both.

3

Kin

ANOTHER qualification here, besides the ambivalence between an heredity of talents versus an heredity of assets, is the very definition of "Family." It is easy to say the family consists of just those bearing the family name. As we all know in personal experience, that is far from being the case. Mother's widowed sister Aunt Tillie is the real power around the house. There may be one hundred thousand Adamses descended from Henry of Braintree. They are not "The Adams Family." But the Homans are, and so are others like them (Perkins, Lovering, etc.), closely connected through marriage and social familiarity. Around those bearers of the name who count spreads what has been already called the root system of kinship and cousinship. In the case of the Adamses it is fairly limited. In the case of the du Ponts it is enormous, but still definite. In the case of the Biddles it is enormous and inextricably confused. For instance it would be generally understood in Philadelphia that Happy Rockefeller (Mrs. Nelson Rockefeller), as a Fitler, would derive much of her family prestige from her Middle Biddle connections. From now on in Philadelphia, the Rockefellers are "kin." The situation is even more acute among the du Ponts, where everybody is so carefully kept track of.

Since these root systems extend for great distances in time and space, it can be pretty well assumed that *any* American family that has had means and gentility for five or more generations is probably very distantly related and connected to every other such family; which of course includes all these five. This is particularly true of families whose descent, if not gentility, begins from some original seventeenth-century settlement. An ingenious genealogist once figured out a "Royal Family" which connected some dozen Presidents through this sort of root system — Washington, Madison, the Adamses, the Harrisons, the Roosevelts, Taft and others. You have to trace right far back, to people like Isaac Allerton of the Banqueting Hall, but it can be done. Other similar bonds exist throughout among these five families, some already mentioned: those Ogdens of New Jersey with their cross-connections to Adamses, Roosevelts and Detroit Biddles, those ubiquitous Randolphs, who rope in everybody — Lees, Biddles, du Ponts, even the Adamses, perhaps, since a Randolph once married a Massachusetts Coolidge back in the earlier nineteenth century, and ever afterwards Proper Bostonians have been marrying Coolidges. Another ubiquitous family has been the Lees of *Massachusetts.* They are prime Essex Junto people, hence related to Cabots, Lowells, Saltonstalls, etc. Theodore Roosevelt's first wife was one of these Lees. Edward Biddle, who married a Drexel, then married such a Lee. A Francis I. du Pont II of recent vintage married a Rosamund Saltonstall Lee, who ought to be related. Another less-recent Massachusetts Lee married a Virginia Tucker, so that living until recently in Richmond, Virginia, was a St. George Tucker Lee who was a *Boston* Lee! What confusion. Finally Arthur Adams, father of the present John Hancock vice president John Quincy, also married a Lee. There must be dozens of other such ties between these families. Anyone with any ancestral claims can spend many a happy hour linking himself by hook or crook to one of these families, and hence to all of them.

However, there are much more direct connections. All these families in fact, except the Adamses, married du Ponts, who thus form a kind of total family mucilage. The first and best established of these linkages was that between Lee and du Pont. To recapitulate: it all began before the Civil War with that unfortunate wedding of rebel Charlotte Henderson (Hendersons already vague Lee kin) to an Eleuthère du Pont, son of Alfred Victor and Margaretta Lammot. Their orphan child was pugnacious Alfred I. Meanwhile Charlotte's father, General Archibald, had married Anne Cazenove. Anne Cazenove's sister Eliza had married a Gardner, and their daughter Anne Gardner married Cassius Lee, descendant of both Stratford and Leesylvania. The son of Cassius, Cazenove Gardner Lee, then married Marguerite du Pont, sister of Alfred I., daughter of Eleuthère du Pont, who had married Charlotte Henderson (round and round). By now the various du Pont Lees and the children of Alfred and his ex-wife Bessie Gardner (such as architect Alfred V., whose name was *not* changed to Dorsey Cazenove) are firmly knit together. The Lees and the du Ponts are *related* (See Appendix V).

Next, and much later chronologically, was the celebrated marriage of Ethel du Pont, granddaughter of President Eugene, to Franklin D. Roosevelt Jr. in 1937; a first, but not last, marriage for both of them. Since at that time the du Pont-supported Liberty League was in full anti-Franklin cry there was a definitely Romeo-Juliet, Montague-Capulet atmosphere about it all; various important du Ponts refused to attend the wedding, and it was a newshawk's field day. The marriage lasted no longer than some other Roosevelt marriages of this generation. After the birth of two sons, FDR III and Christopher du Pont, they were divorced. Franklin junior went on to marry Suzanne Perrin. Ethel married Benjamin S. Warren Jr. She lived in Detroit, and there in a handsome house on Provencal (pronounced Provéncal) Road, within sight of the vast Grosse Pointe Country Club, she committed suicide in 1965. So the blight on Roosevelt marriages has extended to the du Ponts.

The third and latest linkage has been flagrantly dynastic. In 1959 James Biddle, son of Charles of Andalusia, married Louisa Copeland, daughter of Lammot of Mount Cuba. Among younger Biddles, James is now the one likely to be seen in the public eye. He began as curator of the American Wing of the Metropolitan Museum of New York and has gone on to be president of the National Trust with headquarters in Washington. The National Trust, from feeble beginnings as an imitation of the vigorous outfit in England, has grown more and more effective. It devotes itself to preserving noteworthy old houses all over America and encouraging civic beautification and conservation. Backed by Henry of Winterthur and many others, it has been getting lots of newspaper coverage and attracting interest and support, much of this due to the activities of Biddle.

All the children of all these four families — the du Pont Lees, the Franklin Roosevelt Jrs., the James Biddles, and their respective du Pont in-laws — are all cousins.* It is appalling to think of how many other cousins they have — the combined root systems of New England (Delanos, Howlands), New York (Livingstons, Astors, Irvings), Philadelphia (Cadwaladers, Emlens, Shippens via the Lees), Delaware and Maryland (Ridgelys, Bayards), and all of Old Virginia. One big happy Family.

No Adams has yet married a du Pont; but an Adams has married a Morgan, which is pretty much the same thing.

* For just how closely they are related, again see Appendix V.

4

Houses

THE most pleasant memorials these Families have left are their houses. One can follow right up through the architecture of the American country house by taking a tour of Family homesteads. Unfortunately chronology and geography don't quite match. However, start in Virginia with Stratford (the 1730's), especially in spring when all is rich and quiet and green. It has been preserved by a special foundation (Robert E. Lee Memorial Foundation), supported by private funds, and restored as a working plantation. A wonderful sense of space and grace pervades the house, full of fine furniture of the period, and the gardens and fields and woods beyond. There is a glimpse of the Potomac from in back. At that time of year it is hard to imagine the doors chained against creditors, or the macabre last years of Black-Horse Harry. Up the Potomac lie Mount Vernon and Arlington, not of course Lee houses, but with those strong Lee connections — the house where Robert was married, the house where his father-in-law was raised; and a continuation of the architectural survey, a plantation house of the mid-eighteenth century and one of the early nineteenth.

The story is carried on up in Wilmington by the house called the Eleutherian Mills. This is the oldest surviving du Pont homestead, built for Irénée in 1803, supposedly from a design by backer and partner Pierre Bauduy. It was lived in during recent years by the Crowninshields, Mrs. Crowninshield being the sister of Henry of

Winterthur.* The house has now been Winterthurized, beautifully decorated with objects mostly associated with the early days of family history, and is open to the public, but unfortunately (up to the present) only for short periods in spring or fall. It sits on the edge of the tree-choked ravine of the Brandywine, and is surrounded by lands cared for by the Hagley Foundation. In the ravine itself are the remains of the old powder works. Up near the entrance road is Sand Hole Woods Graveyard, where all the original du Ponts are buried.

Next geographically and chronologically comes Andalusia, north of Philadelphia on the otherwise industrialized Delaware. The house is an almost magically preserved example of full Greek Revival, white columns facing lawns down to the river, Napoleonic furniture inside, all dating from the remodeling in 1834–36 by Nicholas the Great and his pet architect Thomas U. Walter. Outside the house are various quaint dependencies, such as a little two-story Grecian pavilion, where Nicholas went to play cards and billiards, and opposite along the water's edge a tiny Gothick chapel built by Nicholas' wife as a sort of antipagan, antigambling, anticlassic protest. Then there is a small bathhouse, which used to contain an ancient marble sarcophagus used by Nicholas and his guests as a tub (cold water only). The tub is now an ornament of the beautiful gardens sheltered by the massive ruined walls completely shrouded in wistaria, that were once part of the famous greenhouses. This particular house is not open to the public, being the only one of these Family houses which is still in Family hands. Sometimes, however, it is available on garden-club tours, etc.

The one missing architectural-chronological link is a true mid-Victorian country house actually built or occupied by one of these families. Sagamore Hill is Victorian enough, but not mid-Victorian. As a substitute, one of the Hudson River houses of a relation might do — Sunnyside, the Washington Irving house in Tarrytown, as

---

* It was the wedding of son John and Fanny Crowninshield that delayed Ambassador CFA's arrival in England in 1861.

Romantic of its period as Andalusia is Classic; the Irvings, after all, became cousins of the du Ponts. Then there is Algonac, the Delano house near Newburgh, though that burned and was rebuilt. Or the numerous Livingston houses up near Rhinebeck, like Rokeby, where once lived the William Astors, in-laws of Franklin Delano of Steen Valletje nearby. However, of these only Sunnyside is open to the public. Lyndhurst, which is Victorian and open, won't do. It belonged to the Enemy, Jay Gould, and is *not* a Family house but a Robber Baron Roost.

In New York City, however, we do have a mid-Victorian house, the brownstone birthplace of Theodore Roosevelt on Twenty-eighth Street. It is of course a town house, not a country house, and it is a restoration, not an original. The family moved northward in 1873 to Fifty-seventh Street (the "cursed" house where Alice and Martha died). In 1896 the older house was sold and was used commercially, the neighborhood having altered. Then in 1919 it was bought back, along with Uncle Bob's old house next door, and refurbished with many of the original pieces. The result is certainly a very fine example of a typical brownstone of the 1850's. Uncle Bob's house is a museum and library. Too bad the house wasn't located just one block east so that, instead of being engulfed by wholesale makers of false fruit, etc., it would be a part of the oasis of Gramercy Park.

Then on Long Island there is Sagamore Hill. One tends to preconceive it in purely Teddy terms — big black halls, mooseheads, stone fireplaces. Actually most of it is in an earlier style, that of the 1880's, and except for the large room built on the back in 1905 (designed by Grant La Farge, son of Henry Adams' bosom friend John), the house is more "old-fashioned" than one would expect, especially "Ethel's room," the dainty front parlor, all light brocade and pastel watercolors, or the picturesquely archaic kitchen. The Sound is almost invisible from the wide piazza these days, due to the growth of the trees, nor are the gardens kept up, but the house is still stuffed with souvenirs and curiosities — African, Japanese,

Amerindian — and the lawns and woods are as they were when Teddy romped about them on his way to strenuous picnics.

Old Orchard next door, the handsome neo-Georgian pre–World War II house of Theodore junior has also been taken over by the National Park Service, like Sagamore Hill. It has no furniture in it, merely various Roosevelt family exhibits. A record of what it was like in its days of formal grace under the "other Eleanor" exists in a charming family group painted by that Wyeth of the salon, John Koch, now in the possession of Theodore junior's daughter-in-law, Mrs. Quentin Roosevelt.

Hyde Park might well do as our example of mid-Victorian country house, except that in the remodeling of 1915 it was split down the middle lengthwise, like a roast chicken, and a handsome neo-Georgian front and wings tacked on. The back of the house, however, is exactly as it was when it was the Springwood of the 1860's — Gothicky gables, brown plaster outside, fussy overupholstered and becurtained decor inside. As at Sagamore Hill, a big, new, paneled living room has been added, with the dignified portraits of Isaac the Patriot and bespectacled James at either end, and a mixture of accumulation in between. The formal false front, so exactly contradictory to Franklin's informal (and many people thought equally false) façade, is still very effective, very dignified; spacious, calm, fronting on a long, flat vista of lawn and trees. The inside will appeal not to decorators but to the nostalgic — a hugger-mugger of inherited furniture and souvenirs of "jaunts abroad." Brass beds, reproductions of Raphael madonnas in the bedrooms, cabinets of curiosities and whatnots in the living rooms. Back of the house the land suddenly drops away to a spectacular view of the river. On the way back to the parking lot is the rose garden, where both Franklin and Eleanor are buried under a block of marble.

Of all these houses, Hyde Park is perhaps the least satisfactory aesthetically and chronologically, but the most livable. It is not quite Victorian enough; but it does, even more than Sagamore Hill, which it so resembles, have a powerful aroma of the American gentry and their nineteenth-century daily living, their avocations, their trips to Europe, their rather uncritical tastes — the delightfully fuggy confusion that no restored house can ever achieve.

Finally we go back to beginnings again with the Adams houses in Quincy. First there are the "birthplaces," two bright-red, small, early-Colonial farmhouses in the crowded center of the modern (though not very modern) town; good, rather primly restored examples of plain New England early eighteenth-century architecture. Then the Old House itself, residence of the family from the time John bought it in 1787 till the death of Brooks in 1927, the last member of the family to live there. Like Sagamore Hill, it is maintained by the National Park Service. It sits in an ample acreage of gardens, fields, pond, shade trees, and is itself a history of the American household interior from 1731, when the rich West Indian merchant Leonard Vassall first built it and paneled the living room with mahogany, through the John Adams addition of the 1790's and the later wings and ells added by JQA and CFA. It is pungent with Adams personality and the charm of their past, cluttered with French furniture from diplomatic days and remarkable family portraits. Outside, by the pretty sampler of an old-fashioned garden stands the small, two-story, stone library, built in 1870 by CFA, which once housed the formidable Adams papers, and now houses a big collection of old family books. On the center table are the latest in that stream of words produced by this word-addicted Family (because it "amused them") — the sociological works of George Homans, inscribed to the library by "a scion."

Except for the comparative unavailability to the public of the Eleutherian Mills and Andalusia, the whole collection leads continuously from the fringes of the seventeenth century (the earliest of the Adams birthplaces) up almost to the present, from the spacious grandeur of Stratford and the forceful quaintness of the Old House to the cluttered charms of Sagamore Hill and Hyde Park; family history in terms of a tapestry of taste and daily living rather than of national events.

5

Summary

"IN AMERICA the aristocratic element has always been feeble from its birth; and if at the present day [1830] it is not actually destroyed, it is at any rate so completely disabled that we can scarcely assign to it any degree of influence in the course of affairs. . . . There is no family or corporate authority, and it is rare to find even the influence of individual character." (This in the Age of Jackson!)

This statement by Alexis de Tocqueville in his admired *Democracy in America* comes as close as any one statement can to defining his attitude towards a real or potential American aristocracy. By "aristocracy" he meant the real thing, power, rulership by an hereditary caste, not just "social superiority." His book is a study in contrast between a Europe he envisages as having once been totally aristocratic and an America he imagines, as of 1830, to be totally democratic. The kind of hereditary aristocracy he sets up as a contradiction to total democracy has indeed been comparatively feeble in America; but only comparatively, as Virginia under Speaker Robinson demonstrates. Most traces of such real aristocracy have certainly been destroyed here as of this particular present (1970). That is, we are definitely not owned and governed by hereditary noblemen. That does not mean, however, that de Tocqueville's kind of total democracy — a totally egalitarian and homogenized social order, a total "tyranny of the majority" — exists or ever has existed. In the frontier Middle West, or the later Middle West of Babbitt, this kind of Procrustean egalitarian version of democracy has perhaps been for a while triumphant.* Some of the more striking aspects of American life as a whole do indeed reflect majority tyranny, but to suppose as de Tocqueville seems to suppose that there are *no* contradictions to this tyranny in America was and is nonsense.

De Tocqueville is most nonsensical in his blind and bland assurance that aristocratical, hereditary and family ideals had no place at all in American life. True, the 1830's were indeed years during which popular reactions against "aristocracy," evidenced by the defeat of J. Q. Adams for President and the defeat of Nicholas Biddle as controller of the economy, were most fervent. However, as the history of these five families should demonstrate, heredity and family continuity, the holding onto family prestige, the leadership of community and country by men of family, the achievement of men of family along hereditary lines are all *characteristic* of America, not exceptional. Certainly one can easily see this emphasis on heredity throughout American society and history as a constant vertical which opposes the tendencies of de Tocqueville's universal horizontal. Whether de Tocqueville and his idolators like it or not, the Lees, for an example, have endured as a family, and with all the appendages of family continuity, for eight, going on nine or ten generations. Such family successions very clearly show that his kind of "aristocratic" tradition — or rather, what I have continually insisted on calling not aristocracy but meritocracy, "rule" by men of family because of their merits — is perfectly compatible with American democracy. Indeed it is one of the results of that democracy. When the Lees or Tuckers turned from landowning to professional

* One sometimes feels in reading de Tocqueville that he spent all his time in Gopher Prairie or Zenith.

life they illustrated a form that the tradition of aristocracy naturally takes in a democratic situation. The Adamses did not make themselves a dynasty by inheriting power and privilege. They did it by following family footsteps with dogged determination. This of course is not at all the same thing as Philip Ludwell Lee's enjoyment of Stratford as eldest son. In fact this succession of merit may not be in any way what de Tocqueville means by aristocratic; but it most certainly is hereditary. It most certainly keeps families going, it most certainly establishes family prestige, it most certainly adds to American society a strong past and present tinge of birth, gentility, tradition, what have you; all those things which are the appendages if not the crude essence of aristocracy.

De Tocqueville evidently could not or would not see any of this. He presumed that the old Federalist mercantile oligarchy of the North and the planters of the South were on their way to extinction. He was right enough as far as he went. As classes they were extinguished. Yet representatives of these classes, the descendants of Federalist Isaac Roosevelt and of planter Thomas Lee, did not necessarily become extinct. Why? Because either plain tenure or a family tradition of individual hereditary merit along either the lines of service, or in the case of the du Ponts, executive and technical ability kept them going through the generations.

De Tocqueville was biased in his picture of American society as a perpetual wheel of shirt-sleeves to shirt-sleeves, a rotation of ill-educated entrepreneurs. God knows there has been plenty of that; his picture was acute and correct as far as it went, a vivid delineation of one very important aspect of democratic civilization. But he was fatally wrong in proposing this as the whole picture.

He does make a few exceptions. He warns against the rise of a capitalist upper class, those "Gold Bugs" who did indeed attempt to take over the country in the Gilded Age as an oligarchy of money power. "I am of the opinion . . . that the manufacturing aristocracy which is growing up under our eyes is one of the harshest which ever existed in the world . . . the friends of democracy should keep their eyes anxiously fixed in this direction; for if ever a permanent inequality of conditions and aristocracy again penetrate into the world, it may be predicted that this is the gate by which they will enter." Henry Adams and Theodore Roosevelt agreed — those two men of Family.

De Tocqueville also makes a rather quixotic exception in the case of lawyers. "In America there are no nobles or literary men, and the people are apt to distrust the wealthy; lawyers consequently form the highest political class and the most cultivated portion of society . . . If I were asked where I place the American aristocracy I should reply, without hesitation, that it is not among the rich, who are united by no common tie, but that it occupies the . . . bench and the bar . . . The lawyers . . . form the most powerful, if not the only, counterpoise to the democratic element." That is, conservative.

This was the age of Clay and Webster, of Marshall and Taney, the high tide of forensic eloquence, of legal luminaries. Nonetheless he did miss the point here. The counterpoise he speaks of is not exclusively legal. The tyranny of the majority he so detests can be resisted from two sides: by the kind of conservative, cautious, well-educated lawyer and professional man and banker (often a man of family tenure) that he is thinking of, and from the other side by the liberal, who may often be a man like Jefferson whose idea of democracy was far from de Tocqueville's, or by leaders of popular opinion like the Roosevelts. The plain conservative opposition to democracy, as evidenced by the typical man of tenure or typical man of wealth, may be useful and inevitable. Conservatism is as important a part of the democratic mechanism as the brake is of the automotive mechanism. De Tocqueville's idea, however, that the steering wheel must be activated purely by a sort of half-educated popular mob or by its ill-chosen representative, in fact that democracy steers itself, is obviously contradicted by history.

Some of the most effective steerers of America have been men of family, members of the meritocracy (but seldom if ever gentlemen of pure tenure). De Tocqueville's failure to account for this, recognize this meritocracy as a fact or a possibility, certainly gives his portrait a very lopsided appearance.

The general outcry at this point might be, "But that's all in the past! What place have such hereditary gentlemen in the present or the future?" There is no doubt that at the moment Adamses, Roosevelts, Biddles, du Ponts and Lees are not what they have been. Perhaps they will never be famous again and this book is in the nature of a memorial. That does not mean that the principle they represent is defunct. As Adams succeeded to Winthrops and Quincys, as Roosevelts to de Lanceys or Biddles to Shippens, so a dynasty like the Kennedys may succeed to them. It is not just the persistence of a certain few families that counts; it is the persistence of the ideal and practice of such family successions that is meaningful. Exactly as in the 1830's, when de Tocqueville visited America, there are in 1970 the same strong currents that run counter to hereditary successions of any kind. Now as then taxes and the division of property by wills threaten the man of tenure and his assets. Now as then genes do dry up, as in the case of the Bizarre Randolphs, and the drive of a dynasty finally falters. There is indeed a widespread suspicion throughout America of anything hereditary, anything that smacks of class superiorities, even superiorities of talent. That meanest of all weaknesses, envious hatred of what is above and contempt of what is below (by no means confined to democracy), will no doubt dishonor America as long as human beings make up its population. Nobody could suggest that Family founding in America is easy or inevitable.

Also, the Mass World that intellectuals so fear and despise, and which technology and democracy seem to favor, is certainly very much opposed to the grim grandeur inherent in the makeup of a John Quincy Adams. The happiness of the largest number seems to have little to do with his sort of family fate. In Aldous Huxley's *Brave New World,* that reactionary satirical-prophetic continuation of de Tocqueville's study of democracy, a character proposes that whenever the masses seize political power, it is "happiness rather than truth or beauty" that matters to them. Was the "decency" that Franklin Roosevelt hoped to achieve for the masses the same as the lobotomized "happiness" of Huxley's new world? Is the "American Way of Life" a happiness to be achieved only at the sacrifice of truth and beauty, of individuality and distinction? Of, in other words, the aristocratic values de Tocqueville cherishes? Many think so. Must we have the aristocratic evils to enjoy these values?

So far American history would seem to prove rather tentatively that we can have our cake and eat it. We can have an hereditary aristocracy of talents without having an hereditary aristocracy of powers. If a family such as the Lees can carry on in America from 1640 to 1970 without any serious break in family continuity despite the total liquidation of the basis of their original class prosperity, there seems to be no sensible reason to believe that other families cannot do likewise — beginning in 1970. This opportunity, like others, is open in a democracy to anyone. Hence the obviously similar dynastic ambitions of a family like the Kennedys. You too can found a Family.

There is no use pretending, however, that following the fate of a dynasty is fun — glory, honor, power, name in newspapers and history books, but hardly "happiness" of the ordinary-guy variety. One can take warning as well as heart by the contemplation of the careers of Adamses, Biddles, Lees (or Kennedys). The greatest of them were scarcely models of mindless good fortune. Happiness had very little to do with the career of Robert E. Lee. If the object of democracy is to make everybody happy and the object of aristocracy is to make a few great, then a family tradition of merit would certainly seem to err on the side of aristocracy.

Still and all, America does not have a true aristocracy, "rule by the best"; even rule by the richest, despite Mr. Lundberg. These families are not hereditary *rulers*. They are just private persons. When they do happen to rule it is largely on their merits; hence meritocracy, "rule by merit." Yet such families do supply and always have supplied those things which de Tocqueville found missing, because perhaps he chose not to see them, in American life: those vertical values of antique tradition (after all, two or three hundred years is quite a long time anywhere), family distinction, breeding, *noblesse oblige* and what have you.

The attempt of the Gold Bugs of the 1890's to set themselves up as an economic *noblesse* centered in New York by means of gaudy palaces, lavish parties, a superficial veneer of cosmopolitanism and foreign marital alliances, was doomed to failure. They could not achieve true aristocracy that way even though they did at the time have the power a real aristocracy ought to have. "Who Killed Society?" asked Cleveland Amory; and failed to answer. The kind of Gilded Age society of Ward McAllister and Harry Lehr killed itself with its own shallowness, vulgarity and lack of true morale. It has a certain raffish glamour and gaudy charm, like any bonanza, but its demise seems unregrettable. Unfortunately most discussions of this whole general area, such as Dixon Wecter's in many ways admirable *Saga of American Society*, tend to mix up that hippogriff "Society," the ostentatious tomfoolery of parvenus, with true family-society, the gentry of tenure and merit. The result is the total confusion of all values, evidenced by the later Cleveland Amory, Stephen Birmingham's *Right People,* and others. If America must have aristocratic traditions (and I think all healthy, normal societies must, so long as they don't overdo it), it is certainly not to the Gold Bugs that it must look for them. Not Vanderbilts and Astors, but their elders and betters constitute a basis for pride of blood. Around families such as these five, different as they are, with their enormous, spreading aura of blood-and-marriage connections, can be created by those who need this kind of thing — the Henry Jameses and T. S. Eliots of the country, who have a horror of the horizontal and featureless — a more-than-sufficient bulwark of gentility. For any purpose *except* that of real hereditary political-economic power, these families will certainly do. As representatives of any of those previously cited "aristocratic values," such as historical glamour or genetical breeding, they embody the antique qualities de Tocqueville regretted, without requiring for their support the antique injustices he deplored. For Americans who choose to be proud of distinction, such families and many others like them should serve to give society a due sense of continuity and honor.

Perhaps a technology-infatuated future will make this kind of heredity difficult or impossible. No one has ever asked who the grandparents of the astronauts were.* From de Tocqueville on it has been universally assumed that time and tide are running against any sort of aristocratic values. Perhaps there are so many levels of American life and so many geographical areas where such values seem nonexistent or laughable or pernicious that it might be rash to say hereditary merit is characteristic of America as a whole. Wiser perhaps to say that it is characteristic only of the upper echelons of the older, east-coastal fringe of the country, but begins to vanish westward. Certainly places like Boston, Philadelphia or Charleston would seem more likely to cherish Families than, say, Los Angeles.

I do not believe this. I think hereditary values are so characteristic of the country that they spring up almost as soon as the soil is planted. Cincinnati is not really a very old city, but what city in the world is more Family-dominated? (Taft, et al.) Idaho as a state has been barely settled for a century, but already the Churches are a political dynasty there. What family could have more hereditary respect than the Youngs in Utah? The automobile business is still wet behind the ears, but already the Ford family has acquired many of the dynastic trappings that the du Ponts have in Delaware. Naturally it takes at least three generations to build up a proper hereditary dynasty, and that requires fifty years at least. But if San Francisco can become as Family-conscious as it is in the hardly-more-than-a-century since 1848, how long should it take L.A.?

* Astronaut Conrad, as a respectable Philadelphian, may well be kin of the Biddles.

As for the Brave New World of astronauts and "happiness," meritocracy has survived Jackson, the Civil War, the Industrial Revolution, the New Deal. In fact, these epochal events have been to a considerable extent engineered by meritocrats. Not being essentially conservative like tenure, merit can easily adapt to changes, or vigorously help reform them. It would be a lot safer to say, on the basis of the past, that the tradition of hereditary merit will flourish as it always has, will be as widespread as America, and will tend to be *more* consciously and universally accepted as the country as a whole ages.*

The fact of the present existence of hereditary merit is unquestionable. There may be questions about those "aristocratic values" themselves. Cannot the tradition of meritocracy turn into a sort of Roman patrician elitism, a fascism of some sort? Enemies were fond of accusing the earlier Adamses of monarchism. There are ominous traces of Hitlerism in the works of later Adamses. Yet one can't really accuse Roosevelts or Kennedys of being reactionary politicians. Actually, all these particular families were famous for their rebels. The fact of the existence of hereditary meritocracy is massive. Presidents and Vice Presidents, cabinet members of all kinds, governors, senators, congressmen, admirals, generals by the score, a few inventors, even some saints and artists stud the ramifications of these family trees in bewildering profusion.† "Blood will tell," though it's sometimes pretty hard to predict just what it will tell. Heredity, whether genetic or environmental, means something. Exactly what it does mean remains a mystery. The *why* is speculation and study; the *what* is history. There is no reason to suppose that it will mean less in the future than it has in the past. It is permanently

---

* The increasing use of III and IV (John Robert Smith III) among upper-echelon Americans seems to indicate an increasingly dynastic feeling. We have a Theodore Roosevelt IV, a Pierre du Pont V, a Livingston Biddle III and a Maurice du Pont Lee III. Any list of Ivy League graduates will confirm the prevalence, far more common nowadays than before the last war. It must mean something — if only the longevity of grandparents.

† See Appendix I.

in the American grain as is rags to riches, say, or riches to rags. In the panorama of the nation's chronicle from Adams to Roosevelt, hereditary meritocracy takes its place securely as one of America's most powerful and respectable traditions.

Appendixes

I

Prominent Officeholders Among
the Five First Families

PRESIDENTS:
J. Adams, J. Q. Adams; Theodore Roosevelt, Franklin D. Roosevelt.

VICE PRESIDENTS:
J. Adams; Theodore Roosevelt.

CABINET MEMBERS:
J. Q. Adams, C. F. Adams III; Charles Lee; Francis Biddle (and all those Roosevelt assistant secretaries).

U.S. SENATORS:
J. Q. Adams; Henry du Pont, T. Coleman du Pont; R. H. Lee, Harry Lee.

U.S. REPRESENTATIVES:
J. Q. Adams, C. F. Adams; James J. Roosevelt, R. B. Roosevelt, James Roosevelt, Franklin D. Roosevelt Jr.; Charles J. Biddle; Richard Bland Lee, Fitzhugh Lee. Various state senators and representatives, aldermen, etc.

CONTINENTAL CONGRESS:
The four Signers (two Adams, two Lees); Edward Biddle; Thomas S. Lee; and others.

STATE GOVERNORS:
Samuel Adams; T. and F. Roosevelt; Thomas S. Lee. Thomas Lee of Stratford and Charles Biddle were acting governors.

DIPLOMATS:
J. Adams, J. Q. Adams, C. F. Adams; R. B. Roosevelt; A. J. D. Biddle Jr.; Arthur Lee, William Lee.

GENERALS:
C. F. Adams II; T. Roosevelt Jr., Elliott Roosevelt; A. J. D. Biddle Jr. and *many* other Biddles; Harry Lee, Robert E. Lee and his sons and neph-

ew. Innumerable officers of army and marines.

ADMIRALS OR COMMODORES: James Biddle; Samuel du Pont; Samuel Phillips Lee, Fitzhugh Lee. Many naval officers.

The professional record is less distinguished (i.e., no Chief Justices, etc.).* Many judges, however, and well-known lawyers. A few well-known doctors (George Bolling Lee; Andrew P. Biddle of Detroit). Even fewer in the arts, sciences and religion (but those two near-saints). These families are more generally political or service families. However, if one wants to extend the family by adding relatives like the Randolphs or the Livingstons, the record becomes fantastic.

* Chief Justice Edward D. White was a descendant of Thomas L. Lee, brother of Richard Henry.

II

Family Members Included in the *Dictionary of American Biography, Who's Who, Who Was Who,* and the *Encyclopaedia Britannica*

NOTE: The years of birth and death (as available: birth and death dates given only as they appear in these reference works) follow the family member's name. In the *Who's Who* column are the inclusive years in which the family member was cited; no one appears before 1899 (the first year *Who's Who* was published) or after 1968 (the most recent volume consulted). The references to *Who Was Who* are from Volume I, covering the years 1607–1896; those to the *Encyclopaedia Britannica*, from the 1967 edition. The number of family members cited in each reference work is given in parenthesis under the column head.

ADAMSES

	DAB (8)	WW (8)	WWW (5)	EB (9)
SAMUEL (1722–1803)	†		†	†
JOHN (1735–1826)	†		†	†
ABIGAIL (1744–1818)	†		†	†
JOHN Q. (1767–1848)	†		†	†
CHARLES F. (1807–1886)	†		†	†
CFA² (1835–1915)	†	1899–1914		†
HENRY (1838–1918)	†	1899–1916		†
BROOKS (1848–1927)	†	1899–1926		†
CFA³ (1866–1954)		1910–1954		†

ADAMSES

	DAB (8)	WW (8)	WWW (5)	EB (9)
ARTHUR (1877–)		1932–1938		
CFA[4] (1910–)		1952–1968		
THOMAS B. (1910–)		1958–1962		
JOHN Q. (1922–)		1968		

BIDDLES

	DAB (4)	WW (18)	WWW (8)	EB (1)
EDWARD (1738–1779)			†	
CLEMENT (1740–1814)	†		†	
NICHOLAS (1750–1778)	†		†	
JAMES (1783–1848)	†		†	
NICHOLAS (1786–1844)	†		†	†
JOHN (1792–1859)			†	
RICHARD (1796–1847)			†	
JAMES STOKES (1818–1900)		1899		
CHARLES J. (1819–1873)			†	
CRAIG (1823–1910)		1899–1910		
JAMES (1832–1910)		1903–1910		
EDWARD WM. (1852–1931)		1914–1930		
WILLIAM P. (1853–1923)		1914–1922		
GERTRUDE (MRS. EDWARD) (1857–)		1914–1952		
JOHN (1859–1936)		1899–1936		
ANDREW P. (1862–1944)		1920–1944		

BIDDLES

	DAB (4)	WW (18)	WWW (8)	EB (1)
AJDB sr. (1874–1948)		1901–1948		
Clement M. (1876–)		1932–1956		
Nicholas (1879–1923)		1922		
George (1885–)		1928–1968		
Francis (1886–)		1936–1968		
Charles J. (1890–)		1954–1968		
Alexander (1893–)		1958–1968		
AJDB jr. (1897–)		1936–1962		
William S. III (1900–)		1958–1966		
James (1929–)		1964–1968		

DU PONTS

	DAB (7)	WW (21)	WWW (4)	EB (2)
Pierre S. (1739–1817)				
Victor Marie (1767–1827)	†		†	†
Eleuthère Irénée (1771–1834)	†		†	
Samuel Francis (1803–1865)	†		†	†
Henry (1812–1889)	†		†	
Henry Algernon (1838–1926)	†	1899–1926		
Thomas Coleman (1863–1930)	† *	1910–1930		

* In Supplement I of *DAB*.

DU PONTS

	DAB (7)	WW (21)	WWW (4)	EB (2)
ALFRED IRÉNÉE (1864–1935)	†*	1934		
PIERRE S. (1870–1954)		1918–1954		
IRÉNÉE (1876–)		1924–1958		
A. FELIX (1879–)		1944–1948		
LAMMOT (1880–)		1932–1952		
HENRY FRANCIS (1880–)		1954–1968		
FRANCIS V. (1894–)		1941–1962		
HENRY B. JR. (1898–)		1944–1968		
EMILE F. (1898–)		1946–1962		
JESSIE (MRS. ALFRED)		1952–1964		
ALFRED V. (1900–)		1944–1968		
ALEXIS F. JR. (1905–)		1958–1968		
EDMOND (1906–)		1954–1968		
WILLIAM JR.		1954–1966		
ALFRED RHETT (1907–)		1954–1968		
PIERRE S. III (1911–)		1954–1968		
IRÉNÉE JR. (1920–)		1960–1968		
ELEUTHÈRE I. (1921–)		1968		
FRANCIS I. II (1927–)		1966–1968		

* In Supplement I of *DAB*.

LEES

	DAB (15)	WW (10)	WWW (13)	EB (5)
RICHARD I (? –1664)	†		†	
RICHARD HENRY (1732–1794)	†		†	†
FRANCIS LIGHTFOOT (1734–1797)	†		†	
WILLIAM (1739–1795)	†		†	
ARTHUR (1740–1792)	†		†	†
THOMAS SIM (1745–1819)	†		†	
HARRY (1756–1818)	†		†	†
CHARLES (1758–1815)	†		†	
RICHARD BLAND (1761–1827)	†		†	
HENRY JR. (1787–1837)	†		†	
ROBERT EDWARD (1807–1870)	†		†	†
SAMUEL PHILLIPS (1812–1897)	†		†	
GEORGE W. CUSTIS (1832–1913)	†	1899–1912		
FITZHUGH (1835–1905)	†	1899–1903		†
WM. H. FITZHUGH ("Rooney") (1837–1891)	†		†	
ROBERT E. JR. (1843–1914)		1906–1914		
BLAIR (1857–1944)		1914–1944		
ROBERT E. III (1869–)		1901–1906		
GEORGE B. (1872–1948)		1926–1948		
EDMUND J. III (1877–)		1930–1954		

LEES

	DAB (15)	WW (10)	WWW (13)	EB (5)
P. BLAIR (1895–)		1948–1966		
FITZHUGH (1905–)		1958–1966		
ARMISTEAD (1916–)		1962–1968		

ROOSEVELTS

	DAB (4)	WW (25)	WWW (3)	EB (3)
NICHOLAS J. (1767–1854)	†		†	
JAMES I (1795–1875)			†	
ROBERT B. (1829–1906)	†	1899–1908		
HILBOURNE (1849–1886)	†		†	
WILLIAM EMLEN (1857–1930)		1906–1928		
THEODORE (1858–1919)	†	1899–1918		†
EDITH CAROW (1861–)		1908–1916; 1944–1948		
HENRY LATROBE (1879–1936)		1928–1934		
*FRANKLIN D. (1882–1945)		1914–1946		†
ANNA ELEANOR (1884–1962)		1930–1962		†
GEORGE EMLEN (1887–)		1932–1962		
THEODORE JR. (1887–1944)		1920–1944		
KERMIT (1889–1943)		1920–1942		
PHILIP J. (1892–1941)		1932–1942		

* Hyde Park branch.

ROOSEVELTS

	DAB (4)	WW (25)	WWW (3)	EB (3)
NICHOLAS (1893–)		1930–1968		
ARCHIBALD B. SR. (1894–)		1936–1950		
*JAMES (1907–)		1938–1968		
*ELLIOTT (1910–)		1940–1968		
ELEANOR (MRS. THEODORE JR.) (1910–)		1950–1960		
*FRANKLIN JR. (1914–)		1954–1968		
THEODORE III (1914–)		1962–1968		
JOHN K.		1956–1968		
*JOHN ASPINWALL (1916–)		1960–1968		
KERMIT JR. (1916–)		1960–1968		
WILLIAM EMLEN JR. (1917–)		1956–1968		
ARCHIBALD JR. (1918–)		1960–1968		
JULIAN KEAN (1924–)		1962–1968		

* Hyde Park branch.

III

Acknowledgments and Book List

Books like this invariably have a preface thanking kind librarians and a bibliography listing many sources. Since this book has no intention of being scholarly and is addressed directly to people, I have as a matter of course dispensed with apparatus, i.e., footnotes and bibliography. In fact the very nature of these families is enough to discourage the typical preface and bibliography. They have been so involved in history that all decent works of reference (notably encyclopedias, the *Dictionary of American Biography,* and *Who's Who*) are chock-full of them (see Appendix II). They are very much in the public domain. With certain few exceptions, everything one would care to know about them is available in any good library. No special kindnesses, then, or private sources have really been necessary except the ordinary and unfailing impersonal kindnesses of the Princeton University Library, the Historical Society of Pennsylvania and such others. I am duly grateful.

A few persons however have been especially kind: Mr. Ludwell Lee Montague, president of the Lee Society, Mrs. Cazenove Lee of Washington, and Mr. Maurice du Pont Lee Jr. Dr. Richmond D. Williams of the Eleutherian Mills Library took me on a surprise personal tour of the homestead. Though not at all in connection with this book, Mr. and Mrs. Charles J. Biddle revealed the beauties of Andalusia to me. Mrs. Quentin Roosevelt gave me a charming glimpse of Cove Neck I would not otherwise have had. Mrs. John Quincy Adams of Dover was cordial. Nicholas Biddle Wainwright, editor of the *Pennsylvania Magazine of History and Biography,* has also been helpful. Meeting Alice Roosevelt Longworth was as memorable an occasion for me as it has been for others; for this meeting I owe thanks to Mr. David L. Mitchell.

Of books about and around these families there is a vast library. Any attempt at a full and detailed bibliography covering all these individuals would produce quite literally a book as fat as this one. Instead, I have made a list of some books that I think readers might like if they choose to go deeper into these family histories. The list does not represent all my sources, but I have used all these books to some extent. The comments are, naturally, just my own personal reactions. The idea has been brevity, not inclusiveness. This is as much as possible a minimum list, yet still comes to over sixty titles. (*Note:* a star* indicates "especially recommended.")

General: History of the United States

*MORISON, SAMUEL ELIOT, *The Oxford History of the American People* (Oxford, 1965). For a good, general historical background to this particular book, nothing would better serve the purpose than this already-mentioned history. It is definitely a history of America in terms of these families. Other such shorter histories, for example, Allan Nevins and Henry Steele Commager, *A Short History of the United States* (Knopf, 1966), might be useful for contrast; none are as firmly authoritative and briskly readable as Morison.

Family in General: The total subject, or families en masse

*WECTER, DIXON, *The Saga of American Society* (Scribner's, 1937). For a good, general historical background to the particular area of Family in America, this sprightly semiclassic is also required reading. It also is fairly authoritative and certainly briskly readable. It suffers from one grave fault, the dangers inherent in that dirty word "Society." No one who tries to write of "Society" can fail to get caught in a bog of confusion. Wecter is no exception. You can't talk of the inanities of the Gilded Age and of Lees and Adamses in one book without getting all mixed up. "Society" *does* connect with Family, but one has to be more careful than Messrs. Wecter, Amory, Birmingham and others have been. But this is still a good and funny book.

SCHRIFTGIESSER, KARL, *Families* (Howell, Sorkin, 1940). As a pioneer in the field, Schriftgiesser has written a nice, compact guide to the histories of ten families, including the Adamses, Lees, du Ponts and Roosevelts. Also included are the James, Astor, Guggenheim and other families, making a nice bouquet of contrasts. Necessarily rather skimpy on each individual family.

HESS, STEPHEN, *America's Political Dynasties* (Doubleday, 1966). Hess, far from being skimpy, is almost incredibly detailed. More information on more families is packed into this book than most people could digest; but it is certainly a mine of information. Hess has been interested only in *political* families, families that have sent a variety of members to Congress. He too, like Schriftgiesser, covers the Lees and Roosevelts, also the Adams, but not du Ponts or Biddles, despite their

Congressional claims. In all, he deals with sixteen names, ranging from obvious ones like Livingstons, Kennedys and Harrisons to obscure ones like Washburns. A bit tough for straight-through reading, despite a lively style, but certainly recommended for anyone with Family interests.

DE TOCQUEVILLE, ALEXIS, *Democracy in America* (try the abridgment, edited by Richard D. Heffner, Mentor MQ788, 1956). A book about America that disdains the very thought of Families there as part of its basic thesis. Essential background, however.

Families in Particular

ADAMSES

*ADAMS, JAMES TRUSLOW, *The Adams Family* (Little, Brown, 1930). JT was not "an Adams," but writes in a spirit of reverence. He writes well and, despite the pervading idolatry, this is still the best of all single-family books.

LEES

*HENDRICK, BURTON J., *The Lees of Virginia* (Little, Brown, 1935). Next to Adams on Adams, this is the best of single-family books; almost as idolatrous, rich in background, a bit wordy and diffuse. These two books are the classics of their kind.

LEE, CAZENOVE G., JR., *Lee Chronicle* (New York University, 1957). For authoritative details on Lee genealogy and history.

ROOSEVELTS

SCHRIFTGIESSER, KARL, *The Amazing Roosevelt Family* (Funk, 1942). This is the daddy of all books about the Roosevelts. It tells one really more than one cares to know about them, but is indisputably "the source."

CHURCHILL, ALLEN, *The Roosevelts* (Harper and Row, 1965). This derives all its earlier history from Schriftgiesser, but is lively and fresh on TR and FDR and is more up-to-date than Schriftgiesser.

PARTRIDGE, BELLAMY, *The Roosevelt Family in America* (Hillman-Curl, 1936). Though written earlier than the others, it does not equal Schriftgiesser as a source, or Churchill for good reading. It does have that genealogical tour de force of "America's Royal Family" in it.

DU PONTS

WINKLER, JOHN K., *The Du Pont Dynasty* (Reynal, 1935). Oldest of the du Pont books for the general reader (as opposed to those strictly for family consumption).

DORIAN, MAX, *The du Ponts* (Little, Brown, 1961). Family history with a pleasant French slant. Nice pictures.

CARR, WILLIAM H. A., *The du Ponts of Delaware* (Dodd, Mead, 1964). This is the latest and best book on the family. Though it borrows, of necessity, from Winkler, it still makes the most informative reading of these three.

However, none of these six books on Roosevelts and du Ponts is equal to Adams's or Hendrick's. Such books as do exist about Biddles are privately printed genealogies and the like. These of course exist for the other four families, notably the magnificent du Pont genealogy. Most of them will be found in big historical-society libraries, listed under the families. Not for general reading obviously. But there is *no* complete printed Biddle genealogy, only a monstrous hand-illuminated scroll of linoleum in the Historical Society of Pennsylvania, impossible to use. Faugh!

Books on Individuals

Here one must sift through a mass. The list on Robert E. Lee alone is a book in itself. Likewise the Roosevelts. Not to mention the Adamses. I have just picked out a few books that are either readable, or essential, or both. I have left out many authoritative works, some that I have used, some that I should have used. In general, I have tried to stick to one or two books per subject.

ADAMSES

In dealing with this family one is faced with The Papers. There are two sets of these, the Old Papers and the New Papers. Where available, the new are always preferable to the old.

The Old Papers are those edited by pious CFA:

Letters of John and Abigail (in various editions)
Life and Works of JA (10 vols.), plus biography
Memoirs of JQA (12 vols.)

Plus some others, among them:

Writings of JQA (8 vols., unfinished), ed. by Worthington C. Ford (Macmillan, 1913–17), which was meant to consist of correspondence, articles, papers, etc.

The New Papers include, as of 1969:

John Adams, *Diary and Autobiography* (4 vols., plus "earliest diaries") and *Legal Papers* (3 vols.)
Charles F. Adams, *Diary* (4 vols., up to 1968)

All these were edited by Lyman Butterfield and published by Harvard. Eventually there will be some hundred volumes and the Old Papers will be obsolete.

Not yet included in these papers are such other volumes of letters as:

New Letters of Abigail Adams, ed. by Mitchell Stewart (Houghton Mifflin, 1947)
CFA² and others, *A Cycle of Adams Letters,* ed. by Worthington C. Ford (Houghton Mifflin, 1920)
Henry Adams and His Friends, ed. by Henry D. Cater (Houghton Mifflin, 1947)

and many more such. Besides all this mass, which is interesting to the extent one is interested, there are plenty of other books, of which these are a selected few:

John and Abigail

SMITH, PAGE, *JA* (2 vols.; Doubleday, 1962). This is as of now the "authoritative biography," but since it was published before the New Papers, it will no doubt be superseded.

*BOWEN, CATHERINE DRINKER, *JA and the American Revolution* (Atlantic–Little, Brown, 1950). This is, to my thinking, the best of all the books listed, in its combination of fictional vividness and historical accuracy. Historians sniff at it because it trembles on the dangerous line of fictionalized biography; but in this one case the result is superb. However it takes John only up through the Declaration. I suspect this book is the origin of John and Abigail as America's Lovers. Read it.

STONE, IRVING, *Those Who Love* (Doubleday, 1965). This, by comparison, is a good bad example of the same technique of fictionalized biography, in which the Adamses are made to talk like modern "just folks" and the earnestly researched detail is made drab by Stone's style, or rather lack of it. However, it was a great best-seller, so people liked it. I did not. There are some other even worse examples of this kind of book about the Adamses.

HARASZTI, ZOLTÁN, *JA and the Prophets of Progress* (Harvard, 1952). A scholarly but still interesting discussion of JA's mental processes and intellectual background as revealed by his reading.

These are only scratches on the surface of the Adams literature. Works fictional and nonfictional about modern America's favorite married lovers continue to pile up. Go see the B'way musical *1776* for further details (and note the sacrilege committed on Richard Henry Lee).

John Quincy

BEMIS, SAMUEL F., Vol. I, *JQA and the Foundations of American Foreign Policy* (Knopf, 1949); Vol. II, *JQA and the Union* (Knopf, 1956). These are the authoritative biographical studies. Not fun; but interesting in places, because of the material.

Charles Francis

DUBERMAN, MARTIN B., *CFA 1807–1886* (Houghton Mifflin, 1961). A sober study; definitive. I found it a dull book about a dull man. But admirable, man and book.

Charles Francis Junior

KIRKLAND, EDWARD C., *CFA, Jr., 1835–1915* (Harvard, 1965). Just like Duberman, but a smaller book about a smaller man. Also definitive — so far. And dull.

Henry

*SAMUELS, ERNEST, *Henry Adams.* Vol. I: *The Young HA* (Harvard, 1965). Vol. II: *The Middle Years* (Harvard, 1958). Vol. III: *The Major Phase* (Harvard, 1964).

Next to Freeman's monument to R. E. Lee, this is by far the best and largest biography of any of the individuals in this book (including the Roosevelts).

Brooks

ANDERSON, THORNTON, *BA: Constructive Conservative* (Cornell, 1951), and BERINGAUSE, ARTHUR, *BA: American Prophet* (Knopf, 1955). These two handle this prickly person with loving care, and in general are apologetic, especially Anderson. Any book about Brooks can't help but be interesting. However, one feels the need of something more solid.

There is lots of other stuff written about Adamses, especially Henry.

ROOSEVELTS

Theodore

*PRINGLE, HENRY F., *TR* (Harcourt, Brace, 1931, 1956). A rather critical revisionist biography of Theodore, but still one of the best of all these individual biographies. Nowadays it is considered the standard work, eclipsing earlier, more laudatory works.

WISTER, OWEN, *Roosevelt: the Story of a Friendship* (Macmillan, 1930). Theodore by a man who knew him well and could write. Some people find him rather offensively fulsome and snobbish too; but this is the original of many of the most telling anecdotes and gives a good picture of Roosevelt's circle.

Franklin

Out of a welter of material:

*SCHLESINGER, ARTHUR, JR., *Age of Roosevelt*, Vol. I: *The Crisis of the Old Order* (Houghton Mifflin, 1957) and Vol. II: *The Coming of the New Deal* (Houghton Mifflin, 1958). These two volumes remain the classic description of the Rise of Roosevelt and give adequate biographical background. If you want to limit your reading to one author, these are the books. Violently pro-Franklin; objectivity is not the characteristic of the FDR literature.

GUNTHER, JOHN, *Roosevelt in Retrospect* (Harper, 1950). Lively, journalistic, a bit slapdash and very idolatrous, but a readable one-volume biography.

PERKINS, FRANCES, *The Roosevelt I Knew* (Viking, 1946). Again idolatrous, but in a very restrained, Yankee way. It remains perhaps the best of the numerous "I remember him" books about FDR.

BURNS, JAMES M., *Roosevelt, the Lion and the Fox* (Harcourt, 1956). Not so idolatrous. Like Pringle on Theodore, the best of the modern revisionist biographies and a wholesome corrective to the fulsomeness of others.

There are innumerable other readable books, such as the notable Robert Sherwood, *Roosevelt and Hopkins: An Intimate History;* but enough is enough.

Two unfinished biographies, which remain fine fragments are:

PUTNAM, CARLETON, *TR* (1 vol. only; Scribner's, 1958) and

FRIEDEL, FRANK, *FDR* (3 vols. [to 1932]; Little, Brown, 1949–). Either of these, if completed, would have been definitive. Another curious case of a family parallel.

BIDDLES

Captain Nicholas

CLARK, WILLIAM BELL, *Captain Dauntless* (Louisiana, 1949). A nice little book, which gets bogged down towards the end in the Charleston Navy Yard. Ends with a bang, though.

Nicholas the Banker

GOVAN, THOMAS P., *Nicholas Biddle (1786–1844)* (Chicago, 1959). A meticulously scholarly defense of Biddle's role as banker and opponent of Jackson. A corrective to the pro-Jackson polemics of Schlesinger and others, but a brief for the defense, not an impartial study. However, it remains the only modern biography.

Anthony J. Drexel

BIDDLE, CORDELIA, and CRICHTON, KYLE, *My Philadelphia Father* (Doubleday, 1955). Good clean fun, a romp of a not very elevated sort, halfway between *Life with Father* and *Auntie Mame*. Created the AJDB myth.

DU PONTS

Pierre

SARICKS, AMBROSE, *Pierre Samuel Du Pont de Nemours* (Kansas, 1965). A serious, scholarly effort to strip the myths and get down to the facts. Of necessity rather pedestrian; but Pierre's life was so eventful that even scholarship fails to make it uninteresting.

Alfred I.

JAMES, MARQUIS, *Alfred I. Dupont, the Family Rebel* (Bobbs-Merrill, 1941). A lively, partial, journalistic biography of this difficult person. James feels he was more wronged than wrong.

LEES

There are *no* good modern biographies of either Richard Henry or Arthur. Why not? The latter particularly needs a defender in the Beaumarchais battle. The other side has had all the say. The previous nineteenth-century books are not much use.

Harry

Two light books:

BOYD, THOMAS, *Light-Horse Harry Lee* (Scribner's, 1931) and GERSON, NOEL, *Light-Horse Harry Lee* (Doubleday, 1966). Readable enough. Not weighty.

Robert E.

*FREEMAN, DOUGLAS S., *Robert E. Lee* (4 vols.; Scribner's, 1934–42). Of all the books about all of these men, this alone stands as *the* definitive biography. Weighty. Anything else written about Robert will be only addenda or revisions. The emotional effects, the "buckets of tears," come across despite the detail and the restrained, even ponderous, style. But of course not light reading.

DOWDEY, CLIFFORD, *Lee* (Little, Brown, 1965). As a supplement to Freeman, gives some details not there available.

Books by Members of These Families
(As big a library as books about them)

ADAMSES

For works by earlier members (JA, AA, JQA, CFA), see the various Adams papers. Two condensations are useful:

KOCH, ADRIENNE, et al., eds., *Selected Writings of JA and JQA* (Knopf, 1946).

NEVINS, ALLAN, ed., *The Diary of JQA* (Longmans, 1928). One volume of selections.

Henry

The book by an Adams is of course:

*ADAMS, HENRY, *The Education of Henry Adams* (Houghton Mifflin, Sentry paperback, 1961). Despite its fascination, both of matter and manner, and the high level of at least the first part as sheer biography, I still feel that this classic has been overadmired for the wrong reasons. The general popularity in modern times of the mixed-up kid, of whom Henry is an early, articulate example, has tended to make people overlook the perverse, *fin-de-siècle* spleen that pervades the work: essence of sour grapes. Though it is good to be a Seeker, one feels that Henry would have rejected any Answer (like Catholicism) in the interests of maintaining his picturesque position as ironist. His other books, *Mont-Saint-Michel* and *Democracy,* and of course the *History,* need no citing from me. I am not sure that they too have not been somewhat overpraised because of the *Education.*

Charles Francis, Jr.

ADAMS, CHARLES FRANCIS, JR., *Charles Francis Adams, an Autobiography* (Houghton Mifflin, 1916). Henry's crusty brother's crusty opinions on Boston, education, businessmen, etc. Fun, in an Adams way.

Brooks

ADAMS, BROOKS, *The Law of Civilization and Decay* (Knopf, 1955). This expresses most forcefully the Adams theories of dissipation of energy, etc.

As for the welter of other Adams writings, the historical researches of CFA², for example, and all those other works of Brooks, they are all usually spiced with Adams salt; but they are also pretty special as to subject. One could spend a lifetime reading Adams; and there are less profitable ways of spending a lifetime.

Abigail Homans

*HOMANS, ABIGAIL ADAMS, *Education by Uncles* (Houghton Mifflin, 1966). The niece of the Brothers in her contribution to the Papers. Delightful.

ROOSEVELTS

Here again, amid a welter, two autobiographies:

Theodore

ROOSEVELT, THEODORE, *An Autobiography* (Macmillan, 1914).

Eleanor

Roosevelt, Eleanor, *This Is My Story* (Harper, 1937).

Neither TR nor ER were Henry Adams; one reads for content rather than style. Theodore wrote semiautobiographical books about his hunting expeditions and Eleanor wrote two later autobiographical volumes, *This I Remember* (Harper, 1949), and *On My Own* (Harper, 1961). But of the three the first is incomparably the best. Theodore was of course a professional writer. Like many other American statesmen, a writer *manqué,* but not because he didn't try. None of his works, however, seems to stand on its own feet without the support of biographical interest in Teddy himself. Though vivid, he's wordy and full of pugnacious prejudices. There are strong passages in the *Winning of the West* and the accounts of the hunting expeditions. As for Eleanor, she wrote and wrote; but she was not a good writer. Her kindly and inquisitive personality comes through in flashes. FDR's speeches and letters are available in print; but are of historical-research, not purely literary, interest. As in the case of the Adamses, one could spend a lifetime reading Roosevelts (don't forget Uncle Bob), but I confess I wouldn't want to.

Also, there are three autobiographies by lesser figures which, though not works of genius, have juicy nuggets in them:

Longworth, Alice R., *Crowded Hours* (Scribner's, 1933).

Roosevelt, Mrs. T. R., Jr., *Day before Yesterday* (Doubleday, 1959).

Roosevelt, Nicholas, *A Front Row Seat* (Oklahoma, 1953).

BIDDLES

There's a refreshing dearth of Biddle material, and what there is is mostly very good of its kind, particularly three autobiographies:

Charles

*Biddle, Charles, *Autobiography* (privately printed, Philadelphia, 1883). This should-be classic account of a seafaring career is not a literary effort; one damn thing follows another. But it ought to be of interest to almost anybody, especially those curious about life at sea in the eighteenth century. It should be reedited and reprinted (attention Mr. Wainwright).

George

Biddle, George, *An American Artist's Story* (Little, Brown, 1939). Self-portrait of a twentieth-century Philadelphia rebel, and a striking if perhaps mannered writer. Groton in the days of FDR, Tahiti, Paris, New York, etc.

Francis

BIDDLE, FRANCIS, *A Casual Past* (Doubleday, 1961) and *In Brief Authority* (Doubleday, 1962). Next to Henry Adams's immortal *Education,* this is the best of all these family's memoirs. It not only gives the Bizarre story in felicitous detail, and covers Biddle family history, but also provides a civilized ramble through the twentieth century and its wars, New Deals, and what have you. Good if leisurely reading.

The other works of George and Francis are equally elegant. They too are writers *manqué;* but it is lack of volume, not of style, that prevents them from being more highly thought of as literary figures. Then there are the works of Katharine Chapin Biddle (poetry) and of Livingston Biddle Jr. (novels), the two pros of this family. Of these five families, the Biddles come after the Adamses as wordsmiths, and are perhaps superior as such to all but Henry himself.

DU PONTS

They do not write, except for laborious, handsomely printed books on family history or company history, useful for purpose of research only. Exception is ornithologist in-law Greenewalt (hummingbirds, etc.).

LEES

Lees have written, but not much or very well. Harry's *Memoirs* and the biographical works of R. H. Lee Jr., who dispersed all his materials, are for research. R. H. Lee Sr.'s *Letters from the Federal Farmer* and his correspondence are in print, but they are not very entertaining either. Robert E. Junior's recollections of his father are well thought of. In modern times the works of Maurice duPont Lee Jr. are addressed to historians of sixteenth- and seventeenth-century Scotland and England, but can claim to be the best Lee writing so far.

This list does not cover *all* the writings of *all* members of *all* these families (those books by the sons of TR for instance, the beautiful books on birds by Clifford Greenewalt). But . . .

Books Relating to These Families or Their Backgrounds

ADAMSES

*Amory, Cleveland, *The Proper Bostonians* (Dutton, 1947). Still the classic of all books of its kind; gives the Adams position in Boston its Proper setting.

ROOSEVELTS

Hagedorn, Hermann, *The Roosevelt Family of Sagamore Hill* (Macmillan, 1954). In this and several other books, Hagedorn has written with enthusiasm of Theodore and his family.

Daniels, Jonathan, *Washington Quadrille* (Doubleday, 1968). Daniels has squatter's rights on the Lucy Mercer story; in this book and others he tells what he can. Also notes on Princess Alice, etc.

BIDDLES

Burt, Nathaniel, *The Perennial Philadelphians* (Little, Brown, 1963). Without undue modesty, let me recommend this as a book on Biddle background. Biddles may disagree.

Schlesinger, Arthur, Jr., *The Age of Jackson* (Little, Brown, 1945). Biddle as villain in a pro-Jackson world.

DU PONTS

There are lots of books involving the du Ponts' role in industry. Though I can certainly not recommend it, the previously mentioned *The Rich and the Super-Rich* by Ferdinand Lundberg has lots to say about the du Ponts.

Canby, Henry S.: *Family History* (privately printed, Cambridge, Massachusetts, 1945). Gives lots of background on *non*-du Pont Wilmington (Canbys, etc.). Full of nostalgic charm. See also other writings by Canby.

LEES

Wilstach, Paul, *Tidewater Virginia* (Blue Ribbon Books, 1929). Old Plantations in Old Virginia. Don't forget the Philip Vickers Fithian diaries too.

BRADFORD, GAMALIEL, *Damaged Souls* (Houghton, 1923). For John Randolph. See also Henry Adams's rather snippy biography, and the novel by J. and A. Walz called *The Bizarre Sisters*.

Almost any book on New England, New York, Pennsylvania, Delaware or Virginia is bound to cross the paths of these families somewhere. Particularly handy and readable are the books in the "Rivers of America" series for local background (Hudson, Delaware, Brandywine, James, etc.). You can hardly avoid these people and their cousins and their in-laws in these areas. There are also many other such biographies of families, some of whom connect and interlock. For instance, John H. Davis's *The Bouviers*, gets into the Drexels (and the Kennedys). Birmingham's *Our Crowd* has no direct connections, but is certainly full of Family parallels.

Fun can be had with *narrative* genealogies, such as that of Owen Biddle's descendants from which I gleaned Middle Biddle items. All sorts of queer stories pop up in them. But then some people like just plain genealogies. I confess I do if they are sufficiently intricate. A form of mathematics? A special taste.

Though I think I have covered most of the well-known biographies, there are many others about some of these men, and some very good. In fact, too many. Yet one is still appalled by the lack of biographical work on some others. One thinks again of Lees in particular: Richard Henry, Arthur, Black-Horse Harry. Another broader and less biased (and perhaps less technical banking) book on Nicholas Biddle is surely due. Nicholas Roosevelt the Steamboater would seem worthy of a real modern biographical effort; or Uncle Robert B. And of course a decent printed Biddle genealogy. In fact some one condensed *central* genealogy of these First Families and their kin is something libraries desperately require. To find out just how various famous people are related is still a tangled business. A *Dictionary of American Genealogy* to parallel and supplement the *Dictionary of American Biography* would be enormously helpful. (Scribner's please note).

IV

Two Poems

As supplementary reading, two poems are appended, one by Nicholas Biddle, the other by his poet friend, John Quincy Adams. The "Ode to Bogle" dates from 1829. The argument reads: "Robert Bogle . . . was a wellknown character in his day, and resided in Eighth near Sansom Street, in the city of Philadelphia. He united the vocations of public waiter and undertaker, frequently officiating at a funeral in the afternoon and at a party on the evening of the same day — presenting on all occasions the same gravity of demeanor. The term 'colorless colored man' was especially descriptive of Bogle, as he was a very light mulatto. The 'fantastic toes' was an allusion to his occasional indulgence, towards the end of an entertainment, in some of the liquids he so decorously dispensed to the guests. 'Johnson' and 'Shepard' were also public waiters of only inferior fame."

ODE TO BOGLE
by Nicholas Biddle

Dedicated, with permission and a piece of mint-stick,
to Meta Craig Biddle,* aged four years.

Bogle! not he whose shadow flies
Before a frighted Scotchman's eyes,
But thou of Eighth, near Sansom, thou
Colorless colored man, whose brow,
Unmoved, the joys of life surveys,
Untouched the gloom of death displays,
Reckless if joy or gloom prevail —
Stern, multifarious Bogle — hail!

. . . .

Scarce seems the blushing maiden wed
Unless thy care the supper spread;

* She who later married her cousin James Stokes Biddle. See Appendix V.

Half christened only were that boy,
Whose heathen squalls our ears annoy,
If, service finished, cakes and wine
Were given by any hand but thine;
And Christian burial e'en were scant
Unless his aid the Bogle grant.

Lover of pomps! the dead might rise
And feast — upon himself — his eyes,
When marshaling the black array
Thou rul'st the sadness of the day,
Teaching how grief may be genteel,
And legatees should seem to feel.
Death's seneschal, 'tis thine to trace
For each his proper look and place, —
How aunts should weep, where uncles stand,
With hostile cousins hand in hand;
Give matchless gloves, and fitly shape
By length of face the length of crape.
See him erect, with loftly tread,
The dark scarf streaming from his head,
Lead forth his groups in order mete
And range them grief-wise in the street;
Presiding o'er the solemn show —
The very Chesterfield of woe.

. . . .

Nor less, stupendous man! thy power
In festal than in funeral hour,
When gas and beauty's blended rays
Set hearts and ball-rooms in a blaze.

. . . .

In flames each belle her victim kills,
And sparks fly upward in quadrilles:
Like iceberg in an Indian clime
Refreshing Bogle breathes sublime —
Cool airs upon that sultry stream,
From Roman punch and frosted cream.

So — sadly social — when we flee
From milky talk and watery tea,
To dance by inches in that strait
Between a sideboard and a grate,
With rug uplift and blower tight
'Gainst the red Demon Anthracite,
Then Bogle o'er the weary hours
A world of sweets incessant showers,
Till, blest relief from noise and foam,
The farewell poundcake warns us home.

. . . .

On Johnson's smooth and placid mien
A quaint and fitful smile is seen;
O'er Shepard's pale, romantic face,
A radiant simper we may trace;
But on the Bogle's steadfast cheek
Lugubrious thoughts their presence speak —
His very smile serenely stern
As lighted lachrymary urn.
In church or state, in bower or hall,
He gives, with equal face, to all
The wedding cake, the funeral crape,
The mourning glove, the festive grape;
In the same tone, when crowds disperse,
Calls Powell's hack or Carter's hearse;
As gently grave, as sadly grim
At the quick waltz as funeral hymn.

Thou, social Fabius! since the day
When Rome was saved by wise delay,
None else has found the happy chance —
By always waiting — to advance.

. . . .

Yet — (not till Providence bestowed
On Adam's sons, McAdam's road) —
Unstumbling foot was rarely given
To man or beast when quickly driven.
And they do say — but this I doubt,

[466]

For seldom he lets things leak out —
They do say — ere the dances close,
His, too, are "light fantastic toes."
Oh, if this be so, Bogle! then,
How are we served by serving men!
A waiter by his weight forsaken!
An undertaker overtaken!

A nice period piece, portrait of the person and the time; note, as of 1829, the introduction of those modern improvements: gas lighting, central heating with anthracite coal, and macadamized roads.

As for the poem by John Quincy Adams, an entry in the diary for February 15, 1807, reads: "Judge Livingston, Mr. Verplanck, and General Van Cortlandt spent the evening here. I finished this day the last fair copy of some stanzas entitled 'A Winter's Day' containing in verse a very minute and exact account of my daily occupations. . . ." (as senator from Massachusetts in Washington).

A WINTER'S DAY
by John Quincy Adams

1

Friend of my bosom! would'st thou know
How, far from thee, the days I spend,
And how the passing moments flow,
To this short, simple tale attend.
When first emerging from the East
The sunbeam flashes on my curtain,
I start from slumber's ties releas'd,
And make the weather's temper certain.

2

Next on the closet's shelf I seek
My pocket Homer, and compel
The man of many wiles, in Greek
Again his fabled woes to tell.
How true he paints the scenes of life!
How sweet the poet's honest prattle!

[467]

Far sweeter than fierce Ilium's strife
  And never-ending fields of battle.

3

At nine, comes Moses to my door,
  And down stairs summons me with ease,
But on my neighbor calls before,
  And knocks, "Miss Kitty — breakfast — please."
Again he louder knocks and stronger,
  Till Kitty answers, "Coming, Moses,"
And then, in half an hour, or longer,
  Comes Kitty, just as breakfast closes.

4

Then forth I sally for the day,
  And, musing politics or rhyme,
Take to the Capitol my way,
  To join in colloquy sublime.
There with the fathers of the land
  I mix in sage deliberation,
And lend my feeble voice and hand
  With equal laws to bless the nation.

5

The labors of the Senate o'er,
  Again, with solitary pace,
Down to Potomac's glassy floor
  My morning footsteps I retrace,
And oft, dejected or elate
  With painful or with pleased reflection,
In thought renew the day's debate,
  And canvass votes by retrospection.

6

At home I find the table spread
  And dinner's fragrant steams invite,
But first the twofold stairs I tread,
  My atmospheric tale to write.
Then, seated round the social board,
  We feast, till absent friends are toasted,

Though sometimes my delays afford
The beef or mutton over-roasted.

JQA in an unexpectedly genial and relaxed light — the Cosmopolitan rather than the Puritan.

V

Genealogies

(All minimal.   □ = no male descent.   △ = male descent of name.   O = male *or* female descent.)

ADAMS

Generations from
Emig.   Esta[...]

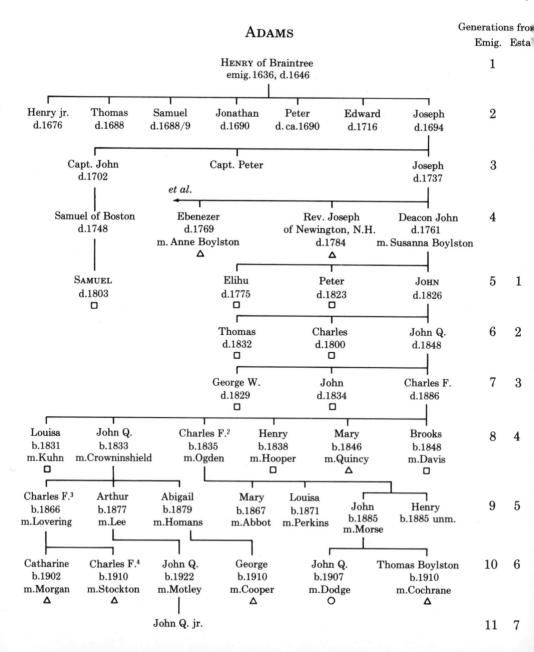

							Emig.	Esta
			HENRY of Braintree emig.1636, d.1646				1	
Henry jr. d.1676	Thomas d.1688	Samuel d.1688/9	Jonathan d.1690	Peter d. ca.1690	Edward d.1716	Joseph d.1694	2	
	Capt. John d.1702		Capt. Peter			Joseph d.1737	3	
	Samuel of Boston d.1748		Ebenezer d.1769 m. Anne Boylston △		Rev. Joseph of Newington, N.H. d.1784 △	Deacon John d.1761 m. Susanna Boylston	4	
	SAMUEL d.1803 □		Elihu d.1775 □		Peter d.1823 □	JOHN d.1826	5	1
			Thomas d.1832 □		Charles d.1800 □	John Q. d.1848	6	2
			George W. d.1829 □		John d.1834 □	Charles F. d.1886	7	3
Louisa b.1831 m.Kuhn □	John Q. b.1833 m.Crowninshield	Charles F.[2] b.1835 m.Ogden	Henry b.1838 m.Hooper □	Mary b.1846 m.Quincy △		Brooks b.1848 m.Davis □	8	4
Charles F.[3] b.1866 m.Lovering	Arthur b.1877 m.Lee	Abigail b.1879 m.Homans	Mary b.1867 m.Abbot	Louisa b.1871 m.Perkins	John b.1885 m.Morse	Henry b.1885 unm.	9	5
Catharine b.1902 m.Morgan △	Charles F.[4] b.1910 m.Stockton △	John Q. b.1922 m.Motley	George b.1910 m.Cooper △		John Q. b.1907 m.Dodge O	Thomas Boylston b.1910 m.Cochrane △	10	6
		John Q. jr.					11	7

ADDENDUM A: Smith–Johnson connection

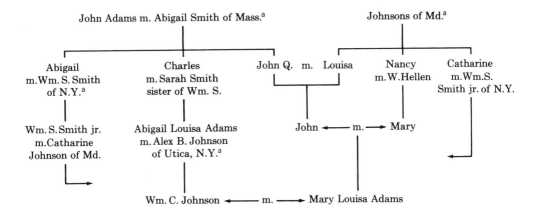

[a]The two Smith families (Mass. and N.Y.) and the two Johnson families (Md. and Utica, N.Y.) were no kin. Louisa, Nancy, and Catharine Johnson of Md. had another sister named Carolina Marylanda Virginia Johnson.

BIDDLE

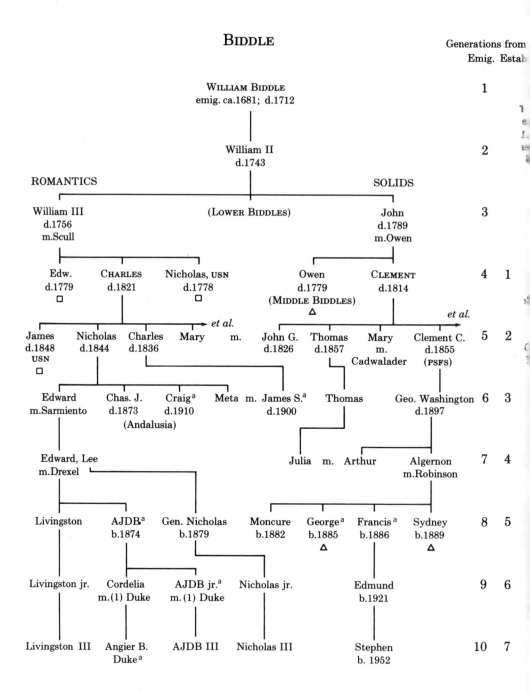

WILLIAM BIDDLE
emig. ca.1681; d.1712 — 1

William II
d.1743 — 2

ROMANTICS   SOLIDS

William III   (LOWER BIDDLES)   John   3
d.1756   d.1789
m.Scull   m.Owen

Edw.   CHARLES   Nicholas, USN   Owen   CLEMENT   4   1
d.1779   d.1821   d.1778   d.1779   d.1814
  □   □   (MIDDLE BIDDLES)
                                              △   et al.
                              et al.

James   Nicholas   Charles   Mary   m.   John G.   Thomas   Mary   Clement C.   5   2
d.1848   d.1844   d.1836   d.1826   d.1857   m.   d.1855
USN   Cadwalader (PSFS)
  □

Edward   Chas. J.   Craig[a]   Meta m. James S.[a]   Thomas   Geo. Washington   6   3
m.Sarmiento d.1873   d.1910   d.1900   d.1897
            (Andalusia)

Edward, Lee   Julia   m.   Arthur   Algernon   7   4
m.Drexel   m.Robinson

Livingston   AJDB[a]   Gen. Nicholas   Moncure   George[a]   Francis[a]   Sydney   8   5
             b.1874   b.1879   b.1882   b.1885   b.1886   b.1889
                                                   △   △

Livingston jr.   Cordelia   AJDB jr.[a]   Nicholas jr.   Edmund   9   6
                 m.(1) Duke m.(1) Duke   b.1921

Livingston III   Angier B.   AJDB III   Nicholas III   Stephen   10   7
                 Duke[a]   b. 1952

[a] See *Who's Who*, 1899-1968 (Appendix II).

ADDENDUM A: Romantic Biddles extended

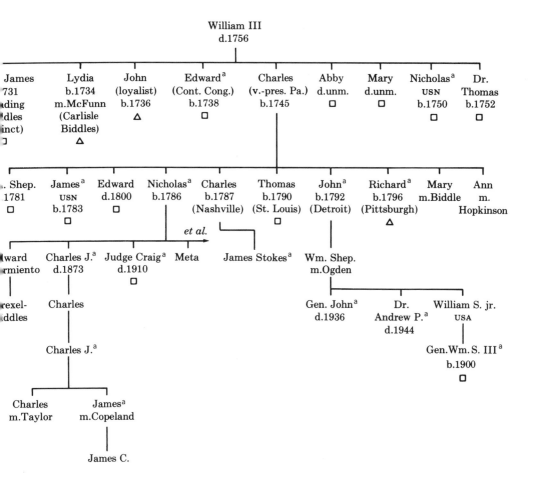

[a] These names appear in the reference works cited in Appendix II. Note the occurrence of two or more in five successive generations.

ADDENDUM B: Randolph–Biddle–Bizarre connection

1.

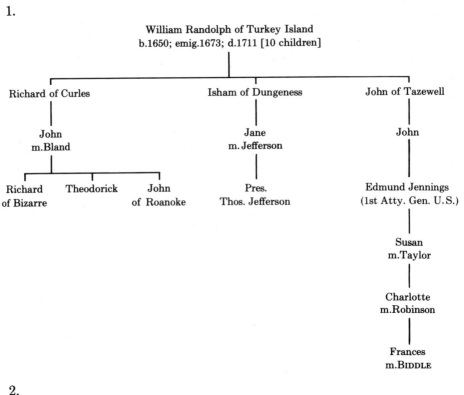

William Randolph of Turkey Island
b.1650; emig.1673; d.1711 [10 children]

Richard of Curles   Isham of Dungeness   John of Tazewell

John m.Bland   Jane m.Jefferson   John

Richard of Bizarre   Theodorick   John of Roanoke   Pres. Thos. Jefferson   Edmund Jennings (1st Atty. Gen. U.S.)

Susan m.Taylor

Charlotte m.Robinson

Frances m.BIDDLE

2.

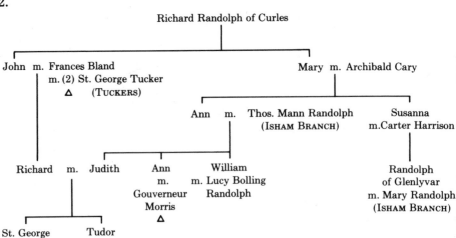

Richard Randolph of Curles

John m. Frances Bland
m. (2) St. George Tucker
△ (TUCKERS)

Mary m. Archibald Cary

Ann m. Thos. Mann Randolph (ISHAM BRANCH)   Susanna m.Carter Harrison

Richard m. Judith   Ann m. Gouverneur Morris △   William m. Lucy Bolling Randolph   Randolph of Glenlyvar m. Mary Randolph (ISHAM BRANCH)

St. George   Tudor

3.

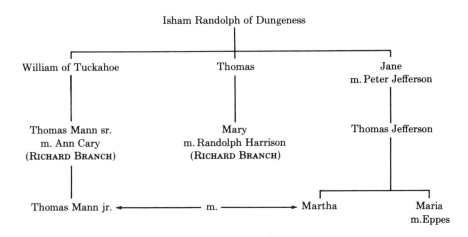

Isham Randolph of Dungeness

William of Tuckahoe

Thomas Mann sr.
m. Ann Cary
(RICHARD BRANCH)

Thomas Mann jr. ◄———————— m. ————————► Martha

Thomas

Mary
m. Randolph Harrison
(RICHARD BRANCH)

Jane
m. Peter Jefferson

Thomas Jefferson

Maria
m. Eppes

This is what is known as "inbreeding." Note the Lee-connected names: Edmund Jennings, Theodorick, Bland, Carter, Bolling, etc.

DU PONT

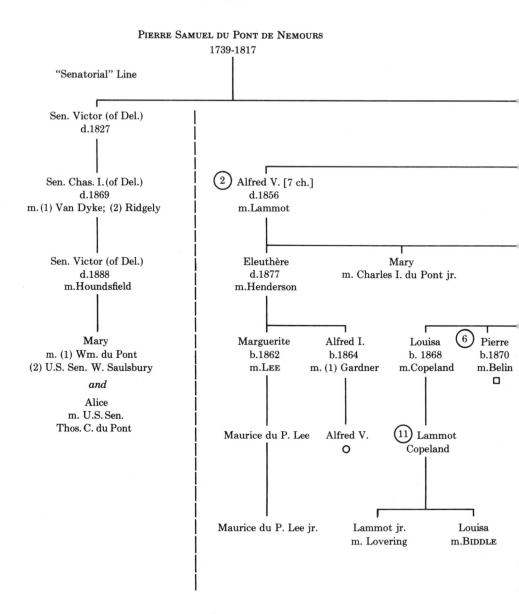

PIERRE SAMUEL DU PONT DE NEMOURS
1739-1817

"Senatorial" Line

Sen. Victor (of Del.)
d.1827

Sen. Chas. I. (of Del.)
d.1869
m. (1) Van Dyke; (2) Ridgely

Sen. Victor (of Del.)
d.1888
m. Houndsfield

Mary
m. (1) Wm. du Pont
(2) U.S. Sen. W. Saulsbury

and

Alice
m. U.S. Sen.
Thos. C. du Pont

(2) Alfred V. [7 ch.]
d.1856
m. Lammot

Eleuthère
d.1877
m. Henderson

Mary
m. Charles I. du Pont jr.

Marguerite
b.1862
m. LEE

Alfred I.
b.1864
m. (1) Gardner

Louisa
b. 1868
m. Copeland

(6) Pierre
b.1870
m. Belin

Maurice du P. Lee

Alfred V.

(11) Lammot
Copeland

Maurice du P. Lee jr.

Lammot jr.
m. Lovering

Louisa
m. BIDDLE

(In the Presidential Line, the circled numbers indicate presidents of the Company in succession.)

"Presidential" Line

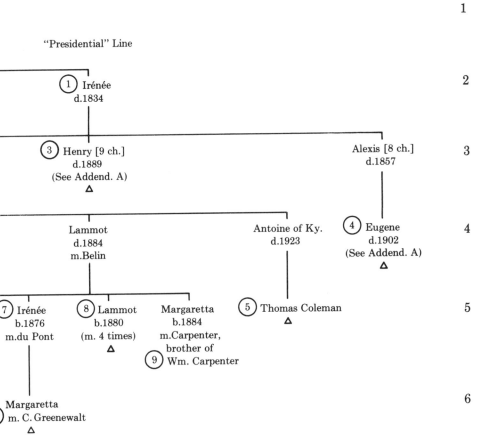

(1) Irénée
d.1834

2

(3) Henry [9 ch.]
d.1889
(See Addend. A)
△

Alexis [8 ch.]
d.1857

3

Lammot
d.1884
m.Belin

Antoine of Ky.
d.1923

(4) Eugene
d.1902
(See Addend. A)
△

4

(7) Irénée
b.1876
m.du Pont

(8) Lammot
b.1880
(m. 4 times)
△

Margaretta
b.1884
m.Carpenter,
brother of
(9) Wm. Carpenter

(5) Thomas Coleman
△

5

Margaretta
0) m. C. Greenewalt
△

6

7

Addendum A: Kinships

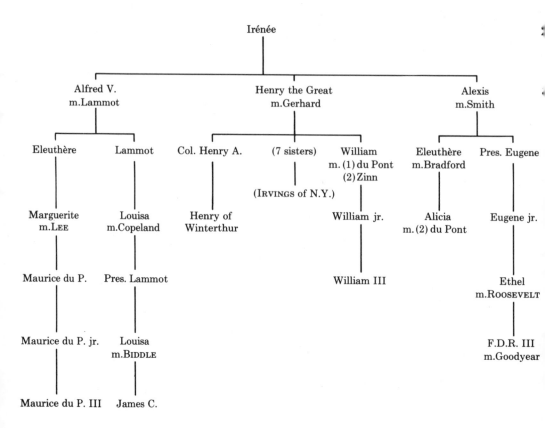

Irénée

Alfred V.
m.Lammot

Henry the Great
m.Gerhard

Alexis
m.Smith

Eleuthère

Lammot

Col. Henry A.

(7 sisters)

William
m. (1) du Pont
(2) Zinn

Eleuthère
m.Bradford

Pres. Eugene

Marguerite
m.Lee

Louisa
m.Copeland

Henry of
Winterthur

(Irvings of N.Y.)

William jr.

Alicia
m. (2) du Pont

Eugene jr.

Maurice du P.

Pres. Lammot

William III

Ethel
m.Roosevelt

Maurice du P. jr.

Louisa
m.Biddle

F.D.R. III
m.Goodyear

Maurice du P. III

James C.

ADDENDUM B: Bradford-du Pont connection

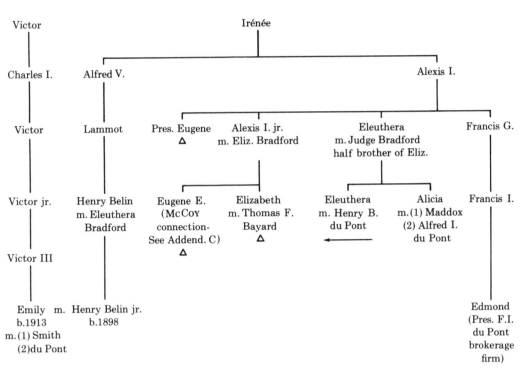

ADDENDUM C: McCoy connections

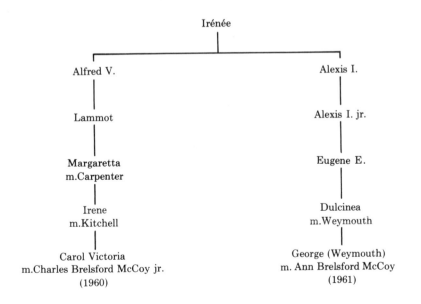

LEE

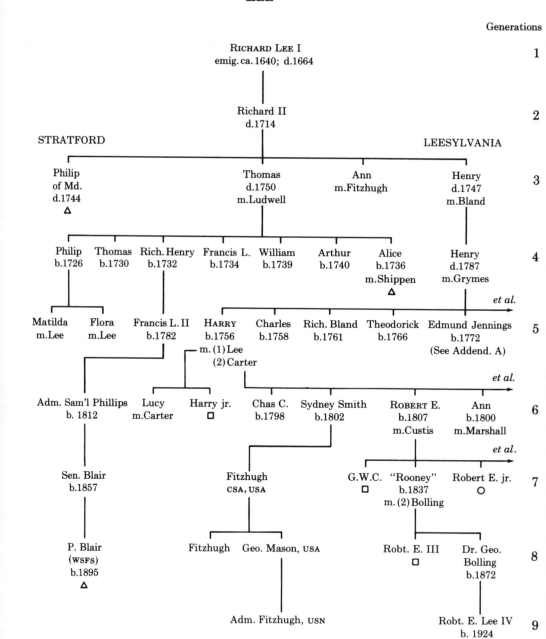

Generations

RICHARD LEE I
emig. ca. 1640; d.1664   **1**

Richard II
d.1714   **2**

STRATFORD   LEESYLVANIA

Philip   Thomas   Ann   Henry
of Md.   d.1750   m.Fitzhugh   d.1747   **3**
d.1744   m.Ludwell   m.Bland
△

Philip   Thomas   Rich.Henry Francis L. William   Arthur   Alice   Henry
b.1726   b.1730   b.1732   b.1734   b.1739   b.1740   b.1736   d.1787   **4**
                                                               m.Shippen m.Grymes
                                                               △
                                                                          et al.

Matilda   Flora   Francis L. II HARRY   Charles   Rich. Bland Theodorick Edmund Jennings
m.Lee   m.Lee   b.1782   b.1756   b.1758   b.1761   b.1766   b.1772   **5**
                                  m. (1)Lee   (See Addend. A)
                                     (2)Carter
                                                                              et al.

Adm. Sam'l Phillips Lucy   Harry jr. Chas C.   Sydney Smith   ROBERT E.   Ann
b. 1812   m.Carter □   b.1798   b.1802   b.1807   b.1800   **6**
                                                                   m.Custis   m.Marshall
                                                                              et al.

Sen. Blair   Fitzhugh   G.W.C.   "Rooney"   Robert E. jr.
b.1857   CSA, USA   □   b.1837   O   **7**
                                                                m. (2)Bolling

P. Blair   Fitzhugh   Geo. Mason, USA   Robt. E. III   Dr. Geo.
(WSFS)   □   Bolling   **8**
b.1895   b.1872
△

                                       Adm. Fitzhugh, USN   Robt. E. Lee IV   **9**
                                                                           b. 1924

ADDENDUM A: Lee-Lee-du Pont connections

1. Lees

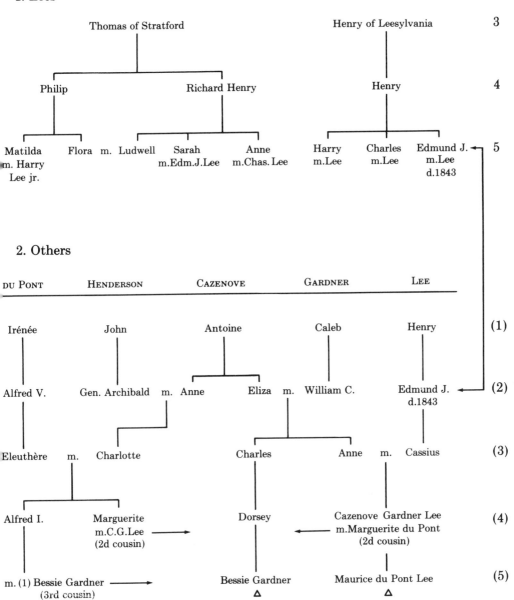

Thomas of Stratford   Henry of Leesylvania   3

Philip   Richard Henry   Henry   4

Matilda   Flora m. Ludwell   Sarah   Anne   Harry   Charles   Edmund J.   5
m. Harry   m.Edm.J.Lee m.Chas. Lee   m.Lee   m.Lee   m.Lee
Lee jr.   d.1843

2. Others

DU PONT	HENDERSON	CAZENOVE	GARDNER	LEE	
Irénée	John	Antoine	Caleb	Henry	(1)
Alfred V.	Gen. Archibald m. Anne	Eliza m. William C.		Edmund J. d.1843	(2)
Eleuthère m. Charlotte		Charles Anne m. Cassius			(3)
Alfred I. Marguerite m.C.G.Lee → (2d cousin)		Dorsey	Cazenove Gardner Lee m.Marguerite du Pont ← (2d cousin)		(4)
m. (1) Bessie Gardner → (3rd cousin)		Bessie Gardner △	Maurice du Pont Lee △		(5)

(2) Alicia Bradford (Maddox)
(2d cousin) (See du Ponts)

(3) Jessie Ball

Roosevelt

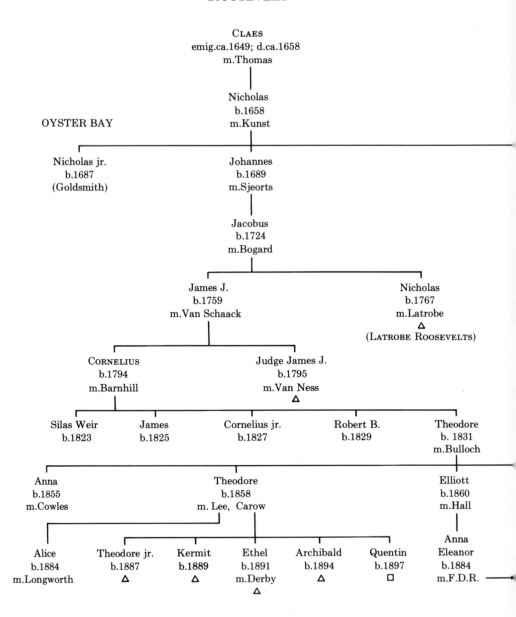

Claes
emig.ca.1649; d.ca.1658
m.Thomas

Nicholas
b.1658
m.Kunst

OYSTER BAY

Nicholas jr.
b.1687
(Goldsmith)

Johannes
b.1689
m.Sjeorts

Jacobus
b.1724
m.Bogard

James J.
b.1759
m.Van Schaack

Nicholas
b.1767
m.Latrobe
(Latrobe Roosevelts)

Cornelius
b.1794
m.Barnhill

Judge James J.
b.1795
m.Van Ness

Silas Weir
b.1823

James
b.1825

Cornelius jr.
b.1827

Robert B.
b.1829

Theodore
b. 1831
m.Bulloch

Anna
b.1855
m.Cowles

Theodore
b.1858
m. Lee, Carow

Elliott
b.1860
m.Hall

Alice
b.1884
m.Longworth

Theodore jr.
b.1887

Kermit
b.1889

Ethel
b.1891
m.Derby

Archibald
b.1894

Quentin
b.1897

Anna
Eleanor
b.1884
m.F.D.R.

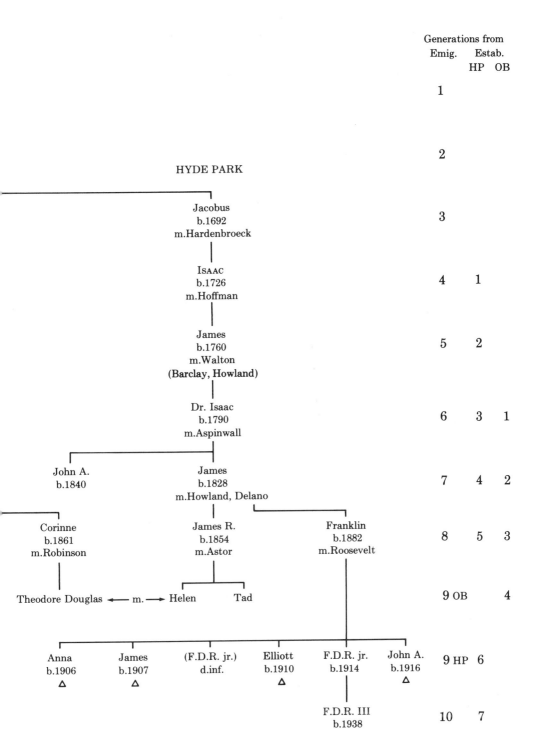

Generations from
Emig.   Estab.
HP OB

1

2

HYDE PARK

Jacobus   3
b.1692
m.Hardenbroeck

Isaac   4   1
b.1726
m.Hoffman

James   5   2
b.1760
m.Walton
(Barclay, Howland)

Dr. Isaac   6   3   1
b.1790
m.Aspinwall

John A.   James   7   4   2
b.1840   b.1828
                  m.Howland, Delano

Corinne   James R.   Franklin   8   5   3
b.1861   b.1854   b.1882
m.Robinson   m.Astor   m.Roosevelt

Theodore Douglas ◄── m. ──► Helen   Tad   9 OB   4

Anna   James   (F.D.R. jr.)   Elliott   F.D.R. jr.   John A.   9 HP 6
b.1906   b.1907   d.inf.   b.1910   b.1914   b.1916
  △   △   △   △

                                          F.D.R. III   10   7
                                          b.1938

ADDENDUM A: Livingston–Roosevelt

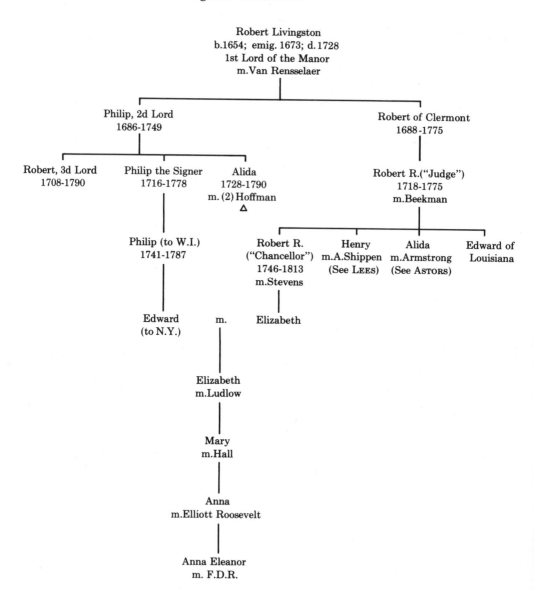

Robert Livingston
b.1654; emig. 1673; d.1728
1st Lord of the Manor
m.Van Rensselaer

Philip, 2d Lord
1686-1749

Robert of Clermont
1688-1775

Robert, 3d Lord
1708-1790

Philip the Signer
1716-1778

Alida
1728-1790
m. (2) Hoffman
△

Robert R.("Judge")
1718-1775
m.Beekman

Philip (to W.I.)
1741-1787

Robert R.
("Chancellor")
1746-1813
m.Stevens

Henry
m.A.Shippen
(See LEES)

Alida
m.Armstrong
(See ASTORS)

Edward of
Louisiana

Edward
(to N.Y.)

m.

Elizabeth

Elizabeth
m.Ludlow

Mary
m.Hall

Anna
m.Elliott Roosevelt

Anna Eleanor
m. F.D.R.

ADDENDUM B: Astor-Roosevelt

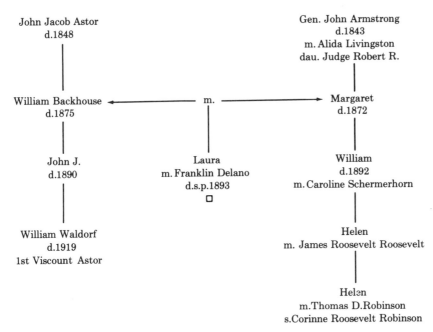

John Jacob Astor
d.1848

Gen. John Armstrong
d.1843
m. Alida Livingston
dau. Judge Robert R.

William Backhouse ← m. → Margaret
d.1875   d.1872

John J.   Laura   William
d.1890   m. Franklin Delano   d.1892
                  d.s.p.1893   m. Caroline Schermerhorn

William Waldorf   Helen
d.1919   m. James Roosevelt Roosevelt
1st Viscount Astor

                                Helen
                        m. Thomas D. Robinson
                        s. Corinne Roosevelt Robinson

ADDENDUM C: Howland-Roosevelt

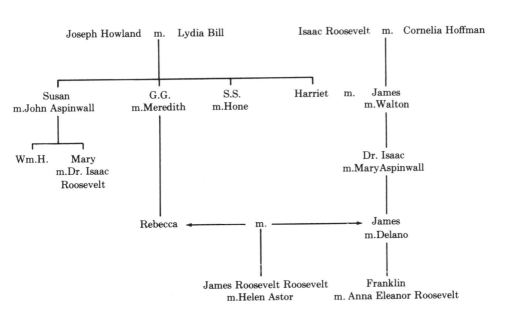

Joseph Howland   m.   Lydia Bill   Isaac Roosevelt   m.   Cornelia Hoffman

Susan   G.G.   S.S.   Harriet   m.   James
m. John Aspinwall m. Meredith   m. Hone   m. Walton

Wm. H.   Mary   Dr. Isaac
        m. Dr. Isaac   m. Mary Aspinwall
        Roosevelt

        Rebecca ← m. → James
                            m. Delano

        James Roosevelt Roosevelt   Franklin
        m. Helen Astor   m. Anna Eleanor Roosevelt

Index